What Readers Are Saying About
Beginning Mac Programming

Helping a complete novice get off the ground building real Mac (and iPhone) apps is daunting—I would have thought impossible—but Tim makes some of the toughest concepts of Cocoa accessible and enjoyable. I get tons of email from people looking to get into Cocoa programming who don't know where to start, and there really hasn't been a good resource to point them to until this book.

▶ **Loren Brichter**
Owner, atebits LLC

Perfect for anyone who is new to Objective-C. It is laid out well, and the examples let you jump right in to developing an application. This will be a well-thumbed reference for me for quite some time.

▶ **David Flagg**
Internet Technology Specialist, National Science Foundation

Isted's book gently places you on the path, giving you the guided tour not just of Mac programming but of programming itself. Simple, evocative examples take care of reinforcing the theory he deftly slips into the conversation. If you want to get into Mac programming quickly, at your own pace, this is your book.

▶ **Uli Kusterer**
Software Engineer, The Void Software

A gentle, practical, and comprehensive introduction to Mac development, which is genuinely suitable for people who have never programmed before. It will not only have you building applications but also understanding how they work.

▶ **Dave Verwer**
Director, Shiny Development Ltd.

If you are new to programming and want to write the next killer app, this is a great place to start. Tim takes you from the very basics of programming to some fairly advanced stuff, all the while never forgetting that you are new to this. The book is filled with great explanations of not only how to do stuff but also why you should do them. I highly recommend this book to people who are new to programming. Especially if you want to build an iPhone application but have never programmed before, this book will take you through a great introduction to programming in general and leave you ready to tackle the iPhone SDK.

▶ **Bill Dudney**
Owner, Gale Factory Software LLC

This book is recommended for anyone starting out with no prior experience with programming or Cocoa development. By introducing fundamental programming principles side by side with a fantastic introduction to the Cocoa frameworks and their tools, Tim gives aspiring developers a foundation on which they can realize their goal of creating software for any modern Apple platform.

▶ **Cathy Shive**
Senior Developer, Sofa B.V.

Tim Isted clearly remembers what it was like when he first learned Objective-C, and it shows. He understands when things will be confusing and when you will be excited you got it all to work.

▶ **Lyndia Zarra**
Owner, LIZography

A book like this is all too rare to find when it comes to beginning programming literature. It focuses on results right from the get-go and has you building applications from the very start, a great way to monitor your progress. All the while it manages to teach you fundamental programming techniques in a clear, concise manner, while not sounding patronizing. An absolute must for anyone considering taking up programming on the Mac platform.

▶ **Danny Greg**
Cocoa Developer, Realmac Software

This book is great; it thankfully eschews the "traditional" dry format of teaching programming and takes you on a journey that will leave you itching to get on and write your own programs.

▶ **Robert McGovern**

I've always been a fan of learning programming by boldly diving in. This book is a prime example of that idea: you create your first program in the second chapter, and create your first objects and code in the third. The traditional fundamentals of programming are there in the middle of the book, and an introduction to Mac application design fills out the end. But I challenge you to be bold. Play with everything, make your own marks, and this book will serve you well on the path to becoming a great Mac programmer.

▶ **Matt Gallagher**
Sole Proprietor, ProjectsWithLove

An extremely gentle introduction to the fundamentals of developing for the Mac. While some beginner books presume knowledge of arcane tidbits, this author has plotted a careful course that starts with a few essentials and then builds upon them bit by bit.

▶ **Daniel Jalkut**
Founder, Red Sweater Software

Before Isted's book, learning how to program and learning how to program Cocoa were sadly two distinct undertakings. The best introductory programming books didn't target Cocoa, and the Cocoa books presumed knowledge of programming. Tackling two separate books wasn't an impossible task for a new programmer, but it was a speed bump along an already steep grade. In this book, Isted offers a seamless, gentle slope towards reaching Mac programming heights. I'm happy I can now recommend Isted's book to those who ask me how they can start programming Apple's lovely machines.

▶ **Jonathan "Wolf" Rentzsch**
President, Red Shed Software Company

Beginning Mac Programming

Develop with Objective-C and Cocoa

Beginning Mac Programming

Develop with Objective-C and Cocoa

Tim Isted

The Pragmatic Bookshelf

Raleigh, North Carolina   Dallas, Texas

Our Pragmatic courses, workshops, and other products can help you and your team create better software and have more fun. For more information, as well as the latest Pragmatic titles, please visit us at

http://www.pragprog.com

ISBN-10: 1-934356-51-4

ISBN-13: 978-1-934356-51-7

Printed on acid-free paper.

P2.0 printing, September 2010

Version: 2010-8-31

Contents

1 Introduction   **1**
  1.1   The Intended Audience 2
  1.2   What's Involved? 2
  1.3   What's Needed? 3
  1.4   Acknowledgments 4
  1.5   Let's Go 5

2 Your First Application   **7**
  2.1   Introducing Xcode 7
  2.2   The Main Event 10
  2.3   The Cocoa Framework 14
  2.4   Application Resources 15
  2.5   Chapter Summary 21

3 All About Objects   **23**
  3.1   The Application Construction Process 23
  3.2   An Introduction to Objects 24
  3.3   Object Inheritance 31
  3.4   Writing Code for Our Own Objects 33
  3.5   Chapter Summary 48

4 Object Messaging   **49**
  4.1   Defining a New Method 49
  4.2   The Target-Action Mechanism 52
  4.3   Sending Messages from Our Code 59
  4.4   Chapter Summary 66

5 Variables and Memory   **67**
  5.1   How Memory Works 67
  5.2   Using Variables 72
  5.3   The Scope of a Variable 81
  5.4   Memory Addressing 83
  5.5   Pointers Again 87
  5.6   Chapter Summary 89

6 Passing Information Around   **91**
  6.1 Returning Values   91
  6.2 Methods and Arguments   99
  6.3 Class Methods   105
  6.4 Passing Values by Reference   109
  6.5 Chapter Summary   111

7 Objects and Memory Management   **113**
  7.1 Memory Considerations   113
  7.2 Allocating Memory for Objects   115
  7.3 Creating Objects in Code   118
  7.4 The Object Life Cycle   123
  7.5 Denying Responsibility   127
  7.6 Initializing with Arguments   131
  7.7 Utility Class Methods   134
  7.8 Chapter Summary   138

8 Collecting Information   **139**
  8.1 Introducing Arrays   139
  8.2 Using Arrays in an Application   142
  8.3 Object Mutability   148
  8.4 A New Application   154
  8.5 Chapter Summary   175

9 Branching Out   **177**
  9.1 Introducing if and else   177
  9.2 All About the Truth   193
  9.3 Stylistic Conventions   196
  9.4 Switching Around   199
  9.5 Writing Init Methods   202
  9.6 Adding Conditional Statements to the Shopping List
       Application   204
  9.7 Chapter Summary   211

10 Looping and Enumerating   **213**
  10.1 Introducing Array Enumeration   213
  10.2 Counting   216
  10.3 Traditional for Loops   219
  10.4 Enumerating an Array with a Traditional for Loop . . .   223
  10.5 Other Types of Loop   226
  10.6 A Simple Change to Our Shopping List Application . .   229
  10.7 Chapter Summary   231

11 Objects, Encapsulation, and MVC   **233**
   11.1 The Main Types of Object 233
   11.2 Designing Model Objects 236
   11.3 Reworking the Shopping List Application 246
   11.4 Creating a Shopping List Item Object 257
   11.5 Reworking the Shopping List Application... Again . . . 264
   11.6 Introducing Objective-C 2.0 Properties 266
   11.7 Chapter Summary 272

12 All About Views   **273**
   12.1 Simple Geometry in Two Dimensions 273
   12.2 Working with Windows and Views 277
   12.3 The View Hierarchy 285
   12.4 Custom Views 290
   12.5 Back to the Shopping List Application 301
   12.6 Views and Cells 305
   12.7 Chapter Summary 313

13 Mac OS X and Cocoa Mechanisms   **315**
   13.1 Delegation 316
   13.2 Notifications 332
   13.3 Working with Events 342
   13.4 Responders and the Responder Chain 354
   13.5 Archiving with NSCoding 362
   13.6 Chapter Summary 369

14 Where to Go from Here   **371**
   14.1 Important Technologies 372
   14.2 Finding Information 377
   14.3 Book Summary 381

A Developing for the iPhone OS   **383**

B Installing Xcode   **399**

C Bibliography   **405**

    Index   **407**

Chapter 1

Introduction

The iPad, the iPhone, the iPod, the iMac...

The world according to Apple is vast and ever-expanding. The Mac and iPhone OS platforms seem to breed passionate users, united in their love for software and hardware that looks beautiful, behaves exactly how they expect, and works without the pains of hardware incompatibilities, driver installations, and convoluted interfaces.

Behind this alluring exterior lies a fascinating world. All computer platforms have communities of software developers, each equally devoted to what they do. What seems to set the Mac platform apart, though, is that so much of the available Mac and iPhone software has been written either by individual developers, working as independents, or for relatively small companies that maintain that "indie" feel. The sense of community is great, newcomers are welcomed and respected, and the indie-developer experience offers many rewards.

What also sets the Mac apart from another, reasonably well-known computer platform, is that the tools to write software come bundled *free of charge* with every Mac. They're even available as free downloads from Apple's website if you happen not to be able to find the original system discs or want the absolutely latest version.

Perhaps the only reasonable excuse not to sit down and write software right away is that the learning curve feels steep. The advice is often to "Go away and learn C, and come back when you're done!" The aim of this book is to offer a different path.

We'll be jumping headfirst into creating applications on the Mac that look and behave like the other Mac applications you're used to. We'll certainly be learning general programming principles, but we will be putting them into practice in real-world situations, right from the start. Over the course of the book, you'll learn enough that you can fend for yourself, with enough knowledge of how the Mac programming world works that you know where to go to fill gaps in your knowledge with information from the right sources.

1.1 The Intended Audience

This book is designed for those of us who don't have a degree in computer science. It's intended to be read by people who've spent time working with the Mac, perhaps as power users of their applications, or at least people with the confidence that they know enough to explain the difference between, say, a menu and a window. Most importantly, the book is intended for people who have little or no previous programming knowledge.

If you already revel in the intricacies of hash tables or take pleasure in analyzing complex algorithms, this book probably isn't for you. Similarly, if you prefer to learn theory first or you work best studying computer stuff away from your computer, it's probably wise to look at some of the other books out there.

Throughout the course of this book, we'll be going over basic programming skills, picking them up as they relate to the language we're learning and to the coding we'll be doing. By the time you reach the end, not only will you have learned enough to start building your own Mac applications, but you'll be confident enough to take on the more advanced literature that's available.

1.2 What's Involved?

So, what will we cover in this book? Well, we'll be learning a programming *language*. On the Mac, this means learning something called Objective-C. Don't worry, it's not too scary, and we won't be trying to learn all of it, all at once. Learning a computer programming language is much easier than learning to speak a foreign language; computers understand only a relatively limited vocabulary and grammar.

For some of the programming principles we'll be learning, we'll introduce concepts using a kind of "pseudolanguage," which is really just standard English made more formulaic. As will quickly become clear, this pseudolanguage isn't too far from what Objective-C actually looks like. Once we've learned to recognize the basic structure of a code project and learned the grammar, or *syntax* used inside the project files, it's not too difficult to work out what's going on in the code.

At the same time that we're learning Objective-C, we'll be learning about a *framework* provided by Apple, called Cocoa, and, obviously, we'll be spending a lot of time using the developer *tools* Xcode and Interface Builder to make Mac software.

The great thing about learning Objective-C for the Mac desktop is that it is also the language used to write software for the iPhone OS, that is, for applications that run on Apple's iPhone and iPod touch devices; toward the end of this book, we'll even take a quick foray into writing iPhone software. The software-building processes we'll learn throughout the book apply just as much on the iPhone as they do the Mac desktop, so we'll be learning skills that open up multiple new worlds of creativity!

1.3 What's Needed?

If you're reading this book, it's probably fairly likely that you either own or have access to a Mac. It doesn't matter whether it's an old PowerPC-based model or the latest top-of-the-line, Intel-based Mac Pro. As long as it runs OS X, you can use it with this book to learn Mac programming.

You won't need to buy any special software. As we've already said, Apple's developer tools are available either on the system discs that came with your computer (or on OS X upgrade discs) or for download from Apple's Developer Connection website. You'll need to register with Apple as a Developer Connection member to download the software, but registration is free.

The developer tools must be installed—they probably won't be available to run on your hard drive unless you've specifically installed them. Installation is very easy; for help, take a look at Appendix B, on page 399.

The only additional considerations are if you want to take iPhone coding further. As a start, the tools used to write for the iPhone OS require an Intel-based Mac. If you want to test and run your software on a real iPhone or iPod touch (rather than in a simulator on your desktop Mac), you'll need to sign up as a registered iPhone Developer; this isn't particularly expensive but, at the time of writing, bears an annual fee of $99 for individuals. Rest assured that you won't *need* to do this to get the most out of this book, though.

The screenshots in this book are taken from version 3.2 of the developer tools—the version that comes with Mac OS X 10.6, Snow Leopard. If you're running Mac OS X 10.5, Leopard, you may find that some parts of Xcode look slightly different, but it shouldn't be too difficult to work out how your version relates to what you see in this book.

1.4 Acknowledgments

Although it's *my* name that's listed on the front, this book would not exist were it not for the work of a very large number of people.

Thankfully, the ever-awesome publisher, Pragmatic Bookshelf, also includes the name of the editor on the cover, which is truly fitting for what Colleen Toporek has put into this project. If I simply used the standard author phrase about "tireless support," it would be one of the biggest understatements of all time. This has been a partnership from beginning to end, and this is as much her book as it is mine.

I have also been lucky enough to have an incredible team of technical reviewers, reading through manuscripts at various stages. The early input from Lyndia Zarra, Bill Dudney, and Rob McGovern requires special mention, as it helped shape much of the book's path and style; they even provided a second set of comments once the first draft was almost complete, for which I doubtless owe an as yet undisclosed number of drinks.

My drawing skills are somewhat lacking, so I'm indebted to David Perkins for his willingness to turn my horrendous scribbles into recognizable shapes. I am also extremely grateful to Dave Verwer, Chris Adamson, Dave Klein, and David Flagg for their support and technical comments on the book as a whole as it got closer to completion, and to Uli Kusterer, Danny Greg, Matt Gallagher, Loren Brichter, Cathy Shive, and Daniel Jalkut for looking over and commenting on the near-final manuscript.

Finally, I'd like to thank all those who submitted errata and forum questions on the book as it went through the Pragmatic Beta process. The Mac and iPhone developer community has to be one of the friendliest, most helpful and supportive groups in existence. We look forward to welcoming you, the reader, into it!

1.5 Let's Go

Writing software for the Mac, and indeed programming in general, can be incredibly rewarding. It doesn't necessarily have to be done at 3 a.m. fueled on coffee or cola, but sometimes it's easy to get carried away knowing that some awesome feature is *so* close to working.

We'll probably manage to avoid some of the blood, sweat, and tears normally associated with learning programming, but even those who have suffered for their art will tell you that it's worth it to use a great piece of software every day and be able to say "I made that!" And, of course, it's even greater to watch other people using and loving (and maybe paying for...) your software too.

So, let's get started!

Chapter 2

Your First Application

Welcome to the world of Mac programming!

Many programming books begin by giving you long histories of programming languages, introducing a lot of very abstract ideas before you actually get to *do* anything. Even when you're eventually allowed to do something at your computer, it's writing code for little command-line tools that output text to a "no user interface" console screen. This book is different.

We're going to begin our journey together by creating a simple but fully functional application that exhibits all the wonderful characteristics of a typical Mac application. Our application will launch like any normal Mac app, display its own window, show its own menu bar, respond to all sorts of user input, and, astonishingly, even allow the user to print to a connected printer. All of this will be achieved without actually writing any code.

In subsequent chapters of this book, we'll use this simple application to demonstrate how to write code. Our aim is therefore not only to learn a new programming "language" but to learn how software is built *from a Mac perspective*, using this language inside a real Mac application, which we'll create using Apple's developer tools.

2.1 Introducing Xcode

If you've done any coding at all on other platforms or maybe dabbled a little with writing or designing web pages, you'll have had a choice of a variety of development environments or coding tools. On the Mac, you'll generally be using *Xcode*, software provided *free of charge* by Apple.

This software comes on the Mac OS X installation CDs as an additional install, or alternatively you can download the most recent version from Apple's Developer Connection website. If you've not yet installed Xcode, please do so now by following the instructions given in Appendix B, on page 399.

Although its name suggests it is used solely to write code, Xcode is what's known in the programming world as an *Integrated Development Environment* (IDE). We'll be using it to organize our code files, launch the interface-editing tools, create an application out of our code, run that application, fix any bugs, and do a whole lot more.

The Xcode Environment

Let's start Xcode right now and create our first programming project. On its first launch, you should be greeted by a Welcome to Xcode window. Close this window for now, and choose the File > New Project... menu item. A template window will appear, as shown in Figure 2.1, on the facing page.

An application is built in Xcode from a large number of different files. Rather than having to add all these to a completely blank project, Xcode offers a variety of template projects that you use as starting points for your own work.

On the left side of this template window, you'll notice many different types of Mac OS X projects. You may also see some template types for iPhone OS projects (shown in Figure 2.1, on the next page); if you haven't installed Xcode with the iPhone SDK, your template window won't show these iPhone OS project types.

We'll talk about some of the different types of projects later in the book, but for now we'll be creating a Mac OS X *application*. Make sure the Application type is highlighted (just under the Mac OS X heading), and you'll see several types of project templates listed in the upper-right half of the window.

A standard Mac application can be one of two fundamental project types—*Cocoa Application* and *Cocoa Document-based Application*. The difference between these two is perhaps best explained with examples. Apple's Pages and Microsoft's Word are examples of document-based applications. iTunes and DVD Player, by contrast, are nondocument applications because they don't work by asking the user to "open a

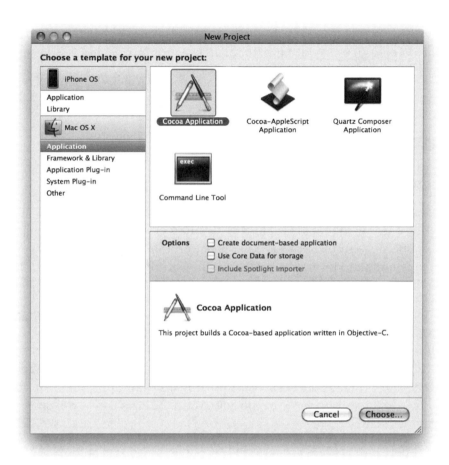

Figure 2.1: THE XCODE TEMPLATE WINDOW

file." The difference isn't always this clear-cut, but that's the basic distinction.

To keep things nice and uncomplicated, we'll create a basic Cocoa application, so make sure the Cocoa Application template is highlighted in the project window, leave the "Create document-based application" checkbox in the lower portion of the window deselected, and click the Choose... button.

At this point, you'll see a standard Save panel asking for a name and location on disk for the project. Note that Xcode will automatically create a new folder with the same name as your application to hold all the project files, so you don't need to do this yourself.

Call the project "TextApp," and click the Save button.

The Project Window

You should see a window appear on screen that looks something like Figure 2.2, on the facing page. Try not to feel overwhelmed at seeing so many items in the Groups & Files list on the left of the window. For most of our time in Xcode, we'll only be worrying about what's under the first group in the list, the TextApp group.

Some of the folders in this group will be empty, but click the triangle next to Other Sources to expand it and view the contents. Two files will appear, one of which is called main.m. Click this file once, and its contents will appear in the lower-main portion of the project window, rather like an email message does in Apple's Mail application. If you double-click the main.m file in the left Groups & Files list, it will open in a new window.

You'll notice that there are several buttons and drop-down boxes along the top of the project window. I'll talk about these as we use them.

2.2 The Main Event

Most introductory programming books that talk about variants of the C language spend most of their time writing code that sits inside this main file. When you're writing standard Mac applications, however, it's actually very rare that you'd want to modify this file. I originally said that we weren't going to *write* any code in this chapter, so we'll stick to that, but it's worth just taking a quick *look* now.

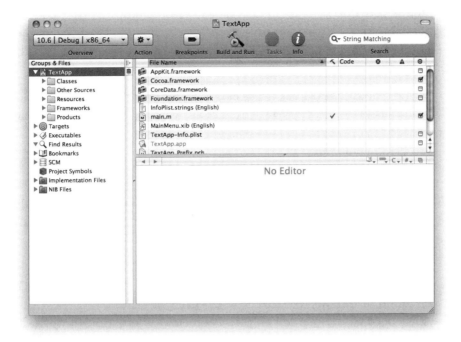

Figure 2.2: THE PROJECT WINDOW FOR TEXTAPP

We'll be going into some serious depth on the layout and language syntax of code later in this book, but let's get a very brief overview of what you're seeing in this particular file. When you double-click the main.m file, you will be looking at a window containing the code listing:

YourFirstApp/TextApp/main.m

```
//
//  main.m
//  TextApp
//
//  Created by Tim Isted on 08/09/2009.
//  Copyright 2009 __MyCompanyName__. All rights reserved.
//

#import <Cocoa/Cocoa.h>

int main(int argc, char *argv[])
{
    return NSApplicationMain(argc, (const char **) argv);
}
```

Assuming you haven't modified Xcode's default settings, the code in this file should appear in a number of different colors. These colors are designed to help you when coding, because they allow you to identify portions of code "at a glance."

Notice that the first few lines are green on your screen. You'll also notice that each of those lines starts with two forward slash characters, like this:

```
// TextApp
```

These lines are *comments* and are completely ignored when the code is run. In this instance, they are used to give information about the file, such as its name, the name of the project, the author, and copyright information. These particular details were provided automatically for us when we used the Cocoa Application project template earlier.

As we'll see throughout this book, comments can be used in all sorts of ways. One of the major uses is to *document* your code. You might, for example, need to perform a complex geometric calculation to work out how to draw a regular star shape inside a set of drawing coordinates. This code might make perfect sense to you while you're writing it, but six months later it might be absolutely impossible to see what's going on without a few comments spread throughout the code to explain what's happening.

Another great feature of comments is to *comment out* particular lines of code. Let's say that your code to draw a star isn't working quite how you'd like. You might decide just to draw a simple rectangle in the place of the star to make sure your coordinate calculations are correct. Rather than deleting all the lines of star-drawing code, you could just comment them out so that it's possible to reintroduce them later, one line at a time.

After the green commented sections, there's a brown and red line starting with **#import**. Don't worry too much about this line just now; instead focus on the last four lines of the file:

```
int main(int argc, char *argv[])
{
    return NSApplicationMain(argc, (const char **) argv);
}
```

Believe it or not, these four lines contain your full-blown Mac OS X application from launch until it quits. To simplify the process somewhat, when a user double-clicks your application in the Finder, the

Keyboard Shortcuts

Most of the menu commands given in the book have their keyboard shortcuts shown, using the symbols commonly found on Mac keyboards. You'll also see references to ^-clicking.

Some Mac keyboards don't show these symbols; if yours doesn't, you may find this table helpful:

^　Control or Ctrl

⇧　Shift

⌥　Option, Opt or Alt

⌘　Command or Cmd

⌫　Delete or Del

↩　Return

⌅　Enter

operating system looks inside the application code to find this **main** portion, and then it runs the code between the curly braces.

As I said before, you don't need to modify the main.m file very often. With that in mind, let's see what happens when we run the application.

Close the main.m file so that you can see the main TextApp project window. Click the Build & Run icon on the toolbar at the top of this window, and sit back while Xcode *builds* your project from the various files in the template and then runs the resulting application.

Assuming all has gone to plan, your application will launch. A blank window should open that you can move around and resize. Notice that the menu bar has changed, displaying "TextApp" as the application name at the top left of your screen. Take a moment to look through the items under each menu. You'll find a standard File menu, with several items like the New and Open commands *grayed out*. The Edit menu contains the standard *pasteboard actions* such as Copy and Paste. The Window menu contains commands that affect the blank window visible on screen. You can minimize it to the Dock or zoom it to fill your screen.

One of the most important principles of building software for the Mac platform is that applications should follow a standard set of interface guidelines set by Apple. One of these guidelines is that certain menu items appear in all applications and in specific groupings. For example, you should always find Cut, Copy, and Paste commands under the Edit menu, always listed in that order. If your application follows these guidelines, it will be much easier for people to use because it behaves in the way they expect.

Quit the TextApp application in any way you choose. You'll find you can pick the Quit TextApp command from the TextApp menu or press its usual keyboard equivalent—the ⌘-Q shortcut. You could also right-click with the mouse (or ^-click) on the Text App icon that has appeared in the Dock at the bottom of your screen and choose Quit. These are all perfectly acceptable ways to exit the application, and you'll find all of them already work for you "out of the box."

2.3 The Cocoa Framework

Remember how we looked inside the main.m file in the previous section and saw one line of code that apparently ran the application from launch until it quit? It seems rather bizarre that this single line could accomplish all the functionality we experienced.

One way to write applications on a computer would be to write code that literally draws every pixel on screen to represent the user interface. Writing TextApp in this way, you'd need to draw a bar across the top for the menus, then display text for each menu, before drawing the window outline and its contents. That's ignoring any need to display what's in the background of the user's screen from their desktop or other applications and forgetting that we need to write code to make those pixels change when the user wants to interact with our application.

Remember how we talked about applications conforming to a standard set of interface guidelines? A *window* has a defined look and feel, for example, and menus all behave in a certain way; there would be a large amount of duplicated functionality between applications if every programmer had to write similar code to achieve the same basic behavior. Imagine what would happen if the guidelines changed slightly—every application would have to be modified to represent the new standard.

The solution to these issues is to use a *framework*. A framework provides a large amount of prewritten code that we can use to avoid having to "reinvent the wheel." When writing Mac software, we use the *Cocoa* framework, provided for us by Apple.

You might recall that when we created our TextApp project, we chose the Cocoa Application template. By creating an application using Cocoa, we're relieved from worrying about the basic functionality exhibited by most Mac applications, and left to worry about writing code only for the features that are unique to our own application.

Open main.m again to take a look at that important line between the curly braces:

```
return NSApplicationMain(argc, (const char **) argv);
```

For now, ignore the fact that this looks rather terrifying in terms of syntax. All this line is actually doing is creating a Cocoa application and giving it control.

2.4 Application Resources

It's all very well just to say that we're giving control over to some Cocoa application, but we still haven't discovered where the menu bar and windows come from.

If you double-clicked the main.m file earlier to open it in a separate window, close that window now so that you return to the Xcode project window for TextApp. In the left side of the window, the Other Sources group should still be expanded. Under this, you'll see another group called Resources. Click the triangle to the left of this to expand it, and you'll see three more files. Click the TextApp-Info.plist[1] file once, and it will appear in the lower-right portion of the project window, looking like Figure 2.3, on the next page.

There's a lot of information in this file, but the line we need to focus on just now is the one called Main nib file base name. You'll see that the Value column for this line contains MainMenu.

The MainMenu.xib File

When you create an application using the Cocoa framework, the framework looks inside the ApplicationName-Info.plist file for this value and uses the file with that name to create the basic interface for the application. Look back in the Resources group on the left of the project

---

1. If you are using an earlier version of Xcode, this file might be called Info.plist rather than TextApp-Info.plist.

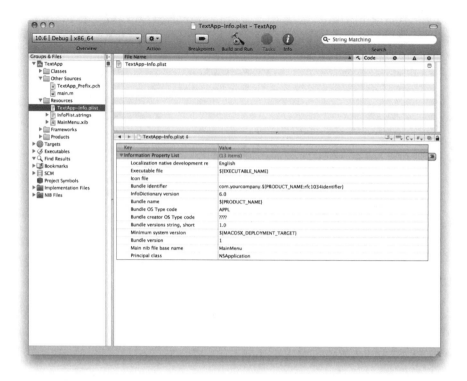

Figure 2.3: THE TEXTAPP-INFO.PLIST FILE

window, and you'll see that the third resource listed is called Main-Menu.xib. Double-click this file to open it.

Xcode launches another Apple developer tools application, called Interface Builder, to edit this file. When it opens, you'll find a number of windows on your screen; the main window looks like Figure 2.4, on the facing page.

This main MainMenu.xib window contains a variety of objects. The two to take notice of right now are Main Menu and Window (TextApp).

Double-click the Main Menu icon to open the menu editor (it may already be open on screen). This menu editor (shown in Figure 2.5, on page 18) contains the menu bar that is displayed when the TextApp application is run. If you click a menu title, that menu will drop down and be displayed so that you can make any changes to the menu items.

Figure 2.4: MAINMENU.XIB OPEN IN INTERFACE BUILDER

Click the TextApp menu once to display it, and then *double*-click the first menu item, About TextApp. You'll find that the menu item title becomes editable, and you can change it to anything you want. Change the name to "About My Wonderful TextApp Application."[2]

Save the MainMenu.xib file in Interface Builder, and switch back to X-code. Click the Build & Run toolbar item once to launch your application. Now when TextApp runs, you'll find that the About menu item appears with its new name, just as we set in Interface Builder. Choose the Quit TextApp command to exit the application.

---

2. Under some earlier versions of Xcode, the project template doesn't name some of the menu items correctly. The About menu item might be About NewApplication, and the Quit command might be Quit NewApplication. If so, you can rename them as described. The application menu itself may also be New Application, but when the application is run, this will change, as if by magic, to TextApp.

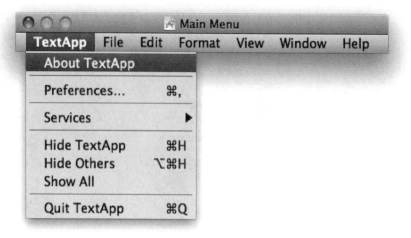

Figure 2.5: THE MENU EDITOR IN INTERFACE BUILDER

Adding to Our Basic Interface

It isn't only basic user interface items like windows and menus that Cocoa provides for us. There are a whole host of other *controls* that we can use to add functionality to our application.

Over the next few chapters of this book, we're going to be needing a place to display some textual information. To demonstrate how much functionality can be provided by the "built-in" controls, we'll use a control right now to allow the user to type text into the window. We'll be using some of the other available controls later in the book.

So, return to Interface Builder,[3] and make sure the MainMenu.xib file is still open. From the Tools menu, open the Library palette. This palette, shown in Figure 2.6, on the facing page, contains the controls that we can either use as is in our projects or extend with extra functionality if needed.

---

3. There's a very useful Mac OS X shortcut to switch quickly between applications; hold down the ⌘-key and press ⇥, and a box will appear allowing you to pick between all open applications. When you release the ⌘ key, the selected application will be brought to the front.

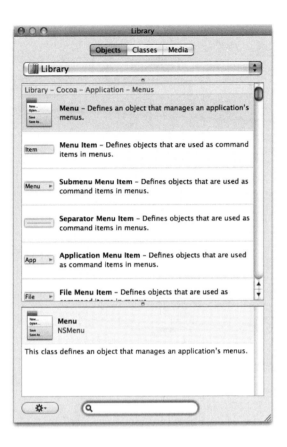

Figure 2.6: INTERFACE BUILDER'S LIBRARY PALETTE

At the bottom of the Library palette is a search box; type "text view" in this box. You'll see that only one item is left inside the palette, and, helpfully, this is the one we are going to use.

We need to add our new text view to TextApp's window. To make sure this window is visible, double-click the icon in the main MainMenu.xib window that's labeled Window (TextApp), and it will open as a blank window on screen.

Drag a Text View object from the Library palette, and drop it in the blank window. As you hover the new object over the window, you'll notice various blue guides appear to help you position it. Line up the top-left corner with the blue lines a short distance inside the top left of the window. Using the little manipulation points around the object,

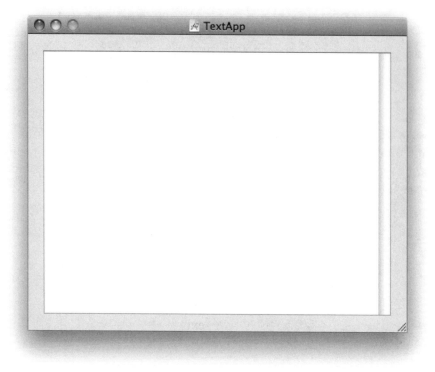

Figure 2.7: THE TEXT VIEW INSIDE THE WINDOW

enlarge it so that its bottom-right corner lines up with the blue lines that appear a short distance from that corner of the window. You should end up with something resembling Figure 2.7.

Let's test our new text view straightaway. Save the Interface Builder file, switch back into Xcode, and click the Build & Run icon. When the application launches, you'll see that the main window now has a text view inside it, eagerly awaiting your input. Notice how you can type anything you like into the text view, select characters with the mouse, drag and drop items, copy and paste to and from other applications, and even change the style of the text using the Fonts palette available in TextApp's Format menu. How amazing is that? We still haven't had to write any code.

2.5 Chapter Summary

We've taken a quick peek into the fantastic world of building Mac OS X applications using Apple's Cocoa framework. Despite not actually writing a single line of code, we've made a reasonably functional application with some impressive text-editing functionality just by working with the resources inside a Cocoa application.

This is all well and good, but to produce applications that are useful and functional in the real world (notice we have no undo capabilities or any file-saving functionality in TextApp), we're going to need to learn how to write some code. We'll be making changes to TextApp throughout the next few chapters, using it to display various bits of useful output, and modifying it to test various features of Mac software development as you learn them.

The next chapter introduces a few basic programming principles, and we'll actually get to start coding. Feel free to experiment with the various objects, palettes, and features provided by Interface Builder, but make sure that you have a clean copy of TextApp to work with for the next chapter.

Downloading the Code

You can download the Xcode projects and code used in this book from the Pragmatic website page for this book:

Pragmatic Bookshelf...................http://www.pragprog.com/titles/tibmac

Chapter 3

All About Objects

In the previous chapter, we walked through the process of building a very simple application. We didn't actually write any code, and although the application was impressive given its ease of construction, it still lacks quite a bit of functionality. From now on, we'll be learning basic programming principles and starting to write code that lets us add the functionality unique to the software we create.

3.1 The Application Construction Process

To build TextApp, we did most of our work in Interface Builder, modifying a menu item and adding a text view to the window. When you're writing your own software, it is often a good idea to begin in the same way—creating the basic interface first. This doesn't mean that you have to decide exactly where every button will go or make it look exactly as it will when finished; it means thinking about, for example, how many windows your application will need or the kind of thing each window will display, along with the types of user interface items you will use.

For TextApp, we needed only a single window, with a single text-editing control inside it. If we were instead writing an application to track financial information or expenses, we might choose to use multiple windows, each displaying different kinds of financial information or allowing the user to import transactions from their bank accounts.

Once the basic layout of the application is agreed, we can add the functionality unique to our application, such as the code that controls what the user interface items display, how they respond to user input, and how they change the underlying data. In Mac applications, this code is written inside *objects*.

3.2 An Introduction to Objects

You have probably heard the phrase *object-oriented programming* (or OOP). When writing software for the Mac or the iPhone using Objective-C and Cocoa, you will be working almost entirely with objects. If "working with objects" sounds overly abstract, don't worry—we've already done quite a lot with objects when building TextApp in the previous chapter, and that wasn't too bad, was it?

You may remember that in the main Interface Builder window (shown in Figure 2.4, on page 17), there were several icons with names like Main Menu and Window. We also dragged a Text View from a library of similar interface items for use in the window. Each of these items (Window, Text View, and so on) is an *object*.

We're about to learn all about objects and how they interact, but before we do, let's take a moment to think about how things could be done in a non-object-oriented way.

Non-Object-Oriented Programming

As we went through the application *resources* in the previous chapter, we briefly examined two ways to draw an application's user interface. One way would be for every application to draw every pixel necessary on screen to represent each portion of the user interface—menu bar, menus, windows, and so on. When the application was launched, we might end up with a sequence like this:

1. Draw a white rectangle at the top of the screen for a menu bar.
2. Draw the Apple icon for the left Apple menu.
3. Move along a few pixels, and draw the application menu.
4. Move along a few more pixels, and draw the File menu.
5. Move along a few more pixels, and draw the Edit menu.
6. Draw a big box on screen to represent the window outline.
7. Draw a small, solid gray box across the top of the window for the title bar.
8. Draw three differently-colored circles for Close, Minimize, and Zoom.
9. Draw the window's title in the center of the bar.
10. Fill out the rest of the window with its content.
11. Wait for the user to do something.

We can break this list down into three sections. The first section covers drawing the menu bar and menus, the second deals with the window and its content, and the final section addresses waiting for the user to do something:

1. Menu bar and menus

    a) Draw a white rectangle at the top of the screen for a menu bar.

    b) Draw the Apple icon for the left Apple menu.

    c) Move along a few pixels, and draw the application menu.

    d) Move along a few more pixels, and draw the File menu.

    e) Move along a few more pixels, and draw the Edit menu.

2. Window and content

    a) Draw a big box on screen to represent the window outline.

    b) Draw a small, solid gray box across the top of the window for the title bar.

    c) Draw three different-colored circles for Close, Minimize, and Maximize.

    d) Draw the window's title in the center of the bar.

    e) Fill out the rest of the window with its content.

3. Events

    a) Wait for the user to do something.

Apart from anything else, this list is much easier to read. If we ever *were* to write an application in this way, it would make sense to split our code into these sections.

Now let's consider what happens if we want to open a second window on screen. All the code for the "Window and content" section would have to be written out again but changed slightly so the new window displays different content from the first. Repetition in software design is always something best avoided, not least because if you need to change the way windows are displayed, you would have to modify the code in multiple places.

There's actually quite a bit of repetition already in our three-part list. Drawing each menu, for example, requires almost identical steps: "Move along a few pixels, and draw the *«menu name»* menu."

We might write out a piece of code that gets called multiple times to display a given menu name in a given position. Something like this:

- Draw the *«menu name»* menu at *«position»*.

We can do something similar to create our windows—write a piece of code to display a window with a given title in a given position:

- Draw a window entitled *«title»* at *«position»*.

This condensing process seems reasonable, but there is another way.

The Object-Oriented Approach

Object-oriented programming makes the assumption that the mechanisms behind computer software can be defined in terms of objects. Rather than the code for an application having hundreds of lines to draw a menu bar, for example, we can instead simply create a "menu bar object" and tell that object to "draw itself."

That's a fairly complicated system introduced in a two-sentence paragraph, so let's delve in a little more deeply. Building a Mac application from an object-oriented perspective involves defining a whole network of objects. Each object in that network has internal functionality (for instance, drawing code) that can be triggered by another object.

Returning to the earlier window example, let's consider defining a Window object. We could code into this object the functionality to draw the background of the window along with its title bar—functionality that would jump into action whenever the object was told to display itself on screen. To display two windows on screen, we end up with something that follows this outline:

1. Create the first Window object entitled *«title»* at *«position»*.

2. Tell this Window object to display itself.

3. Create a second Window object entitled *«title»* at *«position»*.

4. Tell this Window object to display itself.

To create a Window object, we need somehow to decide what makes up such an object. Ideally, we would create a kind of blueprint so that we could create multiple objects with identical structures if needed—as in when we want to create two or more windows.

A Real-World Analogy

There's quite a bit of new terminology, so let's look at an analogy from the "real world" for a moment:

A property developer wants to build a series of houses along a street. These houses will be absolutely identical in size, shape, and internal layout but will have different-colored front doors. An architect is hired to draw up a blueprint plan for a single house that the builders can use to construct multiple, identical houses along the street. The property developer then decides to build three of these houses, referring to them for the moment as Houses A, B, and C.

When it comes time to build the houses, the developer instructs the builders to do the following:

1. Build House A with a red door.

2. Build House B with a blue door.

3. Build House C with a yellow door.

The city officials visit the houses to make sure all is in order, before assigning a street address to each one. The developer records this information for each house:

1. The address of House A is 12 Wisteria Lane.

2. The address of House B is 13 Wisteria Lane.

3. The address of House C is 14 Wisteria Lane.

Finally, the developer requests the builders to affix numbers to each front door representing the house number:

1. Fix the house number of House A to its front door.

2. Fix the house number of House B to its front door.

3. Fix the house number of House C to its front door.

Let's think about this simplified house-building exercise from an *object* perspective. The general house blueprint describes the floor plans and measurements, and so on. Each house built from the blueprint has two *assignable values*: the door color and the house address. In programming terms, the blueprint has a large amount of fixed *functionality* and *data*, such as describing the house foundations, walls, and roof, along with the two changeable *attributes*. We might define such a house blueprint like this:

- **Name:** House

- **Assignable attributes:** doorColor, address

- **Functionality:** foundations, walls, roofing

In object-oriented programming, this blueprint is called a *class description*. All houses that are built from this class description are then referred to as *instances* of the House *class*. This is important terminology, and you need to make certain you understand the distinction between a "class" and any "instances" of that class. So, in our real-world example, we have our House class (the architectural blueprint for any houses belonging to that class) and the instances—houses A, B, and C.

The process of building a house would therefore be something like this:

1. Tell builders to create a new House instance with doorColor set to "red."

2. When building is finished, send out the city official to the house for approval and request an address.

3. Set the address of the house instance as given by the city official.

4. Tell builders to go back to the house and add the house number to the front door.

I mentioned earlier that object-oriented software is built from a network of objects; let's expand our example a little with some extra classes: a PropertyDeveloper class, a Builder class, and a CityOfficial class. These objects need to be able to communicate with each other; for example, the developer needs to know when a house is finished so the city official can be sent there.

Let's look at the class description for the PropertyDeveloper class as an example:

- **Class name:** PropertyDeveloper

- **Assignable attributes:** name

- **Responds to messages:** houseHasBeenBuilt, houseHasBeenApprovedWith-AnAddress, numbersHaveBeenFixedToDoor

Here's the Builder class description:

- **Class name:** Builder

- **Assignable attributes:** name

- **Responds to messages:** buildHouse, fixNumberToDoor

And finally, here's the CityOfficial class description:

- **Class name:** CityOfficial

- **Assignable attributes:** name

- **Responds to messages:** approveHouseAndAssignAddress

If we make up a bit of pseudo-code, we can see that all it takes to start the process is for the developer to create a house object and tell a builder to construct it:

```
buildANewHouse
{
    create a new house instance
    set the door color to "red"
    find builder with name "Acme House Construction Inc"
    tell builder to 'buildHouse'
}
```

At this point, the builder gets to work and starts putting up the house. When the house is finished, the builder calls the developer object, sending the message houseHasBeenBuilt. When it receives this message, the developer does the following:

```
houseHasBeenBuilt
{
    find friendly city official
    tell city official to 'approveHouseAndAssignAddress'
}
```

The city official approves the house, assigns an address, then calls the developer object back with the message houseHasBeenApprovedWith-AnAddress, at which point the developer does this:

```
houseHasBeenApprovedWithAnAddress
{
    set address of house as given by official
    tell builder to 'fixNumberToDoor'
}
```

The builders add the numbers to the door and let the developer know, confirming that numbersHaveBeenFixedToDoor, at which point the developer knows the house is finished and ready to sell.

```
numbersHaveBeenFixedToDoor
{
    tell the world that the house is ready to buy
}
```

One of the many advantages to this approach is that we can *factor out* all the different parts of the process. In the real world, the property developer doesn't need to know the internal processes necessary for a city official to approve a house and give it an address. And, in this pseudocode, the PropertyDeveloper object has no knowledge of what happens when the CityOfficial is told to approveHouseAndAssignAddress. All either object knows is what messages can be sent between them.

If we were to try to write these objects in real code, we could easily let someone else write code for the CityOfficial class; we don't care what's happening behind the scenes, as long as a CityOfficial object responds to the message approveHouseAndAssignAddress with a valid address.

Back to the Programming World

Now let's translate our knowledge of classes and instances back to the world of Mac programming, returning to the window example introduced earlier in this chapter. The class description for a Window object looks something like this:

- **Class name:** Window

- **Assignable attributes:** title, backgroundColor, positionOnScreen

- **Responds to messages:** drawOnScreen

To create and display a window on screen, then, we could use the following pseudocode in our application:

```
displayAWindow
{
    create a new window object
    set its window title to "My Beautiful Window"
    set its background color to "sea green"
    set its shape to be a rectangle
        500 pixels wide
        300 pixels high
        centered on screen
    tell the window to 'drawOnScreen'
}
```

Because it's working with a window object, the application doesn't need to know anything about how a window actually draws itself on the screen. All the application cares about is that it can create a window object, set various attributes to describe the window, and send the object a drawOnScreen message. Similarly, the window needs to know nothing about *why* it has a particular title or background color. It simply needs to know how to draw itself when it's instructed to do so.

Remember that back in our TextApp application, we worked with a Window object that already existed in the Interface Builder file. We could have created that window by writing code instead, replacing the window instance we were given. Creating an object instance in Interface Builder is very much like creating an object in code, but instead of setting attributes on the object by coding them, we can use the Interface Builder *Inspector palettes* to edit them "visually."

3.3 Object Inheritance

We're very close to actually making our own objects, but there's one quite important point we need to cover—objects can *inherit* characteristics from other objects.

Let's return to our housing system for a moment. The property developer decides that it also wants to build offices, shops, and apartment blocks. Obviously, these are all different types of Buildings, and all share a number of similarities with our current House object. Each building has a front door and address, for example, but obviously they also differ in many ways, too.

If we defined new classes for a Shop and an ApartmentBlock in the same way that we defined our House class, there would be a large amount of duplicated general *building* information appearing in each class. To avoid this duplication, we can define a class description for a generic Building object and let the House class and other building types inherit those base characteristics.

So, let's define a class description for a Building. It's actually just the old House class description with a new name:

- **Class name:** Building

- **Assignable attributes:** doorColor, address

- **Responds to messages:** accessFoundationSpecifications, accessWallSpecifications, accessRoofSpecifications

We can now redefine our House class as simply being a subclass of the Building class; put another way, the House class *inherits from* the Building class:

- **Class name:** House

- **Inherits from:** Building

The House class doesn't need to add any attributes of its own in our simplified house-building world, so we can just leave the class description at that. Because the attributes are inherited, any house instance also has a door color and address.

When one class inherits from another class, it not only inherits all the attributes in the parent class but also inherits all the messaging functionality. Any instances of our House class, therefore, will respond to the accessFoundationSpecifications messages along with *all* the other functionality defined by the Building class.

Given what we've done so far, you shouldn't be surprised to discover that we can define the ApartmentBlock class like this:

- **Class name:** ApartmentBlock

- **Inherits from:** Building

- **Assignable attributes:** numberOfApartments

- **Responds to messages:** accessIndividualApartmentSpecifications

Here we've added an attribute for the number of apartments within the apartment block and said that this new object will respond to a new message requesting the specifications of an individual apartment.

A problem arises, however, since the general specifications for an apartment building are going to be different from those of a house. We need some way to make the specification access methods return different information for each class.

Overriding Inherited Behavior

When one class inherits functionality from another class (known as the *superclass*), the new class has the option to provide code to respond to the *same messages* as the superclass. This is known as *overriding* the inherited behavior. As a result, it is possible to provide code in the House class that supplies house-specific information about the walls, for example. Similarly, the ApartmentBlock class needs to provide apartment-specific information about walls.

When a class overrides behavior, it replaces the superclass's behavior entirely. At the moment, the House and ApartmentBlock classes have to provide complete responses to the requests for specifications. But, a wall is a wall—there are definitely going to be a few bits of information common across all the different types of buildings. At the very least, each needs to provide the requested information in some kind of uniform way. If we consider pseudocode for the House and ApartmentBlock responses to the accessFoundationSpecifications messages, we might get something like this:

Code for House class:
```
    accessFoundationSpecifications
    {
        generic
          specification layout and design
            code here

        generic
              foundation
            code here

        house-specific code here
    }
```

Code for ApartmentBlock class:
```
    accessFoundationSpecifications
    {
        generic
          specification layout and design
            code here

        generic
              foundation
            code here

        apartment-block-specific code here
    }
```

Rather than having this duplicated generic code appear in each Building subclass, it would be much better to keep the generic code in the superclass so that it's defined only once but can still be used by each subclass. Thankfully, we *can* do this quite simply, as we'll soon see.

3.4 Writing Code for Our Own Objects

Now that we have a basic understanding of objects, let's start writing our own. We're going to write a very simple object whose only job in life is to let us know when it is created. Along the way, we'll be learning about the Objective-C programming language and its syntax.

I promised in the previous chapter that we wouldn't spend too much time talking about programming history, so we won't. It is just worth knowing that when we're writing code, we need to write in a very formulaic language that the computer can understand. This language provides rules for writing instructions, performing calculations, and so on. We can choose from a number of different languages, but the most common for writing code on the Mac platform is called Objective-C. It is based on one of the most famous and popular programming languages of all, called C, with some additional object and messaging features added by Apple (which is why it has the *Objective* part). We'll be learning the Objective-C language throughout the rest of this book.

Objects and Objective-C

Let's jump straight in and write a class description for our new object now. If you don't have Xcode running, launch it, and open the TextApp project from the previous chapter.

When the project window opens, look at the Groups & Files structure on the left. If you need to, click the triangle to the left of each item to expand it so that you can see the Classes group. This is where we'll add our new class description.

Right-click (or ^-click) the Classes group, and choose Add > New File.... The New File window should appear, looking like Figure 3.1, on the next page.

Again, we'll be using Xcode's templates to save us from having to write basic contents in each file. On the left of this window, click Cocoa Class, and find the template called Objective-C class. Make sure this template is selected, and click the Next button. You'll be greeted by a window looking like Figure 3.2, on page 36.

Change the filename to NotifyingClass.m, and make sure the "Also create 'NotifyingClass.h'" checkbox is selected. When you click Finish, you should find that Xcode has created two files, listed under the Classes group in your project window. The first of these, NotifyingClass.h, should be showing in the source code panel of the project window, as shown in Figure 3.3, on page 37.

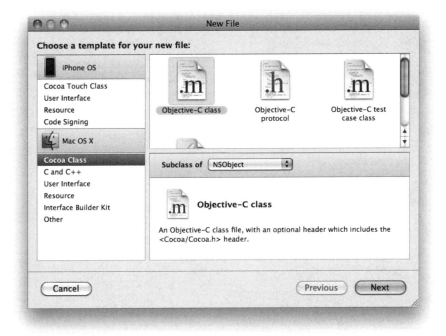

Figure 3.1: THE NEW FILE WINDOW IN XCODE

Objective-C File Types for a Class

It is perfectly possible to define a class using just a single file,[1] but it generally makes more sense to split the class into two separate files. Remember the *class descriptions* we used earlier in the chapter? These are used to determine the attributes belonging to a class and to specify which messages the class can respond to. This class description generally goes inside a file with an .h extension, known as a *header* file. The other file, with an .m extension, contains the lines of code, or *methods*, that are called when messages are sent to a class. Don't worry if this isn't immediately clear—it will become easier to understand as we begin to create our class.

We're going to be writing a very simple class that just notifies us when it is created and destroyed. It doesn't need to maintain any attributes

---

1. Or even to define multiple classes within one single file.

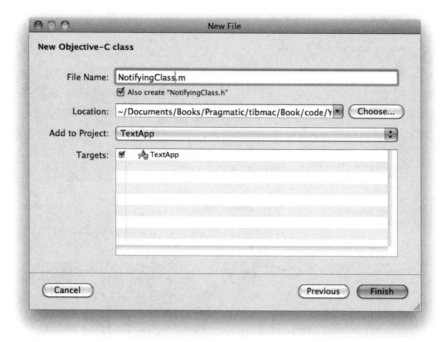

Figure 3.2: THE NEW FILE PANE IN XCODE ASKING FOR A FILENAME

at all, so if we follow the format from before, our *class description* might look something like the following:

- **Class name:** NotifyingClass

- **Assignable Attributes:** *none*

- **Responds to messages:** createObject

Our notifying class is a very simple class that doesn't do very much, so it might seem like we don't need to inherit any behavior from any "superclass." In fact, this isn't the case.

You'll remember in the previous chapter that we talked about using a framework to provide common functionality without having to duplicate code, and that on the Mac we use the Cocoa framework, provided by Apple. The menus and window displayed in our TextApp application all come from classes in the Cocoa framework, and in order for this framework to function, it expects to find certain behavior common to

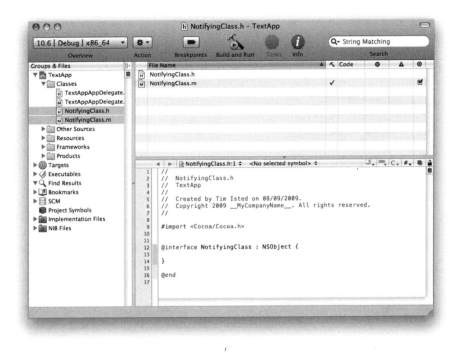

Figure 3.3: NOTIFIYINGCLASS.H VISIBLE IN THE PROJECT WINDOW

all objects it encounters; this behavior is provided for us by a *base object* class that is called NSObject.

As we explore the classes provided by the framework, we'll see that the majority of the classes have the characters *NS* at the start of their names. To avoid conflicts of class names (*object* is a pretty common word, for example), it's common practice to prefix names with characters that are likely to make them unique. We'll discuss this more later, but for now, don't worry that our own NotifyingClass doesn't have a prefix.[2]

Creating a new class that inherits from another is called *subclassing*. By subclassing NSObject, we inherit a number of "memory management" features. We will be talking in great depth about memory

---

2. If you're wondering why Apple has chosen the letters *NS* for its framework classes, they actually stand for "NeXT Step," a computer platform that preceded Mac OS X and from which quite a lot of functionality was ported.

The NSApplication Object

You might remember that when we took a quick peek inside the main.m file in the previous chapter, there was a single line of code inside those curly braces:

```
{
    return NSApplicationMain(argc, (const char**) argv);
}
```

Notice the *NS* in there, on the front of the word NSApplication-Main? This code actually creates an instance of an *application object* that is defined for us by the Cocoa framework. As you might have guessed, the name of the class for this application object is NSApplication. When this application object is created, a whole heap of functionality leaps into action, as defined by the Cocoa NSApplication class. This was why we ended up with so much functionality apparently taking place in a single line of code.

management later in the book; for now, let's look at a few basic messages that can be sent to an NSObject instance related to its creation and destruction.

Object Initialization Messages

When an instance of a class is created in Objective-C, it is immediately sent a message to initialize itself. This message is helpfully called init and is generally used to set initial values (or *default* values for any instances of the class). In the earlier house examples, we might set a default door color and address for the house in case the property developer forgets to set them later.

Setting Up Our Class Description

We now need to revise our NotifyingClass class description in light of what we've learned about NSObject. The class needs to inherit from NSObject and will be responding to one message—init:

- **Class name:** NotifyingClass
- **Inherits from:** NSObject
- **Assignable attributes:** *none*
- **Responds to messages:** init

Make sure that you are looking at the NotifyingClass.h file. It should look like this:

`AllAboutObjects/TextApp/NotifyingClass.h`

```
//
//  NotifyingClass.h
//  TextApp
//
//  Created by Tim Isted on 08/09/2009.
//  Copyright 2009 __MyCompanyName__. All rights reserved.
//

#import <Cocoa/Cocoa.h>


@interface NotifyingClass : NSObject {

}

@end
```

As I mentioned in the previous chapter, the green lines with the // characters at the start are comments and are ignored. Again, these lines simply state the name of the file, its containing project, and information about the file's creator. Some people prefer to remove these lines altogether—you may find them helpful for now to be sure you're editing the right file at any particular time.

Under the comment lines, there's a line beginning with **#import**, and then we get a section starting with the keyword **@interface** and ending, pretty unsurprisingly, with the keyword **@end**. These two keywords should be pink.

This portion of the file is where our class description goes. In the Objective-C language, we refer to a class having a public *interface*, describing the messages that can be sent to that class. The **@interface** line looks like this: ·

```
@interface NotifyingClass : NSObject {
```

This line states that this is the **interface** for a class called NotifyingClass. Putting a colon after the name of the class specifies that this class should inherit from another class, specified in this case as NSObject. Because it's such a common requirement, the Xcode file templates for an *Objective-C class* are set up to inherit from the Cocoa framework's base class.

Curly braces are used in Objective-C to indicate *blocks* of code. In this particular **@interface** section, they are used to specify attributes that belong to a class. In our house example, we would put information between these curly braces to indicate that the House class has attributes for a door color and address. Since our NotifyingClass doesn't have any of its own attributes, we can leave this part blank.

The last thing left to include from our class description is the list of messages the class can receive. These go between the closing curly brace and the final **@end** keyword.

Looking back at our class description, we see that we will be writing code to respond to the init message. From this, we might assume that we need to list this now. In fact, we originally decided to write code for this message because it is called automatically when an instance of NSObject is created. The interface file for the NSObject class *already* lists this message, so we don't really need to do it again here.

If you're feeling adventurous, choose the File > Open Quickly... menu item in Xcode, and type "NSObject.h" to find its interface file. You'll then be able to open this file by clicking the Open button. Don't be too intimidated by its contents—if you scroll down until you find the green Base class comment, you'll see the **@interface** declaration for the NSObject class, as shown in Figure 3.4, on the facing page.

We'll be returning to this file in a little while, but for now, click the NotifyingClass.h file in the Groups & Files list to go back to the interface file for our own rather simpler class.

The Syntax to Define an Interface

Class descriptions written in the Objective-C language always follow this pattern, or *syntax*:

```
@interface «nameOfClass» : «nameOfClassToInheritFrom» {
    «attribute information»
}

«list of messages responded to»

@end
```

Because we're only going to be writing code to respond to the init message and the init message is already listed in the interface of NSObject, we don't need to make any changes to our NotifyingClass.h file at all.

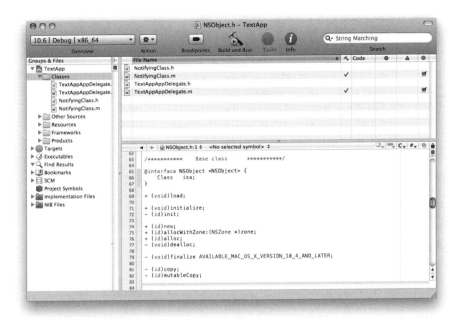

Figure 3.4: THE NSOBJECT.H INTERFACE FILE

Creating an Instance of Our NotifyingClass

Before we go and put in our notifying behavior, let's test our object quickly by creating an instance of it.

Given our knowledge so far, the easiest way for us to create the instance is by using Interface Builder. In the same way that the Window, Menu, and Text View objects were created by our work in MainMenu.xib, we can *instantiate* a new NotifyingClass object "visually."

Open MainMenu.xib in Interface Builder again by double-clicking the file in the Resources group in the Groups & Files list.

Locate Interface Builder's Library palette, and find the Object icon. It looks like a blue cube, as shown in Figure 3.5, on the next page.

Drag this icon to the main MainMenu.xib window (that's the one with the Main Menu, Application, and other objects in it), and drop it after the other objects. At the moment, having this "Object" in our file will generate an instance of the standard NSObject base class when the application is run. We want to modify it so that our own NotifyingClass class gets instantiated instead.

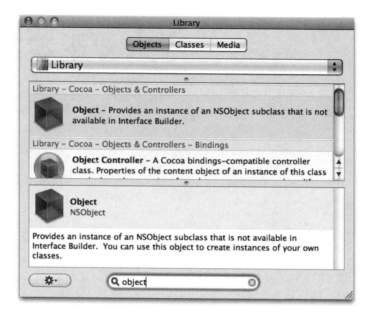

Figure 3.5: The Object icon in the Library palette

Choose Tools > Identity Inspector, and you'll see that the first option in this palette is Class. It currently shows NSObject in the adjoining text field. Change this field to say "NotifyingClass." You should find that as you start typing, Interface Builder guesses the rest of the class name. There is complex integration between Apple's developer applications such that when you create and define an object in Xcode, Interface Builder automatically knows about it.

At this point, we've created an instance of our object in MainMenu.xib—this instance will be created when the application is run, so let's try to run the application now.

Save the MainMenu.xib file in Interface Builder, return to Xcode, and click the Build & Run button.

Unless you accidentally typed something in the NotifyingClass.h file, you should find that TextApp launches exactly as it did before—absolutely nothing appears to have changed. For now, you'll just have to have faith that there really is an instance of our NotifyingClass existing between application launch and application exit.

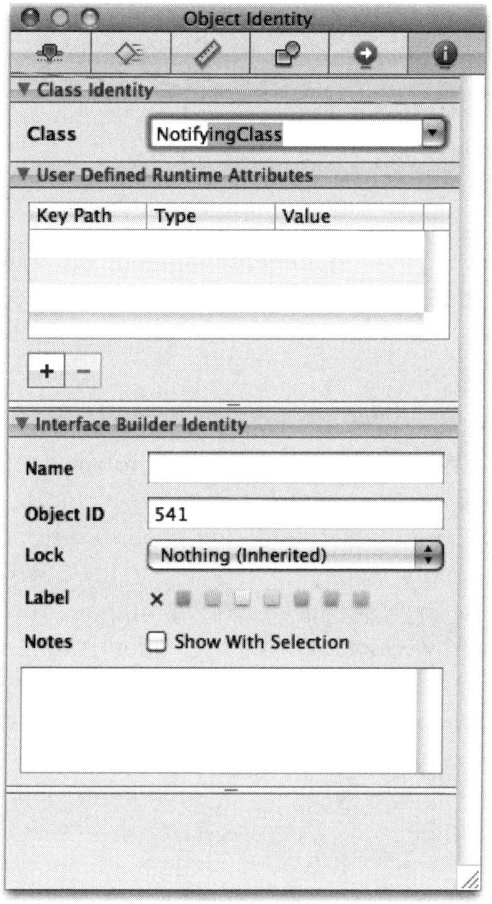

Figure 3.6: The Identity inspector for our NotifyingClass

Adding Our Notifying Behavior

Now we're finally going to get our teeth into some code. We'll be writing a *method*—methods are the blocks of code that get *executed* when a particular message is received.

Open the NotifyingClass.m file in a new Xcode window by double-clicking it in the Groups & Files list. You should see a file with the usual descriptive comments at the top, followed by this code:

```
#import "NotifyingClass.h"

@implementation NotifyingClass

@end
```

This .m file contains the *implementation* for the object. The method we're going to write will go inside the **@implementation** section of this file, before the final **@end**.

The method we need to write should tell us when the object is first initialized. It is the method called in response to the init message, currently defined by the NSObject base class implementation. So that our code is called instead, we need to make sure the name and relevant information on this message is exactly the same as that from the interface for NSObject. So, select File > Open Quickly... from Xcode's menu bar, and again type in "NSObject"—you should see the NSObject header file (NSObject.h) that we looked at before. Open this file once more, and scroll down the contents until you find the relevant lines inside the NSObject Base Object interface that define the messages. One of these lines should be the following:

```
- (id)init;
```

Copy this line to the clipboard, and go back to the NotifyingClass.m file. Paste the line in between the **@implementation** and **@end** keywords.

Don't worry for now about the "- (id)" bit before init—we'll be talking more about what this means in the next chapter. Do, however, notice that there is a semicolon (;) at the end of this line.

The Objective-C programming language has punctuation just like natural languages do. A semicolon is used to indicate the end of a particular programming statement, like a period or "full stop" does in English. In the **@interface** section, this line was used to show that NSObject implements an init method. That was as much information as was needed in an **@interface**, so a semicolon is included to "end the statement."

Whitespace in Objective-C

Some programming languages use "new lines" to denote ends of statements. For the most part, Objective-C doesn't care whether you put one statement all on one line or split it over multiple lines. It uses the "punctuation" such as semicolons and braces to indicate where statements begin and end.

We could put the opening curly brace on the end of the - (id)init line like this:

```
- (id)init {
}
```

or on a new line like this:

```
- (id)init
{
}
```

and it wouldn't make any difference. You'll see both ways of defining methods used throughout the programming community. You may, for example, have noticed that the opening curly brace used in the template-generated NotifyingClass.h interface is on the same line as the **@interface** keyword.

In our implementation, however, we need to specify the lines of code for the init method. We'll be providing more information here than just the name of the method, so the convention is to remove the semicolon at the end of the line.[3]

As I said earlier, curly braces are used to denote blocks of code. In our implementation file, we need to use them to indicate the code to be run for this particular method. So, on the line immediately underneath our newly pasted - (id)init line, put in an opening and a closing curly brace like this:

```
- (id)init
{
}
```

Code blocks using curly braces are the exception to the rule of needing semicolons. In general, where you have something defining a block of

---

3. It's also perfectly acceptable to leave the semicolon in method implementations—some people like to do this because it makes it easier simply to copy and paste the method signatures from the interface file to the implementation file.

code in curly braces like this init method, the closing curly brace is enough to confirm the end of the "statement," so a semicolon isn't used.

Introducing NSLog

Since the purpose of our new object is to let us know when it is created, we need to decide on a suitable way for it to notify us. An incredibly useful and very simple way is to *log* a message to the console. This may sound a little scary, but it's actually quite straightforward. In Xcode, open the Debugger Console by choosing the Run > Console menu item. You will probably see a series of message looking like this:

```
Loading program into debugger...
Program loaded.
run
[Switching to process 3618]
Running...

Debugger stopped.
Program exited with status value:0.
```

These messages show when TextApp was loaded and run and when it stopped and exited (that is, quit).

To write a message to this log, we can use NSLog(). This isn't actually an object, despite having the *NS* initials, but instead is what's called a *function*. We'll talk more about these later in the book, but we'll use this particular function right now. Change your NotifyingClass.m implementation by adding the following line:

```
@implementation NotifyingClass

- (id)init
{
    NSLog(@"Hello World! I'm a new NotifyingClass instance!");
}

@end
```

This line will log a friendly message to the console—don't forget to include the final semicolon to indicate that this is the end of the logging statement.

One Final Thing

For this to work, we need to add one final line of code at the end of this method; we'll find out exactly what this line does in a couple of chapters' time. After the NSLog call, add the following line of code (again, don't forget the ending semicolon):

```
- (id)init
{
    NSLog(@"Hello World! I'm a new NotifyingClass instance!");

    return self;
}
```

Make sure that the Debugger Console window is still visible, and click Build & Run.

When the application is run, you should find that our notifying message appears in the log:

```
Running...
2009-09-08 17:48:25.003 TextApp[3642:a0f] Hello World!
                                I'm a new NotifyingClass instance!
```

At the moment, we're completely overriding the init method provided by the NSObject base class in order to make this demonstration as simple as possible. In reality, you will need to write a lot more into this method if you override it—for a start, you'll need to be sure to call the original, overridden init behavior so that the inherited NSObject base is initialized properly. We'll revisit this method in our chapter on memory management. For now, don't worry about it, other than noticing that this is the only time you'll have an init method that looks as short and simple as the one in NotifyingClass.m!

Creating Another Instance

Just to make absolutely certain that we're happy about classes and instances, let's add a second instance of our NotifyingClass to the application. You might like to think about what you expect to see happen when the application is launched...

Quit the TextApp application if it is still running. Go back into Interface Builder, and drag out another base Object (that blue cube icon) from the Library palette. Again, go to the Identity inspector, and change its class to "NotifyingClass," just like we did for the other instance created.

Save the file, and return to Xcode. Make sure the Debugger Console is still visible, and click the Build & Run button to launch the application.

Hopefully, you predicted that you would see a second "Hello" message in the Console log—sure enough, you now should be looking at something like the following:

```
Running...
2009-09-08 17:49:05.963 TextApp[3661:a0f] Hello World!
                                I'm a new NotifyingClass instance!
2009-09-08 17:49:05.965 TextApp[3661:a0f] Hello World!
                                I'm a new NotifyingClass instance!
```

We've now instantiated two separate NotifyingClass instances, both of which log their message to the console when they are created at application launch.

3.5 Chapter Summary

Over the course of this chapter, we've looked at an overview of object-oriented programming. Once the basic principles were laid out, we created our own object class description, set up an instance of this class using Interface Builder, and implemented some very basic functionality for the object by writing code that is called in response to the init message.

In the next chapter, we'll be looking at how objects interact by sending messages to each other.

Chapter 4

Object Messaging

Now that you have an understanding of objects, it's time to look a lit-tle further into how messages can be sent between them. Our TextApp application is built using a number of objects, including the Notifying-Class object we created in the previous chapter, but they aren't doing very much once the application has loaded. To introduce new function-ality to the application, we need a way to send messages between our objects.

Currently, our NotifyingClass object responds to the init message sent automatically when the object is created. In this chapter, we're going to change TextApp by adding a button to the interface. When this button is clicked, it will send a message to our NotifyingClass to do something. In the previous chapter, we used NSLog( ) to log a message to the debugging console in Xcode. This time, we'll have our NotifyingClass communicate with the text view inside TextApp to display the message.

4.1 Defining a New Method

You already know that we use the NotifyingClass.h header file to define an **@interface** for our NotifyingClass object. Our current class description is very basic and shows only that our class inherits from NSObject.

We're going to define a new method called displaySomeText that will be called when a button is clicked in the application's interface. Remem-ber how we didn't put anything in our class description to inform the world that our object would respond to the init message because that method was already defined in the NSObject class description? By con-trast, displaySomeText is a new method, not provided by NSObject, so we *will* need to list it in our class description.

Open the NotifyingClass.h file in Xcode. If you glance back to Section 3.4, *The Syntax to Define an Interface*, on page 40, you'll see that the «*list of messages responded to*» goes after the closing curly brace and before the **@end** keyword. This is where we need to define the new method.

To make sure we get the correct *signature* for a basic message, let's take another look at some of Apple's own Cocoa method signatures. Once again, use Xcode's Open Quickly... command (⇧-⌘-D) to open the NSObject.h header file, and scroll down to find the **@interface** for NSObject; some of the signatures you'll find look like this:

```
+ (void)load;

+ (void)initialize;
- (id)init;

+ (id)new;
+ (id)allocWithZone:(NSZone *)zone;
+ (id)alloc;
- (void)dealloc;
```

You should recognize that we copied a line from here when we implemented a method to respond to the init message in the previous chapter. Notice how each message signature listed conforms to a similar format:

```
-         (id)     init;
+         (id)     allocWithZone: (NSZone *)zone;
«+ or -»  («word») «messageName» «some optional bits»;
```

The «+ *or* -» at the start of the signature describes whether the message can be called on an *instance* of the class or *on the class itself*. We'll be seeing more about what are known as *class methods* later, but for now we just want to define the behavior of our *instance* when it receives the displaySomeText message. This requires us to use a minus (-) sign, just like we saw before on init.

The «*word*» in brackets before the message name specifies whether the method will return some information when it's called. For our theoretical House class from the previous chapter, for example, a house instance would be expected to respond to the accessFoundationSpecifications message by sending back the requested information. Our Notifying-Class doesn't need to respond with any information when it's called—it just needs to do something in response to the message.

Glancing at the code extract from NSObject.h earlier, notice how each of those signatures listed uses either **void** or **id**. We'll be talking about **id** later in the book, but, given the everyday definition of "void," it shouldn't come as much of a surprise that **void** is used to specify that a method returns nothing.

So, our method signature might look like the following:

```
- (void)displaySomeText;
```

This specifies that an instance of NotifyingClass does something in response to the displaySomeText message and that it doesn't provide any information in return. Make your NotifyingClass.h file look like this:

```
#import <Cocoa/Cocoa.h>

@interface NotifyingClass : NSObject {

}

- (void)displaySomeText;

@end
```

Implementing Our New Method

Next, we're going to write some code to be executed in response to the displaySomeText message. Open NotifyingClass.m, and remove all the code for the existing init method, leaving behind the **@implementation** and **@end** keywords.

To make sure we get our method correct, let's copy its signature from our header file. As a quick shortcut in Xcode, you can switch between header and implementation files for a class by using the little Go to Counterpart icon (shown in Figure 4.1, on the next page) or by using the keyboard shortcut ⌥-⌘-↑.

Copy the method signature to the pasteboard:

```
- (void)displaySomeText;
```

Switch back to the implementation file, and paste the copied method between **@implementation** and **@end**. Remember that when we're implementing a method, we usually remove the semicolon? Do that now, and add opening and closing curly braces so that you end up with the method looking like this:

```
@implementation NotifyingClass

- (void)displaySomeText
{

}

@end
```

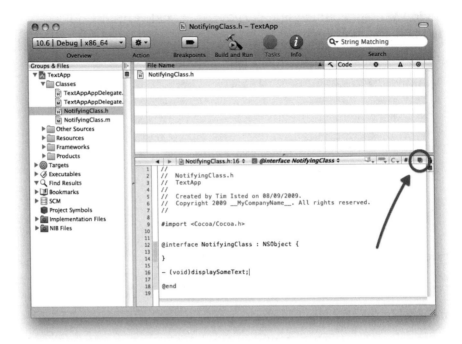

Figure 4.1: THE GO TO COUNTERPART QUICK-SWITCH ICON IN XCODE

For now, we'll just output a message to Xcode's debugger console to let us know when this method is called, so add the following line of code:

```
- (void)displaySomeText
{
    NSLog(@"displaySomeText just got called!");
}
```

If you Build & Run at this point, you'll find that TextApp launches fine, but no friendly messages appear in the debugger console. We removed the code responding to the init message earlier, and at the moment our new displaySomeText method never gets called. All we've done so far is define the code that would be called *if* the displaySomeText message was received, but it never is.

4.2 The Target-Action Mechanism

Our aim is to send the displaySomeText message to our NotifyingClass object when the user clicks a button in our TextApp application. The

Cocoa framework provides us with a nifty little technique to help with this, called *target-action*.

Certain objects offered by the Cocoa framework allow you to provide them with a *target* object and specify an *action*—a message to be sent to that object. One of the objects supporting such a mechanism is an NSButton. This class is used to create a number of different types of Mac OS X buttons; its default style is the one we'll be using shortly when we add a button to TextApp's user interface. Once we've created an NSButton instance in Interface Builder, we can tell the button about our NotifyingClass instance and specify that the relevant *action* is to call its displaySomeText method when the user clicks the button.

At this point we need to make a couple of small changes to our existing method definition for displaySomeText so we can use it with Interface Builder and target-action. For Cocoa desktop applications on the Mac, a method to be called in a target-action situation needs to conform to a specific signature format. The method needs to be able to accept a single *argument* on it.

We'll discuss arguments in Chapter 6, *Passing Information Around*, on page 91, but if you take a quick look back now to earlier in this chapter at the format for a message signature, you'll see that there are "optional bits" that can be put on the end of the signature style we've seen so far, as in one example from NSObject.h:

```
+ (id)allocWithZone:(NSZone *)zone;
```

If a message name has a colon on the end of it (that's : rather than the end-of-line *semi*colon ;), it means that it accepts one or more arguments. An argument is used to pass some information along with a message. Back in our housing example, when the property developer object sends a message to the builder object to buildHouse:, it needs to specify which house to build. This would be offered as an argument, like this:

```
- (void)buildHouse:(House *)houseToBeBuilt;
```

After the colon comes something in parentheses with an asterisk— (House *)—that specifies what kind of information is being provided, followed by a name to be assigned to the provided information. Don't worry if this isn't immediately clear in your head; we'll be covering various things in the next chapter that will help you to understand it. We'll continue using it in this chapter, though, so at this point, just follow along with the syntax.

```
+ (id)                    allocWithZone:(NSZone *)              zone;
- (void)                  buildHouse: (House *)                 houseToBeBuilt;
± («type expected in return»)methodName:(«type of info provided»)«name for info»;
```

The buildHouse: method (notice we're putting the colon on the end of it to indicate it accepts an argument) expects to receive a House object when it's called, identifying the particular house to be built. Similarly, the allocWithZone: method expects an NSZone object to identify the zone to be used.

Returning to target-action, I stated a little earlier that a method needs to accept a single argument to work for target-action. This argument happens to be used to identify the object that sent the message in the first place. When we connect a button in TextApp to target our Notifying-Class instance, the *button* would send the message and specify that *it* was the sender. The signature therefore needs to look something like this:

```
- (void)displaySomeText:(id)sender;
```

The **id** keyword here is used to specify that *some kind of object* will be provided as the sender. Again, we'll be talking more about **id** later.

There's just one last thing we need to change slightly on this method declaration, since we're going to be using Interface Builder to connect the target and action on a new NSButton object.

Communication Between Xcode and Interface Builder

Remember how we created an object instance in Interface Builder (that blue cube thing) in the previous chapter and set its class to Notifying-Class in the inspector? When we did that, Interface Builder managed to guess the rest of the class name after we'd typed only a few characters. This is because Interface Builder and Xcode "talk to each other" behind the scenes. Some things happen automatically (like IB having knowledge of classes for which you've provided class descriptions in an Xcode project), whereas other things happen when you use specific keywords in your code files.

This is one case where we need to use such a keyword. To specify that our method is an action that can be connected to a control object (like an NSButton) in Interface Builder, we need to change the **void** keyword into **IBAction**:

```
- (IBAction)displaySomeText:(id)sender;
```

As far as the *code compiler* is concerned, **IBAction** is synonymous with **void**. This keyword simply alerts Interface Builder that there's an *action* available in a class description.

It's time to modify our code for this purpose. First, we need to change the interface for our NotifyingClass object, so open NotifyingClass.h in X-code. Change it so that the method follows our new action signature:

```
@interface NotifyingClass : NSObject {
}

- (IBAction)displaySomeText:(id)sender;

@end
```

Next, we need to change our implementation method signature in Noti-fyingClass.m, so switch to this file, and make it look like this:

```
@implementation NotifyingClass

- (IBAction)displaySomeText:(id)sender
{
    NSLog(@"displaySomeText just got called!");
}

@end
```

Notice that we don't need to do anything with the sender attribute—we can quite safely ignore it altogether. And, since **IBAction** is just a keyword meaning **void** as far as the compiler is concerned, we don't have to worry about giving any information back at the end of the method.

Make sure you save all your modifications before proceeding. If you hold down the ⌥ key on your keyboard and go to Xcode's File menu, you'll see that a few of the items have changed, and there is now a Save All... command (with keyboard shortcut ⌥-⌘-Ⓢ.) If there are any unsaved changes in any of the project's files, use this command to save them all at once.

Connecting the Action in Interface Builder

Now that we've defined our NotifyingClass class instances to respond to an action message for displaySomeText, we'll use Interface Builder to connect things visually.

Let's start by adding a button to our existing TextApp window. Open MainMenu.xib, and make sure TextApp's Window object with the text

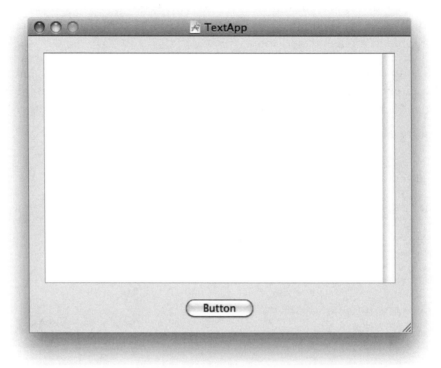

Figure 4.2: THE NEW PUSH BUTTON IN OUR TEXT APP MAIN WINDOW

view is visible. If you need to reopen the Window, double-click the Window (TextApp) object in MainMenu.xib.

You will need to make that text view a little smaller by dragging up the bottom handle so there's room for a button underneath it (make sure you resize the text view rather than just moving it higher in the window). Next, find a standard Push Button object in the Library palette, and drag one out onto the window. You should end up with something resembling Figure 4.2.

Next, remove one of the existing NotifyingClass instances from the MainMenu.xib file by selecting it and pressing the ⌫ key.

We're now ready to connect our button to the remaining NotifyingClass instance, and Interface Builder provides a great interface for doing this. Bring the MainMenu.xib document window to the front in Interface

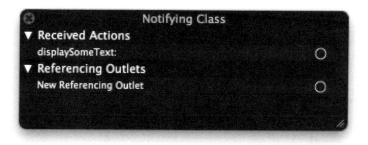

Figure 4.3: THE CONNECTIONS HUD FOR OUR NOTIFYINGCLASS INSTANCE

Builder, but keep the window with the button in it visible on screen. Right-click (or ^-click) the Notifying Class blue cube. You'll find that a black mini-window pops up (known as a *heads-up display*, or HUD), as shown in Figure 4.3.

If everything has gone to plan, you should find that this HUD window shows one option under the heading "Received Actions"—our displaySomeText: action message. To the right of this line is a little circle; click and drag from the circle, and you'll find a line extends out and follows your movements on screen. Drag down to our new Button object, and you'll find IB highlights and identifies the button. Release your mouse, and you should find that the HUD display now shows a connection to our Push Button, as in Figure 4.4, on the next page.

If you now bring the application's window to the front, click the push button to select it, and then right-click (or ^-click) on it, you'll find that another HUD window will appear, showing a connection to our NotifyingClass object's action under the "Sent Actions" heading, as in Figure 4.5, on page 59.

It really is as simple as that! Interface Builder has now set up our button with a reference to the notifying object and has set up the requested action for us, all with just a simple click-and-drag motion.

Save your file in Interface Builder, and switch back to Xcode to Build & Run. TextApp will launch, and when you click the button in the window, you'll see a message appear each time in the Xcode console window. Woo-hoo!

Figure 4.4: CONNECTING OUR BUTTON TO THE ACTION

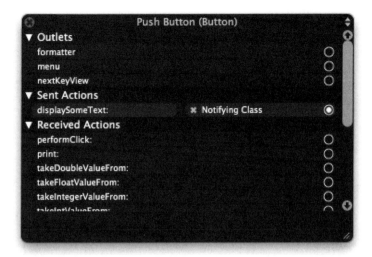

Figure 4.5: THE ACTIONS SENT BY OUR PUSH BUTTON

4.3 Sending Messages from Our Code

The target-action mechanism we explored in the previous section is awesome for connecting up buttons and *receiving* messages in certain situations, but we need to *send* messages to objects from our code too. Our next step for TextApp is to stop using the debugger console to display information and instead be able to send a message to the text view to change its text to something we specify.

A Quick Note About Pointers

For the rest of this chapter, we will be using *pointers*. Pointers can be nontrivial to understand, and a large portion of the next chapter is devoted to them. For now, just think of the pointers we're using here as being like a "link" to an object instance in memory.

To be able to send a message to the text view, we need to have some kind of handle on that specific text view instance so we can "talk" to it; this is a bit like needing a cell phone number to send a text message to a friend.

A pointer looks like this:

```
NSTextView *aTextViewInstance;
```

Notice the asterisk (*) involved here.[1] This particular syntax *declares* a pointer to a text view object (naturally bearing the class name NSText-View) that is called aTextViewInstance. Once this pointer is "connected" to a text view, we can use the pointer to send messages to the text view. In the same way that you need to activate a cell phone before it will accept calls or messages, you need to link up a pointer to the object it "points to." In this chapter, we'll be linking our pointer using Interface Builder.

A Pointer to Our Text View

Our NotifyingClass object needs to be able to talk to the NSTextView in TextApp's user interface. That means that we need our object to have access to a pointer to the text view. With this in mind, open Notifying-Class.h in Xcode.

The text view pointer will be an attribute for the NotifyingClass class description, so it needs to go between the curly braces like this:

```
@interface NotifyingClass : NSObject {
    NSTextView *textView;
}

- (IBAction)displaySomeText:(id)sender;

@end
```

But, because we are going to use Interface Builder to link it up to the actual object, we need to use another IB communication keyword. Putting **IBOutlet** in front of the pointer declaration tells Interface Builder that we need access to that pointer so we can hook it up to something. This kind of "hook-up-able" pointer is known as an *outlet*, which is why it's called **IBOutlet**.

Modify your NotifyingClass.h file so that the **@interface** looks like this:

```
@interface NotifyingClass : NSObject {
    IBOutlet NSTextView *textView;
}

- (IBAction)displaySomeText:(id)sender;

@end
```

---

1. You probably noticed these earlier in this chapter when we were looking at attributes on methods.

Because we're declaring this pointer inside the NotifyingClass class description, it becomes one of those "assignable attributes" we saw before in class descriptions, and we would be able to use it from within any method implemented by the class. We have only one method at the moment (displaySomeText:), but it's worth mentioning all the same.

Connecting Outlets in Interface Builder

Save your work in Xcode, and then switch to Interface Builder to edit the MainMenu.xib file. Once again, right-click (or ^-click) the Notifying-Class object, and you'll see a new addition in the HUD window that appears. There is now an Outlets group in the HUD, and it contains one item—our textView outlet that we just created in Xcode.

Make sure that you can see the main window for TextApp in Interface Builder with its text view. Guess how we link up the outlet? Yep, drag from the little circle in the HUD over to the text view—it should highlight, as shown in Figure 4.6, on the next page. You'll need to drag right up to that highlighted area at the top, which is the actual text view. The rest of the area with scroll bars is really an enclosing scroll view.

That's all there is to it![2] Our pointer/outlet is now linked up to the text view ready for us to start sending messages. Save your work in Interface Builder, and then switch back to Xcode.

Sending a Message to an Object

To get the text view to display some text, we need to know exactly what message to send it. There are several ways to find out which messages an object will accept; this time, let's use the documentation system built into Xcode. Choose the Help > Developer Documentation menu item (⌥-⌘-?), and the Developer Documentation window will appear. In the Search textbox, enter "NSTextView." You should find that "NSTextView Class Reference" appears in the main portion of the window, as in Figure 4.7, on page 63.

This may look like a scary document, but it's actually not all that bad. It lists the messages that an NSTextView object will respond to; since we're looking to insert some text in the text view, scroll down until you find a

---

2. Under earlier versions of the Developer Tools, an NSTextView object created in Interface Builder starts out life filled with *Lorum Ipsum* placeholder text. If you have this text showing in your text view, you'll probably want to remove it before continuing. Accomplishing this can be a little fiddly, but, essentially, click three times over the existing placeholder text until all the text (and only the text) is selected. Once you've selected it, you can edit it like you would any text in any application.

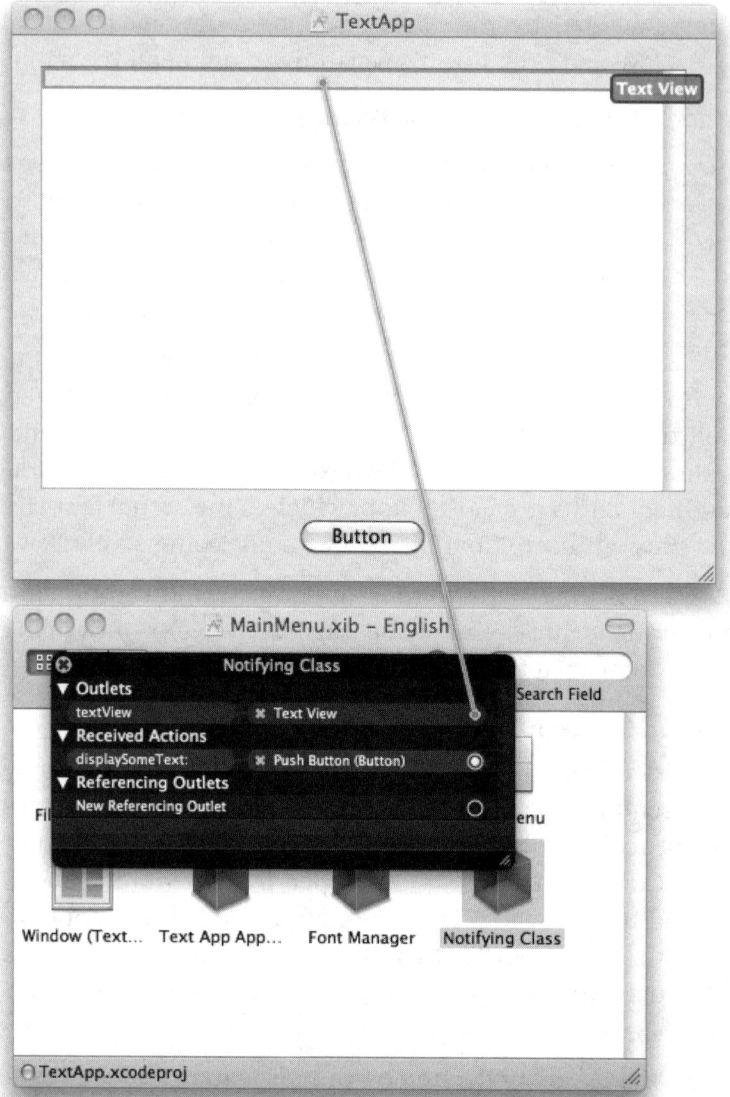

Figure 4.6: CONNECTING OUR OUTLET TO THE TEXT VIEW

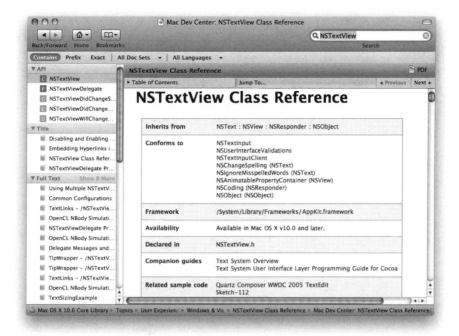

Figure 4.7: THE XCODE DOCUMENTATION WINDOW

list of messages under the "Inserting Text" heading. The first message listed is the helpfully named insertText: method. If you click this link, you'll jump down to read the documentation for it.

The insertText: method takes one attribute—a string object. In programming, a *string* refers to a string of characters such as "this is a medium-length string" or "hello!" You'll generally see strings defined in programming code between single or double quotation marks.

Now that we know what message to send to the text view, the last thing we need to learn is the syntax used to do that in Objective-C. It's actually quite simple and involves the use of square brackets ([and]). Close the documentation window, and open NotifyingClass.m. Change your displaySomeText: method to look like this:

```
- (IBAction)displaySomeText:(id)sender
{
    [textView insertText:@"displaySomeText just got called!\n"];
}
```

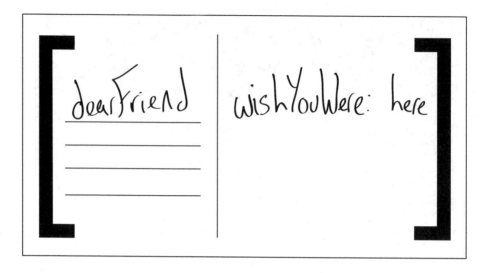

Figure 4.8: Sending messages to objects in Objective-C

We've replaced the use of NSLog with a message to the text view object to insert the text. Notice that there are no *parentheses*—(and)—in use here; we're now using *square brackets* to indicate that we're sending a message. Notice also that we've added the characters \n (that's a back-slash, not the more frequently used forward slash) on the end of the string. This is a **new line** specifier, rather like the carriage return at the end of a paragraph in a text document. It means that any subsequent text should display on the next line down.

An analogy might be helpful at this point. For example, you could think of the line of code as being like a rectangular postcard (Figure 4.8). The first word on the card addresses the object to which the message will be sent (textView); next comes the name of the message to send (insertText:), followed by any parameters that are needed (@"displaySomeText just got called!\n"):

```
[«receiving object» «message»«:optional parameters»];
```

Assuming you haven't mistyped anything, TextApp will launch when you click Build & Run. When you click the button, you should see the message appear in the text view; every time you click, a new message will appear!

Just to show that this isn't some kind of fluke, let's send a message to another object that we can access. Remember when we redefined our displaySomeText: method to have a sender variable for use with the target-action mechanism? This sender is a pointer that will be linked to the object that sent us the message—in TextApp, it will be the push button.

If you wish, look up the class reference for NSButton like you did for NSTextView. You'll find it has a method called setTitle: that, unsurprisingly, sets the title of the button to the string you specify.

Change your displaySomeText: method by adding a call to setTitle: on the sender object. The syntax is the same as before and looks pretty similar to our existing call to the text view:

```
- (IBAction)displaySomeText:(id)sender
{
    [textView insertText:@"displaySomeText just got called!\n"];

    [sender setTitle:@"Clicked"];
}
```

This time when you Build & Run, the text on the button will change once it has been clicked. Obviously, it will appear to change only the first time—subsequent times, we're setting the text to the value it already has.

You can also disable the button from this method so it can be clicked only once. Open the class reference for NSButton again in the documentation viewer. At the top of the file, you'll see a list of classes that it "inherits from." The first of these listed is the NSControl class. Click this class, and you'll jump into its class reference. Scroll down a little way until you find the task heading "Enabling and Disabling the Control." There's a helpful method listed called setEnabled:, which looks like it will do what we want. If you click this, you'll jump down to the documentation for the method; its signature looks like this:

```
- (void)setEnabled:(BOOL)flag
```

The keyword **BOOL** refers to a *Boolean* value—one that is either true or false. Open the NotifyingClass.m file, and change the displaySomeText: method to the following:

```
- (IBAction)displaySomeText:(id)sender
{
    [textView insertText:@"displaySomeText just got called!\n"];

    [sender setTitle:@"Clicked"];
    [sender setEnabled:NO];
}
```

The keyword **NO** states that we *don't* want the button to be enabled—see how readable the Objective-C language can be? This time, when you Build & Run the application, you'll find you can click the button only once. When our displaySomeText: method is called, it disables the button. This also confirms what we discussed in the previous chapter: not only can we call methods that are specifically defined by an object (like setTitle:), we can also call methods *inherited* from parent objects (like setEnabled:).

4.4 Chapter Summary

You've learned quite a lot in this chapter. First, we defined our own message for our class. We looked at the target-action mechanism and redefined this new method to work as an action. Using keywords to help Interface Builder identify our action method meant that we were able to hook up this action, visually, to the push button we created in our interface.

Next, we touched briefly on pointers before setting up an IB-connected outlet from our notifying object to our text view object. Once the pointer was connected, we covered how to send a message to insert some text in TextApp's text view on screen. We also made use of the sender parameter provided to us in our action, linking to the object that sent us the message.

It's now time to delve a little more deeply into pointers, attributes, and parameters by looking at how information gets stored in memory.

Chapter 5

Variables and Memory

You've traveled a long way into the world of Mac OS X programming. Before you can go much further, though, you need to learn a little about how computers work with memory to keep track of useful information.

In the first part of this chapter, we'll look at how a computer actually stores information in its memory, before moving on to talk about how we can declare *variables* to hold basic values for us. We'll modify our current TextApp application to store some values temporarily in memory, perform a calculation or two, and then output the values to see what was stored.

5.1 How Memory Works

Your computer contains a number of physical storage places for information. Some are for *persistent* storage (such as hard disks, CD/DVD drives, and so on), and some are for temporary use while the computer is running (RAM). It's the RAM that we are talking about for this chapter—the memory available for use by your application at runtime.[1]

In the previous chapter, we used *pointers*—references to objects that were held in memory. For the first part of this chapter, however, we'll be looking at storing very simple pieces of information such as integer and decimal numbers. These are known as *scalar types* and are handled very differently from the *objects* we've been used to up until now. We

---

1. *Runtime* refers to the time at which the finished application is launched by a user. It differs from other "types of time" that a programmer might be interested in, such as *compile time*, which is the time at which the Objective-C code that you've written gets *compiled* into machine-understandable language and linked together into an application.

can't send messages to these scalar types; they just exist as a value in memory that you can access when needed.

Before we dive in and start looking at how we use and access memory from Objective-C code, let's take a brief look at how information gets stored inside a computer's physical memory. This is valuable background for our next steps, so hang in there! We'll start with very basic integer numbers.

Bits and Bytes

You might like to think of the RAM inside your computer as a giant collection of switches. Each switch is either "on" or "off," meaning that it can be used to represent one of only two possible values. When you're programming, you'll find these values are used in many different ways. Numerically, they can be 0 and 1; they can also be used to represent "true" and "false," or even the words "yes" and "no."

Clearly, a single switch, or *bit*, is not going to be much help storing numbers greater than 1, quite aside from large objects, so computers use groups of these bits to represent larger numbers in *binary* notation. Representing numbers in binary is actually very similar to the way you currently think about numbers, using *decimal* notation, but instead you only have the digits 0 and 1 to worry about. Let's analyze our standard decimal notation first.

Decimal Notation

Consider for a moment what we're doing when we write down a number like 2,568. When counting "normally," we're used to working with the numbers 0 through 9. Multiple digits are used to represent values greater than 9, and each of these digits specifies a multiplier for a *power of ten*. This all sounds incredibly complicated given that counting, say, from 99 to 101 seems so natural to us, but for now let's look at what each individual digit represents in the number 2,568 by splitting its digits into a table format like this:

10,000	1,000	100	10	1
0	2	5	6	8

Notice that each column in the table is a *power of 10* (each column header is equal to the previous column header multiplied by 10), where 10 is the number of possible digits that we can use from 0 to 9. The maximum number we can represent with a certain number of columns would be when each column contains the highest possible digit (9). If we were using only three columns (100, 10, and 1), the maximum number we could represent would be 999, which also happens to be 1 less than the next highest column header (1,000).

We can rework the table to show how we "build up" a final number from the digits in each column like this:

$$
\begin{array}{rcrcr}
0 & \times & 10,000 & = & 0 \\
2 & \times & 1,000 & = & 2,000 \\
5 & \times & 100 & = & 500 \\
6 & \times & 10 & = & 60 \\
8 & \times & 1 & = & 8 \\
& & \text{Total} & = & 2,568
\end{array}
$$

Binary Notation

Since in binary we can use only two possible digits (0 and 1), we are going to be working with column headers that are *powers of 2*. If we make a similar table to our first *decimal* table from earlier in the chapter, keeping the same relationship between consecutive column headers as before, we would end up with this:

16	8	4	2	1
0	1	1	1	0

It's quite easy to work out what this number, written as 01110 in binary notation, would be in decimal notation. We simply need to build the number using the second table style shown earlier to give this:

$$
\begin{array}{rcrcr}
0 & \times & 16 & = & 0 \\
1 & \times & 8 & = & 8 \\
1 & \times & 4 & = & 4 \\
1 & \times & 2 & = & 2 \\
0 & \times & 1 & = & 0 \\
& & \text{Total} & = & 14
\end{array}
$$

So, the number 01110 in binary is the number 14 in decimal.

Groups of Bits

When we ask a computer to store a decimal number like 2,568, the computer would need to convert that number to binary format first before storing it, in this case giving the result 101000001000. Representing this number therefore needs a chain of 12 individual bits. Storing the number 29, however, would take only 5 bits (11101).

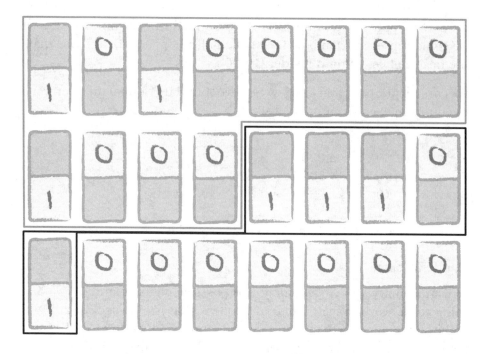

Figure 5.1: A GRAPHICAL REPRESENTATION OF OUR NUMBERS STORED USING SWITCHES IN MEMORY

It might seem that the most efficient way to store numbers in memory would be to use only as many bits as were needed, but this actually poses a problem. Consider a large bank of these switches set up to represent our chosen data. With the two values stored, we might end up with something looking like Figure 5.1.

The problem with this approach is that in order to make sense of the 1s and 0s in memory, we need to know how many bits are taken by each number. To retrieve our first number, we would need to ask for "a number represented by the first 12 bits;" to get our second number, we then need to ask for "a number represented by the next 5 bits." Not only is this system confusing, it also requires us to store the "number of bits used" along with the number itself in order to be able to retrieve our information. We'd then need another "number of bits used" for the "number of bits used" number, and so on!

Bytes

An easier way is to decide that we'll work using blocks of a specific number of bits. In the C programming language and therefore in Objective-C, the basic bit-block size is 8. These 8-bit blocks are called *bytes*.

As an example, the number 29 requires 5 bits to be set and so could be represented using a single byte. The unused bits in a byte are set to zero, so 29 would be 00011101 in a byte.

The maximum number representable in a byte can be worked out in two ways; either we can set all 8 bits to 1 to work it out:

128	64	32	16	8	4	2	1
1	1	1	1	1	1	1	1

1	×	128	=	128
1	×	64	=	64
1	×	32	=	32
1	×	16	=	16
1	×	8	=	8
1	×	4	=	4
1	×	2	=	2
1	×	1	=	1
		Total	=	255

or, the easier way, we can simply look at what the next column header would be (256) and subtract 1 from it (to give 255.)

Since we know that storing our larger number 2,568 would need a minimum of 12 bits, we are going to need to use two bytes to represent it—00001010 00001000, or:

32,768	16,384	8,192	4,096	2,048	1,024	512	256
0	0	0	0	1	0	1	0

128	64	32	16	8	4	2	1
0	0	0	0	1	0	0	0

The largest number representable using two bytes would be the next high column header (65,536) minus 1 (65,535).

Next Steps

So far, we've only looked at basic integer numbers that are greater than zero, or *positive* numbers. Clearly this excludes two ranges of numbers—those that are not integers (that is, are not whole numbers) and those that are less than zero. We'll look at number types such as these later in the chapter, but for now, let's get back to coding and start storing and using some integer values.

5.2 Using Variables

To work with simple scalar types in code, we use *variables*. Variables are used to hold basic values in memory and, as the name implies, can *vary*. Do you remember how we used pointers to keep track of our objects back in the previous chapter? Our original Interface Builder outlet *declaration* for a pointer to the text view looked like this:

```
NSTextView *textView;
```

Pointers, like textView here, are actually a very specific type of variable and, as you have already seen, are denoted by the asterisk (*) symbol. Variables for simple scalar types look very similar but do not have an asterisk. The code to declare a simple integer variable looks like this:

```
int myFirstIntegerVariable;
```

Just like our NSTextView pointer example, the first word is used to specify the *type* of the variable, followed by a *name* to refer to the variable. Unsurprisingly, the keyword **int** is used in the C language to specify a variable that can hold an integer value.

Working with Variables in TextApp

Let's declare a new variable right now. Open Xcode with your TextApp project from the previous chapter, and find the NotifyingClass.m file with its declaration for the displaySomeText: method. Add a variable into the top of this method:

```
- (IBAction)displaySomeText:(id)sender
{
    int ourVariable;

    [textView insertText:@"displaySomeText just got called!\n"];
}
```

If you want, you can Build & Run to see whether anything has changed. You'll find that nothing appears any different in the application since we don't do anything with the variable we just declared. We also never give this variable any value. Xcode will generate a *warning*, as shown in Figure 5.2, on the next page, that you have an "unused variable 'ourVariable'"—Xcode gets concerned when you declare a variable to hold some information but then never refer to it again.

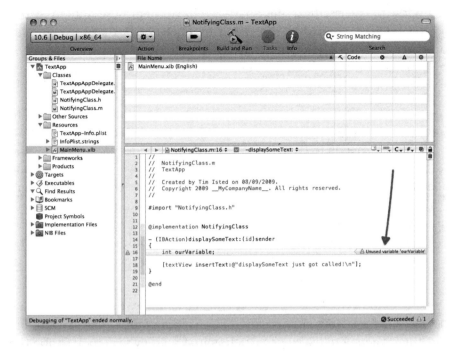

Figure 5.2: A WARNING SHOWING IN XCODE

Let's change this behavior right now by *assigning* a value to the variable and outputting that value to our text view. This code is beginning to get more complicated, so be sure to double-check that you haven't mistyped anything! Replace the code that inserts text in the text view so it looks like this:

```
- (IBAction)displaySomeText:(id)sender
{
    int ourVariable;
    ourVariable = 25;

    [textView insertText:[NSString
        stringWithFormat:@"The value of the variable is: %i\n",
                    ourVariable]];
}
```

Common typos here could be missing semicolons, forgetting the @ sign, or not having enough closing square brackets at the end of the line (there should be two). You also do not need to have the line breaks in the middle of the insertText: message—we have them here only to fit the code on the page. Remember from earlier in the book that the compiler doesn't care about whitespace in a statement? As long as the statement has a semicolon at the end, you could split the code into as many lines as you wanted.

If you want to condense the statement into a single line, you will need to replace the line breaks with at least a single space. Each code "word" in the statement needs to be separate; there must be a space between the [NSString and the stringWithFormat:; otherwise, Xcode would try to compile those two words as a single word, [NSStringstringWithFormat:, which isn't a valid expression and will generate an error that stops your code from compiling. Because there is a comma after the %i\n" and before ourVariable, you don't necessarily need the space—the comma punctuates the two code pieces. Generally, you should choose to format your code in the way that makes it most readable to you.

Just like before, the first line of code declares the variable—named ourVariable—and specifies that it will hold an **integer** value. The second line uses the *assignment operator* (which is just a fancy way to describe the = sign) to assign a value to that variable.

The remaining lines use an NSString object—this is an object that holds a *string* of characters. We'll be working with NSString objects quite a bit in a later chapter, but, for now, all you need to know is that by using the code [NSString stringWithFormat:@"The value of the variable is: %i\n", ourVariable], the %i part will be substituted with the value of our variable.

Notice that we haven't had to worry about specifying any values in binary. You never have to worry about conversion into binary for memory storage—you can supply a number in decimal notation, and the conversion is handled for you.

Changing the Value of the Variable

Once we have a variable for use, we can change the value that it holds as many times as we want. Modify your code so it looks like this:

```
- (IBAction)displaySomeText:(id)sender
{
    int ourVariable;
    ourVariable = 25;
    ourVariable = 35;
    ourVariable = 49;
    ourVariable = 58;
```

```
    [textView insertText:[NSString
        stringWithFormat:@"The value of the variable is: %i\n",
                        ourVariable]];
}
```

No prizes here for guessing what will be output to our text view—since the last value that we assign is 58, that's what you should see in the text view.

We can also use the *assignment operator* (the = sign again) to set a value for one variable using the value from another variable:

```
- (IBAction)displaySomeText:(id)sender
{
    int ourVariable;
    ourVariable = 25;

    int anotherIntegerVariable;
    anotherIntegerVariable = ourVariable + 10;

    [textView insertText:[NSString
        stringWithFormat:@"The value of the variable is: %i\n",
                        anotherIntegerVariable]];
}
```

Here we declare a second variable called anotherIntegerVariable and set its value to be that of our first variable, plus 10. When you Build & Run, you should find that your output gives the value of the variable to be 35.

If we wanted to, we could reuse our first ourVariable variable and simply add 10 to it:

```
- (IBAction)displaySomeText:(id)sender
{
    int ourVariable;
    ourVariable = 25;

    ourVariable = ourVariable + 10;

    [textView insertText:[NSString
        stringWithFormat:@"The value of the variable is: %i\n",
                        ourVariable]];
}
```

When you run the app this time, you should find that you still see the same output—the value of the variable gets set to 35 before it is displayed in the text view.

Using this fancy assignment operator therefore follows this pattern:

«set the value of the thing on this side» = «to what's on this side»

Other Types of Variables

Now that we've seen how to use **int** variables to hold integer values, let's look at a few other types of variables to hold different types of numbers.

Signed and Unsigned Numbers

When I was talking earlier about storing numbers in memory, I limited the discussion to numbers that were greater than zero, or *positive* numbers. It's not immediately obvious from that discussion how a computer could store a number that was less than zero, or *negative.*

The answer is actually pretty simple. Consider what you do when communicating with other human beings (!) to indicate whether a number is negative or positive: to state the obvious, you generally take any number that has no + or - sign to be positive and use a - sign to indicate that a number is negative:

Negative numbers   -5,235   -78   -784,122,564
Positive numbers   4,876   694   224,387,471

Representing positive and negative numbers on a computer isn't really any different; we can simply use a single bit to represent the minus sign, or "whether a number is negative or not." This reduces the maximum number representable in, for example, a single byte, because it means we would only have 7 bits remaining to specify the number; with two bytes, we would have 15 bits to use; four bytes leaves 31 bits; and so on.

In the programming world, numbers that are defined as negative or positive in this way are called *signed* numbers. Numbers that don't make use of a bit for *signing* are, you guessed it, called *unsigned* numbers.

Up until now we've used the **int** keyword to define our variables, and as such, we have actually been defining variables that are signed. To demonstrate this, change the number we store and output to be a negative number:

```
- (IBAction)displaySomeText:(id)sender
{
    int ourVariable;

    ourVariable = -50;
```

```
[textView insertText:[NSString
    stringWithFormat:@"The value of the variable is: %i\n",
                    ourVariable]];
}
```

You'll find that our negative number is happily accepted and displayed correctly in the text view.

Sometimes, however, you might know in advance that a variable will only ever contain positive values. On these occasions, you can specify a variable that doesn't allow signed numbers using, somewhat predictably, the keyword **unsigned**.

Change the code again so that it looks like this:

```
- (IBAction)displaySomeText:(id)sender
{
    unsigned int ourVariable;

    ourVariable = 50;

    [textView insertText:[NSString
        stringWithFormat:@"The value of the variable is: %u\n",
                        ourVariable]];
}
```

Notice that we've also changed the text view output string substitution from the original %i to a %u to specify that we are providing an **unsigned** variable.

If you run the application now, you'll find that it outputs our value quite correctly. Just to see what happens, try changing the value of the unsigned variable to a negative number:

```
- (IBAction)displaySomeText:(id)sender
{
    unsigned int ourVariable;

    ourVariable = -50;

    [textView insertText:[NSString
        stringWithFormat:@"The value of the variable is: %u\n",
                        ourVariable]];
}
```

This time when you run the application, you'll find that the value of the variable is reported incorrectly, saying that "The value of the variable is: 4294967246." This is because we have allocated memory for an unsigned variable; given it an illegal, signed negative value; and then tried to output the value as if it were unsigned. This is an incredibly common source of errors in programming—trying to access something in memory thinking it's one type of value when it's actually another.[2]

Floating-Point Numbers

Another type of number we haven't yet considered is non-integers, such as 1.235 or -25.784637. These are numbers that have a *decimal point.*

There are certain types of numbers (like currencies) for which it might make sense to provide a specific number of digits after the decimal point. In some currencies, we might need to store values with exactly two digits after the decimal point. But, even with a currency, there are many reasons why you might actually need extra digits—tax calculations, for example. Ideally, we would like to be able to specify the number of digits that we need *before and after* a decimal point.

This type of number is referred to as a *floating-point* number because the decimal point can "float left and right" along the digits. Exactly how these numbers are stored using bits and bytes is outside the scope of this chapter, but it is worth saying that a floating-point number uses bits slightly differently since it records both the digits and the location of the decimal point.

To declare a decimal value in our code, we can use the variable type **float**:

```
- (IBAction)displaySomeText:(id)sender
{
    float approxValueForPi;
    approxValueForPi = 3.14159265;

    [textView insertText:[NSString
        stringWithFormat:@"The value of the variable is: %f\n",
                    approxValueForPi]];
}
```

Provided you've copied the code correctly, remembering to change the %u substitution string to %f to specify that we're outputting the value of

---

2. If you're wondering where the apparently arbitrarily high number 4,294,967,246 has come from, try converting it into binary; it's the incredibly long value 11111111111111111111111111001110. Next, try converting the number 50 into binary; it's the more manageable 110010. When negative numbers are stored using signed numbers, we store what's known as the *two's complement*, formed by inverting all the digits (changing 1s to 0s, and vice versa) and adding one. This turns 110010 into 001110. That really long number has these six bits on the end but has *all* the other bits set to 1. When you try to interpret all those 1s as an unsigned number, you end up with the value 4,294,967,246.

a **float** variable, you should find that you can store and output decimal numbers to your heart's content!

Storing Other Information

You've now seen how numbers can be stored in memory using bits and bytes, but it's not obvious how you might represent text characters like A or ! in binary. The answer is to assign each text character a *number* and just store that instead.

You may have seen the acronyms ASCII or UTF-8 written with reference to websites or email encoding. These refer to standards that define which letter corresponds to which number. If you know that a particular series of bits in memory refers to a character and what type of encoding has been used, you can work out what character we need. If you're given the decimal number 65 (01000001 in binary), for example, you might find that this is the letter *A* in a particular encoding.

Just as you don't have to worry about supplying numbers in binary notation, the great news for characters is that you don't need to worry about converting them into numbers or back again—the conversion happens automatically. As a result, you can think of characters as characters and trust that everything will work!

We can declare a variable for a single character like this:

```
- (IBAction)displaySomeText:(id)sender
{
    char ourVariable;
    ourVariable = 'a';

    [textView insertText:[NSString
        stringWithFormat:@"The value of the variable is: %c\n",
                    ourVariable]];
}
```

Here we assign the letter *a* to our character variable (declared using the **char** keyword) and specify the letter inside single quotes (') to denote a single character. Be sure to change the substitution string to %c to display a character!

When you're developing Objective-C applications for the Mac, you'll find that you don't need to use **char** variables very often. Most of the time, you'll be working with strings of characters, held by NSString objects. We'll look at these in the next chapter.

Code Readability

Sometimes it makes sense to actually opt for a longer section of code in order to make it readable—readability of code is important because it allows you to return to a project six months later and see quite clearly what is going on. Objective-C is a very readable and *self-documenting* language on the whole, but there are various things you can do to make it even clearer, as we'll see throughout this book.

Combining Declaration and Assignment

Over the course of the book, we've seen several examples of how the Objective-C language doesn't care about whitespace. We've recently seen how a single command can be split across several lines, and it doesn't matter to the compiler. Related to this is the fact that there are frequently several different ways you can achieve the same aim by using either fewer *or more* lines of code.

Up until now, we have been declaring a variable in one line of code and then using a second line of code to do the value assignment for that variable. We can also combine these actions into one single line of code. In this code fragment, we declare and assign two variables—either approach works equally well:

```
{
    int firstIntegerVariable;
    firstIntegerVariable = 56;

    int anotherIntegerVariable = 56;
}
```

Since a variable has an unpredictable value before you assign something to it, it's good practice to combine these statements by using the second approach to avoid any strange behavior. If you declare a variable but don't explicitly assign it a value, the variable will start out life containing the value that currently exists in memory. Feel free to test this out by checking the value of ourVariable but not assigning it a value before outputting it:

```
- (IBAction)displaySomeText:(id)sender
{
        int ourVariable;
```

```
[textView insertText:[NSString
        stringWithFormat:@"The value of the variable is: %i\n",
                         ourVariable]];
}
```

When I run this code, the outputted value of the variable is 1. Yours might be 0, or any arbitrary number. Setting an initial value of a variable when you declare it, like this:

```
int ourVariable = 50;
```

stops you having any weird problems from old 1s and 0s hanging around in memory. We'll be using this approach for most of the rest of the book.

5.3 The Scope of a Variable

Now that you know how to declare and assign a variable, it's worth discovering how long that variable will hang around for you to use. This is known as the *scope* of a variable. The basic rule for variable scope is that a variable is *valid only within the code block in which it is declared.*

Consider this implementation for two methods inside an object:

```
@implementation NotifyingClass

- (IBAction)displaySomeText:(id)sender
{
    int firstVariable = 34;
}

- (IBAction)doSomethingElse:(id)sender
{
    int secondVariable = 54;
}

@end
```

Both of these methods declare a single integer variable for their use, but because those variables are defined in different code blocks (that's the "curly-brace" sections), neither method can access the other's variable. The variable actually ceases to exist when its closing section's curly brace is reached, so for the displaySomeText: method here, the variable firstVariable doesn't really have much of a life before it is cleared from memory.

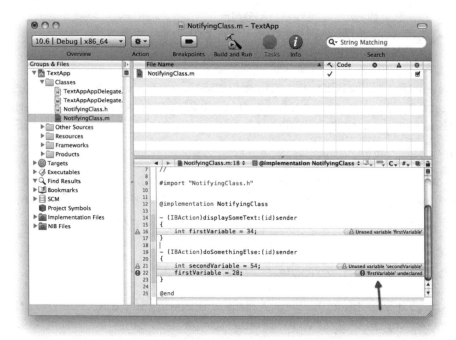

Figure 5.3: AN ERROR IN XCODE FOR A VARIABLE THAT'S OUT OF SCOPE

```
- (IBAction)displaySomeText:(id)sender
{
    int firstVariable = 34; // variable is created and assigned a value
} // variable ceases to exist
```

If you were to add that second method (doSomethingElse:) into your Noti-fyingClass implementation, then try to access the first variable from it:

```
- (IBAction)doSomethingElse:(id)sender
{
    int secondVariable = 54;
    firstVariable = 28;
}
```

you'd find that Xcode prevents your project from compiling and gener-ates an error, as shown in Figure 5.3. Because the variable firstVariable is declared in a different code block, the compiler has no idea what you're talking about when it tries to compile the second method, so it reports that the variable is "undeclared."

This means that you can reuse variable names in other methods without any problem:

```
@implementation NotifyingClass

- (IBAction)displaySomeText:(id)sender
{
    int anInt = 34;
}

- (IBAction)doSomethingElse:(id)sender
{
    int anInt = 54; // this has nothing to do with any other 'anInt'!
}

@end
```

but you cannot "redefine" a variable with the same name as a variable name already used by the same method:

```
- (IBAction)displaySomeText:(id)sender
{
    int anInt = 34;
    int anInt = 54; // you can't do this!
}
```

This code would generate a "redefinition of 'anInt'" error and refuse to compile.

You may remember that in the previous chapter we made use of an **IBOutlet** to a pointer to the NSTextView object in order to send messages to it. We placed this outlet in the class interface, rather than placing it inside one of the methods. Variables placed inside the interface of an object are accessible by *all* the methods of that object (and any subsequent classes that inherit from it).

You'll be seeing a lot more about the scope and life of a variable as you proceed through the book.

5.4 Memory Addressing

Let's turn our attention back to how variables are held in memory again. Take a look at our memory diagram in Figure 5.1, on page 70. Since we now know that we should be using 8-bit bytes to store information, we should really rework this diagram to look like Figure 5.4, on the following page.

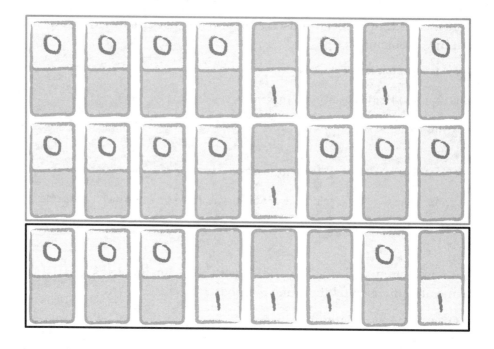

Figure 5.4: OUR NUMBERS STORED IN MEMORY USING BYTES

Think of this large field of 8-bit bytes as being like a parking lot. Each byte is one parking space and can hold a maximum of only one piece of information at a time. Larger items can be "parked" across spaces, by using multiple bytes. We can then work out an address scheme for each parking space; that way our number 29 might be stored in "space 1" and the number 2,568 in "spaces 2–3."

On a computer, bytes are addressed in the same way, but the numbering that is used by the machine is actually given in *hexadecimal* rather than decimal. Try not to throw your hands up in horror at this point, but we're now uncovering yet another numbering system. Hexadecimal works in the same way as decimal and binary, but rather than having 10 or 2 digits, it uses 16 (which are the numbers 0–9 and the letters A–F.)

Thankfully, in the same way that you won't have to worry about binary when you're writing code, you won't really have to worry *too* much about hexadecimal, either. When you do see it being used, you'll find it is normally given a prefix of *0x* in order to differentiate it from decimal.

Checking the Address

To give us a little bit of insight into what's going on inside the "mind" of the computer, let's try finding out the addresses of our variables in memory. Displaying the address of a variable isn't something you'll find yourself doing very often, but it's useful right now to help visualize the situation.

The C language provides us with an easy way to access the address of a variable—we simply specify the name of the variable, preceded by an ampersand, like this: &myVariable.

To try this, let's change the displaySomeText: method to declare an **int** variable and a **float** variable and to output their addresses to the text view:

```
- (IBAction)displaySomeText:(id)sender
{
    int anInt = 15;
    float aFloat = -35.2444;

    [textView insertText:[NSString
        stringWithFormat:@"address of anInt is: %p\n", &anInt]];

    [textView insertText:[NSString
        stringWithFormat:@"address of aFloat is: %p\n", &aFloat]];
}
```

Notice that the substitution string uses %p here—we'll see why this is in a short while!

When you run this code, you'll see an output that looks something like this:

```
The address of anInt is: 0xbfffed4c
The address of aFloat is: 0xbfffed48
```

Your addresses will almost certainly be different, but as promised, you'll be looking at two hexadecimal values with the prefix *0x*—these are the addresses of the physical bytes in memory where our variables are being stored.

How Many Bytes Is That?

In Section 5.1, *Bytes*, on page 71, you saw that values are stored in memory using one or more bytes. Given a base address like 0xbfffed4c, how are you to know how many bytes to make up our value? Well, each variable type uses a specific number of bytes. You don't need to worry about this: the compiler will know what it's doing for you. The only time it becomes a problem is when you need to make sure you don't try to store a number larger than the maximum allowed in a specific variable type. One difficulty is that the sizes can vary depending on the type of machine you are running—there is a difference in the size of some types between, for example, older Macs that use PowerPC processors and newer Macs that use Intel processors.

If you want, you can also check the size of a variable at runtime by using another function, sizeof():

```
- (IBAction)displaySomeText:(id)sender
{
    int anInt = 15;

    [textView insertText:[NSString
        stringWithFormat:@"size of anInt is: %i bytes\n",
                            sizeof(anInt)]];
}
```

Running this on my machine tells me that the "size of anInt is: 4 bytes."

Using Memory Addresses for Access

As I said earlier, it's not often you'll need to *display* the address of a variable. There are, however, many cases when knowing the address of a variable is incredibly useful. One of these is when you need to provide access to a variable that isn't currently "in scope." Consider again those two methods for NotifyingClass that you saw earlier:

```
@implementation NotifyingClass

- (IBAction)displaySomeText:(id)sender
{
    int firstVariable = 34;
}

- (IBAction)doSomethingElse:(id)sender
{
    int secondVariable = 54;
}

@end
```

As we've already discussed, our doSomethingElse: method cannot access the firstVariable from the displaySomeText: method because that variable is not in scope. We could, however, offer up access to the doSomethingElse: method by somehow passing it the address of our variable in memory. The method could check to see what value was currently held in that location and change it if it wanted. We'll see how to do this in the next chapter, in Section 6.4, *Passing Values by Reference*, on page 109, along with a few other ways to pass values between methods.

5.5 Pointers Again

I introduced *pointers* in the previous chapter and used them to keep track of objects so we could send messages. Once again, a pointer declaration for our text view object looked like this:

```
NSTextView *textView;
```

Follow the Pointing Star

You can tell a pointer by the asterisk (*) in front of the variable name. Since the asterisk looks a little like a star, think of the phrase "Follow the pointing star," because that's exactly what a pointer does—it points to something else (hence the name).

I mentioned earlier that a pointer is a specific type of variable, one that is used to hold a memory address. So, we could declare a pointer to an integer variable like this:

```
int *aPointerToAnInteger;
```

This doesn't declare an integer variable to hold an integer *value*; it declares a pointer variable to hold the *address* of an integer value. Where might you get such an address? Well, we saw exactly where in the Section 5.4, *Checking the Address*, on page 85—by using the & symbol. We could create an integer and a pointer to that integer like this:

```
int anInt = 50;
int *aPointerToAnInt = &anInt;
```

If you glance back at the code we used in that section to output the address of an object, you'll see that we used a substitution string of %p to display the addresses of our variables. Now you can see why. The p in %p stands for "pointer."

So, let's display the address of a variable again, this time using a pointer variable. Change the displaySomeText: method to this:

```
- (IBAction)displaySomeText:(id)sender
{
    int anInt = 15;

    int *pointerToAnInt = &anInt;
```

```
[textView insertText:[NSString
    stringWithFormat:@"address of anInt is: %p\n", &anInt]];

[textView insertText:[NSString
    stringWithFormat:@"value of pointerToAnInt is: %p\n",
                        pointerToAnInt]];
}
```

Note that there is no & used when we use the pointerToAnInt pointer in our outputting string. We simply use the value of the pointer variable—which *is* the address.

Again, you should still see the address being output to the text view, looking something like this:

```
address of anInt is: 0xbfffed48
value of pointerToAnInt is: 0xbfffed48
```

Object Pointers

There's another pointer in use in this method. Remember how I stated in the previous chapter that we used pointers to send messages to objects—messages that appear in square brackets? Well, we're sending the insertText: message to our text view object via a pointer called textView. So, let's take a look at the actual value held by that pointer:

```
- (IBAction)displaySomeText:(id)sender
{
    int anInt = 15;

    int *pointerToAnInt = &anInt;

    [textView insertText:[NSString
        stringWithFormat:@"address of anInt is: %p\n", pointerToAnInt]];

    [textView insertText:[NSString
        stringWithFormat:@"address of textView is: %p\n", textView]];
}
```

The output displayed should look like this:

```
address of anInt is: 0xbfffed48
address of textView is: 0x125910
```

Now we're seeing the address of the text view object referenced by our textView pointer.

This might make you wonder, given that you can do this:

```
int anInt;
int *pointerToAnInt = &anInt;
```

whether you can also do something like this:

```
NSTextView aTextView;     // This won't work!
NSTextView *pointerToATextView = &aTextView;
```

to create a new text view object, but, sadly, you can't. There's a big difference between objects and simple scalar types, and we'll see how to create objects like these in Chapter 7, *Objects and Memory Management*, on page 113.

What's the Point?

OK, enough with the pointer jokes already. Seriously, you'll be using pointers extensively when you write code on the Mac, for many reasons, some of which will become clear in later chapters. You could think of pointers as being a lazy and memory-efficient solution to avoid having to store information multiple times or having to keep writing it out. Rather than saying "Here is some object and these are all its values, etc.," you can simply say, "There's an object at address XXX—go take a look for yourself."

5.6 Chapter Summary

This has been a long chapter, containing quite a lot of theory. If you've followed along, you're beginning to understand that you can declare *variables* that contain basic, *scalar* values such as numbers and that you can use *pointers* to reference the addresses in memory of other variables or of objects.

In the next chapter, we'll revisit object methods by looking at how we can pass information around using *arguments* and pass back information using *return values*.

Chapter 6

Passing Information Around

In the previous chapter, you saw how computers store information in memory and how you make use of variables to hold and access that information. You also saw how the scope of a variable prevents one method from accessing a variable declared in another method. In this chapter, you'll see how methods can pass information to each other, first by returning information after the method has run and second by providing arguments passed in when a method is called.

6.1 Returning Values

Let's go straight into Xcode and start coding. Open your TextApp project, and find the displaySomeText: method inside the NotifyingClass.m file. Change it to look like this:

```
@implementation NotifyingClass

- (IBAction)displaySomeText:(id)sender
{
    float someValue = 10.0;

    [textView insertText:[NSString
        stringWithFormat:@"The value is: %f\n", someValue]];
}

@end
```

You should be able to tell that this code simply declares a **float** variable called someValue, assigns it a value, and displays that value in our text view. If you wish, Build & Run the project to check that this is what is happening.

We're going to create a new method inside NotifyingClass that will generate a value and then pass it back to our displaySomeText: method for display.

A Method with a Return Type

Take a quick look back at Section 4.1, *Defining a New Method*, on page 49. In that section, we looked at a number of method signatures that follow this pattern:

```
«+ or -»   («word»)  «messageName» «some optional parts»;
```

Later in that section, I mentioned that the «*word*» portion was used to indicate the type of information being returned by the method. With this in mind, let's create a new method, called generateValue, that is going to pass back our decimal value for output. Since the method is returning a floating-point number, we need to use the keyword **float** to specify this.

First, open the header file for NotifyingClass, and modify the interface by adding the following method signature:

```
@interface NotifyingClass : NSObject {
    IBOutlet NSTextView *textView;
}


- (IBAction)displaySomeText:(id)sender;
- (float)generateValue;

@end
```

Next, copy the method signature to the clipboard, and switch back to the implementation file. Paste the method signature inside the Notifying-Class implementation (before the final **@end**), remove the semicolon, and add curly braces to make the method:

```
@implementation NotifyingClass

- (IBAction)displaySomeText:(id)sender
{
    float someValue = 10.0;

    [textView insertText:[NSString
        stringWithFormat:@"The value is: %f\n", someValue]];
}

- (float)generateValue
{

}

@end
```

If you build the project now without changing anything else, you should find the application runs exactly as before, but you'll receive a warning from Xcode saying that "control reaches end of non-void function." This is because the signature for generateValue indicates that the method will return a **float** value, but no value is actually being returned.

Returning a Value

To eliminate this warning and do what we originally intended (return a value at the end of the method), we need to make use of another coding keyword called—drumroll please—**return**. Change the generateValue method to look like this:

```
- (float)generateValue
{
    return 5.0;
}
```

We can now go back and change the displaySomeText: method to set the value of its someValue variable to the value returned by the generate-Value method.

Talking to Ourselves

Earlier in the book, we saw how to send messages to other objects using the square bracket notation:

```
[«receiving object» «message»«:optional parameters»];
```

We've been using this ever since to send messages to the text view. What we didn't discuss at the time was how an object might send a message to itself. The answer is, as usual, not terribly surprising. We can use the keyword **self**. Every object that you use in Objective-C can use this keyword to refer to itself—it's essentially just a placeholder for a pointer containing the address of the object.

With that in mind, change your displaySomeText: method to this:

```
- (IBAction)displaySomeText:(id)sender
{
    float someValue = 10.0;
    someValue = [self generateValue];

    [textView insertText:[NSString
        stringWithFormat:@"The value is: %f\n", someValue]];
}
```

Here we leave the original declaration of the someValue variable and assign it the value 10.0. We then assign it the value returned by the generateValue method using our trusty assignment operator, before outputting the result as before. If you Build & Run the project again, you'll find that the value output to the text view is now the value returned by the generateValue method (5.0).

Returning Variables

You might be wondering why we bothered to create a method just to return a value. For our example so far, the purpose was just to illustrate how a method can return a value. In reality, such a method might generate a value based on something the user had inputted or from some basic data source like a file on disk or a response from an Internet server.

To add some interest to our generateValue method, let's change it to calculate the circumference of a circle given a radius. For now, we'll hard-code the radius into a variable in the code. Later, we'll spice this up a little.

If you remember any of your math classes from school, the formula $2\pi r$ is probably etched permanently onto your brain. So, change your generateValue method to look like this:

```
- (float)generateValue
{
    float radius = 5.0;
    float circumference = 2 * pi * radius;

    return circumference;
}
```

We declare a new **float** variable to hold our radius and assign it a value. We then declare a second **float** variable to hold the circumference and set its value by multiplying our radius variable by 2 * pi. pi in this instance is a *constant* defined in low-level math library files that you don't need to worry about. It exists exactly for uses like this.

To return the final circumference value, we use the code return circumference;—this simply returns the value held by the variable rather than doing anything fancy to return the actual variable itself by address, and so on. As always, once the end of the method is reached, the circumference variable will cease to exist, so this is exactly the behavior we require.

When you Build & Run the application, the output should indicate a generated value of 31.415926.

To make the output a bit clearer, you might like to change the displaySomeText: method to specify that it is outputting a circumference. And, to make the code tidier, let's rename the variable used in this method to circumference, also getting rid of our initial, unused assignment. Change your method to look like this:

```
- (IBAction)displaySomeText:(id)sender
{
    float circumference = [self generateValue];

    [textView insertText:[NSString
        stringWithFormat:@"The circumference is: %f\n", circumference]];
}
```

Build & Run the application again to make sure you haven't broken anything!

Adding Spice

I said earlier that we'd spice up this example; let's do that now by allowing the user to specify a value for the radius.

Use the Xcode Project Browser to find the MainMenu.xib file, and open it with Interface Builder. We'll make use of a *text field* to get a value typed in by the user. Start by opening the editor for the application's Window. At the moment, it just contains our big text view and button.

Shrink the text view a bit by clicking it once and dragging down the top *handle*. Move the button up into the space left at the top of the window. Double-click the button to enable you to change its title, and set it to "Calculate Circumference"—your window should look something like Figure 6.1, on the following page.

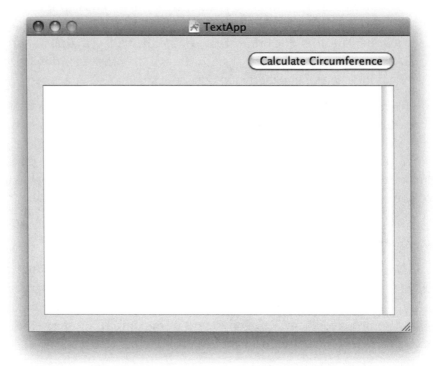

Figure 6.1: INTERFACE WITH THE TEXT VIEW AND RENAMED BUTTON MOVED

Next, we'll add a *text field* to the window. Find the Text Field object in the Library palette, and drag an instance onto the window. Be sure to use the right object—you want the Text Field object, not the Text Field Cell object.

We'll also add a label to our window indicating that this new text field should contain a value for a radius. Once again, locate a Label object in the Library palette, and drag one onto the window. Double-click its text, and set the label to "Radius:"—rearranging your items to look like Figure 6.2, on the next page.

Linking the Interface

Think back to the basic procedure for accessing an interface object from code. We need to add an **IBOutlet** to our NotifyingClass and then connect

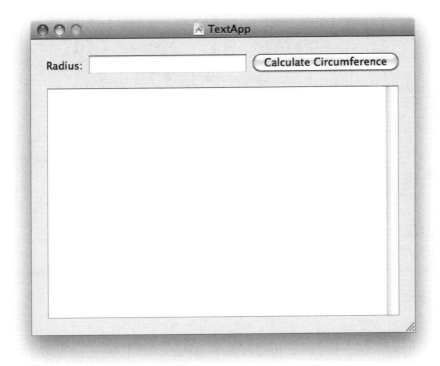

Figure 6.2: Interface with added text field and label

this in Interface Builder. We only need to provide access to the new text field—the label doesn't need to be modified from code.

Switch to Xcode, open the NotifyingClass.h interface file, and add an **IBOutlet** pointer to an NSTextField object:

```
@interface NotifyingClass : NSObject {
    IBOutlet NSTextView *textView;
    IBOutlet NSTextField *textField;
}

- (IBAction)displaySomeText:(id)sender;
- (float)generateValue;

@end
```

Save that file, and switch to Interface Builder. In the main window for the MainMenu.xib file, right-click (or ^-click) the NotifyingClass object, and

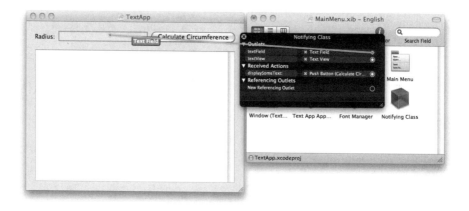

Figure 6.3: LINKING THE NEW TEXT FIELD TO THE TEXTFIELD VARIABLE

you should see the newly added NSTextField object. Link this to the new text field you created earlier, as in Figure 6.3.

Switch back into Xcode, and find the generateValue method inside the NotifyingClass.m implementation. We need a way to set the value of our radius variable to the value held inside the text field. It turns out that this is incredibly simple. In yet another demonstration of the power of the Cocoa framework, we can ask the text field for its value as a **float** by sending it the floatValue message. It will respond with a **float** value, just like our own generateValue method does, set to the value held inside the text field.

With this in mind, change the generateValue method to the following:

```
- (float)generateValue
{
    float radius = [textField floatValue];
    float circumference = 2 * pi * radius;

    return circumference;
}
```

It really is as easy as that—Build & Run the application, enter a number in the Radius text field, and click the Calculate Circumference button. You should see the expected value appear inside the text view.

Even More Spice

Just to demonstrate how easy it is to add some expected functionality to this basic application, let's make our app a little more Mac-like. It would be great if the radius-calculation code was called whenever the user pressed the ↵ or ⌤ key.

In ye olden days, this would have involved hugely complicated code to intersect keystroke events sent from the keyboard, checking to see what they were, and responding accordingly. Happily, we can instead accomplish this in our own application without having to write any code at all.

Open Interface Builder once again, and select the text field in the interface. Take a look at the Connections palette (⌘-⑤), and you'll find a "selector" connection in the Sent Actions section. Drag a connection from the circle next to this selector over to the NotifyingClass object, and release the mouse button. A pop-up window will appear containing the possible action messages for NotifyingClass—in this case, our displaySomeText: action. Click this action in the pop-up, and the selector will be linked to the action.

This *selector* is a link to the action that will be called on a particular target when something happens. The button in our interface has its selector set to the displaySomeText: method, called when the button is clicked. There are a couple of options on a text field to specify when the action is called; we'll use the one that sends the action when the ↵ or ⌤ key is pressed.

So, switch to the Attributes palette for the text field (⌘-①), and change the Action drop-down box value to "Sent on Enter only."

Now when you Build & Run the application from Xcode, you'll find that the circumference calculation is carried out whenever the user presses ↵ or ⌤.

Hooray for the Cocoa framework!

6.2 Methods and Arguments

Now that we've seen how to return information at the end of a method, let's look at how to pass in information when a method is called.

So far, we've mostly been working with methods that don't accept any such information. In the previous section, we wrote the generateValue method that was called with the code [self generateValue].

Back in Section 4.2, *The Target-Action Mechanism*, on page 52, we did see that some methods take arguments, specified after a colon (:)—and we have been working within just such a method ever since. The code for the displaySomeText: method looks like this:

```
- (IBAction)displaySomeText:(id)sender
{
    «code for method»
}
```

It was written to work using the target-action mechanism and thus accepts a single argument. We'll return to this method a little later, but for now let's add a new method to our NotifyingClass interface.

Defining a New Method with an Argument

At the moment, our generateValue method handles the simple task of generating the circumference itself. For the sake of this demonstration, let's *factor out* the circumference-generation code into a separate method. This new method should return a circumference calculated from the radius it is given. The method therefore needs to accept a single argument (the radius) for which it can return the correct value.

Naming Conventions

It's worth taking a minute to talk about *naming conventions*. Hopefully you've noticed that, up until now, we've been naming variables and methods in a very specific way. If a method name or variable is made up of multiple words, those words are run together, but with the first letter of each subsequent word made into a capital letter—e.g., "displaySomeText." This is known as *camel case* and is a convention you should follow when you write your own code. For method names and variable names, you should *not* capitalize the first word (so "DisplaySomeText" would be incorrect), but you *should* capitalize the first word in names of classes (e.g., "NotifyingClass").

For methods that take arguments, there are some further conventions you might like to follow. For a start, it's *usually* a good idea to identify the arguments you expect in the name of the method, like this:

```
- (void)buildHouse:(House *)houseToBeBuilt
```

Having said that, one obvious exception is the naming of target-action methods, like our displaySomeText:(id)sender method. The way that we have named it is potentially confusing; it looks like we should display some text that is provided as an argument. We can just about get away with this, however, because target-action methods are always *expected* to accept a single argument (a pointer to the object that triggered the action). For our new circumference-calculation method, however, we should definitely try to use a convention-driven name.

Given that we return a value calculated *from* a given *radius*, let's call this method circumferenceFromRadius: such that the argument supplied is identified as being that necessary radius.

Method Syntax

We did look very briefly at the syntax for defining the arguments on a method, back in Section 4.2, *The Target-Action Mechanism*, on page 52. To add an argument, you need to add the colon, specify the type of information being provided, and provide a name for that information.

The signature for our current generateValue method looks like this:

```
- (float)generateValue;
```

Since our new method also needs to return a float variable, and bearing in mind the syntax for defining arguments, the signature for our new method needs to look like this:

```
- (float)circumferenceFromRadius:(float)radius;
```

The (float)radius part identifies a single argument that will be provided to the method, specifying that it will hold a **float** value. The radius specifies the name of a variable that will then be assigned that value. We can access this radius variable from within the method as if we had defined it ourselves. Given that our previous generateValue method looks like this:

```
- (float)generateValue
{
    float radius = [textField floatValue];
    float circumference = 2 * pi * radius;

    return circumference;
}
```

we can write our circumferenceFromRadius: method like this:

```
- (float)circumferenceFromRadius:(float)radius
{
    float circumference = 2 * pi * radius;

    return circumference;
}
```

Adding the New Method

So, let's add this new method right away. Start by adding the method signature into the interface for NotifyingClass:

```
@interface NotifyingClass : NSObject {
    IBOutlet NSTextView *textView;
    IBOutlet NSTextField *textField;
}

- (IBAction)displaySomeText:(id)sender;
- (float)generateValue;
- (float)circumferenceFromRadius:(float)radius;

@end
```

And then add the method to the implementation file before the final **@end**:

```
@implementation NotifyingClass

«other methods»

- (float)circumferenceFromRadius:(float)radius
{
    float circumference = 2 * pi * radius;

    return circumference;
}

@end
```

Next, we need to change our generateValue method so that it uses this new method rather than doing the calculation itself.

Calling a Method with Arguments

Once again we need to make use of **self** to call the method, just as we called [self generateValue] earlier. To supply the value for the radius argument, we specify it after a colon, like so:

```
[self circumferenceFromRadius:5.0];
```

With this in mind, let's change our existing generateValue method to use the new circumferenceFromRadius: method. Since we're using the radius provided by the user of the application, change your code to this:

```
- (float)generateValue
{
    float radius = [textField floatValue];

    float circumference = [self circumferenceFromRadius:radius];

    return circumference;
}
```

Check that the application still functions as expected by building and running it.

Code Consolidation

If it bothers you that we have turned what was originally a couple of lines of code into a whole string of extra methods and code lines, then there are a few things to keep in mind.

First, putting the circumference generation code into a separate method aids in making the code "self-documenting." Although the calculation to generate a circumference is quite simple, consider what might happen if this were some incredibly complex quantum physics calculation.

By writing the calculation code into a method called circumferenceFrom-Radius, we don't need to add a code comment to explain what we're doing. Similarly, since the new method is properly named, we don't need to add a comment inside it, either—a method called circumference-FromRadius is obviously going to take a radius and generate a circumference. If a method was named energyOfObjectWithMass:, it's pretty clear what that method would do, and you might even have some idea of how it would be written.[1]

Second, we could consolidate the lines of code in each method and avoid having to use any additional variables. The generateValue code currently looks like this:

```
- (float)generateValue
{
    float radius = [textField floatValue];

    float circumference = [self circumferenceFromRadius:radius];

    return circumference;
}
```

---

1. Hint: it uses a pretty famous equation relating E, m, and c....

However, there isn't really any particular reason to define a specific radius variable to hold the value in the textField. We could instead *nest* the square-bracket method calls and replace the use of the radius variable with [textField floatValue], like this:

```
- (float)generateValue
{
    float circumference = [self circumferenceFromRadius:[textField floatValue]];

    return circumference;
}
```

This code still does exactly the same thing but gets rid of the extra radius variable declaration. We could consolidate even further and remove the use of the circumference variable, too; the **return** keyword indicates that we are returning a value that we specify as the next word. We can therefore replace the circumference variable with the code that generates its value, like this:

```
- (float)generateValue
{
    return [self circumferenceFromRadius:[textField floatValue]];
}
```

It's entirely up to you how much you consolidate your code. You might find it easier, particularly while you're still learning, to use lots of variables to show what's going on in the code.

Similarly, it wouldn't detract too much from the readability of the circumferenceFromRadius: method to rewrite it like this:

```
- (float)circumferenceFromRadius:(float)radius
{
    return 2 * pi * radius;
}
```

You might like to put that calculation inside normal brackets to confirm in your mind that we're returning the result of a calculation:

```
- (float)circumferenceFromRadius:(float)radius
{
    return (2 * pi * radius);
}
```

Any of the methods in this section are perfectly acceptable when coding; it's all a matter of personal preference and what looks best to you.

6.3 Class Methods

You have just seen how to refactor the code for circumference generation into a separate method. It seems a little strange, however, to have
that method as part of the NotifyingClass object. Mathematical calculations don't seem to have much to do with notifying the user.

Furthermore, this circumference calculation is the kind of thing we
might want to reuse in the future. We might have another part of our
application (or even a different application altogether) that needs to
calculate a circumference given a radius, and it would be strange to
have to link to or generate a NotifyingClass object just to perform this
calculation.

The alternative is to factor the circumferenceFromRadius: method into a
separate utility class, and we'll do that now. We can also avoid having
to get hold of an instance of that new class by writing our code into
what is known as a *class method*.

Rather than calling the method on an *instance* of the object like this:

```
[someInstanceOfNotifyingClass circumferenceFromRadius:5.0];
```
e.g.,
```
[self circumferenceFromRadius:5.0];
```

we can just call the method on the *name* of the class itself, like this:

```
[ClassName circumferenceFromRadius:5.0];
```
e.g.,
```
[MathUtilities circumferenceFromRadius:5.0];
```

If we write a class called MathUtilities, we don't need to create an instance
of that class to use its class methods.

Writing a New Class

Let's try this out now by creating a new class in the current project.
Right-click (or ^-click) the Classes group in the Xcode project browser
for TextApp, choose Add > New File..., and pick *Objective-C class*. Name
this new class "MathUtilities," and tell Xcode to generate the necessary
.h file for you.

Once the files are created, we can add a new method signature into the
interface for the MathUtilities class. Back in Section 4.1, *Defining a New
Method*, on page 49, we saw a selection of method signatures from the
NSObject interface. Some of these had a + sign at the front, and some
had a - sign. It is this + or - that specifies whether a method is a class

method or an instance method. So far we've been working with methods with a - at the front, like this:

```
- (float)generateValue
{
    «generation code»
}
```

which are methods that can be called on an *instance* of the class. To write our math utility method, however, we're going to need to use the + *class* method specifier.

We're now working with two separate classes, each with an interface and an implementation file. Take care to make sure that you put the right code in the right file! Change the interface for the MathUtilities class (MathUtilities.h) by adding the following:

```
@interface MathUtilities : NSObject {

}

+ (float)circumferenceFromRadius:(float)radius;

@end
```

Next, write the method implementation (MathUtilities.m) like this:

```
@implementation MathUtilities

+ (float)circumferenceFromRadius:(float)radius
{
    float circumference = 2 * pi * radius;
    return circumference;
}

@end
```

Finally, we need to change our NotifyingClass code to call this new class method. We should probably remove the old circumferenceFromRadius: code from this class to avoid any confusion, so first remove the method signature in the interface file (NotifyingClass.h) so it looks like this:

```
@interface NotifyingClass : NSObject {
    IBOutlet NSTextView *textView;
    IBOutlet NSTextField *textField;
}

- (IBAction)displaySomeText:(id)sender;
- (float)generateValue;

@end
```

To call our new circumferenceFromRadius: class method, we need to change the call inside the NotifyingClass's generateValue method from [self circumferenceFromRadius:radius] to [MathUtilities circumferenceFromRadius: radius].

It should now be pretty clear why it's so important to follow the naming convention of capitalized class names and noncapitalized variable names. It's possible, for example, to realize instantly that [MathUtilities circumferenceFromRadius:radius] is a call to a class method because of the capitalization of MathUtilities.

Change your implementation for NotifyingClass (NotifyingClass.m) so that it looks something like this:

```
@implementation NotifyingClass

- (IBAction)displaySomeText:(id)sender
{
    float circumference = [self generateValue];

    [textView insertText:[NSString
        stringWithFormat:@"The circumference is: %f\n", circumference]];
}

- (float)generateValue
{
    float radius = [textField floatValue];
    float circumference = [MathUtilities circumferenceFromRadius:radius];
    return circumference;
}

@end
```

With these changes made, let's try to build the project and run the application to make sure everything still works. Sadly, you'll be greeted by an error in Xcode, as shown in Figure 6.4, on the following page stating "error: 'MathUtilities' undeclared"—this is a slightly strange error, but it indicates that Xcode has no idea what a MathUtilities object is within this NotifyingClass file.

To solve this problem, we need to tell Xcode what the *interface* to a MathUtilities object looks like. How do we do this? Well, we need to tell it to look inside the MathUtilities.h *interface file*. Back near the beginning of the book, you might remember that you saw a statement looking like this:

```
#import <Cocoa/Cocoa.h>
```

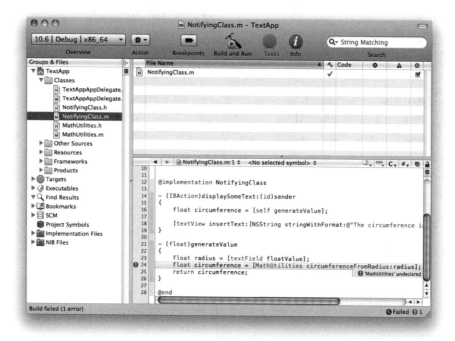

Figure 6.4: THE ERROR IN XCODE ABOUT OUR USE OF THE MATHUTILITIES
CLASS

This appeared in the main.m file for the project. Subsequently, you might have noticed **#import** statements like this one at the top of each file we've worked with. The NotifyingClass.m file, for example, includes the statement #import "NotifyingClass.h" at the top to tell the compiler to include the interface description for the NotifyingClass class.

So, to tell the compiler about the MathUtilities class, we just need to add in an **#import** statement for the MathUtilities.h interface file like this:

```
#import "NotifyingClass.h"
#import "MathUtilities.h"

@implementation NotifyingClass
«implementation continues»
```

Now, when you build the project, the error disappears, and everything behaves as expected.

If we wanted, we could reuse the MathUtilities class in any future project just by including its interface and implementation files and using the relevant **#import** statement.

Class Method Limitations

Class methods are great when you have useful utility code, but since they aren't attached to any particular instance of a class, they obviously have no access to any of the instance variables on a class. If we'd defined a class method for NotifyingClass, for example, that method wouldn't have been able to access the textView or textField outlets, since those outlets have to be set for each particular instance. If you tried to access them, Xcode would complain and refuse to compile your code.

We'll see a number of examples of class methods in later chapters of this book when we use several Apple-provided utility methods for classes in the Cocoa Framework.

6.4 Passing Values by Reference

You might remember from Section 5.4, *Using Memory Addresses for Access*, on page 86 that we mentioned it was possible to allow methods to access variables that aren't currently "in scope" by letting them know the *address* of the variable.

One of the main uses of this is to allow you to return more than one value when a method finishes. Our current generateValue method just returns the calculated circumference. It might be nice to be able to pass back the value that was used to generate the circumference in the first place, but a **return** statement only can be used to return a single value or object.

The solution in this case is to declare a variable in our displaySomeText: method that will eventually hold the radius supplied by the user. We'll pass the address of this variable when we call the generateValue method so that the generateValue method can change the value of the variable held at that address.

Let's start by changing the method signature for generateValue. It needs to accept the address of a *scalar* variable (i.e., a pointer) as its only argument. Since we're dealing with a **float** variable, that's the type of pointer we need to use.

Change the interface for NotifyingClass so that the signature for the generateValue: method looks like this:

```
@interface NotifyingClass : NSObject {
    IBOutlet NSTextView *textView;
    IBOutlet NSTextField *textField;
}

- (IBAction)displaySomeText:(id)sender;
- (float)generateValue:(float *)originalValue;

@end
```

Next, change the method implementation to match the method signature we just wrote:

```
- (float)generateValue:(float *)originalValue
{
    «existing code»
}
```

Now we need to pass in the address of a variable whenever we call this method. Let's modify the displaySomeText: method by declaring a new variable called radius, assigning it a default value of 0.0 and passing its address to the generateValue: method:

```
- (IBAction)displaySomeText:(id)sender
{
    float radius = 0.0;
    float circumference = [self generateValue:&radius];

    [textView insertText:[NSString
        stringWithFormat:@"With a radius of %f, the circumference is: %f\n",
                         radius, circumference]];
}
```

Notice that we've also changed the output string so that it displays the value of this radius.

If you want, check that everything works by building and running the application. When you enter a radius in the box and click the button, you should see output like this:

```
With a radius of 0.000000, the circumference is: 31.415926
```

Since we never actually change the value of the radius variable, it stays at our default value of 0.0.

To change the value of a variable when we have a pointer to that variable, we need to *dereference* the pointer—this all sounds pretty complicated, but it's really quite simple. We use the asterisk symbol again (remember to "follow the pointing star?") and set its value just like any other variable. So, change the generateValue: method to this:

```
- (float)generateValue:(float *)originalValue
{
    float radius = [textField floatValue];
    *originalValue = radius;
    float circumference = [MathUtilities circumferenceFromRadius:radius];
    return circumference;
}
```

By prepending an asterisk to the front of a pointer, we can access the variable to which it points. Build & Run the project, and you'll find that the output is as expected:

```
With a radius of 5.000000, the circumference is: 31.415926
```

Possible Pitfalls

One very important thing to note: dereferencing a pointer can be a dangerous business. Consider the following code fragment:

```
{
    int *aPointerToAnInt;

    *aPointerToAnInt = 30;
}
```

This snippet declares a pointer to an **int** variable and then dereferences that pointer and assigns a value. Where is that value going? Well, as you saw in Section 5.2, *Combining Declaration and Assignment*, on page 80, when you create a *variable* but don't assign a value, it has an unpredictable value at runtime. The same goes for *pointers*—if aPointerToAnInt points randomly to some memory currently in use by an object in your application, or another variable, and you change what's held in that memory, your application will either crash or, at the very least, behave very strangely.

6.5 Chapter Summary

We've written quite a lot of code in this chapter. We've looked at how methods can pass information back once they've been called and how a method can accept argument values. We modified our TextApp application to accept a value from the user and perform a calculation on that value. We even added some extra Mac-like behavior without having to write any extra code.

We also discussed naming conventions for methods and classes and saw how to use class methods for code that doesn't need to apply to a specific instance of a class.

In the next chapter, we'll be talking about how to create new object instances in memory using *code* rather than *instantiating* them in Interface Builder. With the power to create comes the need to manage the memory that those objects use, so look forward to learning about both the creation of new objects in memory and how to decide when an object has reached the end of its life and is ready to be destroyed.

Chapter 7

Objects and Memory Management

You've been working with objects all the way through the book so far. Right at the beginning, you saw how the objects that represent TextApp's menu bar and window are instantiated based on the contents of the MainMenu.xib resource file. You've since created class descriptions for your own custom objects and generated instances of those objects in that same file using Interface Builder.

It's now time to see how you can create objects *programmatically*, or by writing code.

7.1 Memory Considerations

Back in Chapter 5, *Variables and Memory*, on page 67, we saw how information is stored and accessed in a computer's memory. We concentrated our discussion on simple *scalar* types, such as basic integer and decimal numbers, seeing how we write code to allocate a named variable and then assign a value to that variable. We either used two lines of code, like this:

```
int someWonderfulNumber;
someWonderfulNumber = 42;
```

or amalgamated them like this:

```
int someWonderfulNumber = 42;
```

Near the end of that chapter, we considered whether we could create objects using code like this:

```
NSTextView aTextView;
```

but stated that we couldn't. To see why not, let's find out what's involved in creating an object, by analyzing what an object is actually made of.

The Structure of an Object

An object is an instance of a class. As described by its class description, an object has functionality (the *methods*) that typically work with some sort of information held in memory (the *instance variables*). In our NotifyingClass example from the previous chapters, we make use of **IBOutlet**-tagged instance variables (declared in the **@interface**) to maintain links to the user interface items we need to communicate with.

Just like declaring a pointer to a *scalar* value in this way:

```
- (void)randomMethod
{
    int *aPointerToAnInt;
}
```

requires some memory to hold the address to which that pointer points, declaring an *object* pointer in an object interface like this:

```
@interface NotifyingClass : NSObject {
    IBOutlet NSTextView *textView;
}
```

is also going to require memory.

Remember also how objects can inherit from other objects? We've been working so far with *subclasses* of NSObject, and whenever one class inherits from another class, it *inherits both the functionality and all the instance variables from the parent class.*

Earlier in the book, we looked at the interface header file for NSObject. Its **@interface** looks like this:

```
@interface NSObject <NSObject> {
    Class isa;
}
```

It's worth mentioning briefly at this point that you can think of the isa variable as being used to keep track of the type of class the object is—as in, "This particular object *isa* NSObject object, but this other object *isa* NotifyingClass object."

If we define the NotifyingClass class like this:

```
@interface NotifyingClass : NSObject {
    IBOutlet NSTextView *textView;
    IBOutlet NSTextField *textField;
}
```

then any NotifyingClass instance is going to need enough memory to hold the three variables isa, *textView, and *textField. If we were then to declare another class like this:

```
@interface BetterNotifyingClass : NotifyingClass {
    int someReallyCoolNumber;
    NSString *someAmazingString;
}
```

the instances of BetterNotifyingClass would need enough memory to hold all the variables from NotifyingClass, plus the extra someReallyCoolNumber and *someAmazingString.

When we want to create an object programmatically, therefore, we need to make sure enough memory is allocated to hold *all* the instance variables, inherited or declared.

7.2 Allocating Memory for Objects

Thankfully, this seemingly incomprehensible task is handled extremely easily in Objective-C. To allocate the necessary memory for an object, NSObject provides us with a *class method* called alloc. You never need to override this method; it "just works" and always allocates enough memory for any particular object:

```
NSObject *someNewObject = [NSObject alloc];
```

What's actually happening in this line of code is that the alloc method (notice it's definitely a class method because we're calling it on the NSObject class) is assigning an area in memory big enough to contain an NSObject instance and then returning the address of that memory to the someNewObject pointer.

We could allocate memory for one of our own NotifyingClass objects in just the same way:

```
NotifyingClass *myFavoriteNotifier = [NotifyingClass alloc];
```

As well as allocating memory for the object, alloc also has the effect of setting all the instance variables to zero or (for pointers) nil, but it does no further object "setup" work. Before the object can be used, it needs to be initialized properly.

Object Initialization

You might remember in Section 3.4, *Object Initialization Messages*, on page 38, where I said that "When an instance of a class is created in Objective-C, it is immediately sent a message to initialize itself." You then learned that this message is the init message and made use of it to log a message to the console:

```
- (id)init
{
    NSLog(@"Hello World! I'm a new NotifyingClass instance!");
    return self;
}
```

You may also remember that when we wrote this code, we did so with the disclaimer that it wasn't a *complete* initialization method—in a few moments, we'll discover one of the reasons why this is the case.

Calling the init Method

So that an object is always properly initialized ready for use before doing anything else, the init method needs to be called on an object immediately after allocation.

It would be reasonable to assume, therefore, that you should do this:

```
{
    NotifyingClass *myFavoriteNotifier = [NotifyingClass alloc];
    [myFavoriteNotifier init];

    «do something with the myFavoriteNotifier object»
}
```

This code allocates memory for the object and then sends the object a message to initialize itself.

In fact, initializing objects in this way is *not* a good idea, and we'll get to see why a little later in the book. Instead, just like we use one line of code to declare *and* initialize scalar types, like this:

```
int luckyForSome = 13;
```

we can (and *should*) amalgamate our object allocation and initialization code, like this:

```
NotifyingClass *myFavoriteNotifier = [[NotifyingClass alloc] init];
```

Here we make use of *nested* square brackets, such that the "inside" command allocates an object and the "outside" command initializes that object. What is eventually returned to our myFavoriteNotifier pointer is a properly initialized NotifyingClass instance, ready for use.

Returning self

Back in Section 3.4, *One Final Thing*, on page 46, we added an extra line to our very first init method, stating return self;. I said that I'd later explain why this was; hopefully, you now have some idea.

Because we are nesting our alloc and init calls into one line, like so:

```
ClassName *pointerToObject = [[ClassName alloc] init];
```

we need the init method to **return** the address of the initialized object back for assignment to the pointer.

Initializing with Inheritance

When the init message is sent to an object, it is important that the *whole* object is initialized properly. If we were to make a glorified number-storing object, like this:

```
@interface WonderfulNumber : NSObject {
    float storedNumber;
}
```

and write its init method like this:

```
- (id)init
{
    storedNumber = 42;

    return self;
}
```

all would seem to be perfectly reasonable. If you created one of these objects, like this:

```
WonderfulNumber *someWonderfulNumber = [[WonderfulNumber alloc] init];
```

the storedNumber variable would be set to 42.

The difficulty comes if you remember what we've said about inheriting instance variables and behavior. When an object initializes its own instance variables, it needs to make sure that its inherited instance variables have been initialized properly too.

We need a way to allow the NSObject part of our object to initialize itself, *before* we continue initializing the rest of the object.

We do this by "passing up" the init message to super, like this:

```
- (id)init
{
    [super init];

    storedNumber = 42;

    return self;
}
```

This time, when the init message is sent to our WonderfulNumber object, it first calls the original, overridden init method from its parent class (NSObject) to initialize the inherited parts and then carries on initializing itself as expected.

It happens to be the case that the init method for NSObject *doesn't* do any initialization—the isa instance variable is actually set up in alloc. It's possible that the design of NSObject might change in the future, though, so it's good practice to keep all your init methods in the same format—you should *always* call [super init] when you inherit from *any* class.

If another class were to inherit from our WonderfulNumber class, for example, it would need to implement its init method in the same way, and we would end up with a *cascade* of inits—the new init method calls the WonderfulNumber's init method, which in turn calls the NSObject init method, kind of like the woman who swallowed a bird to catch the spider to catch the fly—with the object effectively getting initialized "from the top down."

7.3 Creating Objects in Code

Now that we've talked through some theory about objects and allocations, let's start putting that theory into practice by defining a new object and creating instances of it in TextApp.

We'll design a class description for our WonderfulNumber class; this class will be used to store a **float** number. We'll be able to set and access that float number by sending messages to the WonderfulNumber object; later we'll even add the capability to be able to extract the number as a text string.

Adding a New Class

As usual, open the TextApp project in Xcode, and then right-click (or ^-click) the Classes group, choosing Add > New File… to add a new Objective-C class called WonderfulNumber.

When the WonderfulNumber.h file appears, change the interface to look like this:

```
@interface WonderfulNumber : NSObject {
    float storedNumber;
}

- (void)setStoredNumber:(float)newNumber;
- (float)storedNumber;

@end
```

This interface specifies that we will initially be responding to two messages: a message to set the value of the number being stored and a message asking for the value to be returned.

Next, we'll write the implementation for the class, so copy the two method signatures from the interface, switch to the WonderfulNumber.m implementation file, and paste them in, making them into methods with their curly braces. Since the actual code inside the methods is very simple, let's write it straightaway:

```
@implementation WonderfulNumber

- (void)setStoredNumber:(float)newNumber
{
    storedNumber = newNumber;
}

- (float)storedNumber
{
    return storedNumber;
}

@end
```

The setStoredNumber: method simply sets the storedNumber instance variable to the value provided in the newNumber variable; the storedNumber method just returns the stored number. Pretty straightforward!

Before we create any instances of our new class, let's add an init method to set an arbitrary initial value for the storedNumber instance variable.

```
@implementation WonderfulNumber

- (id)init
{
    [super init];

    storedNumber = 42;

    return self;
}

- (void)setStoredNumber:(float)newNumber
«code continues»
```

Allocating an Instance of Our New Object

Now that we've made a class description for our WonderfulNumber, let's
create an instance of it in our NotifyingClass's displaySomeText: method.
Remember that this is the method called when the user clicks the button in the interface? We'll reuse this code for now to generate a WonderfulNumber instance and then output the value of its stored number to
the text view.

Open the NotifyingClass.m file, and change the displaySomeText: method to
this:

```
- (IBAction)displaySomeText:(id)sender
{
    WonderfulNumber *myWonderfulNumber = [[WonderfulNumber alloc] init];

    float wonderfulValue = [myWonderfulNumber storedNumber];

    [textView insertText:[NSString
        stringWithFormat:@"My Wonderful Value = %f\n", wonderfulValue]];
}
```

Here we allocate and initialize a new WonderfulNumber object, then we
allocate a float variable to hold its stored value, before displaying that
value in the text field.

There's one extra thing we need to do before we can build the application; in order for the NotifyingClass object to be able to use a Wonderful-
Number object, we need to **#import** the interface file for the WonderfulNumber class at the top of the NotifyingClass.m file:

```
#import "NotifyingClass.h"
#import "MathUtilities.h"
#import "WonderfulNumber.h"

@implementation NotifyingClass
«code continues»
```

If you Build & Run, you should find that the text field displays the following output when you click the Calculate Circumference button:

```
My Wonderful Value = 42.000000
```

This might seem like a whole lot of work to output a simple number, but it is a useful exercise!

Remember that we can *set* the value held by a WonderfulNumber object too? Let's try that now by adding a line of code:

```
- (IBAction)displaySomeText:(id)sender
{
    WonderfulNumber *myWonderfulNumber = [[WonderfulNumber alloc] init];

    [myWonderfulNumber setStoredNumber:pi];

    float wonderfulValue = [myWonderfulNumber storedNumber];

    [textView insertText:[NSString
        stringWithFormat:@"My Wonderful Value = %f\n", wonderfulValue]];
}
```

It's not too hard to predict what gets output this time:

```
My Wonderful Value = 3.141593
```

It might be irritating you that the button you click in TextApp is still called Calculate Circumference. Let's change this now. Open MainMenu. xib in Interface Builder, and change the text on the button to "Display Value." While we're here, let's change the label next to the text field too so that it simply says "Input Value:"—this way we can use the text field later to accept input from the user.

A Hidden Problem

So, we've successfully allocated, initialized, and made use of an object, entirely by writing code. That really wasn't too bad, was it?

Unfortunately, there is a problem with our current code. To find out what it is, let's take a quick look at the documentation for NSObject in the Xcode Documentation Browser.

If you browse through the methods on NSObject related to "Creating, Copying, and Deallocating Objects," you'll find that NSObject has a dealloc method. The documentation states that "You never send a dealloc message directly. Instead, an object's dealloc method is invoked indirectly through the "release" NSObject protocol method."

This won't make much sense right now, but the basic idea is that an object is sent the dealloc message when it is about to be removed from memory. We'll get to understand all that release protocol stuff in just a few sections.

Let's implement the dealloc method on our new object so we can do some checking. We'll log a message to the console (rather than the text view) to show when it's being called. We'll also add a message log in the init method so that we see when the object is first initialized. Make these changes to our WonderfulNumber implementation:

```
@implementation WonderfulNumber

- (id)init
{
    [super init];

    storedNumber = 42;

    NSLog(@"A WonderfulNumber object was initialized!");

    return self;
}

- (void)dealloc
{
    NSLog(@"A WonderfulNumber object was deallocated!");

    [super dealloc];
}

- (void)setStoredNumber:(float)newNumber
«code continues»
```

We're back to our old friend, NSLog()—before you Build & Run, make sure that the Debugger Console is open in Xcode (⇧-⌘-R).

When you run the application and click the button a few times, you should see something like this in the console:

```
2009-05-26 18:41:56.981 TextApp[2471:10b] Object was initialized!
2009-05-26 18:41:57.948 TextApp[2471:10b] Object was initialized!
2009-05-26 18:41:58.437 TextApp[2471:10b] Object was initialized!
2009-05-26 18:41:58.861 TextApp[2471:10b] Object was initialized!
2009-05-26 18:41:59.076 TextApp[2471:10b] Object was initialized!
```

OK, so now the "hidden" problem is becoming more apparent. We've stated that the dealloc method is called on an object just before it is removed from memory, but since we're never seeing the output in the console, the dealloc method is clearly never being called, from which we can infer that the object isn't being deallocated.

Given what you know about the scope of a variable, this seems bizarre. Here's the code again that creates the WonderfulNumber object:

```
- (IBAction)displaySomeText:(id)sender
{
    WonderfulNumber *myWonderfulNumber = [[WonderfulNumber alloc] init];

    [myWonderfulNumber setStoredNumber:pi];

    float wonderfulValue = [myWonderfulNumber storedNumber];

    [textView insertText:[NSString
        stringWithFormat:@"My Wonderful Value = %f\n", wonderfulValue]];
}
```

The myWonderfulNumber object instance is created in the first line of the method. Surely it ceases to exist when the method's closing brace is reached?

In fact, what ceases to exist when the method ends is the *pointer* to the object, as in the *actual myWonderfulNumber pointer*. The object that it points *to* is still in existence, left in some kind of limbo with no reference to it at all, like having a cell phone without a phone number. This explains why we never see the message from the dealloc method—the object is never deallocated.

This is what's known as a *memory leak* and is something you will likely spend much of your programming life trying to eradicate. Although it's maybe not so much of an issue to waste a few bytes worth of memory on a WonderfulNumber object given that today's computers typically have several gigabytes of physical RAM, this obviously could become a major issue if you start leaking thousands of particularly large objects. It becomes *really* serious on the iPhone, where your application has very limited available memory.

So, we need some way to specify that an object is no longer needed in order that it can be deallocated. It's important, though, to reiterate Apple's advice that you should *never* call dealloc directly.

7.4 The Object Life Cycle

To come up with a strategy for "getting rid" of objects from memory, we need to make sure that we know when they are no longer needed.

Reclaiming Your Memory

If you're concerned at this point that you've somehow lost a few bytes of your computer's RAM, never to be seen again, you needn't worry.

When an application terminates (that is, the user chooses to quit the app or the operating system decides to terminate it for them), *all* the memory used by the application is released.

This is why we didn't need to worry previously about getting rid of those NotifyingClass instances we added to our application back in Chapter 3, *All About Objects*, on page 23.

In our example of using a WonderfulNumber object earlier, it might make sense to do something like this:

```
- (IBAction)displaySomeText:(id)sender
{
    WonderfulNumber *myWonderfulNumber = [[WonderfulNumber alloc] init];

    «work with myWonderfulNumber»

    [myWonderfulNumber removeYourselfFromMemory];
}
```

However, there is no removeYourselfFromMemory method—and for good reason.

Maintaining an Interest

A lot of the time, you will be working with objects that are needed for longer than just the duration of one method. Frequently, you'll create an object, do something with it, pass it as an argument on messages to other objects, and although you might be finished with it in one place, another piece of code might still want to have access.

Let's consider a hypothetical (and rather convoluted) application that displays a number on screen. When a menu item is chosen in the application, a WonderfulNumber object is created, and its number is displayed in a window. The user can open lots of new windows if they want, and each time, the new window will show the number held by the WonderfulNumber object. Only when all the windows are closed is the WonderfulNumber object no longer needed.

In this particular case, we can't call some kind of removeYourselfFrom-Memory method at the end of the code that creates the WonderfulNumber object, because it will still be needed. The problem is that we don't know how long it will be needed or by how many other objects.

We need some way of keeping track of how much "interest" there is in an object—in other words, how many other objects are interested in keeping a specific object in memory for them to talk to.

Introducing Reference Counting

The solution offered by the Cocoa framework is through a technique called *reference counting*. This technique allows objects to declare that they have an interest in some specific object and also to confirm when they no longer have that interest.

To get the terminology correct here, if an objectA wants to declare interest in some objectB, objectA is said to "retain" objectB. When objectA decides it no longer has any interest in objectB, objectA is said to "release" objectB.

Reference counting works by maintaining a *retain count* on every object. When an object is retained, the retain count is incremented by one. When an object is released, the retain count is decremented by one. If the retain count on an object reaches zero, it automatically gets deallocated from memory.

From our earlier number-displaying window example, each time a new window is opened to display the WonderfulNumber object, that window retains the WonderfulNumber object. Whenever a window is closed, that window releases the object. When all the windows are closed, the retain count will be zero, so the object will be deallocated.

The Retain Count After Allocation

So, how does all this retain/release business fit in with our memory leak on our WonderfulNumber object? Well, since we're making use of the object, we might think that we should retain it after we've created it, and then at the end of the method we should release it.

Before we go ahead and modify our displaySomeText: method, let's take a quick minute to check our theories on allocation and deallocation. We've just said that when an object's retain count is zero, it gets deallocated from memory, but given that we know our WonderfulNumber object *wasn't* being deallocated, its retain count must have been greater than zero to start with.

The reason for this is that when an object is allocated, it begins life with a retain count of 1. So, when we wrote the line

```
WonderfulNumber *myWonderfulNumber = [[WonderfulNumber alloc] init];
```

not only did we allocate memory for the object, but we also effectively declared our interest in using the object, so we didn't explicitly need to retain it.

Another way of looking at this is that because we created an object using alloc, we "agreed" to *take responsibility* for it. We agreed that we would *release* it when we were finished using it.

With this in mind, let's take up our burden of responsibility as object creators and release the object at the end of the method:

```
- (IBAction)displaySomeText:(id)sender
{
    WonderfulNumber *myWonderfulNumber = [[WonderfulNumber alloc] init];

    [myWonderfulNumber setStoredNumber:pi];

    float wonderfulValue = [myWonderfulNumber storedNumber];

    [textView insertText:[NSString
        stringWithFormat:@"My Wonderful Value = %f\n", wonderfulValue]];

    [myWonderfulNumber release];
}
```

Now that we're sending the release message to the object, let's check what happens when we Build & Run. You'll see something like this in the debugger log:

```
2009-05-27 19:01:47.466 TextApp[1848:10b] Object was initialized!
2009-05-27 19:01:47.467 TextApp[1848:10b] Object is being deallocated!
2009-05-27 19:01:50.849 TextApp[1848:10b] Object was initialized!
2009-05-27 19:01:50.850 TextApp[1848:10b] Object is being deallocated!
```

Each time you click the button, a WonderfulNumber object is allocated and initialized, used (to output the value to the text view), then released, et voilà! It is deallocated.

Hooray! Now we are being good memory citizens, creating objects and releasing them from memory when no longer needed.

7.5 Denying Responsibility

Given the title of this section, you can probably guess that there are times when this whole "responsibility for an object" thing isn't so clear-cut.

To find one such occasion, let's implement some functionality I mentioned earlier. We'll add a method to our WonderfulNumber class that returns the stored number as an NSString object. You'll recall that *string* refers to a string of printable characters—such as hooray for responsibility!—so by "converting" a number into a string, we mean that we are providing its representation as physical characters rather than numerical value. We could represent the number 42, for example, as a two-character string, made up of the printable characters 4 and 2.

Let's start by adding a new method to the WonderfulNumber class **@interface** (in WonderfulNumber.h):

```
@interface WonderfulNumber : NSObject {
    float storedNumber;
}

- (void)setStoredNumber:(float)newNumber;
- (float)storedNumber;
- (NSString *)storedNumberAsString;

@end
```

In the implementation for this new method, we're going to need to allocate a new string object based on the value of a **float** variable. Let's examine the documentation for NSString to see what might be available to us.

Initializing Strings

Looking at the class reference for NSString in the Xcode documentation viewer, we find there are various routes we might take. The relevant section is titled "Creating and Initializing Strings."

Notice that after the basic init method, there are a number of initialization methods that take arguments, such as initWithFormat:. These methods work just like a standard init method but take the supplied argument to set up the string in some way as it is initialized. We'll see how to make our own initWithSomething: methods in the next section.

We're going to make use here of the initWithFormat: initializer. If you click the link to read the documentation for the method, you'll see that it "Returns an NSString object initialized by using a given format string as a template into which the remaining argument values are substituted."

If you look down a little way, you'll find a link to the "String Format Specifiers" information, which lists the kinds of things you can substitute into a string. What this really means is that if you were to write code like this:

```
{
    float firstVariable = 55.0;
    int secondVariable = 11;

    NSString *newString = [[NSString alloc]
        initWithFormat:@"Value of firstVariable is %f, secondVariable is %i",
                                            firstVariable,
                                            secondVariable];
}
```

the newString that you'd end up with would have those values substituted into it, so it would be as follows:

```
Value of firstVariable is 55.000000, secondVariable is 11
```

You might recognize that we're already using a format string like this in our displaySomeText: method to output the values of our variables to the text view in the user interface.

Since we just want to return a string representing the value of the variable, we can use a simple format string of @"%f" and provide our float variable as an argument.

So, let's implement our new storedNumberAsString method (in Wonderful-Number.m), like this:

```
- (NSString *)storedNumberAsString
{
    NSString *stringToReturn = [[NSString alloc]
                                initWithFormat:@"%f", storedNumber];

    return stringToReturn;
}
```

This method *allocates* and *initializes* a new string and returns that string at the end of the method. With any luck, you might have alarm bells ringing in your head at this point. We're allocating a new object, but we're not releasing it—we are not fulfilling our responsibility for the object that we've created.

If we were to release the object before the end of the method, like this:

```
- (NSString *)storedNumberAsString
{
    NSString *stringToReturn = [[NSString alloc]
                                    initWithFormat:@"%f", storedNumber];

    [stringToReturn release]; // Uh-oh!

    return stringToReturn;
}
```

the object would be deallocated after the call to release, so by the time we return it, it wouldn't exist anymore. We'd be returning an invalid object.

Note that we also don't want to have to release the string in any other method that ever has to use this storedNumberAsString—unless we've called alloc] init] or retain on an object, we don't want to have to release it. Using code like this:

```
{
    WonderfulNumber *myWonderfulNumber = [[WonderfulNumber alloc] init];

    [myWonderfulNumber setStoredNumber:pi];

    NSString *numberString = [myWonderfulNumber storedNumberAsString];

    «do something with numberString»

    [numberString release]; // Uh-oh!
}
```

is not a good idea—apart from anything else, we'd have to leave some kind of instruction for anybody ever using our WonderfulNumber object that they must always release any string that they accessed via stored-NumberAsString.

We need a way of passing an object on to someone else, but doing so in a way that explicitly "washes our hands" of any responsibility for it.

Introducing autorelease

Cocoa offers this ability through something called *autoreleasing*.

By calling autorelease on an object rather than release, we can *delay* the object release until the next run through the *event loop*. This sounds scarier than it is; what it really means is that the object will persist during the currently executing code (which applies across methods), but once the code finishes executing and your application goes back to waiting for the user to do something, the object will be released. If the retain count at that point is zero, it will be deallocated.

So, let's change the storedNumberAsString method to this:

```
- (NSString *)storedNumberAsString
{
    NSString *stringToReturn = [[NSString alloc]
                                    initWithFormat:@"%f", storedNumber];

    return [stringToReturn autorelease];
}
```

Because we're returning the string as autoreleased, it will be released once the current code finishes executing.

This means that we can now safely make use of the string generation method in our NotifyingClass's displaySomeText: method, so rewrite it like this (in NotifyingClass.m):

```
- (IBAction)displaySomeText:(id)sender
{
    WonderfulNumber *myWonderfulNumber = [[WonderfulNumber alloc] init];

    [myWonderfulNumber setStoredNumber:pi];

    NSString *numberString = [myWonderfulNumber storedNumberAsString];

    [textView insertText:numberString];

    [myWonderfulNumber release];
}
```

Here, after creating our WonderfulNumber object, just like before, we create a pointer to a string object, numberString, assign it the storedNumber string from that myWonderfulNumber object, and insert it into the text view.

The only release call we need to make is to the myWonderfulNumber object, because that's the only object we've *allocated* in the method. Once the displaySomeText: method finishes, the numberString pointer will go out of scope, and since this is the "end of the line" as far as this particular event-response is concerned, the string object that was returned by storedNumberAsString will be released and subsequently deallocated.

Cool, huh?

If this section isn't absolutely 100% clear in your mind right now, try not to worry too much. Understanding "manual" memory management is one of the most difficult things you'll have to deal with in Cocoa. It's definitely one of those things, though, that once you get it, it really doesn't seem so hard.

It's also worth mentioning something called *garbage collection*, which is a feature you can enable in your code that will automatically hunt around in your application for any objects that aren't needed anymore, getting rid of them for you so you don't have to worry about all this manual memory management stuff.

We'll mention this again later in Section 14.1, *Garbage Collection*, on page 374, but it's definitely worth persevering with retain and release right now so that you have an enhanced understanding of what's going on behind the scenes. And, at the time of writing, garbage collection is available only on the Mac desktop, not on the iPhone. If you want to write software for the iPhone, you're going to need a very good understanding of manual memory management.

7.6 Initializing with Arguments

Let's take a step back for a moment, to look at our object initialization code. We've been making use of an initWithFormat: method on NSString that enabled us to create a string object using a substitution.

We're currently creating a WonderfulNumber object with one line of code and then using a second line of code to set the value of its stored number. It would be great if we could provide an initialization method for any newly allocated WonderfulNumber objects to begin life with a specified value.

In other words, just like we declare and assign a numerical value with code like this:

```
{
    float luckyForSome = 13;
}
```

let's merge these two lines of code:

```
{
    WonderfulNumber *myWonderfulNumber = [[WonderfulNumber alloc] init];

    [myWonderfulNumber setStoredNumber:pi];
}
```

into one.

Rewriting the init Method

All we have to do is to provide an init method that accepts an argument and proceed just like we did before. With this in mind, let's change the existing init method in WonderfulNumber.m into this one:

```
- (id)initWithNumber:(float)newNumber
{
    [super init];

    storedNumber = newNumber;

    NSLog(@"Object was initialized!");

    return self;
}
```

You'll recall from Section 3.4, *Setting Up Our Class Description*, on page 38 that because init is listed in the interface for NSObject, we didn't need to list it in our inherited class descriptions. Now that we have a new initialization method called something other than init, we need to list it in the interface for WonderfulNumber so that objects can use it.

Add the new method signature into WonderfulNumber.h:

```
@interface WonderfulNumber : NSObject {
    float storedNumber;
}

- (id)initWithNumber:(float)newNumber;

- (void)setStoredNumber:(float)newNumber;
- (float)storedNumber;
- (NSString *)storedNumberAsString;

@end
```

Next, let's modify NotifyingClass's displaySomeText: method (in Notifying-Class.m) to use it:

```
- (IBAction)displaySomeText:(id)sender
{
    WonderfulNumber *myWonderfulNumber = [[WonderfulNumber alloc]
                                          initWithNumber:pi];

    NSString *numberString = [myWonderfulNumber storedNumberAsString];

    [textView insertText:numberString];

    [myWonderfulNumber release];
}
```

Note that we've removed the line that explicitly sets the number value because, obviously, we're now doing it when we allocate the object instance.

If you Build & Run to check everything works, you should find that the application still functions as expected.

A Small Problem

This is all very well, but what happens if someone comes along and tries to allocate an instance of our new WonderfulNumber object by using a basic init? We can't stop them from using init because init is the *standard* initialization method. And, since it exists as an inherited method from NSObject, the following code will appear to work just fine:

```
{
    WonderfulNumber *dodgyNumber = [[WonderfulNumber alloc] init];
}
```

The problem is that our object is never properly initialized; none of the initialization code that we had written for it (which, admittedly, is only a single line to set the initial value for the storedNumber variable) is ever being called. In a large object with lots of important instance variables, this could be a big problem.

The Designated Initializer

This is where the idea of the "designated initializer" comes in. You decide what your optimum initialization method would be like (for example, [[SportsCar alloc] initWithColor:@"red"]) and then provide a basic init method that calls that optimum method, supplying some "default" value.

We need, therefore, to add a basic init method back into our Wonderful-Number implementation that calls our initWithNumber: initialization method, supplying the original arbitrary number. So, add this additional method into WonderfulNumber.m:

```
@implementation WonderfulNumber

- (id)init
{
    return [self initWithNumber:42];
}

- (id)initWithNumber:(float)newNumber
«code continues»
```

Now, if someone uses init to initialize a WonderfulNumber class rather than our preferred initWithNumber: method, everything will still be OK.

7.7 Utility Class Methods

When you looked at the documentation for NSString, you might have noticed that there were some additional *class* methods listed after the initWithSomething: initialization methods, looking like this:

```
+ stringWithFormat:
+ localizedStringWithFormat:
+ stringWithCharacters:length:
+ stringWithString:
```

These are utility class methods that can be called on the NSString class itself and provide you with a ready-made and initialized object. The advantage of using these methods is that they autorelease the object they return, so you don't need to worry about taking any responsibility. This means that you can generate an NSString instance without using alloc, and therefore you don't have to call release. Because they return a ready-built object, they are often referred to as *factory* methods.

To get a better understanding of how these methods work, we'll write our own class factory method for WonderfulNumber in a moment. First, though, let's change our existing storedNumberAsString method to use one of the NSString factory methods:

```
- (NSString *)storedNumberAsString
{
    NSString *stringToReturn = [NSString stringWithFormat:@"%f", storedNumber];

    return stringToReturn;
}
```

Because the NSString class method returns an already-autoreleased string object, we don't need to autorelease when we pass it back. We've cunningly avoided having to worry about responsibility.

Writing Our Own Class Factory Method

Now that we've used one of these methods from NSString, let's write our own for the WonderfulNumber object. By convention, these sorts of class methods always take the following form:

«*objectType*»**With**«*optional arguments:*»

just like the stringWithFormat: method we've already used.

Following this convention on our own object, we'll call the class method wonderfulNumberWithFloat:. This makes it clear that we will return an autoreleased WonderfulNumber object, initialized using a provided float argument.

First add the new method to the interface:

```
@interface WonderfulNumber : NSObject {
    float storedNumber;
}

- (id)initWithNumber:(float)newNumber;

+ (id)wonderfulNumberWithFloat:(float)newNumber;

- (void)setStoredNumber:(float)newNumber;
- (float)storedNumber;
- (NSString *)storedNumberAsString;

@end
```

Then implement it like this:

```
+ (id)wonderfulNumberWithFloat:(float)newNumber
{
    WonderfulNumber *numberToReturn = [[WonderfulNumber alloc]
                                            initWithNumber:newNumber];

    return [numberToReturn autorelease];
}
```

Remember to use a + on the front because it is a class method.

This code creates a new WonderfulNumber object, just like we are currently doing in the displaySomeText: method, and then returns the autoreleased object.

Planning for the Next Generation

Although this code will work just fine right now, it's wise to think about the future. It's entirely possible that someone might come along and want to subclass our WonderfulNumber class, maybe calling it EvenMore-WonderfulNumber.

Because the new class will inherit the methods from the parent class, it would be possible to call [EvenMoreWonderfulNumber wonderfulNumber-WithFloat:55.4];. Under the existing code, this would allocate and return a new *WonderfulNumber* object rather than the expected *EvenMoreWonderfulNumber* object.

To ensure that the correct object is always returned for any particular class, we need a way to refer to the class itself. Back in Section 6.1, *Talking to Ourselves*, on page 93, we saw how the **self** keyword is used to refer to the object *instance* on which a method has been called. The Objective-C language allows us to use **self** in a class method too, but in this case to refer to the *class* itself.

With that in mind, change the wonderfulNumberWithFloat: method to this:

```
+ (id)wonderfulNumberWithFloat:(float)newNumber
{
    id numberToReturn = [[self alloc] initWithNumber:newNumber];

    return [numberToReturn autorelease];
}
```

Note that we've also changed the type of the numberToReturn pointer to **id**, our friendly generic object pointer,[1] since we don't know exactly what type of object we're going to get back from the [[self alloc] initWithNumber: newNumber] method call. This also explains why these class factory methods always have a return type of **id**, rather than hard-coding the type of the class.

Using the new code, if wonderfulNumberWithFloat: were called on a Even-MoreWonderfulNumber subclass, the method would still return the correct object.

Using the Method

We can now change NotifyingClass's displaySomeText: method to use our new WonderfulNumber class factory method:

```
- (IBAction)displaySomeText:(id)sender
{
    WonderfulNumber *myWonderfulNumber =
                    [WonderfulNumber wonderfulNumberWithFloat:pi];

    NSString *numberString = [myWonderfulNumber storedNumberAsString];

    [textView insertText:numberString];
}
```

Notice how this method has suddenly become much shorter! We no longer need to call release on the WonderfulNumber object (make sure

---

1. Check that your code is id numberToReturn rather than id *numberToReturn—because id means "a pointer to an object," you don't want the asterisk on the front of the variable name. If you leave the asterisk on, you're actually declaring a pointer to a pointer to an object!

you've removed it), because it has already been autoreleased for us. If you want to make it even shorter, you can remove the need to use a numberString variable to hold the string to display:

```
- (IBAction)displaySomeText:(id)sender
{
    WonderfulNumber *myWonderfulNumber =
                    [WonderfulNumber wonderfulNumberWithFloat:pi];

    [textView insertText:[myWonderfulNumber storedNumberAsString]];
}
```

When to Use alloc and When to Use Factory Methods

Knowing when to use a class factory method and when to create an object using alloc isn't always very clear. Right now, it might seem really appealing to use class methods all the time.

Sometimes, though, you'll need an object to persist in memory for a while; just leaving an object alive for the current run through the event loop isn't going to work out. As an example, if you define an object that has as one of its instance variables a pointer to another object, and it needs that object to exist right from initialization until deallocation, you would typically create the second object using alloc] init] in the first object's init method and then release it in the dealloc method.

Additional Cool String Stuff

The NSString class has some pretty amazing functionality, some of which we'll take advantage of right now to output a proper message to the text view.

One of the methods provided is called stringByAppendingString:. The method name is fairly self-explanatory; you call it on an existing string object and provide a string to append, and it returns a new string instance accordingly. Again, because there's no alloc call involved, the returned string object doesn't have to be released.

Let's use it in our displaySomeText: method to write out a more informative string:

```
- (IBAction)displaySomeText:(id)sender
{
    WonderfulNumber *myWonderfulNumber =
                    [WonderfulNumber wonderfulNumberWithFloat:pi];

    NSString *stringToOutput = @"The value is: ";
```

```
    stringToOutput = [stringToOutput
        stringByAppendingString:[myWonderfulNumber storedNumberAsString]];

    [textView insertText:stringToOutput];
}
```

We're doing various things here. First, we create a new NSString object using the special notation @" ". We've seen this style of string creation before, but it's worth explaining now that this is a special shorthand way of creating an NSString object from a basic string of characters.

Next, we take the stringToOutput pointer and *reassign* it to the result of calling the stringByAppendingString: method on the original stringToOutput object. This is equivalent to using code like this:

```
{
    NSString *stringToOutput = @"The value is: ";

    NSString *changedString = [stringToOutput
        stringByAppendingString:[myWonderfulNumber storedNumberAsString]];

    stringToOutput = changedString;
}
```

As an exercise, you might like to try adding a reassignment to append the special *newline* character to the string (tip: you need to append @"\n"). This will mean that successive button presses will result in each output appearing on a new line.

7.8 Chapter Summary

Wow, this has been a long and intense chapter. It's going to need a lot more experience, caffeine, or both to fully understand much of the content. Try not to worry if some of the concepts seem a little hazy right now; they should soon become second-nature once you've spent some time writing code. The main thing to take away from this chapter is that if you allocate an object using alloc, you need to take responsibility for releasing it when you're done.

Chapter 8

Collecting Information

In previous chapters you spent time working with simple scalar variables holding basic numbers, along with strings of characters held as NSString objects. In the real world, it's common to need to work with *collections* of data, such as a shopping list of items, rather than just the odd single string of text here and there.

When writing software, there are various ways to work with collected information. You could just define a new class that has variables to hold a specified number of "pieces of information"—such as a simple Patient object, for example, that provides string variables for the patient's first and last names and a date variable for their date of birth. Or, you could define a shopping list object that had variables for up to ten items. For a lot of the time, however, it's common not to know exactly how many items will need to be maintained as a group; normal shopping lists could potentially contain tens or hundreds of items, and a patient might have a seemingly unending list of medical problems.

8.1 Introducing Arrays

In programming terms, a simple collection of objects is held as an *array* of information. An array can hold as many items as you'd like, and once you've established an array with content, you can subsequently walk through its items, or *iterate* over it.

In the Cocoa world, you will work with arrays using instances of a class called (can you guess?) NSArray. Think of an NSArray instance like a multistory building. Each level of the building has space for exactly one object (well, actually a pointer to that object).

Arrays in Code

Let's jump straight in and look at some code. When we want to create an NSArray instance, we have several options. Open the Xcode documentation browser, and find the documentation for the NSArray class. You'll see that either you can allocate and initialize an array using one of these methods:

```
- initWithArray:
- initWithArray:copyItems:
- initWithContentsOfFile:
- initWithContentsOfURL:
- initWithObjects:
- initWithObjects:count:
```

or you can use one of the class factory methods:

```
+ array
+ arrayWithArray:
+ arrayWithContentsOfFile:
+ arrayWithContentsOfURL:
+ arrayWithObject:
+ arrayWithObjects:
+ arrayWithObjects:count:
```

Notice the similarity between the names of the methods in these two lists—we looked at naming conventions in the previous chapter, and as you might imagine, the class method + arrayWithArray: simply returns an autoreleased array, allocated and initialized using the - initWithArray: method.

As an example, let's look at the code to generate a simple array of items to be used as a shopping list. We'll hold the names of the items as strings, in NSString objects, and build an array to keep track of those strings. We'll use one of the arrayWith... class factory methods for now to avoid having to worry too much about memory issues.

Looking at the list of options, the likeliest candidate seems to be the method arrayWithObjects:. If you click through to view the documentation for this method, you'll find, as expected, that it *creates and returns an array containing the objects in the argument list.*

This uncovers some behavior you haven't seen before—the ability to pass in more than one piece of information to a method.

Passing Multiple Values to a Method

We can pass multiple values into a method in two ways. First, if we know exactly how many values there will be, we can specify them as expected variables in the name of the method, like this:

```
+ (void)personWithFirstName:(NSString *)firstName lastName:(NSString *)lastName;
```

As you might be able to guess, this would be a class factory method on a Person class that builds a Person object with the specified firstName and lastName. You could call it like this:

```
{
    Person *somebody = [Person personWithFirstName:@"Jane" lastName:@"Doe"];
}
```

Previously, we've often been referring to methods by their *names*, as in stringByAppendingString: or generateValue. When a method takes multiple arguments, you get the *name* of the method by stripping out the variable bits and pieces. The name of our earlier Person factory method would therefore be personWithFirstName:lastName:.

Specifying multiple variables in a method name is all very well, but it doesn't seem to apply to the method responsible for constructing our shopping list array. The name of the method we want to use is just arrayWithObjects:—it's not arrayWithObject1:object2:object3:, and so on. This obviously makes sense in theory because an array can hold an arbitrary number of objects.

Because of the way the Objective-C language works, it's possible for a method to use some underlying C functionality to accept a varying number of arguments. It requires a little more knowledge of the underpinnings of Objective-C before you can see how to do this in your own methods, but the basic idea is that a method can accept a list of multiple values, provided the last "value" supplied is nil.

With that in mind, you can now see what is meant in the documentation by the method definition for arrayWithObjects: being as follows:

```
+ (id)arrayWithObjects:(id)firstObj, ...
```

with the accompanying explanation specifying that firstObj, ... is "a comma-separated list of objects ending with nil."

Creating an Array

The code to create an array, therefore, is actually pretty simple. For our shopping list example, we just need to create the objects we want to put in the array and then create the array using those objects, like this:

```
{
    NSString *firstObject = @"Milk";
    NSString *secondObject = @"Eggs";
    NSString *thirdObject = @"Butter";

    NSArray *shoppingListArray =
        [NSArray arrayWithObjects:firstObject, secondObject, thirdObject, nil];
}
```

We end up with a newly created shoppingListArray object, containing the three shopping items. We can do various things with this array, such as sorting its items into alphabetical order, checking to see whether some specified object is being held, or *iterating* over every item stored.

8.2 Using Arrays in an Application

Let's add some array-handling code to our TextApp application. A little later into this chapter, we'll start a completely new project for a simple shopping list application, but for now there are still a few things we need to cover, and we'll learn these by working with TextApp.

First, we'll make some small changes to the existing interface for TextApp so that it makes more sense for our work in this and subsequent chapters. With the TextApp project open in Xcode, start by opening MainMenu.xib in Interface Builder. In the previous chapter, we changed the title of the button to "Display Value," so for this chapter let's change it to "Generate Text." The TextApp window should end up looking like Figure 8.1, on the facing page.

Next we'll modify the code that gets called in response to the Generate Text button being clicked—that's the displaySomeText: method in our NotifyingClass. To begin with, let's create our shopping list array and output the array's description to the text view.

Change the displaySomeText: method to this:

```
- (IBAction)displaySomeText:(id)sender
{
    NSString *firstObject = @"Milk";
    NSString *secondObject = @"Eggs";
    NSString *thirdObject = @"Butter";
```

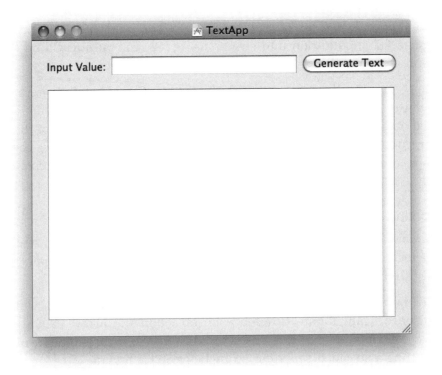

Figure 8.1: MAKING TEXTAPP'S INTERFACE EVEN MORE GENERIC

```
NSArray *shoppingListArray = [NSArray
        arrayWithObjects:firstObject, secondObject,
                         thirdObject, nil];

NSString *stringToOutput = [NSString
        stringWithFormat:@"shoppingListArray = %@", shoppingListArray];

[textView insertText:stringToOutput];
}
```

When you run the app and click the button, the text view should display
the objects in the array like this:

```
shoppingListArray = (
    Milk,
    Eggs,
    Butter
)
```

Once again, we're making use of stringWithFormat:, along with the string format specifier %@, to "output" the array. When we supply Objective-C objects for substitution into strings using %@, the output will be the result of calling the description[1] method on that object.

The NSArray implementation of the description method helpfully iterates over the objects in the array, calling NSString's description method on each object in turn; for our array of strings, we see the values of those strings in the output. We'll see how to do this ourselves when we cover loops and array iteration in Chapter 10, *Looping and Enumerating*, on page 213.

Working with Some Additional NSArray Functionality

To make this example a little more interesting, let's work with one of NSArray's built-in methods to output the strings as a comma-separated list of items.

NSArray provides us with the componentsJoinedByString: method, which will once again iterate through each object in the array, calling its description method, but this time it builds a new string from the results, inserting a specified *separator* string between each item.

Change the method once again:

```
- (IBAction)displaySomeText:(id)sender
{
    NSString *firstObject = @"Milk";
    NSString *secondObject = @"Eggs";
    NSString *thirdObject = @"Butter";

    NSArray *shoppingListArray = [NSArray
            arrayWithObjects:firstObject, secondObject,
                                thirdObject, nil];

    NSString *stringToOutput = @"The shopping list is: ";

    stringToOutput = [stringToOutput
        stringByAppendingString:[shoppingListArray
                                componentsJoinedByString:@", "]];

    [textView insertText:stringToOutput];
}
```

This time, the text view will show the array contents like this:

```
The shopping list is: Milk, Eggs, Butter
```

---

1. If available, it will actually be the *localized* output, using descriptionWithLocale:.

The Index of an Item

When you create an array of objects, like our earlier shoppingListArray example, the objects will be stored in the order they are provided— notice how the items on the shopping list are output in the order in which they were stored.

Because an array is an ordered list of objects, it's possible to ask for the object at a specific *index* in that order. The *index* is a number representing the *position* that the object occupies in the array.

Let's demonstrate this by asking the array for the first item in the list. NSArray provides us with an objectAtIndex: method that should do the trick; it accepts an integer index and returns the object stored at that index. Let's test it by adding the following lines of code:

```
- (IBAction)displaySomeText:(id)sender
{
    «beginning of method»

    stringToOutput = [stringToOutput
            stringByAppendingString:[shoppingListArray
                        componentsJoinedByString:@", "]];

    [textView insertText:stringToOutput];

    stringToOutput = @"\n\nThe first item in the list is: ";

    stringToOutput = [stringToOutput
                stringByAppendingString:[shoppingListArray objectAtIndex:1]];

    [textView insertText:stringToOutput];
}
```

The new output string starts out by inserting two new lines, and we then append the result of the objectAtIndex: method, passing in an index of 1. When you run the application and click the button, you'll see the following:

```
The shopping list is: Milk, Eggs, Butter

The first item in the list is: Eggs
```

Huh? That's not right. The first item in the list is Milk, not Eggs. What's going wrong? Well, it turns out that the index on arrays is *zero-based*. This means that the first item in the array has an index of 0, not 1. Change the relevant line of code:

```
stringToOutput = [stringToOutput
        stringByAppendingString:[shoppingListArray objectAtIndex:0]];
```

This time you should see the correct output:

```
The shopping list is: Milk, Eggs, Butter

The first item in the list is: Milk
```

Here's where it helps to think of an array as a multistory building. Having grown up living in the United Kingdom, I still have the odd confusion when I use an elevator over in the United States. In the United Kingdom, the *ground level* of a multistory building is known as the *ground floor*. The floor above that is the *first floor*, the one above that is the *second floor*, and so on. In the United States, on the other hand, what I know as the *ground floor* is referred to as the *first floor*. It takes me a while to work out which elevator button to press to get back to the lobby of a hotel. The United Kingdom uses a *zero-based* indexing for its floors, with the U.K. *ground floor* being the 0 floor, while the United States uses a *one-based* index, calling the ground floor "level 1."

So, always imagine that you're in the United Kingdom when working with arrays—the first item does *not* have an index of 1; it starts at 0. We can double-check this by asking for the index of an object in an array using the indexOfObject: method. Add the following lines of code:

```
- (IBAction)displaySomeText:(id)sender
{
    «beginning of method»

    stringToOutput = @"\n\nThe first item in the list is: ";

    stringToOutput = [stringToOutput
              stringByAppendingString:[shoppingListArray objectAtIndex:0]];

    [textView insertText:stringToOutput];

    int indexOfObject = [shoppingListArray indexOfObject:secondObject];

    stringToOutput = [NSString
      stringWithFormat:@"\n\nIndex of the second object is: %i", indexOfObject];

    [textView insertText:stringToOutput];
}
```

This time, you should see the following, confirming the situation:

```
The shopping list is: Milk, Eggs, Butter

The first item in the list is: Milk

Index of the second object is: 1
```

Counting the Items in an Array

It's also possible to ask an array how many items it is holding by sending it the count message. Let's try this next.

Add the following lines of code:

```
- (IBAction)displaySomeText:(id)sender
{
    «beginning of method»

    stringToOutput = [NSString
        stringWithFormat:@"\n\nIndex of the second object is: %i", indexOfObject];

    [textView insertText:stringToOutput];

    int numberOfItems = [shoppingListArray count];

    stringToOutput = [NSString
        stringWithFormat:@"\n\nThere are %i items in the shopping list",
                        numberOfItems];

    [textView insertText:stringToOutput];
}
```

This should generate the expected output:

```
The shopping list is: Milk, Eggs, Butter

The first item in the list is: Milk

Index of the second object is: 1

There are 3 items in the shopping list
```

Note that the number returned by the count message is *not* the index of
the last item in the array—in a U.K. building with twenty-five stories,
the top story is the twenty-fourth. The *index* is zero-based, but the
count is the number you would use in the real world to say, for example,
"There are twelve months in a year."

So far, we've worked with what's known as a *static* array—its items are
set when we create the array, and we haven't tried to add or remove
any items. It turns out that NSArray is designed *only* to work as a static
array, and we couldn't make any changes if we tried.

8.3 Object Mutability

We've actually been working with two types of unchanging object so far—NSString and now NSArray. Both have their contents set when they are created, like this:

```
NSString *fixedString = @"This is a non-changing string";

NSArray *fixedArray = [NSArray arrayWithObjects:fixedString, nil];
```

To create new strings from old strings, we've been using an NSString method called stringByAppendingString: in code like this:

```
NSString *fixedString = @"This is a non-changing string";

fixedString = [fixedString
    stringByAppendingString:@" even if we add something to it..."];
```

Rather than append the new string to the existing string, this method returns a whole new string, with its contents made up from the old string plus the new string stuck on the end.

NSArray provides some similar methods for deriving new arrays—such as arrayByAddingObject:. We could, for example, do something like this:

```
NSString *firstItem = @"Milk";
NSString *secondItem = @"Eggs";

NSArray *shoppingListArray = [NSArray arrayWithObjects:firstItem, secondItem, nil];

NSString *thirdItem = @"Butter";

shoppingListArray = [shoppingListArray arrayByAddingObject:thirdItem];
```

Just like we reassigned the fixedString variable to a new, fixed string, here we are reassigning the shoppingListArray variable to a completely new array, containing the items from the previous array plus the additional object tagged on the end.

This is all well and good for our simple shopping list example with only a few items, but if our array were to end up with several thousand objects, this would be extremely inefficient. It would be much nicer if we had some way of adding an object to the *existing* array object.

Mutable Arrays and Strings

This is where the term *mutable* comes in. If an object is *mutable*, its contents are *dynamic* and can change.

Cocoa provides us with several mutable classes, based on its standard fixed-content classes. There is, for example, an NSMutableString class and, luckily for us, an NSMutableArray class.

By using NSMutableArray instead of NSArray, we gain the use of various methods to add extra objects on the end, like addObject:, or insertObject:atIndex: to insert an object into the middle of an array at a specified index. There are also corresponding methods to remove objects from the array when necessary.

To create an NSMutableArray, we have several options. Because the NSMutableArray class inherits from NSArray, we can use our old friend arrayWithObjects: to set up a new mutable array with the specified objects. We could also create a new, empty array using the array class method from NSArray, to which we could add each object individually, like this:

```
NSMutableArray *changingArray = [NSMutableArray array];

// changingArray is currently an empty array
// calling [changingArray count] at this point would return 0

NSString *firstObject = @"The first string";
[changingArray addObject:firstObject];

NSString *secondObject = @"The second string";
[changingArray addObject:secondObject];
```

Array Efficiency

If we know in advance how many items we're eventually going to be storing in the array, we can use either the initWithCapacity: initializer or the corresponding arrayWithCapacity: class factory method. These do all sorts of nifty things behind the scenes to set us up with an empty array that's ready to store the specified capacity most efficiently. You can still add additional items if you want, but the items that occupy the *original* capacity will be stored most efficiently:

```
NSMutableArray *smallArray = [NSMutableArray arrayWithCapacity:2];

// smallArray is currently an empty array
// calling [smallArray count] would still return 0

[smallArray addObject:firstObject];
[smallArray addObject:secondObject];

// smallArray now has two items, stored efficiently

NSString *thirdObject = @"The third string";
```

```
[smallArray addObject:thirdObject];

// the third object might not be stored so efficiently
```

What do I mean by *efficiently*? Well, because an array is a list of pointers to objects, it would ideally be one big block of memory in which each pointer gets stored one after another in that big block.

Sometimes there isn't enough memory to allocate a block big enough to store all the pointers in one place, or we add extra items beyond the original capacity. In these cases, the array object has to keep track of multiple blocks of memory storage containing its object pointer contents.

Changeable Contents

It's worth pointing out that an array simply stores a series of pointers to other objects; it does not store copies of the objects themselves. Having said this, let's take a look at some potentially confusing situations. Consider this code:

```
NSString *firstObject = @"Milk";
NSString *secondObject = @"Eggs";

NSArray *fixedArray = [NSArray arrayWithObjects:firstObject, secondObject, nil];

secondObject = @"Bread";

NSLog(@"Contents of Array = %@", fixedArray);
```

What do you think would be output to the console if you ran this code?

Since the array stores pointers to the objects, it might appear at first glance as if the output would be this:

```
Contents of Array = (
    Milk,
    Bread
)
```

Actually, the output is this:

```
Contents of Array = (
    Milk,
    Eggs
)
```

What's going on? Why isn't the second object changing? There are two issues at play here—first, if you add an object to an array, the array maintains what's known as a *strong* reference to the object. This means that the array retains the object that is added so that, as long as the array exists, the objects inside that array will be retained as necessary.

The second problem is that we *reassign* the secondObject variable with a new string. We tell the array to store the first secondObject string value, and when we reassign the variable, it will end up at a different address in memory that, as far as the array is concerned, is a different variable altogether, so nothing changes.

If we change our example to use *mutable* string objects instead, let's see what happens this time:

```
NSMutableString *firstObject = [NSMutableString stringWithString:@"Milk"];
NSMutableString *secondObject = [NSMutableString stringWithString:@"Eggs"];

NSArray *fixedArray = [NSArray arrayWithObjects:firstObject, secondObject, nil];

[secondObject setString:@"Bread"];

NSLog(@"Contents of Array = %@", fixedArray);
```

When this code is executed, the log shows what we hoped for:

```
Contents of Array = (
    Milk,
    Bread
)
```

You'll see from this that working with mutable strings requires quite a bit more code. Also notice that although it's not possible to *add* or *remove* objects in a standard NSArray instance, the objects that it contains can change as much as they like, provided their memory address stays the same!

Advanced String Stuff

It might be worth pointing out a few things that we've been taking for granted up until now. In the original C language, a string is defined like this:

```
"this is a C string"
```

The notation we've been using all the way through the book so far—@"string"—is an Objective-C shorthand where the @ character takes the string that follows it and passes back an NSString object set to the value of what's between the quotation marks.

It's perfectly possible to create an Objective-C string using code like this:

```
NSString *string = [NSString stringWithCString:"this is a C string"
    encoding:«some encoding»];
```

so you might like to think of the @"string" notation as being roughly equivalent to typing out all of the previous code. The encoding part of that line shown earlier is used to determine how the characters should be interpreted, as described briefly in Section 5.2, *Storing Other Information*, on page 79.

Thankfully, the NSString class is so amazing that you probably won't need to worry about any of the behind-the-scenes C stuff. It's just worth mentioning that every time you use the @"string" Objective-C notation, you are effectively using a class factory method to generate an autoreleased string (and not an NSMutableString) with a set value that cannot change. This is why you couldn't, for example, do this:

```
NSMutableString *aMutableString = @"Try and change me...";

[aMutableString setString:@"I'm trying to change you"]; // this won't work
```

Although the aMutableString pointer looks like it should point to an NSMutableString object, it actually points to an *immutable*, plain NSString instance, because that's what the earlier code assigned to it.

Adding Items to Our Array in TextApp

Now that you know how to add items to our arrays, let's write some extra functionality for TextApp to allow us to add an item to our shopping list. We'll take a string typed into the text field and add it to the end of the shopping list before we display the array contents in the text view.

Let's start by thinning down our existing code, changing back to an NSArray, and adding a line to create a new array with the string value in the text field:

```
- (IBAction)displaySomeText:(id)sender
{
    NSString *firstObject = @"Milk";
    NSString *secondObject = @"Eggs";
    NSString *thirdObject = @"Butter";

    NSArray *shoppingListArray = [NSArray
            arrayWithObjects:firstObject, secondObject,
                        thirdObject, nil];
```

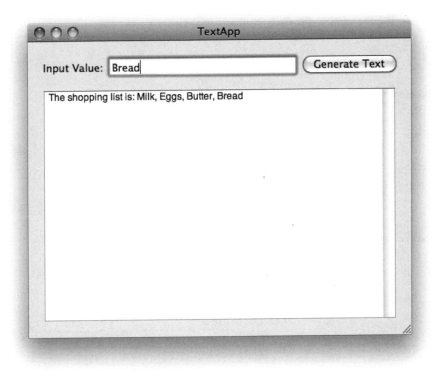

Figure 8.2: ADDING AN ITEM TO THE SHOPPING LIST

```
    NSString *typedValue = [textField stringValue];
    shoppingListArray = [shoppingListArray arrayByAddingObject:typedValue];

    NSString *stringToOutput = @"The shopping list is: ";
    stringToOutput = [stringToOutput
            stringByAppendingString:[shoppingListArray
                            componentsJoinedByString:@", "]];

    [textView insertText:stringToOutput];
}
```

When you test the application this time, you should see something like Figure 8.2.

Why not test your Cocoa prowess now and see whether you can get the application to accomplish the same thing using an NSMutableArray?

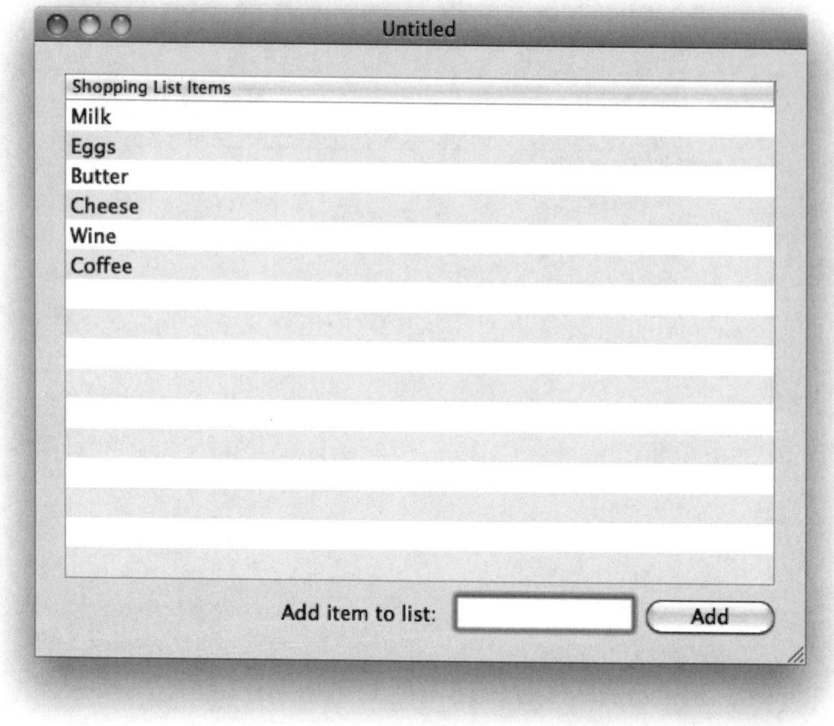

Figure 8.3: THE NEW SHOPPING LIST APPLICATION THAT WE'LL CREATE

8.4 A New Application

Our work in TextApp is all very well for learning about arrays, but it doesn't really behave like a real-world application since we created a new array each time the Generate Text button was clicked. In a standard Mac OS X application, we'd expect the values that were added by the user to persist. Let's move on and build a more Mac-like application that does that right now. We'll put our newfound knowledge to the test and write a simple shopping list application. It's going to look like Figure 8.3.

We'll be covering several new ideas throughout this section, including how to work with a document-based application. By the time we've finished, we'll ideally have reinforced lots of other Cocoa and Objective-C techniques as well.

Creating the Project

Close anything that's currently open in Xcode, and select File > New Project.... We're going to be writing an application that can deal with *multiple* shopping lists, so it makes sense to create a *document-based* application.

Make sure that you have a Mac OS X Cocoa Application selected in the New Project window, and select the "Create document-based application" box. Click the Choose... button, and call the new project "Shopping List."

When working with a document-based application, there are several differences from what we've seen before. First, if you expand the Resources group in the project browser, you'll find that there are now *two* different XIB files—MainMenu.xib that we've seen before and a new MyDocument.xib file.

If you also expand the Classes group, you'll find that there are the relevant files defining a class called MyDocument.

Before doing anything else, click the Build & Run button to see what functionality we get from this template project. You should be greeted by a window looking like Figure 8.4, on the next page.

If you select File > New, you'll find that another window opens, identical to the first one you saw. These windows are the visual representations of the MyDocument class. Whenever you choose the New command, the template application will create a new object instance of the MyDocument class.

You'll find that there are various options to Save and Open files, but these don't do anything at the moment. Quit the application, and return to Xcode.

The MyDocument Class

Let's take a look inside the MyDocument.h file to see how the new document class is set up. The existing interface is extremely simple:

```
#import <Cocoa/Cocoa.h>

@interface MyDocument : NSDocument
{
}
@end
```

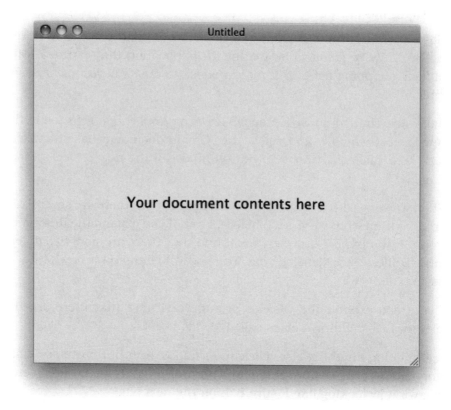

Figure 8.4: An unchanged document-based template application

It just defines a class called MyDocument that inherits from the NSDocument class.

Unsurprisingly, NSDocument is the basic Cocoa class for a document object, and it provides all sorts of useful functionality relevant to documents. As usual, you can override various methods to add your own features, and several methods actually *need* to be overridden to provide the behavior of your application that a template project can't generalize, such as saving and opening files.

Switch to the MyDocument.m file, and you'll be greeted with various prewritten methods that override the basic NSDocument behavior.

The first of these is a trusty init method, and it looks like this:

```
- (id)init
{
    self = [super init];
    if (self) {

        // Add your subclass-specific initialization here.
        // If an error occurs here, send a [self release] message and return nil.

    }
    return self;
}
```

Notice that it starts and ends in the same way as our previous init methods that we've written but adds a code block in the middle starting with if. This is the first time we've seen a *conditional* statement; we'll be looking at these properly in the next chapter. For now, all you need to know is that the code between the inner curly braces is executed only if a condition is met. In our init method, it will be executed if the object is created successfully, which should be most of the time!

The next method is relatively short and straightforward:

```
- (NSString *)windowNibName
{
    // Override returning the nib file name of the document
    return @"MyDocument";
}
```

This is the document equivalent of what you saw, way back in Section 2.4, *The MainMenu.xib File*, on page 15. It returns the name of an Interface Builder file containing the interface for the document, which is why you saw the extra file back under the Resources group in the project browser.

We're seeing the easiest way to work with an NSDocument object here—where there is only one window per open document. It's perfectly possible to work with documents that use multiple windows, maybe to show different views into the same data, but that involves a slightly different approach from the one we're using, which is unfortunately outside the scope of this chapter.

The third method listed is windowControllerDidLoadNib:—it allows us to tap in and do any necessary additional interface setup after the interface has been loaded from the resource file. We won't be needing it here, and we'll also ignore for now the other methods that have something to do with reading and writing data to disk.

What's the Difference Between Nib and Xib?

You might have noticed that the Interface Builder files we're using have an .xib extension, although we've seen a couple of places where the file is referred to as a *nib* file.

Nib stands for "NeXT Interface Builder" and was the original binary file format for the files. When Apple released Xcode version 3.0, and with it Interface Builder 3.0, it moved to an XML-format. To differentiate between the two interface file types, the XML-format uses the .xib extension.

You'll often see Interface Builder files referred to as *nib files*, even when they have the .xib extension. When you're dealing with these files from a code perspective, though, you'll likely always see the word *nib* to maintain backward compatibility.

The NSDocument class is an example of a *controller* class. This means that it acts as a mediator between the view (that's the user interface created in Interface Builder) and the underlying data (that's an NSMutableArray in this instance). We'll talk more about the separation of model, view, and controller classes a little later in the book, in Chapter 11, *Objects, Encapsulation, and MVC*, on page 233.

Creating the Interface

Now that you know how the interface for a document is created from the MyDocument.xib file, let's open it in Interface Builder and start creating our shopping list interface.

When you open the file, you'll find that the template project has stuck a label on the Window, saying "Your document contents here"—the first thing to do is to select this label and delete it.

Introducing Table Views

We want to display our shopping list in a tabular format, and it just so happens that Cocoa provides us with the perfect class to do this: NSTableView.

A table view is an object used to display data in columns and rows; it's a little bit like a spreadsheet at first glance, although it doesn't behave in quite the same way. You'll find examples of table views throughout the

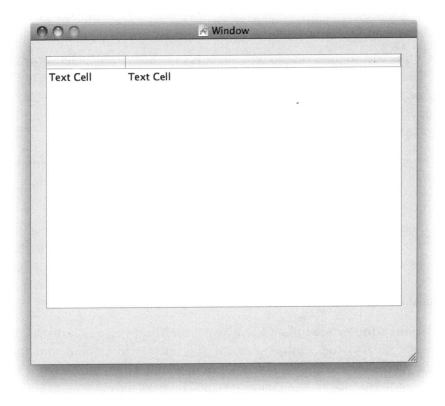

Figure 8.5: A BASIC TABLE VIEW

software on your Mac. When you look at your list of emails in Apple's Mail application, for example, you're looking at a table view.

Let's drag one onto the interface now to take a look at some of its features. Type "table" into the Object Library palette search box, and you should find the Table View object ready to drag out. Drag one onto the document window, and resize it so it looks like Figure 8.5.

You'll see that at the top of the table view is a *header bar*. You typically use this bar to label the columns that appear below it—just like the From, Subject, and Date Received column headers in Mail.

Underneath the column headers are two *cells*. These define how information gets displayed in each row of each column. By default, the cells in the table view are *text cells*, which display a string of text. Since we want to display the string values of each item in our shopping list array, this will do just fine.

It's important to understand why there is only one row of cells shown in Interface Builder—it's because the cell that you see there acts as a *prototype* cell, from which all the rows of data will eventually be displayed when the application is run. We'll see how to supply our shopping list information to the cells in the table view a little later.

Although it's not immediately apparent, the table view that's been generated is actually enclosed in a scroll view—the scroll bars will show up only if there is too much data to fit inside the box.

To make it easier to see the structure of what we have so far, take a look at the Interface Builder window for our file, titled "MyDocument.xib – English." Use the toolbar inside this window to change the "View Mode" to "List View" (that's the middle of the three options, with several horizontal lines).

With this window set to List View, you'll find that there is a disclosure triangle next to the Window item; if you click it to expand and then click each subsequent disclosure triangle that appears, you will see something that looks like Figure 8.6, on the next page.

If you have enough space on your screen, try to rearrange the Interface Builder windows so that you can see both this MyDocument.xib window and the actual Window window displaying the table view. Try double-clicking one of the table columns in the list view, and you'll find that Interface Builder highlights the column in the display.

Since we need only one of the columns, you can select one of the existing Table Column items in the list view and press ⌫; both the column and its internal Text Field Cell should disappear from the two windows. You could also achieve the same thing by selecting the Table View and decreasing the number of columns on the Attributes tab of the inspector.

To make the table view display its rows over an alternating background, select the Table View in the list, and select the Alternating Rows box in its attribute inspector.

Next, select the remaining Table Column in the list view, and change the Title of the column in the inspector to be "Shopping List Items" to give our users a clue about what they should be putting in the column.

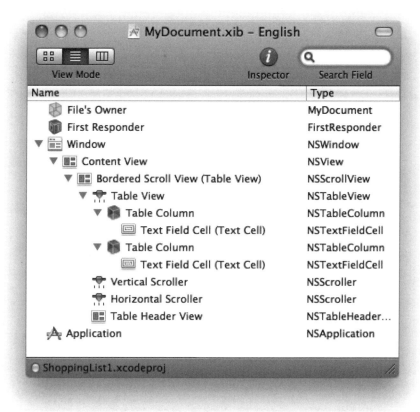

Figure 8.6: INTERFACE BUILDER'S LIST VIEW

Adding the Rest of the Interface

With our table view in place, it's time to add the remaining items to the interface. We need a Label object, titled "Add item to list:"; a Text Field object; and a Push Button titled "Add"—set these items up so that they look like Figure 8.7, on the following page.

Linking the Interface to the Controller

If you cast your mind back to when you created TextApp, you made a new class called NotifyingClass that took care of handling a button press in the window, and talked to the various interface items through their relevant **IBOutlet**s.

Figure 8.7: THE SHOPPING LIST APPLICATION INTERFACE

Because the NotifyingClass acted as an intermediary between the interface items and contained the functionality to display data (various bits of text) in the text view, that class is a *controller* class. You could generate a completely new class in the Shopping List application to handle the interactions between the interface items, but you might remember that you already have a controller object available—the MyDocument object.

Introducing File's Owner

When we created our first instance of NotifyingClass, back in Section 3.4, *Creating an Instance of Our NotifyingClass*, on page 41, we added one into the Interface Builder file so that an instance would be created when the interface was loaded.

If we did the same thing with our MyDocument class, we'd actually end up with two MyDocument objects for every open document window; the application template will already have created a MyDocument instance for us, before reading and instantiating the interface objects from the MyDocument.xib file.

This time, we need to use the *File's Owner* object in our interface file. When an interface file is opened to set up the contents of an interface, the File's Owner object is set to the object that *owns* the interface contents. In this particular case, it will be the MyDocument object, because it's the job of the inherited NSDocument class to open the interface file when a new document is created.

Adding Outlets and an Action

You'll remember from before that in order for a controller object (previously the NotifyingClass instance, now our MyDocument instance) to be able to work with the user interface, we need to add **IBOutlet**s for each item and add an **IBAction** to be triggered when a button is clicked.

Open the MyDocument.h file, and add outlets for the table view and the text field, along with an action for the Add button:

```
@interface MyDocument : NSDocument
{
    IBOutlet NSTableView *shoppingListTableView;
    IBOutlet NSTextField *newItemNameTextField;
}

- (IBAction)addNewItemToShoppingList:(id)sender;

@end
```

Switch to Interface Builder, and right-click (or ^-click) the File's Owner object in MyDocument.xib. When we used the project template to create this application's project files, Xcode already set up this file correctly so that File's Owner was set to our MyDocument class. You should, therefore, now see the two outlets and the action listed—connect these to the relevant interface items, as in Figure 8.8, on the following page.

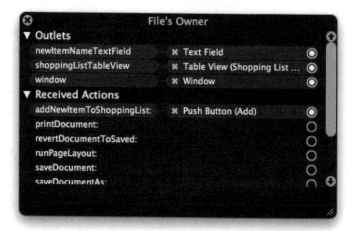

Figure 8.8: CONNECTING THE SHOPPING LIST INTERFACE ITEMS

Once this is done, we need to *implement* the new action method in MyDocument.m. Copy the method declaration from MyDocument.h, and paste it into the top of the MyDocument.m implementation, changing it into a method, like so:

```
@implementation MyDocument

- (IBAction)addNewItemToShoppingList:(id)sender
{

}

- (id)init
{
    «code continues»
```

It would be wise to build the application now, just to check that you haven't made any typographical errors. Choose the Build command from the Build menu in Xcode, and if all is in order, you should see the word "Succeeded" in the bottom-right of the Xcode project window.

Setting Up the Array

Now that we have our basic interface created, it's time to think about how we're going to keep track of the items in our shopping list.

Clearly, we're going to use an array, just like before, but we need that array to hang around, or *persist*, as long as the document (and therefore its window) is open. In the earlier parts of this chapter, we were working with code that established an array for use in the scope of a single method, using a class factory method; the array was deallocated at the end of the method. For our Shopping List application, however, we need it to stay in memory for the lifetime for the MyDocument object. We're also going to need to have access to the array from several methods in the MyDocument implementation.

If you cast your mind back to Section 7.7, *When to Use alloc and When to Use Factory Methods*, on page 137, I hinted briefly about storing a pointer to one object as an instance variable of an another object. I suggested that we could use the init method of the *containing* object to create and initialize the *contained* object and to release it from memory in the containing object's dealloc method. This is exactly what we want to do here.

So, open the MyDocument.h interface file, and add an instance variable for a pointer to an NSMutableArray, like this:

```
@interface MyDocument : NSDocument
{
    IBOutlet NSTableView *shoppingListTableView;
    IBOutlet NSTextField *newItemNameTextField;

    NSMutableArray *shoppingListArray;
}

- (IBAction)addNewItemToShoppingList:(id)sender;

@end
```

We can now access this object pointer from any of MyDocument's methods. First, let's create the array itself in init. Switch to the MyDocument.m implementation file, and change the method to this:

```
- (id)init
{
    self = [super init];
    if (self) {
        shoppingListArray = [[NSMutableArray alloc]
                initWithObjects:@"Milk", @"Eggs",
                                @"Butter", nil];
    }
    return self;
}
```

We're doing several things differently here, and are now creating the array using an alloc] init...] call rather than using a class factory method. At this point, you should be shaking with concern that we are taking responsibility for an object but haven't yet put in a call to release it anywhere. We'll correct that in just a moment.

The code sets up the array with three string objects to start with, so that we'll have something to see when we get our table view displaying data in the next section. We're doing it slightly differently this time, though, putting the @"string" objects directly into the method without creating variables to hold them. Remember from Section 8.3, *Advanced String Stuff*, on page 151 how using the @"string" notation was equivalent to using something like [NSString stringWith...]? We're just passing the *object* provided by the @"string" straight into the initWithObjects:... call without using a named variable.

Notice also that we've put this code inside the conditional if statement's curly brace section. This code will be executed only if the MyDocument object is created successfully.

To put us out of our object responsibility misery, we need to release the array object. When should we do that? Since we need the array to last as long as the MyDocument object, we use its dealloc method. This will be called when the MyDocument object is deallocated from memory.

By default, the project template files for the MyDocument class do not include a dealloc method; we'll need to add one ourselves. The dealloc method needs to work like a "backward" init method. First it should release any instance variables that were retained or alloc] init]ed earlier, and then it needs to pass the dealloc message up the inheritance chain, using [super dealloc], to continue the deallocation of the whole object.

Add the following method just under the existing init method in the implementation:

```
- (void)dealloc
{
    [shoppingListArray release];

    [super dealloc];
}
```

At this point, we've added a reference to the *model* for our data—a simple mutable array. Once again, choose the Build command (⌘-B) just to make sure everything is OK. If you run the application itself, it won't look like much is happening because we still haven't done anything about populating the table view with the shopping list items.

Working with Table Views

When we created the interface for the Shopping List application, we gave it a table view with one column. In Interface Builder, this column appeared with a single Text Cell as its only row. It's now time to see how we get the table view to display our data.

There are several ways to work with table views; the one we'll use for this application is fairly straightforward and very similar to the way you work with a table view on the iPhone. You provide the table view with an object to act as a *data source*, and the table view will then ask that object for the information it needs to populate its rows and columns.

What object should we use to act as the data source in this application? Well, think where the data for our document is currently being held—yes, in a mutable array held by the MyDocument object. So, first things first—let's tell the table view to use the document object as its data source.

Go back to the MyDocument.xib file in Interface Builder, and use the object list view to find the table view object. Right-click (or ^-click) this object to reveal its connections; you should see the dataSource outlet near the top. Link this to the File's Owner object, as in Figure 8.9, on the next page.

Implementing the Required Methods

Now that our data source is connected, we need to know which messages we should respond to in order to supply the data back to the table view. When working with classes that respond to certain messages specific to other classes, you're said to be implementing a *protocol*—something defining the way that classes interact with each other. We'll look more at protocols a little later in the book—there are various coding conventions and bits and pieces that we won't worry about right now. All you need to know is that the *name* of the protocol you need to work with for this situation is NSTableViewDataSource. You might already be able to spot a naming convention going on here!

If you search in the Xcode reference library for *NSTableViewDataSource*, you'll find the protocol reference. This lists "the methods that an instance of NSTableView uses to provide and access the contents of its data source object."

Figure 8.9: CONNECTING THE TABLE VIEW DATA SOURCE

The first two methods listed are as follows:

```
- numberOfRowsInTableView:
- tableView:objectValueForTableColumn:row:
```

When a table view wants to display its data, it initially needs to know how many rows there will be. If it has a data source set up, it will send the data source object the message numberOfRowsInTableView:, to which the object should respond with an integer number specifying the number of rows.

Let's implement this method first. How do we know how may rows there will be? Well, we can simply ask the shopping list array how many items it has by sending the array the count message. Given that this message will return an integer value, we can just pass this value straight back in response to the data source protocol method.

Copy the method signature from the documentation, and add this method into the MyDocument implementation:

```
- (NSInteger)numberOfRowsInTableView:(NSTableView *)aTableView
{
    return [shoppingListArray count];
}
```

Notice that when this method is called, it has a single argument that specifies which table view sent the message. If we had one object acting as a data source to multiple table views, we could check to see which table view had sent the message and respond accordingly. Since we're working with only one table view, we can just ignore that argument.

To provide the details to be displayed in each row of the table view, we need to implement this method:

```
- (id)tableView:(NSTableView *)aTableView
            objectValueForTableColumn:(NSTableColumn *)aTableColumn
            row:(NSInteger)rowIndex
```

Once again, the first argument we see is the table view that sent us the message, and as before, we can just ignore that information. The next argument tells us which table column we're supplying with information. Since we have only one column, we can just ignore this as well. The only argument we are interested in is the rowIndex argument.

The tableView:objectValueForTableColumn:row: method will be called once for each row in the table view; that is, it will be called as many times as we specified in the numberOfRowsInTableView: method. The rowIndex argument specifies the index of the row for which we need to provide an object; the good news is that this is a zero-based index, just like our array.

Remember in Section 8.2, *The Index of an Item*, on page 145 how we asked the array for its first item, using [shoppingListArray objectAtIndex:0]? We can do exactly the same thing here to ask the array for the object specified by the rowIndex argument and just pass the object we get back as the object to be displayed.

Once again, copy the method signature from the documentation, and implement it like this:

```
- (id)tableView:(NSTableView *)aTableView
            objectValueForTableColumn:(NSTableColumn *)aTableColumn
            row:(NSInteger)rowIndex
{
    return [shoppingListArray objectAtIndex:rowIndex];
}
```

If you Build & Run the application at this point, you should find that a table view appears in each document window, correctly populated with those initial contents of our shopping list array.

Adding New Items

The next functionality to sort out is the ability to add new items to the list when the user clicks the Add button. Before we write the method, let's take a moment to plan what needs to happen:

1. We start by getting the string value from the text field and add it into the array.

2. Next, we should clear the text field so that it's ready to accept another item from the user.

3. Finally, to make sure that the new item shows up in the table view, we need to tell the table view to reload its contents. This will cause the table view to talk to its data source and repopulate its rows with the additional item.

Implement addNewItemToShoppingList: with the following code:

```
- (IBAction)addNewItemToShoppingList:(id)sender
{
    NSString *newItem = [newItemNameTextField stringValue];

    [shoppingListArray addObject:newItem];

    [newItemNameTextField setStringValue:@""];

    [shoppingListTableView reloadData];
}
```

This is all fairly self-explanatory. We get the new item string from the text field, add it to the array, set the string in the text field to a blank string (@""), and then send the table view the reloadData message.

If you Build & Run the application once again, you should be able to add items to the shopping list as you want.

Editing the Items

It would be nice if we provided the ability to edit items already in the shopping list. We could go about implementing this functionality in various ways; if the user double-clicked a row in the table view, we might pop up a new window asking for a new string value. As it happens, there is an even easier way.

If you try double-clicking an item in the table view right now, you'll find that there is a built-in editing capability. A text field will appear in the cell at that point, allowing you to change the value that's currently in the cell. If you click out of the text field or press the ↵ key, you'll find that the text in the cell unfortunately jumps straight back to what it was before.

Take a look once again at the documentation for the NSTableViewData-Source protocol. You'll see that there is another data source method, tableView:setObjectValue:forTableColumn:row:, that looks like it will help us here. It's a message to tell us that we should replace the object we currently have to represent the data in a particular column and row with the new object provided.

As before, we can ignore the arguments specifying the table view and table column that this applies to—we're only interested in the new object value and the index of the row. If you now look at the documentation for NSMutableArray, you'll find that it offers us a method, replaceObjectAtIndex:withObject:. We can use this to swap out the existing string at the specified index with the one that has been typed by the user. Copy the method signature for the protocol method, and implement it like this:

```
- (void)tableView:(NSTableView *)aTableView
          setObjectValue:(id)anObject
          forTableColumn:(NSTableColumn *)aTableColumn
                     row:(NSInteger)rowIndex
{
    [shoppingListArray replaceObjectAtIndex:rowIndex withObject:anObject];
}
```

This time when you test the application, you should be able to edit the items in each row of the table view, and they'll stay at the values you set. That was pretty easy, wasn't it?

Adding Spice

We started out by creating a document-based application. At the moment, users can create as many new documents as they like, but they can't save or open files. Anything that is typed into the shopping list is lost once a document window is closed or the application exits. In another demonstration of the awesome power of the Cocoa framework, let's add the ability to save and open shopping list files.

The NSDocument class provides us with various ways to work with files. At the time of writing this book, the standard template files contain two file-related methods, dataOfType:error: and readFromData:ofType:error:. These methods get called when the user tries to save or open a document and are designed to let the programmer simply provide a data object to be saved or receive a data object to be read into a document being opened. We're going to approach this from a slightly different perspective for our Shopping List application, so delete both these methods from the template file.

Saving a Shopping List

Let's start by adding the ability to *save* shopping list files. Consider first of all what needs to be saved. All the data relevant to the shopping list document is contained within the mutable array; wouldn't it be great if we could just get the array to save itself to a file?

Take a look at the documentation for NSArray. You'll find that under the methods dealing with descriptions for the array object, there are two methods listed:

```
- writeToFile:atomically:
- writeToURL:atomically:
```

It sounds like one of these might do the trick. But what's the difference between a file and a URL? Don't URLs have something to do with the Internet, like http://www.apple.com? Yes, a URL on the Internet does take that form, but we can also work with URLs on the desktop to simplify working with filenames and locations.

In order to see whether we want to use writeToFile:atomically: or write-ToURL:atomically:, let's take a look at the documentation for NSDocument to see what options we have for file saving. Under the "Reading From and Writing to URLs" section, there are various methods that look hopeful. The simplest one looks like it will be writeToURL:ofType:error:. Check the documentation for this method to find out what the various attributes do.

The type attribute for this method is used if the application is able to save multiple file types, such as saving a text file in plain text, in rich text, or as a PDF. Since we're working with only one file type, we can ignore this. The error attribute is for us to supply an object describing some sort of error that occurred while writing the file to disk. We'll ignore this as well, for simplicity; in a real-world application, your saving mechanism would probably be more complicated than we are about to implement, and you would definitely want to investigate how to deal properly with errors.

The remaining attribute for this method provides us with a URL, specifying the location on disk to which we want the document to be written. When the user asks to save the shopping list, the built-in functionality in NSDocument will pop up a standard Mac OS X Save dialog box; if the user successfully navigates to a location and chooses a name, our writeToURL:ofType:error: method will be called. We can then just pass the URL along to the writeToURL:atomically: method on NSArray.

Before we implement this, notice that the writeToURL:ofType:error: method on NSDocument is expected to return a BOOL value indicating whether the write was successful. A BOOL can have a value of either YES or NO. We don't need to worry too much about this, however, because the writeToFile:atomically: method from NSArray will pass us a BOOL value to indicate its success, and we can just **return** this straight back in our saving method.

You might want to check the documentation for NSArray to see what the *atomically* means in writeToFile:atomically:. It has to do with whether the document is saved straight to a location on disk or whether it is saved to a temporary file first and then that temporary file gets moved to the correct location. This can be used to avoid data loss if the application crashes during a save—if the save has been to a temporary location, it won't have had any effect on an existing original document. We'll make use of this atomic behavior.

Copy the method signature for writeToURL:ofType:error:, and implement it like this:

```
- (BOOL)writeToURL:(NSURL *)absoluteURL
          ofType:(NSString *)typeName
           error:(NSError **)outError
{
    return [shoppingListArray writeToURL:absoluteURL atomically:YES];
}
```

It doesn't get much simpler than that! Try saving a shopping list by selecting File > Save, and you should find a file is created where you specify. Now all we need to do is figure out how to open it again.

Opening a Saved Shopping List

In the documentation for NSDocument, you will find that there is a method called readFromURL:ofType:error:. This is clearly the corresponding document-opening method to our writeToURL:ofType:error: we just used, so it would probably make sense to use this method, if possible.

What needs to happen when we read from a file? Well, the contents of the shopping list array need to be set to the saved contents in the file. How do we do that? Take a look at the documentation again for NSArray, and you'll find that it's possible to initialize an array using the method initWithContentsOfURL:. Let's use this to initialize a new shopping list array for our document.

One problem arises, however, in that we already have an array allocated and initialized—if we *reassign* the shoppingListArray instance variable with another array, we'll have leaked the array that was already created by the init method. So, we should first release the old shoppingListArray before assigning the instance variable to the newly opened file.

The readFromURL:ofType:error: method is also expected to return a BOOL value to confirm whether the document was opened safely. We really ought to do some kind of check to make sure that we got back a proper array from the initWithContentsOfURL: initializer, but for now let's just return a value of YES to indicate success. Copy the method signature for readFromURL:ofType:error:, and implement it like this:

```
- (BOOL)readFromURL:(NSURL *)absoluteURL
            ofType:(NSString *)typeName
             error:(NSError **)outError
{
    [shoppingListArray release];

    shoppingListArray = [[NSMutableArray alloc]
                         initWithContentsOfURL:absoluteURL];

    [shoppingListTableView reloadData];

    return YES;
}
```

If you now run the application and open the file by selecting File > Open, or drag the file onto the application's icon on the Dock, the saved shopping list will appear, as if by magic. Pretty cool, huh?

A Few Caveats

It's important to point out a few issues with the Shopping List application. First, we do very limited error checking, as discussed along the way. We also don't support the standard functionality of marking the document as *dirty* whenever a change is made.

At the top left of most windows, you'll typically see the three "traffic-light" buttons to close, minimize, and maximize the window. When there are unsaved changes to a document, the document is said to be "dirty," and the red close button displays a big dot inside.

To implement this behavior, we would need to let the document object know that it was dirty whenever an item was added using the Add button or changes were made by the user double-clicking a shopping list item. This would also have the effect of asking the user whether they want to save their changes when they closed a document window; at the moment, you can easily lose any changes you make by closing the window without saving first.

NSDocument responds to the updateChangeCount: message—you would need to insert a call to this method, passing it a *constant* value of NSChangeDone, in both the addNewItemToShoppingList: and tableView:setObjectValue:forTableColumn:row: to solve this problem.

We've also not added any functionality to remove items from the list completely. You might like to try implementing this yourself; you'd need a Remove button in the interface, connected to an action that asked the table view for the row that is currently selected. You'd then need to remove the object at that row index from the array, before telling the table view to reload its data.

8.5 Chapter Summary

You've accomplished quite a bit in this chapter, and you should be gaining confidence in working with objects, the Objective-C language, and the Cocoa framework.

By creating a completely new application, you're moving toward putting your knowledge into development of applications that have more advanced functionality and behavior, and work more as you expect Mac OS X applications to work.

You're now reasonably familiar with the concept of an array as an object to hold a collection of other objects. There are other collection objects available to us in the Cocoa framework, including NSSet, which behaves in a similar way to NSArray but just collects objects together without maintaining any order. You can't ask for an object at a specific index in a set, and objects will likely be returned to you in a different order than they were stored. There is also an NSDictionary object, which allows you to use a *key* string rather than an index to keep track of its collected objects. We'll be looking at dictionaries in Section 11.2, *Dictionaries of Information*, on page 238.

In the next chapter, we'll take a look at those conditional statements we hurried over earlier in this chapter, seeing how to execute different blocks of code depending on the outcome of a decision or the value of a variable.

Chapter 9

Branching Out

Life is full of decisions. You're always having to choose between two or more options, making educated guesses about which might be better and then worrying endlessly, "What if I'd chosen option B?"

In the programming world, decisions are simplified. You generally get to decide exactly *what* will happen, based on absolute criteria, such as "The user clicked this button" or "This computer doesn't have Internet access." And you get to decide the plan of action taken by your software for each of the possible criteria matches.

In this chapter, we look at how to write code that takes different paths depending on the values of logical statements.

9.1 Introducing if and else

Consider the following pseudocode:

```
deleteSomethingImportant:
{
    display a dialog box asking if the user is sure they want to delete

    if they click the Delete button
        then delete the important information
    otherwise if they click the Cancel button
        then don't do anything
}
```

This pseudocode represents behavior that might be placed in an application as a fail-safe mechanism to make sure users are absolutely sure they want to delete some vital piece of information. In Apple's Address Book application, for example, a dialog box is displayed if you try to delete a contact, as shown in Figure 9.1, on the following page.

Figure 9.1: MAKING SURE THE USER WANTS TO DELETE A CONTACT FROM THEIR ADDRESS BOOK

In the C language, the simplest branch construction uses if and else. It takes this form:

```
if( «logical expression evaluates to true» )
{
    // execute this code
}
else
{
    // execute this code
}
```

We'll look at how to write logical expressions in just a minute; right now, it's important to understand the construction shown earlier. The code in the first block (that is, between the first set of curly braces) will be run if the expression evaluates to true; if the expression evaluates to false, the code in the second block will be run instead.

The else part of the branch is optional, so we could also write this:

```
if( «logical expression evaluates to true» )
{
    // execute this code
}
```

As you might expect, the code between the curly braces will be executed *only* if the expression is true; otherwise, the entire code segment will effectively be ignored.

Logical Expressions

If all this talk about "logic" sounds a bit intimidating, don't be put off. A logical expression is just something that ends up with a value that's either *true* or *false*.

Often, an expression will be some kind of construction that checks a variable to see whether it has a particular value. If it does, the expression will evaluate as true; if it doesn't, the construction will evaluate as false.

Let's look at this type of expression first. Assume we've got an integer variable called someVariable and we need to check whether it has a value of "1" or not:

```
if( someVariable == 1 )
{
    // Hooray! someVariable has a value of 1
}
```

The logical expression in the previous code is the bit between the parentheses: someVariable == 1.

Notice how there are *two* "equals" signs in this expression. These two symbols form the part of the expression known as the *logical operator*. They define how the part on the left should be checked against the part on the right; in this case, you're looking at the *equality operator*, used in a logical expression to signify "is equal to." So, you might *read* the previous code as "if someVariable *is equal to* 1..."

This brings up a *very* common source of confusion. The equality operator is similar to the *assignment* operator. Take a look at this code:

```
int someVariable = 5;

if( someVariable = 10 )
{
    // Oooo! someVariable has a value of 10
    «do something about it»
}
```

At first glance, you might assume that whatever code was written in response to someVariable having a value of 10 would not be called. Let's find out!

We're going to start with a little experimentation using TextApp to learn more about conditional branches, and then later in this chapter we'll make some changes to our new Shopping List application.

Open your TextApp project in Xcode and find the NotifyingClass.m file, then change your displaySomeText: method to this:

```
- (IBAction)displaySomeText:(id)sender
{
    NSString *stringToOutput = @"Everything seems normal.";

    int someValue = 5;

    if( someValue = 10 )
    {
        stringToOutput = @"The value was 10!";
    }

    [textView insertText:stringToOutput];
}
```

By this point, you should be reasonably confident about what is happening at the beginning and end of this method; we set up a variable pointing to a string object with the phrase "Everything seems normal" and display the string at the end of the method in the text view. We also create an integer variable, called someValue, with an initial value of 5.

The conditional if statement then changes the value of the stringToOutput variable, if a condition is met. In this case, the condition is what looks like a test to see whether the value of our someValue variable is 10, which it isn't.

Build & Run the application, and click the Generate Text button. Guess what appears:

```
The value was 10!
```

Huh? We're seeing one of the first potential pitfalls of working with very basic logical expressions. We've used the wrong operator by mistake. The *assignment* operator (=) is very different from the *equality* operator (==). Change your code to use the correct logical operator:

```
- (IBAction)displaySomeText:(id)sender
{
    NSString *stringToOutput = @"Everything seems normal.";

    int someValue = 5;

    if( someValue == 10 )
    {
        stringToOutput = @"The value was 10!";
    }

    [textView insertText:stringToOutput];
}
```

Phew! You should now see the expected output:

```
Everything seems normal.
```

So, to check whether one value is equal to another value, you need to use the *equality* operator with *two* equals signs.

Let's make this a little bit more interesting; we'll check whether a number entered by the user in the text field has a certain value:

```
- (IBAction)displaySomeText:(id)sender
{
    NSString *stringToOutput = @"Everything seems normal.";

    if( [textField intValue] == 42 )
    {
        stringToOutput = @"You entered the magic number!";
    }

    [textView insertText:stringToOutput];
}
```

Build & Run the application again, and enter any number or phrase you like in the text field; assuming you didn't enter "42," you'll see our assurance that everything is normal. Type "42" into the text field and click the button again, and you'll see the message about the magic number, as shown in Figure 9.2, on the next page.

Let's try something else:

```
- (IBAction)displaySomeText:(id)sender
{
    NSString *stringToOutput = @"Everything seems normal.";

    if( [textField stringValue] == @"Danger" )
    {
        stringToOutput = @"Warning! Danger ahead!";
    }

    [textView insertText:stringToOutput];
}
```

Build & Run the app again, and this time enter the word "Danger" in the text field. When you click the button, you would expect to see the warning message, but you don't—for some reason, the logical expression [textField stringValue] == @"Danger" is evaluating to false.

Comparing Objects in Expressions

The reason for this is that the equality operator checks the equality of the *values* on either side of it. The left side of the expression, [textField stringValue], returns a pointer to a string object; the right side of the

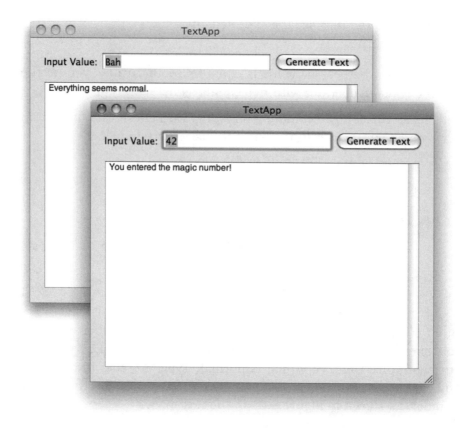

Figure 9.2: ENTERING THE MAGIC NUMBER

expression, @"Danger", also returns a pointer to a string object, as discussed in Section 8.3, *Advanced String Stuff*, on page 151. Remember what a pointer is? It's a variable that holds as its *value* an address in memory. So, the operator checks to see whether the address held on the left side is the same as the address held on the right side.

In this case, they won't be the same, because you're dealing with two separate string objects: one is the string you typed in the box, and the other is the string object created by typing @"Danger". In other words, when you use the equality operator with *objects*, you're asking to check whether the objects are actually the *same* object in memory, not whether the objects both contain some identical internal *value*.

In the earlier example that checked the intValue of the text field, the call to [textField intValue] returned an **int** value—the equality operator was then used to check whether this value was equal to another value, the number 42.

Remember from earlier how the sender variable passed to any IBAction method points to the object that sent the message? Let's use this to make sure that the user clicked the Generate Text button in the interface.

First you'll need an outlet for the button in the **@interface** for the NotifyingClass. So, switch to the NotifyingClass.h file, and add an NSButton outlet:

```
@interface NotifyingClass : NSObject {
    IBOutlet NSTextView *textView;
    IBOutlet NSTextField *textField;
    IBOutlet NSButton *generateTextButton;
}

- (IBAction)displaySomeText:(id)sender;
- (float)generateValue:(float *)originalValue;

@end
```

Open the MainMenu.xib file in Interface Builder, and connect this outlet to the button, as shown in Figure 9.3, on the next page, and then save the file.

Now that the outlet is set up, we can use it to check whether the sender object is equal to the generateTextButton button outlet. Change your displaySomeText: method to this:

```
- (IBAction)displaySomeText:(id)sender
{
    NSString *stringToOutput = nil;

    if( sender == generateTextButton )
    {
        stringToOutput = @"You clicked the button!";
    }
    else
    {
        stringToOutput = @"Illegal Access!";
    }

    [textView insertText:stringToOutput];
}
```

Figure 9.3: Connecting the button outlet in Interface Builder

Notice that we've added an else statement in this example. If the user does click the button to call this method, we'll output a suitable message; in *all other cases*, we'll output a message about illegal access.

Build & Run the application to try this; click the button, and you will see the relevant button message. Remember in Section 6.1, *Even More Spice*, on page 99 how we set up the text field to call the displaySomeText: method as its action, sent when the user presses the ↵ key? Well, try typing something in the text field of the app now and pressing ↵; you'll be warned about illegal access, because the sender in the displaySome-Text: method will be the text field, not the button.

Remembering the Scope of a Variable

We've talked quite a bit in the past about the scope of a variable; the general rule is that a variable is in scope inside the code block in which it is declared. This means that you wouldn't be able to do something like this:

```
- (IBAction)displaySomeText:(id)sender
{
    if( sender == generateTextButton )
    {
        NSString *stringToOutput = @"You clicked the right button!";
    }
    else
    {
        stringToOutput = @"Illegal Access!";
    }

    [textView insertText:stringToOutput];
}
```

Notice how the code declares the string variable in the if block, changes it in the else block, and outputs it at the end of the method? This won't work at all.

For a start, the stringToOutput variable used in the else block isn't even in scope; you can declare as many variables as you like within an if or else block, but they won't be valid *outside* of that block. You might be tempted to try to do something like this:

```
- (IBAction)displaySomeText:(id)sender
{
    if( sender == generateTextButton )
    {
        NSString *stringToOutput = @"You clicked the right button!";
    }
    else
    {
        NSString *stringToOutput = @"Illegal Access!";
    }

    [textView insertText:stringToOutput];
}
```

but it still won't work. Even though you've defined what looks like the same variable in each conditional block, the variable isn't valid or accessible outside those blocks, so the insertText:stringToOutput call doesn't know what you're talking about. As far as code is concerned, the fact that the variables in the two code blocks have the same name is totally irrelevant; they're two separate variables, *in scope* only within the code block in which they are declared.

The correct way to work with a variable that needs to be accessed inside and outside the if/else blocks is the one we used earlier:

```
- (IBAction)displaySomeText:(id)sender
{
    NSString *stringToOutput = nil;

    if( sender == generateTextButton )
    {
        stringToOutput = @"You clicked the right button!";
    }
    else
    {
        stringToOutput = @"Illegal Access!";
    }

    [textView insertText:stringToOutput];
}
```

Declare the variable before the if/else, and it will be accessible both within the conditional blocks and after the relevant block of code has been executed.

Notice that we also changed the declaration of the stringToOutput variable so that it has an initial value of nil. We *could* have just declared it as NSString *stringToOutput;, but remember from Section 5.2, *Combining Declaration and Assignment*, on page 80 that if you don't assign an initial value to a variable, it starts life with an unpredictable value. This happens not to matter for the code we're working with right now, because we assign a value in *both* the if and the else block. Consider what might happen with this code, however:

```
- (IBAction)displaySomeText:(id)sender
{
    NSString *stringToOutput; // No Initial Value

    if( sender == generateTextButton )
    {
        stringToOutput = @"You clicked the button!";
    }

    [textView insertText:stringToOutput]; // Danger!!!
}
```

If the displaySomeText: method is called with a sender *other* than the generateTextButton, the text view will end up being passed an uninitialized

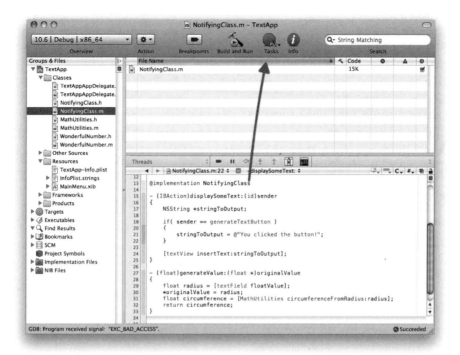

Figure 9.4: STOPPING TEXTAPP FROM XCODE

stringToOutput, which will almost certainly crash the application. This is a bug that might not show up while you're coding unless you specifically test what happens if you have a sender other than what you expect. The moral of the story is always to initialize your variables when you declare them, as a pointer either to an object or to nil.

If you test this, you'll need to *kill* your application manually if it crashes by using the big, red Stop Tasks button in the Xcode project window, shown in Figure 9.4.

The "EXC_BAD_ACCESS" error at the bottom of the Xcode project window means that your code has tried to access something it shouldn't. If you shared a buggy TextApp with someone who isn't running it through Xcode, the operating system would kill the application automatically when it crashed, probably leaving the user rather annoyed and unimpressed.

Further Conditions

So far, we've seen how to use if to check a single logical expression, executing one of only two possible paths. What happens if we need to check for more than one expression?

As an example, we might want to write the displaySomeText: method such that we're happy to accept either the button or the text field as the sender, but not any other object. We need the ability to test for more than one logical possibility.

There are several ways to perform this check; the first we'll look at is to add an if statement alongside the else, like this:

```
if( «first logical expression» )
{
    // do something if the first expression is met
}
else if ( «second logical expression» )
{
    // do something if the second expression is met
}
else
{
    // do something in all other cases
}
```

With this in mind, let's change the displaySomeText: method in TextApp to the following:

```
- (IBAction)displaySomeText:(id)sender
{
    NSString *stringToOutput = nil;

    if( sender == generateTextButton )
    {
        stringToOutput = @"Access Granted!";
    }
    else if( sender == textField )
    {
        stringToOutput = @"Access Granted!";
    }
    else
    {
        stringToOutput = @"Illegal Access!";
    }

    [textView insertText:stringToOutput];
}
```

When you Build & Run the application this time, you'll get the "Access Granted!" message *either* by clicking the button *or* by pressing ↵ from the text field.

Combining Logical Operators

In the previous example, we're effectively doing the *same thing* in two different if code blocks—setting the stringToOutput to @"Access Granted!". In a real-world application, we would probably be doing a great deal more than just setting the value of a string, so it would be much better not to have to write out the same thing twice.

It would be nice if we could somehow *combine* the two conditional checks into a single logical expression for a single code block; in other words, something like this:

```
if( firstExpression is true OR secondExpression is true )
{
    do this
}
```

In the C language, we can accomplish this by building up our logical expressions using multiple operators. So far, we've seen only one example of a logical operator, used for testing equality. Many more are available, including operators to test whether two given logical expressions are *both* true and an operator to test whether one *or* both are true.

Let's use the **OR** operator:

```
«first expression» || «second expression»
```

This operator is specified using two vertical bars; if you haven't typed a vertical bar before, it might take a while to find it on your keyboard. For many keyboard layouts, it's located on the right side of the keyboard near ↵ or on the backward slash \ key.

Let's change our displaySomeText method once again to combine the checks for the sender into one combined expression:

```
- (IBAction)displaySomeText:(id)sender
{
    NSString *stringToOutput = nil;

    if( sender == generateTextButton || sender == textField )
    {
        stringToOutput = @"Access Granted!";
    }
```

```
    else
    {
        stringToOutput = @"Illegal Access!";
    }

    [textView insertText:stringToOutput];
}
```

If you were to read the expression aloud, you might read it as "If sender *is equal to* generateTextButton **or** sender *is equal to* textField, then..."

It's also possible to use parentheses to make it clearer which components make up each individual part of the whole logical expression, like this:

```
if( (sender == generateTextButton) || (sender == textField) )
```

but if having lots of parentheses only seems to confuse the issue, don't worry about them!

More Logical Operators

Let's look at a few more logical operators. One that's very similar to the || operator is &&. As you might be able to guess, it's the *AND* operator, used to test whether two logical expressions both evaluate as true, like this:

```
if( «first expression» && «second expression» )
{
    // do something only if both expressions are true
}
```

We can use the && operator to test whether the user entered a certain number *and* used the ↵ key to call the displaySomeText: method:

```
- (IBAction)displaySomeText:(id)sender
{
    NSString *stringToOutput = nil;

    if( sender == textField && [textField intValue] == 42 )
    {
        stringToOutput = @"Access Granted!";
    }
    else
    {
        stringToOutput = @"Illegal Access!";
    }

    [textView insertText:stringToOutput];
}
```

If you test this code, you'll find that you only get the "Access Granted" message if you type the number 42 and press ↵. If you type anything else or press the button, you'll get the "Illegal Access" message.

Let's complicate things even further by saying that we want access to be given if the text field contains the number 42, **AND** the user either presses ↵ **OR** presses the button. We now *need* to use parentheses, this time to indicate the *scope* of each expression:

```
- (IBAction)displaySomeText:(id)sender
{
    NSString *stringToOutput = nil;

    if( [textField intValue] == 42
            && (sender == textField || sender == generateTextButton) )
    {
        stringToOutput = @"Access Granted!";
    }
    else
    {
        stringToOutput = @"Illegal Access!";
    }

    [textView insertText:stringToOutput];
}
```

If we didn't use the extra parentheses, instead writing the if statement like this:

```
if( [textField intValue] == 42
        && sender == textField || sender == generateTextButton )
```

it's not clear what we mean. If you change your code and test it, you will find that the access granted message is displayed either by pressing the button with any value in the text field or by entering "42" and pressing ↵.

In mathematics, the various mathematical operations like addition and multiplication have different importance. In modern mathematics, writing "2 + 4 * 5" would be interpreted as "2 + 20" rather than "6 * 5" because multiplication should be carried out before addition. The same is true of logical expressions. The **AND** operator will be interpreted before the **OR** operator, meaning that the confusing expression earlier is actually equivalent to this:

```
if( ([textField intValue] == 42 && sender == textField)
        || sender == generateTextButton )
```

Rather than try to remember the order in which operators will be evaluated, it's easier just to use parentheses in the first place. It also makes your code more readable, which is generally a good thing! An expression within parentheses will be evaluated before parts of an expression outside parentheses.

If your head feels like it's about to explode from overexposure to logical expressions and parentheses, you'll be grateful to know that we're moving back to simpler expressions now in order to introduce a couple more operators.

That's So Not True

Sometimes you're going to need to know when something is *not* the case, and luckily, there's an operator for that too. In fact, there are several ways to express **NOT**. One of these is to say that something *is not equal* to something else; the operator looks like this:

```
«left hand value» != «right hand value»
```

Let's say that we wanted to do something in our displaySomeText: method only if the sender was **NOT** the button:

```
- (IBAction)displaySomeText:(id)sender
{
    NSString *stringToOutput = nil;

    if( sender != generateTextButton )
    {
        stringToOutput = @"You didn't press the button!";
    }
    else
    {
        stringToOutput = @"Access Granted!";
    }

    [textView insertText:stringToOutput];
}
```

When you Build & Run the application this time, you'll be informed if you don't use the button to call the method (that is, you press the ↵ key from the text field).

I said that there were several ways to express **NOT**; generally they involve the exclamation point (!), but before I go into any more detail, you need to know a little more about truth and falsehood when programming.

9.2 All About the Truth

In a couple of places earlier in the book, you've encountered what's known as a *Boolean* value, which can have a value of either YES or NO. A Boolean value of YES is synonymous with *true*, and a value of NO is synonymous with *false*.

When working in Objective-C, you use a **BOOL** variable to hold either YES or NO:

```
BOOL enabled = [sender enabled];
```

You might use code like this in the displaySomeText: method to check whether whatever object sent you the message is currently *enabled*. The **BOOL** variable would then have a value of YES or NO to indicate the state of the sender.

Because a **BOOL** variable is effectively either true or false, you can use it in conditional statements, like this:

```
BOOL enabled = [sender enabled];

if( enabled )
{
    // It was enabled!
}
```

There's no apparent operator being used here: all that happens is the value of the variable is checked to see whether it's true or false. If it's true, the code will be executed; otherwise, it won't.

Using if(enabled) in the previous context is the same as saying if(enabled == YES).

If you want to check whether a **BOOL** value is NO, you could obviously use the code if(enabled == NO), or even if(enabled != YES), but there is another way:

```
BOOL enabled = [sender enabled];

if( !enabled )
{
    // It wasn't enabled
}
```

Placing ! on the front of a variable or expression has the effect of *negating* that variable. If the variable was false, ! will make it evaluate as true, and vice versa.

So, the following logical expressions are all equivalent:

```
(enabled == YES)
```

```
(enabled != NO)
```

```
(!enabled == NO)
```

```
!(enabled == NO)
```

Notice the difference between the third and fourth expressions shown in the previous code. Putting the ! on the front of a variable negates the evaluation of that *variable*; putting the ! on the front of a bracketed logical expression negates the result of the *whole expression* inside the brackets.

Every Value Is a Winner

There's another useful feature in the C language, in that any value other than zero will evaluate as true.

This includes pointers to objects. If you declare a pointer to an object, like this:

```
NSObject *someObject = [[NSObject alloc] init];
```

you can "evaluate" someObject, like this:

```
if( someObject )
{
    // the someObject pointer is pointing to an address in memory
}
```

You can check to see whether an object pointer is nil in several ways:

```
if( someObject == nil )
{
    // the someObject pointer hasn't yet been set to an address
}
```

```
if( !someObject )
{
    // the someObject pointer hasn't yet been set to an address
}
```

These two conditional statements are equivalent; nil, like zero, will evaluate as *false*, so !nil will evaluate as *true*. You'll see more examples of this later in the book when we look at methods dedicated to accessing instance variables in an object, called *accessor methods*.

Comparing Objects

Earlier in this chapter we tried to compare two strings using this code:

```
- (IBAction)displaySomeText:(id)sender
{
    NSString *stringToOutput = @"Everything seems normal.";

    if( [textField stringValue] == @"Danger" )
    {
        stringToOutput = @"Warning! Danger ahead!";
    }

    [textView insertText:stringToOutput];
}
```

Because the **==** operator compares the values on either side of it, this code checks to see whether the address of an object on the left is the same as the address of the object on the right; in other words, it checks whether the two objects on either side are actually the same object. Clearly, there are going to be occasions when we do want to check whether two distinct string *objects* contain the same string of *characters*. So, how do we do that?

Objects can provide methods to check whether their contents are equal to some other object's contents, usually taking the form isEqualTo…:. NSString, for example, provides us with a method called isEqualToString:. This method will return a **BOOL** value indicating whether two string objects are equivalent.

Change your displaySomeText: method to look like this:

```
- (IBAction)displaySomeText:(id)sender
{
    NSString *stringToOutput = @"Everything seems normal.";

    NSString *textFieldString = [textField stringValue];

    if( [textFieldString isEqualToString:@"Danger"] )
    {
        stringToOutput = @"Warning! Danger ahead!";
    }

    [textView insertText:stringToOutput];
}
```

In this code, we first get a pointer to the string object held in the text field and then ask that object whether it is equal to the string @"Danger". If you Build & Run the application, you'll find that it behaves as expected—the output will now indicate a warning if you type "Danger" into the text field.

9.3 Stylistic Conventions

It's worth taking a moment now to point out a few stylistic conventions and optional shorthands.

You may recall from seeing code like [[NSObject alloc] init] that we can combine calls to object methods using *nested* square brackets. The inner bracket methods are called before the outer methods, so in the case of object allocations, alloc is called on NSObject, and init is called on whatever object is returned by the alloc call.

With this in mind, we can rewrite our displaySomeText: method, avoiding using the textFieldString variable, like this:

```
- (IBAction)displaySomeText:(id)sender
{
    NSString *stringToOutput = @"Everything seems normal.";

    if( [[textField stringValue] isEqualToString:@"Danger"] )
    {
        stringToOutput = @"Warning! Danger ahead!";
    }

    [textView insertText:stringToOutput];
}
```

There are also some points worth noting about if statements. First, the general rule about placement of curly braces applies, so you might prefer to put the opening curly brace on the same line as the if statement itself:

```
- (IBAction)displaySomeText:(id)sender
{
    NSString *stringToOutput = @"Everything seems normal.";

    if( [[textField stringValue] isEqualToString:@"Danger"] ) {
        stringToOutput = @"Warning! Danger ahead!";
    }

    [textView insertText:stringToOutput];
}
```

Second, if you have only a single statement inside a conditional block, you don't need the curly braces at all.

```objc
- (IBAction)displaySomeText:(id)sender
{
    NSString *stringToOutput = @"Everything seems normal.";

    if( [[textField stringValue] isEqualToString:@"Danger"] )
        stringToOutput = @"Warning! Danger ahead!";

    [textView insertText:stringToOutput];
}
```

Whatever code statement appears immediately after the if statement will be executed only if the evaluation is true.

The same applies to any other conditional blocks:

```objc
- (IBAction)displaySomeText:(id)sender
{
    NSString *stringToOutput = nil;

    if( [[textField stringValue] isEqualToString:@"Danger"] )
        stringToOutput = @"Warning! Danger ahead!";
    else
        stringToOutput = @"Everything seems normal.";

    [textView insertText:stringToOutput];
}
```

Generally, you'll see the relevant statement on the line after its condition, as shown earlier, indented using spaces or tabs. If you have a particularly short statement, however, you can even place it all on the same line, like this:

```objc
- (IBAction)displaySomeText:(id)sender
{
    NSString *stringToOutput = @"Everything seems normal.";

    if( [[textField stringValue] isEqualToString:@"Stop"] ) return;

    [textView insertText:stringToOutput];
}
```

In this particular example, we use the **return** keyword to end the method immediately at that point, *return*ing to whatever was happening when the method was called. If you try this code in your application, you'll see the "Everything seems normal" message whenever the method is called, unless you type the word "Stop" in the text field. If the string evaluates as equal to "Stop," the method will end, and nothing will be output at all.

Fastest First

When writing code that uses multiple **if** conditional statements or a compound expression made up of multiple logical tests, always put either the fastest or most *eliminatory* test first.

If we are testing whether two statements both evaluate as true using an **&&** operator, the statement will fail instantly if the first statement evaluates as false and won't bother testing the second statement at all.

As an example, if we were to write an application that kept track of parents and school children and wanted to write some sort of expression to check whether a particular person in the records was a man with three or more children, we might use something like this:

```
if( [person hasMoreThan3Children] && [person isMale] )
{
    // Found someone!
}
```

From a performance perspective, if we ran this test on every single person in the database, we would waste a lot of time by running the hasMoreThan3Children test before the isMale test. A check to count how many children someone has is going to require looking up all the records for a person's children and counting how many there are. The check to see whether someone is male is a simple test of what is probably a **BOOL** value. The isMale evaluation will execute far more quickly than the hasMoreThan3Children test, so it would be much better to perform them in this order:

```
if( [person isMale] && [person hasMoreThan3Children] )
{
    // Found someone!
}
```

By writing the tests this way around, we'll probably cut the time taken to run the query by half since it's likely that around 50 percent of the people in the database won't pass the isMale test. For anybody who is female, the [person hasMoreThan3Children] test will never be run.

The same principle applies to the || operator too; consider a logical statement that requires at least one of two evaluations to be true, such as:

```
- (IBAction)displaySomeText:(id)sender
{
    NSString *stringToOutput = @"Everything seems normal.";

    if( sender == generateTextButton
                || [[textField stringValue] isEqualToString:@"Danger"] )
    {
```

```
            stringToOutput = @"There may be trouble ahead!";
        }

        [textView insertText:stringToOutput];
}
```

The first test to see whether the sender is the generateTextButton is a simple test to check whether one value is equal to another value (the address in memory of the objects). The second test, checking the equality of two character strings, is more complicated and will take more computer processor cycles to complete. By putting the faster test first, the slower test will be evaluated only if the faster test fails, thereby maximizing performance where possible.

9.4 Switching Around

Earlier in this chapter, we saw how it was possible to do multiple checks for conditional statements, using code like this:

```
if( sender == generateTextButton )
{
    // first case
}
else if( sender == textField )
{
    // second case
}
else
{
    // all other cases
}
```

If there were other possible sender values to check, we'd need multiple else if (...) statements that all perform the same test but try different values. The C language offers an alternative to using else if: the *switch* statement. It looks like this:

```
switch( «variableToTest» )
{
    case «firstPossibleValue»:
        // first case
        break;

    case «secondPossibleValue»:
        // second case
        break;

    default:
        // all other cases
        break;
}
```

This construction executes a particular code *case*, chosen based on a given value of a variable. As an example, let's say we've asked the user for an integer value representing the current day of the week, *zero-based*, of course, between 0 and 6, and we want to translate this number into a string representing the name of the day. Change the displaySomeText: method to the following, filling in the rest of the day numbers in the same style:

```
- (IBAction)displaySomeText:(id)sender
{
    int dayNumber = [textField intValue];
    NSString *stringToOutput = nil;

    switch (dayNumber)
    {
        case 0:
            stringToOutput = @"Sunday";
            break;
        case 1:
            stringToOutput = @"Monday";
            break;
        case 2:
            stringToOutput = @"Tuesday";
            break;
        case 3:
            stringToOutput = @"Wednesday";
            break;

        «Other Day Checks Go Here»

        default:
            stringToOutput = @"Unknown Day";
            break;
    }

    [textView insertText:stringToOutput];
}
```

When you Build & Run the application and enter a number between 0 and 6, you'll see the relevant name of that day output in the text view. Otherwise, you'll get the "Unknown Day" message.

Falling Down

When we use **switch-case** constructions like this, the **break** at the end of each **case** is extremely important. Try removing the **break** from the first case 0: section, and run the application again. If you type a zero into the text field, you'll see the apparently incorrect output of "Monday."

This is a curious but extremely useful feature—if we miss the **break** statement, the code continues through the next case, until it reaches a **break**. So, in the previous case, the stringToOutput variable is set to @"Sunday" by the case 0: code, but then falls through and gets set to @"Monday" by the case 1: code.

Although it can often be a cause of unintended bugs, this behavior is useful when we want to have a number of cases all execute the same code, like this:

```objc
- (IBAction)displaySomeText:(id)sender
{
    int dayNumber = [textField intValue];
    NSString *stringToOutput = nil;

    switch (dayNumber)
    {
        case 0:
        case 1:
        case 2:
        case 3:
            stringToOutput = @"You entered a valid day number";
            break;

        default:
            stringToOutput = @"Unknown Day";
            break;
    }

    [textView insertText:stringToOutput];
}
```

In this code, if the dayNumber variable has a value between 0 and 3, the output indicates a valid day number; otherwise, it outputs "Unknown Day." We can even do super-exciting things like this:

```objc
switch (dayNumber)
{
    case 0:
        NSLog(@"You chose the secret number!");
    case 1:
    case 2:
    case 3:
        stringToOutput = @"That is a valid day number";
        break;

    default:
        stringToOutput = @"Unknown Day";
        break;
}
```

With this code, the same output appears in the text view for any value between 0 and 3. For the special case value of 0, the secret message will *also* be output to the console log but *only* for that special case.

Just the Values

The **switch-case** construction can *only* be used to test the *value* of an integer. Sadly, we can't use it to test for multiple sender objects, and we can't use it to test for different string contents of an NSString object.

9.5 Writing Init Methods

Now that we've seen a variety of ways to write conditional code, or code that gets executed depending on certain conditions being met, it's time to revisit our understanding of init methods for objects.

In the previous chapter, in Section 8.4, *The MyDocument Class*, on page 155, we looked briefly at the init method generated for us by the Xcode Document-based Application template. We added code to this method to set up our initial array in the Shopping List application, ending up with the following method:

```
- (id)init
{
    self = [super init];
    if (self) {
        shoppingListArray = [[NSMutableArray alloc]
                initWithObjects:@"Milk", @"Eggs",
                                @"Butter", nil];
    }
    return self;
}
```

It should be clear by now what's happening in this method: first self is set to the value returned by [super init]; then we check to see whether self is a valid object. If it is a valid object, we set up the shoppingListArray object by creating a new mutable array.

If self has failed to be allocated and initialized properly, it will be nil, and whatever is located between the curly braces won't be executed. Instead, the method will just return the value of self (that is, nil) straight back from the method.

Why bother to perform this check? Well, if the object has failed to initialize properly, there won't be any instance variables to set. If we still choose to allocate and initialize a mutable array at this point, we would *leak* that array, since there would be no valid reference to it after it was created.

You will see init methods written in a variety of ways. The other interesting case that you will encounter is this one:

```
- (id)init
{
    if (self = [super init]) {
        shoppingListArray = [[NSMutableArray alloc]
                initWithObjects:@"Milk", @"Eggs",
                                @"Butter", nil];
    }
    return self;
}
```

Assuming you've been following along, alarm bells should be ringing when you see the conditional expression if(self = [super init]). Surely we shouldn't be using an assignment operator in a logical expression?

In fact, using an assignment operator in this case is useful. Think about what is actually happening.

The logical expression is self = [super init]. If this evaluates to true, the conditional block will be executed. What is *true*? Well, any value other than nil. If the [super init] portion returns nil, then self will be set to nil, and the whole expression will evaluate as false.

If [super init] returns a non-nil value (the address of the object that has been initialized), then self will be set to that non-nil value, and the whole expression will evaluate as true.

There has been a lot of heated discussion about how best to write an init method. If you are particularly interested in learning all the grisly details, do a search on the Internet for an article by Mike Ash called "The How and Why of Cocoa Initializers." If you just want to make sure that you're doing the Right Thing, then it's best to follow the advice given by Apple. At the time of writing, this is to use the format we saw earlier:

```
- (id)init
{
    self = [super init];
    if (self) {

        «object setup goes here»

    }
    return self;
}
```

Following Apple's recommendations is usually the best way to proceed, since it ensures that whatever you're doing will continue to work with whatever top-secret things Apple has planned for the future.

9.6 Adding Conditional Statements to the Shopping List Application

To see conditional statements working in a real-world example, let's add some extra capabilities to our Shopping List application. At the end of the previous chapter, I mentioned that it would be nice to be able to remove objects from a shopping list. You might have had a go at implementing a mechanism for this; either way, let's now take a look at one way to do it, asking the user to confirm the deletion before we actually remove the item.

If the TextApp project is still open in Xcode, close it. Also, quit Interface Builder to close any open interface files.

Adding a Remove Button

Open the Shopping List Xcode project from the previous chapter, and double-click the MyDocument.xib file to open it in Interface Builder. We'll start by adding a new button to the interface.

In Interface Builder's Library palette, find the NSButton object called Square Button. Drag one of these out onto the document Window interface, and make it about half the default size. If you hold down the ⇧ key while dragging on the object handles, you'll find that the size is constrained to a perfect square.

With the button still selected, find the Image attribute in its Attributes inspector. Use the drop-down box for this attribute to select the NSRemoveTemplate image. You should end up with something looking like Figure 9.5, on the facing page.

We now need to write the method to set as the action for our new button.

Adding the Remove Item Method

Switch back into Xcode, and open the MyDocument.h header file.

Figure 9.5: THE NEW REMOVE BUTTON IN THE SHOPPING LIST INTERFACE

Add a new **IBAction** method signature for a method called removeItem-
FromShoppingList:, like this:

```
@interface MyDocument : NSDocument
{
    IBOutlet NSTableView *shoppingListTableView;
    IBOutlet NSTextField *newItemNameTextField;

    NSMutableArray *shoppingListArray;
}

- (IBAction)addNewItemToShoppingList:(id)sender;
- (IBAction)removeItemFromShoppingList:(id)sender;

@end
```

Copy the method signature to the clipboard, and change to the MyDoc-ument.m implementation file.

Paste the new method between the addNewItemToShoppingList: action method and the init method, and add curly braces:

```
- (IBAction)removeItemFromShoppingList:(id)sender
{

}
```

Before we work out how to delete an item from the shopping list array, let's first use this method to display an *alert* to the user, asking him whether he is sure he wants to delete the item.

Displaying an Alert

There are several ways to display alerts and dialog boxes in Cocoa. One of the simplest is to use an object called—yes!—NSAlert.

To use an NSAlert, we create an alert instance, add some button names to the alert object (along with a message and some informative text), set the alert style, and then *run* the alert. Add the following code to the removeItemFromShoppingList: method:

```
- (IBAction)removeItemFromShoppingList:(id)sender
{
    NSAlert *alert = [[NSAlert alloc] init];
    [alert addButtonWithTitle:@"Delete"];
    [alert addButtonWithTitle:@"Cancel"];
    [alert setMessageText:@"Delete the shopping list item?"];
    [alert setInformativeText:@"Deleted items cannot be restored."];
    [alert setAlertStyle:NSWarningAlertStyle];

    [alert runModal];

    [alert release];
}
```

Before we do anything else, be sure to connect the new Remove button in Interface Builder to target this action method. By now you should feel pretty confident in doing this: right-click the File's Owner object in the Interface Builder project window (this will be the MyDocument object), and find the removeItemFromShoppingList: method; drag from the little circle next to it, and release when you reach the button.[1]

---

1. If you've already done this, instinctively, after adding the method in the previous section, give yourself a pat on the back!

Figure 9.6: THE "DELETE THE SHOPPING LIST ITEM?" ALERT

Once the button is connected, Build & Run the application from Xcode, and test the new Delete button. You should find that an alert is displayed on-screen, as shown in Figure 9.6.

The Delete button is blue, indicating that it is the *default* button (the first button that you supply to an alert is taken to be the default button). If you press the ↵ key on your keyboard, this default button will be selected; pressing ⌷Esc⌷ will select the cancel button. At the moment, neither button will have any effect other than to dismiss the alert from the screen.

Finding the Item to Delete

Before we work out how to remove the item, let's first check that the user has actually selected an item in the shopping list. We can get the *index* of the selected *row* in the shoppingListTableView by asking it for its selectedRow.

If the selectedRow index is -1, no row is selected. In this case, we don't want to display the alert; we just want to return immediately from the removeItemFromShoppingList: method without doing anything.

With this in mind, add the following lines:

```
- (IBAction)removeItemFromShoppingList:(id)sender
{
    int selectedItemIndex = [shoppingListTableView selectedRow];

    if( selectedItemIndex == -1 ) return;

    NSAlert *alert = [[NSAlert alloc] init];
    [alert addButtonWithTitle:@"Delete"];
    «method continues»
```

Notice that we're using a conditional statement consolidated into one line; if no item is selected, we return—without creating or displaying the alert. Build & Run the application again, and you will find the alert is displayed only if an item is selected in the shopping list.

Finding Which Alert Button Was Pressed

Assuming users have selected an item in the shopping list and pressed the Remove button, we need to find out whether they then clicked the Delete or the Cancel button in the alert.

We do this by checking the value returned by the runModal method; this will be an integer value indicating the number of the button that was pressed. Apple helpfully defines some *constants* for us to use here; the relevant values are NSAlertFirstButtonReturn or NSAlertSecondButtonReturn. Since we only care about doing something if the Delete button is pressed, we just need to check for the NSAlertFirstButtonReturn. Add the following code to our removeItemFromShoppingList: method:

```
- (IBAction)removeItemFromShoppingList:(id)sender
{
    int selectedItemIndex = [shoppingListTableView selectedRow];

    if( selectedItemIndex == -1 ) return;

    NSAlert *alert = [[NSAlert alloc] init];
    [alert addButtonWithTitle:@"Delete"];
    [alert addButtonWithTitle:@"Cancel"];
    [alert setMessageText:@"Delete the shopping list item?"];
    [alert setInformativeText:@"Deleted items cannot be restored."];
    [alert setAlertStyle:NSWarningAlertStyle];

    int returnValue = [alert runModal];
    if( returnValue == NSAlertFirstButtonReturn )
    {
        // we need to delete the item
    }

    [alert release];
}
```

Deleting the Relevant Shopping List Item

At this point, we're ready to write the code that removes the selected item from the array. Once the item has been removed from the array, we'll need to reload the table view so that the deleted item disappears.

We can use the removeObjectAtIndex: method on our shoppingListArray, and because both the table view and the array use zero-based indexing for their objects and rows, we can just pass the selectedItemIndex value straight to the removeObjectAtIndex: method. Replace the item deletion comment with this:

«beginning of method»

```
int returnValue = [alert runModal];
if( returnValue == NSAlertFirstButtonReturn )
{
    [shoppingListArray removeObjectAtIndex:selectedItemIndex];
    [shoppingListTableView reloadData];
}
```

«end of method»

Build & Run the application to make sure you can delete items from the list. Items should be removed only if you choose the Delete button; if they also get deleted when you click Cancel, make sure that you have used the == equality operator and not the = assignment operator in the conditional expression!

It's worth mentioning that we could also use a **switch-case** construction here, since the value of the returnValue variable is an integer:

«beginning of method»

```
int returnValue = [alert runModal];
switch( returnValue )
{
    case NSAlertFirstButtonReturn:
        [shoppingListArray removeObjectAtIndex:selectedItemIndex];
        [shoppingListTableView reloadData];
        break;

    case NSAlertSecondButtonReturn:
        // do something in response to the Cancel button being pressed
        break;

    default:
        // this won't happen unless you add a third button to the alert
        break;
}
```

«end of method»

Additional Conditionals

Let's make one last addition to the Shopping List application for this chapter. We'll assume that you've been so excited by your achievements in creating such an amazing application, you decide to show it to your friends. One of these friends isn't as confident using a Mac as you are and is terribly disconcerted to find that when he types a value into the New Item text field, the value disappears from that text field when he clicks the Add button. He would much prefer it if the value remained after clicking the button, ready to be deleted before typing something else. The rest of your friends all zip along adding new items by typing into the Add box but are dismayed to find that they can't add items just by pressing the ↵ key. They don't want to have to fiddle around with a mouse to press a button.

There are two issues here; let's deal with the easy one first. Switch to Interface Builder, and set the action for the New Item text field to be the addNewItemToShoppingList: method. You'll need to right-click (or ^-click) the text field and connect the selector outlet to the File's Owner object's addNewItemToShoppingList: action method. Use the Identity inspector for the text field to set its Action as "Sent on Enter Only."

This solves the problem of adding new items by pressing the ↵ key. Your Mac-experienced friends are delighted. The fact that the New Item text field is emptied each time means they can type an item, add it by pressing ↵, and start typing a new one straightaway.

How might you go about appeasing your slower and less experienced friend? Well, you can check to see which object *sent* the addNewItem-ToShoppingList: message and respond accordingly. You only want to empty the text field if the sender was the newItemNameTextField. So, change the addNewItemToShoppingList: method to this:

```
- (IBAction)addNewItemToShoppingList:(id)sender
{
    [shoppingListArray addObject:[newItemNameTextField stringValue]];

    if( sender == newItemNameTextField )
        [newItemNameTextField setStringValue:@""];

    [shoppingListTableView reloadData];
}
```

With one simple **if** statement, the text field will be emptied only if the user pressed the ↵ key. Now all your friends are happy, which means you are satisfied that you've achieved a thorough understanding of conditional statements.

9.7 Chapter Summary

You have covered quite a lot in this chapter. Conditional statements appear throughout code in real-world applications; understanding how to work with **if** and **else** is extremely important when you start writing your own code.

I hope you've recovered from looking at so many logical expressions and operators, such as **==**, **&&**, and **||**. You'll see these, and the **!** operator appearing throughout the rest of the book.

We'll be adding more functionality to the Shopping List application in the next chapter when we learn all about the joys of looping and iteration, see how to get the same code to run multiple times, and access each value in an array in turn to check its contents.

Chapter 10

Looping and Enumerating

In the previous chapter, you saw how to execute different blocks of code depending on certain conditions being met. Sometimes, though, you need to be able to execute the *same* block of code, multiple times.

Say you wanted to display the names of the months of the year: you could write code that output each month name in turn using twelve separate segments of code, each effectively doing the same thing, just with a different value. Then think what happens if you decide to change the way we display each month; you'd have to go through and change twelve different sections. The margin for error, let alone the level of annoyance, would be high!

It would make much more sense if you could write only a single code segment and get that segment to run multiple times. You'd need a way of providing each code segment with the value necessary to display each month, and you'd need to know how many values there were to display in order to run the code the right number of times.

10.1 Introducing Array Enumeration

Back in Chapter 8, *Collecting Information*, on page 139, we looked at storing collections of objects using arrays. We wrote code for TextApp to generate a simple array containing three shopping list items, with an additional item typed by the user into the text field. We then output a string built from the items in the array, using the NSArray method componentsJoinedByString:.

That code looked like this:

```
- (IBAction)displaySomeText:(id)sender
{
    NSString *firstObject = @"Milk";
    NSString *secondObject = @"Eggs";
    NSString *thirdObject = @"Butter";

    NSArray *shoppingListArray = [NSArray
                                  arrayWithObjects:firstObject, secondObject,
                                  thirdObject, nil];

    NSString *typedValue = [textField stringValue];

    shoppingListArray = [shoppingListArray arrayByAddingObject:typedValue];

    NSString *stringToOutput = @"The shopping list is: ";

    stringToOutput = [stringToOutput
       stringByAppendingString:[shoppingListArray componentsJoinedByString:@", "]];

    [textView insertText:stringToOutput];
}
```

As an alternative to using the componentsJoinedByString: method on NSArray, we could instead walk through each item in the array, or *enumerate over* the items, outputting them individually. In Objective-C, as of version 2.0[1] of the language, we have access to something called *fast enumeration*, which gives us easy access to exactly what we need.

Let's use TextApp, as usual, to learn how to use fast enumeration. We'll change the displaySomeText: method to set up an array containing the names of the months of the year so that we have a reasonable number of items to enumerate. We'll continue to use the componentsJoined-ByString: method for now, just so we can make sure we set up the array correctly.

Open the TextApp project in Xcode, and find the usual NotifyingClass.m file. Change the displaySomeText: method to this:

```
- (IBAction)displaySomeText:(id)sender
{
    NSArray *monthsArray = [NSArray arrayWithObjects:@"January", @"February",
                            @"March", @"April", @"May", @"June",
                            @"July", @"August", @"September",
                            @"October", @"November", @"December", nil];
```

---

1. Objective-C 2.0 is the language available to us from any release of Mac OS X Leopard onward.

```
    NSString *stringToOutput = [monthsArray componentsJoinedByString:@", "];

    [textView insertText:stringToOutput];
}
```

This simple code creates a new array containing twelve string objects, one for each month of the year, and then outputs a new string built from the array's objects, joining each component with a comma and space. Make sure that you remember what you learned in Section 8.1, *Passing Multiple Values to a Method*, on page 141, and include nil on the end of the list of items in the array, or your code will crash! And, since you're using the @"string" string object shorthand, also check that you've got the @ on the beginning of each string, or, again, your code will crash.

Build & Run the application to check that the simple list of months is output when you click the button.

Fast Enumeration Syntax

We're now ready to change our code to walk through and output each item in the array *separately*, instead of using the componentsJoined-ByString: method. In pseudocode, what we want to achieve is this:

```
run this code block for each string object in the months array:
{
    output the string object to the text view
}
```

The Objective-C syntax is this:

```
for( «ObjectType» *«variableName» in «collection» )
{

}
```

In other words, you supply an object type and variable name for the items in the collection. The code block will then be executed for every item in the collection, with the variable set to the relevant item for each *loop* through that code block.

It's probably easier to understand this by seeing it used in code; so, change the displaySomeText: method to the following:

```
- (IBAction)displaySomeText:(id)sender
{
    NSArray *monthsArray = [NSArray arrayWithObjects:@"January", @"February",
                                @"March", @"April", @"May", @"June",
                                @"July", @"August", @"September",
                                @"October", @"November", @"December", nil];
```

```
for( NSString *eachMonth in monthsArray )
{
    [textView insertText:eachMonth];
}
}
```

Build & Run the application to see what happens. When you click the button, the output will be the following:

```
JanuaryFebruaryMarchAprilMayJuneJulyAugustSeptemberOctoberNovemberDecember
```

That single [textView insertText:eachMonth]; line is executed for every month in the array. On each pass through the loop, the eachMonth variable is set to the relevant month, and we output it. After all twelve iterations, we've output all twelve of the strings in the array. Since the process happens extremely quickly, it looks like we output all the strings as one very long word.

It would be much nicer to output the months in a slightly more readable way, so change the method to this:

```
- (IBAction)displaySomeText:(id)sender
{
    NSArray *monthsArray = [NSArray arrayWithObjects:@"January", @"February",
                            @"March", @"April", @"May", @"June",
                            @"July", @"August", @"September",
                            @"October", @"November", @"December", nil];

    for( NSString *eachMonth in monthsArray )
    {
        [textView insertText:[NSString
                stringWithFormat:@"%@ is a nice month\n", eachMonth]];
    }
}
```

This time you should see the output shown in Figure 10.1, on the facing page.

10.2 Counting

Sometimes you need to keep track of how many times you've been through the loop. Let's say we want to generate output that says something like "Month 1 is January, Month 2 is February," and so on. We need to maintain a counter variable that is changed in each pass through the loop.

The usual *variable scope* rules also apply to loops; if a variable is declared within the inner loop code block, it's in scope only within that code block, and it's valid only during each iteration through the loop.

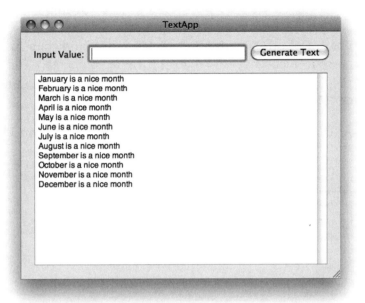

Figure 10.1: OUTPUTTING EACH MONTH OF THE YEAR

To maintain a counter variable, we need to declare it outside the loop, with an initial value before the loop starts, and then increment the value after each pass through the loop. Change your code to look like this:

```
- (IBAction)displaySomeText:(id)sender
{
    NSArray *monthsArray = [NSArray arrayWithObjects:@"January", @"February",
                            @"March", @"April", @"May", @"June",
                            @"July", @"August", @"September",
                            @"October", @"November", @"December", nil];

    int counter = 1;

    for( NSString *eachMonth in monthsArray )
    {
        [textView insertText:[NSString
                stringWithFormat:@"Month %i is %@\n", counter, eachMonth]];

        counter = counter + 1;
    }
}
```

This code sets up a new counter variable with an initial value of 1. Each time through the loop, we output a string using this number (the loop pass will output "Month 1 is January"), and then in the last line of the code block, we add 1 to the value of counter. The second time through the loop will start with this incremented counter, i.e., outputting "Month 2 is February" and so on.

When you Build & Run, you'll see the following when you click the button:

```
Month 1 is January
Month 2 is February
Month 3 is March
Month 4 is April
Month 5 is May
Month 6 is June
Month 7 is July
Month 8 is August
Month 9 is September
Month 10 is October
Month 11 is November
Month 12 is December
```

Shorthand Counting

It's so common to need to increment a value by 1 that the C language has a simple shorthand, using another operator: **++**.

Putting **++** after a variable is a shorthand way of saying "increment by 1," so these two lines of code both have the same effect:

```
variable = variable + 1;

// is the same as

variable++;
```

Change the displaySomeText: method so that it uses this shorthand:

```
for( NSString *eachMonth in monthsArray )
{
    [textView insertText:[NSString
            stringWithFormat:@"Month %i is %@\n", counter, eachMonth]];

    counter++;
}
```

Build & Run the application to check that the output is still the same.

Decrementing a Value

If we have access to an operator **++**, it makes sense that there might be an operator **--** too. Let's test that theory by changing the increment code counter++ to counter--:

```
for( NSString *eachMonth in monthsArray )
{
    [textView insertText:[NSString
            stringWithFormat:@"Month %i is %@\n", counter, eachMonth]];

    counter--;
}
```

Take a guess at what you expect to see in the output, and then Build & Run to make sure.

When you click the button, you'll see the following:

```
Month 1 is January
Month 0 is February
Month -1 is March
Month -2 is April
Month -3 is May
«... etc ...»
```

The **–** operator is used to decrement a value, meaning that these two code lines both achieve the same result:

```
variable = variable - 1;
   // is the same as
variable--;
```

10.3 Traditional for Loops

Earlier in the chapter, I said that fast enumeration was only introduced with Objective-C 2.0. This begs the question, what was available before Objective-C 2.0?

In the standard C language, there are several looping techniques, all of which are also available in Objective-C. Probably the most common of these is the standard **for** loop, which forms the basis for the fast enumeration syntax. It looks like this:

```
for( «pre-loop statement»; «condition»; «statement for after each loop pass»)
{

}
```

This syntax is a little more complicated than that of fast enumeration and might take a while to get your head around. There are effectively three mini-statements within the main **for** statement:

- The pre-loop statement is a statement that is executed before the loop starts looping. It's usually an initial assignment to a counter variable.

- The condition is a condition that will be checked each time through a loop. As long as the condition is met, the loop will continue. If the condition is not met, the loop will stop.

- The statement for after each loop pass will be executed after the code within the loop, each time through the loop. It's usually an increment operation on a counter variable.

Let's look at a few examples. We'll start by writing a **for** loop that will run exactly five times.

To do this, we're going to need a counter variable that is incremented on each pass through the loop, and we're going to need a condition to check whether that counter has reached a value of 5.

Even More Conditionals

In the previous chapter, you were introduced to several conditional operators, used to test for equality and inequality between two variables. There are also *comparative* conditional operators, used to check how one variable *compares* to another.

To decide how many times the loop should run, you need to be able to write a condition that checks whether one value is less than another. There's one potential comparator available to us that looks like this:

«*firstValue*» < «*secondValue*»

This expression will be true only if firstValue is *less than* secondValue. It's even helpful that the operator *looks* like its meaning. The value next to the small, pointy part represents the "lesser" side, while the value next to the wide open part represents the "greater" side.

Predictably, there's also a *greater than* comparison operator, which looks like this:

«*firstValue*» > «*secondValue*»

For this operator, the expression is true only if "the value on the left is *greater than* the value on the right."

Working with for Loops

Now that you know about comparison conditions, we can start to write our simple loop to execute a statement five times.

Change the displaySomeText: method to this:

```
- (IBAction)displaySomeText:(id)sender
{
    // monthsArray is unused at the moment...
    NSArray *monthsArray = [NSArray arrayWithObjects:@"January", @"February",
                            @"March", @"April", @"May", @"June",
                            @"July", @"August", @"September",
                            @"October", @"November", @"December", nil];

    int counter;
    for( counter = 1; counter < 5; counter++ )
    {
        [textView insertText:@"This should appear 5 times\n"];
    }
}
```

Here we get to see a real example of the three parts in the **for** statement. We start by setting the initial value of our counter variable to 1. This will happen before the loop starts running.

Each time through the loop, the counter < 5 condition will be checked to see whether the counter variable still has a value less than 5. Assuming it does, the code block will be run, after which the counter variable will be incremented, as specified by that third counter++ part.

Build & Run the application to check the output. You'll see a warning in Xcode that the monthsArray variable is unused (Xcode is worried that we've declared an array but never use it again), but ignore this because we'll reintroduce code to use the array a little later. Once TextApp is running, click the button, and you'll see this:

```
This should appear 5 times
This should appear 5 times
This should appear 5 times
This should appear 5 times
```

Your eyes are not deceiving you: the statement appears only four times, not five. What's going on?

Remember how I said earlier that the < operator is used to check that one value is less than another? Well, let's analyze exactly what's going on during our **for** loop:

1. Start by setting counter to 1.

2. Check whether counter (value of 1) is less than 5; it is, so output the string, and then increment counter.

3. Check whether counter (value of 2) is less than 5; it is, so output the string, and then increment counter.

4. Check whether counter (value of 3) is less than 5; it is, so output the string, and then increment counter.

5. Check whether counter (value of 4) is less than 5; it is, so output the string, and then increment counter.

6. Check whethercounter (value of 5) is less than 5; it's not, so stop the loop.

The *less than* operator means exactly what it says. 5 isn't less than 5, it's *equal to* 5, so the condition is false, and the loop stops.

Several options are available to us to correct our code:

- We could use a zero-based counter, using the initial statement to set counter = 0. The text would be output five times, for counter values 0, 1, 2, 3, 4.

- We could change the condition to check that the counter variable had a value less than 6, rather than 5. The text would be output five times, for counter values 1, 2, 3, 4, 5.

- We could use a different operator to check *less than or equal to.*

Yet More Operators

As well as *less than* (<) and *greater than* (>), there are two further operators available to us:

«*firstValue*» <= «*secondValue*»

and

«*firstValue*» >= «*secondvalue*»

These operators are used to check "less than *or equal to*" and "greater than *or equal to.*"

We can now fix our five-times loop by using <= in our condition:

```
int counter;
for( counter = 1; counter <= 5; counter++ )
{
    [textView insertText:@"This should appear 5 times\n"];
}
```

Build & Run the application once again, and you'll find that the statement is now output five times, as we originally intended.

10.4 Enumerating an Array with a Traditional for Loop

Now that you've seen how to use a traditional **for** loop to run a specific block of code multiple times, you have another alternative available to enumerate the contents of an array.

Fast enumeration, as described in Section 10.1, *Introducing Array Enumeration*, on page 213, was only introduced in Objective-C 2.0. Before that, it was possible to enumerate arrays either by using a traditional **for** loop or by using one of the other C looping techniques. Let's look at **for** loops first.

Counters and Array Indices

In the previous section, we saw how to get our **for** loop to execute exactly five times. If we want to enumerate an array, we'll need the code to run as many times as there are elements in the array.

Back in Section 8.2, *Counting the Items in an Array*, on page 147, we saw how to count the number of items in an array using its count method. With this in mind, our condition to check whether the loop should continue is going to involve one of the comparator operators to check a counter variable against the number of items.

Remember that an array uses a zero-based index? And, remember how we can access a specific element in an array using objectAtIndex:? Putting all this together means that we can use a counter variable, initially set to 0, to access each element during the **for** loop. And, because the array index is zero-based but the count method will return the actual number of items, we need to use the *less than* operator rather than *less than or equal to*—the last item in an array of 12 items will have an index of 11.

So, change the displaySomeText: method to enumerate our old monthsArray using a traditional **for** loop:

```
- (IBAction)displaySomeText:(id)sender
{
    NSArray *monthsArray = [NSArray arrayWithObjects:@"January", @"February",
                            @"March", @"April", @"May", @"June",
                            @"July", @"August", @"September",
                            @"October", @"November", @"December", nil];
```

```
int currentIndex;
for( currentIndex = 0; currentIndex < [monthsArray count]; currentIndex++ )
{
    NSString *eachMonth = [monthsArray objectAtIndex:currentIndex];

    [textView insertText:[NSString
                    stringWithFormat:@"%@ is a nice month\n", eachMonth]];
}
}
```

Notice that we've renamed our counter variable to currentIndex. This is purely for aesthetic reasons; it's just to make the code a little more self-documenting, which is always a good thing.

Build & Run the application; when you click the button, you'll see the same output as you saw when we used fast enumeration:

```
January is a nice month
February is a nice month
March is a nice month
«... etc ...»
```

Optional Parts

It may interest you to know that the mini-statements inside the **for** statement are all optional. It's perfectly acceptable to write this:

```
for( ; ; )
{
    // do something forever
}
```

Note that the semicolons are still required, but this time no initial assignment is made, no condition is checked, and no per-loop incrementation is being performed. Whatever is contained within the code block will execute forever.

This means you can use a **for** loop to execute a block of code multiple times, but you can handle all the conditional checking, counter incrementation, and so on, yourself, like this:

```
int currentIndex = 0;
for( ; ; )
{
    if( !(currentIndex < [monthsArray count]) )
        break;

    NSString *eachMonth = [monthsArray objectAtIndex:currentIndex];

    [textView insertText:[NSString
                stringWithFormat:@"%@ is a nice month\n", eachMonth]];

    currentIndex++;
}
```

Break and Continue

We've seen the **break** keyword used to stop a loop altogether. Sometimes, you'll want to skip the rest of a code block during one loop pass but have the loop continue with the next loop pass. The keyword for this is, helpfully, **continue**.

If we wanted to display every month from our monthsArray except the one with an index of 3, for example, we could use this code:

```
int currentIndex;
for( currentIndex = 0; currentIndex < [monthsArray count];
                                          currentIndex++ )
{
    if( currentIndex == 3 )
        continue;

    NSString *eachMonth =
        [monthsArray objectAtIndex:currentIndex];

    [textView insertText:[NSString
        stringWithFormat:@"%@ is a nice month\n", eachMonth]];
}
```

If the currentIndex variable has a value of 3, the loop skips the output code and continues with the next run through. It would have the effect of outputting all the months except April (the month with a zero-based index of 3).

In this code, we set the initial value of the currentIndex variable before the loop starts. At the beginning of each run through the loop, we check to see whether the currentIndex variable is *not* less than the number of items in the monthsArray. If it is "not less"—in other words, greater than or equal to—we use the **break** keyword to stop the loop.

Back in Section 9.4, *Switching Around*, on page 199, we saw **break** used in **switch** statements to dictate where the code for each **case** should end. In a **for** loop, the **break** keyword is used to break the loop, causing it to stop execution.

At the end of the loop code block, assuming we haven't "**break**ed," we increment the currentIndex, ready for the next pass.

We've effectively written out "in full" what happens when using a traditional **for** loop. Note that it might make the code easier to read if we changed the condition check to currentIndex == [monthsArray count] rather than negating the result of a *less than* comparison. Once the currentIndex reaches the value of [monthsArray count], we can stop the loop.

Initial Assignment and Single-Line Loops

If the counter variable used during a **for** loop isn't needed for anything outside the loop, it's also acceptable to make the actual variable assignment in the head of the **for** loop itself, like this:

```
for( int counter = 0; counter < 5; counter++ )
{

}
```

And, just like we saw with **if** statements in the previous chapter, when there is only one line of code in the **for** loop block, we don't need to use the curly braces:

```
for( int counter = 0; counter < 1; counter++ )
    NSLog(@"Hello!");
```

Test your loop knowledge and understanding of conditionals by working out how many times that Hello! message will be output to the console log.

10.5 Other Types of Loop

Rather than having a portion of code run a certain number of times, we often need to have a loop continue for as long as some condition is true. Given that the parts of a **for** statement are optional, we could accomplish this using a **for** loop:

```
for( ; shouldContinue == YES; )
{
    // do something until shouldContinue is NO
}
```

but the C language has another loop construction that's more suitable in this case, the **while** statement. It looks like this:

```
while( «condition» )
{

}
```

The code between the braces will keep looping as long as the condition is met.

The **while** equivalent of the earlier example would be this:

```
while( shouldContinue == YES )
{
    // do something until shouldContinue is NO
}
```

A similar loop that you might encounter is the **do...while** loop, which looks like this:

```
do
{
    // whatever needs to be done
}
while «condition»;
```

This loop operates just like the **while** loop, but the code within the braces will *always* be executed at least once because the condition is checked at the *end* of each loop, rather than at the beginning.

Consider these two examples:

```
BOOL shouldContinue = NO;
while( shouldContinue == YES )
{
    NSLog(@"This will never be shown");
}

do
{
    NSLog(@"This will be shown once");
}
while( shouldContinue == YES );
```

The code block for the **while** statement in this example will never be shown because the condition is checked *before* the code is executed. The code block for the **do...while** statement, however, will be executed once because the condition is checked only *after* the code is executed.

Other Ways to Enumerate

The **while** loop can also be used for yet another way to enumerate an array. Apple provides us with a Cocoa class called NSEnumerator. To use it, you ask the array for an objectEnumerator and then keep asking that enumerator for its nextObject. The enumerator will continue to return you the objects in the array until it runs out of objects; at that point, it will return nil.

To display the months from the monthsArray using an NSEnumerator, we could use this code:

```
NSEnumerator *enumerator = [monthsArray objectEnumerator];
NSString *eachMonth = nil;
while( eachMonth = [enumerator nextObject] )
{
    [textView insertText:[NSString
                    stringWithFormat:@"%@ is a nice month\n", eachMonth]];
}
```

In another rare example of when we use the *assignment operator* (=) in a condition, this code will keep setting the eachMonth variable to the next object retrieved from the enumerator. As long as an object is returned, the eachMonth = [enumerator nextObject] assignment will evaluate as **true**. When there are no more objects and the nextObject method returns nil, the assignment will evaluate as **false**, and the loop will stop altogether.

It's usually easier now just to use fast enumeration, but there is also a helpful method provided by NSArray, called reverseObjectEnumerator, which will provide an object to enumerate over the array, supplying the objects in *reverse order*.

Running this code:

```
NSEnumerator *enumerator = [monthsArray reverseObjectEnumerator];
NSString *eachMonth = nil;
while( eachMonth = [enumerator nextObject] )
{
    [textView insertText:[NSString
                    stringWithFormat:@"%@ is a nice month\n", eachMonth]];
}
```

will output the months in reverse order:

```
December is a nice month
November is a nice month
October is a nice month
September is a nice month
«... etc ...»
```

If you need to enumerate in reverse but prefer the syntax offered by fast enumeration, you can combine the two and provide an enumerator object instead of an array in the fast enumeration syntax, like this:

```
for( NSString *eachMonth in [monthsArray reverseObjectEnumerator] )
{
    [textView insertText:[NSString
                    stringWithFormat:@"%@ is a nice month\n", eachMonth]];
}
```

This code will again output the months in reverse order.

10.6   A Simple Change to Our Shopping List Application

Let's put our looping knowledge into practice by making a very simple change to our Shopping List application from the last couple of chapters. When the user types the name of an item and tries to add it to the shopping list, we'll enumerate through all the existing items in the array to check whether there is an item with the same name already in the list. If there is, we'll ask the user whether they really want to add a duplicate item.

Close the TextApp project if it is still open in Xcode, and open the Shopping List project. Open the MyDocument.m file from the project, and find the addNewItemToShoppingList: method. At the moment, it looks like this:

```
- (IBAction)addNewItemToShoppingList:(id)sender
{
    NSString *newItem = [newItemNameTextField stringValue];

    [shoppingListArray addObject:newItem];

    [shoppingListTableView reloadData];

    if( sender == newItemNameTextField )
        [newItemNameTextField setStringValue:@""];
}
```

We'll use fast enumeration to walk through the existing shopping list items in the array. If an existing item in the array matches an item typed into the shopping list, we'll just stop the method altogether for now, without duplicating that item in the array. We'll write code to show the dialog box and ask the user after we have this part working.

Change your method to use the following code:

```
- (IBAction)addNewItemToShoppingList:(id)sender
{
    NSString *itemToAdd = [newItemNameTextField stringValue];

    for( NSString *eachItem in shoppingListArray )
    {
        if( [eachItem isEqualToString:itemToAdd] ) return;
    }

    [shoppingListArray addObject:itemToAdd];

    if( sender == newItemNameTextField )
        [newItemNameTextField setStringValue:@""];

    [shoppingListTableView reloadData];
}
```

We start by storing a pointer variable for the string held in the newItem-NameTextField. We then enumerate over all the existing items in the shoppingListArray; if the item typed into the text field matches an item in the array, we use the **return** keyword to end the method at that point.[2]

Build & Run the application to check that this works; you should be prevented from adding any duplicate items into the shopping list. Note that since the method returns straightaway, the newItemNameTextField is not emptied, regardless of whether you press ↵ or push the button. You might think this is useful if a user wants to add a qualifier to what they just typed—like changing "biscuits" into "chocolate biscuits,"—or you might decide that you should empty the text field before **return**ing, ready for an entirely new item to be typed.

Now that our basic duplicate item check is working, we can add the code to display an alert to ask the user whether they want to add a duplicate item, rather than just **return**ing instantly. We saw how to use NSAlert in the previous chapter, so let's use the same technique here and change the method to this:

```
- (IBAction)addNewItemToShoppingList:(id)sender
{
    NSString *itemToAdd = [newItemNameTextField stringValue];

    for( NSString *eachItem in shoppingListArray )
    {
        if( [eachItem isEqualToString:itemToAdd] )
        {
            NSAlert *alert = [[NSAlert alloc] init];
            [alert addButtonWithTitle:@"Duplicate"];
            [alert addButtonWithTitle:@"Cancel"];
            [alert setMessageText:@"This item already exists in
                                        your shopping list."];
            [alert setInformativeText:@"Do you really want to
                                        add a duplicate item?"];
            [alert setAlertStyle:NSWarningAlertStyle];

            int returnValue = [alert runModal];
            [alert release];
            if( returnValue != NSAlertFirstButtonReturn )
                return;
            else
                break;
        }
    }
}
```

---

2. Notice the difference between **return**, **break**, and **continue** when working with **for** loops. The **return** keyword will stop the entire method at that point, the **break** keyword will stop just the loop from looping, and **continue** will stop only the current pass through the loop.

```
    [shoppingListArray addObject:itemToAdd];

    if( sender == newItemNameTextField )
        [newItemNameTextField setStringValue:@""];

    [shoppingListTableView reloadData];
}
```

Build & Run the application once again to test the new behavior. If you type a duplicate item into the text field, you'll be asked whether you really want to duplicate that item. The conditional test in the previous code checks to see whether the button clicked is *not* the Duplicate button. If it's not—for instance, if the user clicks the Cancel button—the method **return**s instantly, just like before. Otherwise, if the user chooses to duplicate the item, we specifically **break** the loop at that point.

We could leave out the else break;, but this would mean that the array enumeration and duplicate item checking would continue, even though the user had already confirmed that he really wants to duplicate an item. Apart from wasting processor cycles for no reason, this would also mean that if the user had *previously* duplicated the item, any subsequent loops through the existing shopping list items will find that second duplicate and display the dialog box once again.

10.7 Chapter Summary

You've covered a lot of theory in these past few chapters. Now that you have a solid understanding of logical and comparison operators, you can write code that branches out or repeats itself as often as you like.

Enumerating through arrays is extremely common when developing Mac software, and we've covered several different ways to enumerate in this chapter, from fast enumeration in **for** loops to reverse enumeration using a **while** loop. We've also seen how to **break** completely out of looped code when needed or **continue** into the next pass through the loop if we want to miss out the rest of a repeated code block during a particular iteration.

Collections of objects appear throughout an application. A user interface consists of collections of controls, for example, the menu bar at the top of the screen displays a collection of menus, each one holding a collection of menu items. If you're writing a data-driven application, you'll probably be working with several collections of data objects. All of this makes it essential to have a good understanding of arrays and looping when writing software with Objective-C and Cocoa.

In the next chapter, we'll be looking again at good object-oriented design in applications, seeing the three different categories of classes in a Cocoa application: model classes describing objects that contain data, view objects that display information on screen, and controllers that liaise between model objects and views.

Chapter 11

Objects, Encapsulation, and MVC

In the past few chapters, we focused on learning the syntax of Objective-C, working with conditional statements and loops. We're going to change tack slightly in the first part of this chapter, taking a step back and looking at the design principles behind Mac OS X applications built using Cocoa.

By designing your own classes to follow the same object-oriented principles and general design standards used by the Cocoa framework, your software will be easier to maintain and fit better into the general scheme for object-oriented Mac OS X applications.

We're also going to spend some time looking at different ways of holding the information in our Shopping List application. We'll be revising its data structure and learning all about another type of collection object, an NSDictionary. Finally, we'll see how best to encapsulate the shopping list items within a dedicated object.

There is quite a lot of theory to get through in this chapter, but we do get to write a whole new application, albeit a small one, and make some interesting changes to the Shopping List application. The information we'll be covering on object encapsulation is essential when writing code that plays well both with Cocoa and with code written by other people.

11.1 The Main Types of Object

We've worked with a large number of different Cocoa classes so far; if we look at some of the ones we've used, such as NSString or NSTableView, it's clear that each class has a definite role for the objects it describes.

An NSString object is designed to hold a string of characters, offering various methods that let us access and query those characters, or even combine one string object with another. The NSTableView class describes an object used to display tabular information; we're using it in our Shopping List application to display the contents of our NSMutableArray collection of shopping list items.

It is extremely important to keep a clear idea of the role of an object when we write our own classes, not least because it keeps the size and complexity of the class description to a minimum. It's much better to write lots of smaller, well-thought-out objects, each working as efficiently as possible, than just to use one giant object that encompasses all the potential behavior we might need.

Along with clearly defined roles, the classes that we work with should generally fit into one of three *types* of class:

- Objects designed to *hold data* are known as **model** objects.

  In our Shopping List application, we're currently using an NSString object to hold the name of each item in the list and holding those items in a collection using an NSMutableArray.

- Objects used to *display information* on screen are known as **view** objects.

  We use an NSTableView class to display our Shopping List. In Text-App, we've been using an NSTextView to display the output from our code; we also used an NSTextField to accept input from the user.

- Objects that *handle the interaction* between an application's model objects and its views are known as **controller** objects.

  In TextApp, we have a NotifyingClass object to respond when the user clicks a button (NSButton is a view object), changing information (held in an NSString model object) and asking the NSTextView object to change its displayed text.

The Shopping List application offers us a great example of the interaction between these three types of class. Consider what happens when the user wants to add a new item to the list:

1. When the user clicks the Add button (view), the button sends an action message to its target, the MyDocument object (controller).

2. The MyDocument class asks the item name NSTextField (view) object for its stringValue and holds this in an NSString (model).

3. It then adds the string into the NSMutableArray (model) and tells the main NSTableView object (view) to reload.

4. When it receives the message to reload its data, the NSTableView asks MyDocument for the number of objects it will be displaying; the MyDocument asks the NSMutableArray how many objects are currently being held and passes the number to the NSTableView.

5. The NSTableView then asks the MyDocument object for the value to be held in each row of each column; the MyDocument asks the NSMutableArray for the object held at the index of the requested table row and passes back the value to the NSTableView.

This separation between model and view is extremely useful. The fact that the NSTableView object will be displaying a shopping list is completely irrelevant to the table view; all it cares about is the fact that it will be displaying tabular information, held in columns and rows, and that some other object will provide it with the information (in our case, an NSString) for each *cell* to be displayed in the table. The table view never talks directly to the model, and the model never talks directly to the table view.

It would be possible to define a complete ShoppingList class that looked after its own shopping list items, displaying those items on screen straight out of its internal storage; this would obviously end up being a large and complex object from a code perspective, and if we did create an object like that, we wouldn't have much opportunity to reuse it. If we needed to have a multicolumn display of shops and locations, we'd have to define a whole new class, with some functionality common to the ShoppingList but with a different way of storing the information for multiple columns.

In the previous chapter, I introduced code to our Shopping List application to check whether an item to be added already existed in the shopping list. In this chapter, we'll change the Shopping List application so that it also has an option to enter a quantity for an item, such as "5 apples" or "25 candy bars."

To implement this change, we're going to need an extra column in our table view to display the new quantity value. Before we start writing code or changing the interface, though, we must decide how best to change our underlying data model in order to store the new quantity information.

11.2 Designing Model Objects

At the moment, our shopping list model is extremely simple: we have a single NSMutableArray to hold a collection of NSString objects. Our user interface is extremely simple, too—we have a single-column table view designed to display one string in each row.

Let's familiarize ourselves with the code that supplies the information to the table view. Open the Shopping List project in Xcode, and find the MyDocument.m file.

Considering how the information is *displayed* in the table view, these are the two methods directly relevant:

```
- (NSInteger)numberOfRowsInTableView:(NSTableView *)aTableView
{
    return [shoppingListArray count];
}


- (id)tableView:(NSTableView *)aTableView
            objectValueForTableColumn:(NSTableColumn *)aTableColumn
                                  row:(NSInteger)rowIndex
{
    return [shoppingListArray objectAtIndex:rowIndex];
}
```

The first method returns the number of items currently held in our shopping list. The second method returns the value to be displayed for the requested row.

When we originally wrote the second method, we decided just to ignore the aTableColumn value because we had only one column in the table view. Clearly, this is going to have to change if we add a new Quantity column. We're going to want to do something like this:

```
{
    if( aTableColumn == «itemNameColumn» )
    {
        return «name of item at rowIndex»;
    }
    else if( aTableColumn == «quantityColumn» )
    {
        return «quantity for item at rowIndex»;
    }
    else // Unknown Column!
    {
        return nil;
    }
}
```

We need to check which column is requested and respond accordingly.

One of the easiest ways to implement this would be to add a second array, a shoppingListQuantitiesArray. It would need to have the same number of rows as the main shoppingListArray (we should probably rename this to shoppingListItemNamesArray to avoid confusion) and store a collection of objects containing the quantity number for each item.

If we used this implementation, the earlier method would look like this:

```
{
    if( aTableColumn == «itemNameColumn» )
    {
        return [shoppingListItemNamesArray objectAtIndex:rowIndex];
    }
    else if( aTableColumn == «quantityColumn» )
    {
        return [shoppingListQuantitiesArray objectAtIndex:rowIndex];
    }
    else // Unknown Column!
    {
        return nil;
    }
}
```

There's nothing particularly bad about this implementation, but it will make our lives more difficult when we need to write the information to a file if the users want to save their shopping lists. We'd need to archive two separate arrays, and we could no longer use the convenient writeToURL: and initWithContentsOfURL: methods provided by NSArray.

Another possible implementation is to use an *array of arrays*.

Using our multistory building analogy for an array, this means that rather than just having one string per story, we would instead have *another array* in each story. These new arrays would contain the information to be displayed in each row, so we might set the first object for the item name and set the second object as the quantity.

In code terms, our tableView:objectValueForTableColumn:row: method would now need to look like this:

```
{
    NSArray *itemInfoArray = [shoppingListArray objectAtIndex:rowIndex];

    if( aTableColumn == «itemNameColumn» )
    {
        return [itemInfoArray objectAtIndex:0];
    }
    else if( aTableColumn == «quantityColumn» )
    {
        return [itemInfoArray objectAtIndex:1];
    }
```

```
        else // Unknown Column!
        {
            return nil;
        }
}
```

We start by extracting the array of shopping list item information held at the relevant index in the main shoppingListArray. Depending on the column that we're asked for, we then return either the first or the second object in this itemInfoArray.

Again, there's nothing really wrong with this implementation, and it definitely allows for expansion in the future if, say, we decide we want to store an extra piece of information for each shopping list item, such as the store that sells it.

One criticism, however, is that the code isn't very readable. Keeping track of which object is at which index at which point is pretty confusing, even when we're storing only two pieces of information for each shopping list item.

We can make the code easier to follow if we can somehow refer *by name* to the information we need, such as itemName and quantity, rather than index:0 and index:1. As it happens, there's a Cocoa object designed exactly for this purpose.

Dictionaries of Information

Earlier, in Section 8.5, *Chapter Summary*, on page 175, I mentioned in passing that there was another type of collection object in Cocoa, an NSDictionary. This collection object behaves rather like an array, but instead of holding objects at numeric indices, it keeps track of objects through string *keys*.

To understand how dictionaries work, we're going to create a new application called "LookItUp." It's a document-based application—like Shopping List—that lets the user store and retrieve information using a dictionary. It looks like Figure 11.1, on the next page.

Close any open projects in Xcode before continuing (if you hold down the ⌥ key and click the File menu, you'll find there's a Close All item— ⌥-⌘-Ⓦ).

Create a new Cocoa Application project, making sure the "Create document-based application" checkbox is selected. Call it "LookItUp."

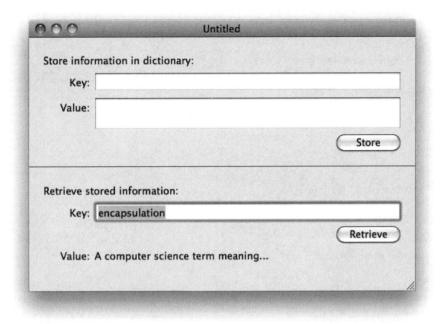

Figure 11.1: The LookItUp application in action

We'll jump straight in and set up the interface first. When the LookItUp project window opens in Xcode, expand the Resources group in the Groups & Files list, and double-click the MyDocument.xib file to open it in Interface Builder.

Remove the existing "Your document contents here" placeholder in the document's Window interface, and add new controls to the window so that it looks like Figure 11.2, on the following page.

We've used most of these controls before. In the upper half of the window, the text field next to the "Value" Label is a Multiline Textfield object; the item used to display the Value in the lower half of the window is a Multiline Label object. The line across the middle of the window is a Horizontal Line object; it's actually an instance of an NSBox object, used to draw...yes!...a box. It's just been collapsed to a single pixel in height so that it displays a flat line.

Next, we need to add outlets for all these user interface items into a controller object, along with actions for the two buttons. As with the

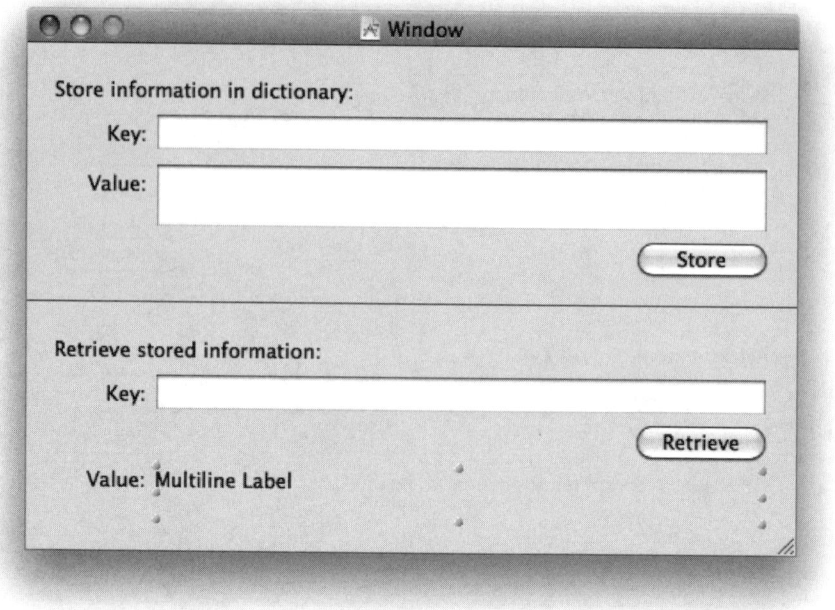

Figure 11.2: THE LOOKITUP DOCUMENT INTERFACE IN INTERFACE BUILDER

Shopping List application, the MyDocument class is fine as the controller for this application. If our document had multiple windows or we had a particularly complicated interface in one window, it might make more sense to create separate controllers for each window or one controller for each area of functionality within the main window.

Switch to Xcode, and open the MyDocument.h file. Add outlets for each of the text fields and the multiline label, along with the two action methods:

```
@interface MyDocument : NSDocument
{
    IBOutlet NSTextField *keyToStoreTextField;
    IBOutlet NSTextField *valueToStoreTextField;

    IBOutlet NSTextField *keyToRetrieveTextField;
    IBOutlet NSTextField *retrievedValueLabel;
}
```

Control Types

If you're wondering why the different types of text field and label are all NSTextField outlets, it's because all those objects really are instances of the NSTextField class.

Many of the control classes in the Cocoa framework can be configured in different ways; a label, for example, is an NSTextField with its editable flag set to false (and a few other settings related to its display). When you drag an item out of the Interface Builder library, that item has all the flags pre-set so that the control displays in the right way.

Because there's so much functionality shared between a label and an editable text field (essentially, the display of a string of characters, with various optional features such as selection or editing), it makes sense for them both to be represented by one class, rather than multiple classes with overlapping behavior.

The NSButton class is another example of a class with various faces in Interface Builder; there are a wide variety of different looks for a push button, for instance, all specified by setting various NSButton properties. Even a *checkbox* is an instance of an NSButton!

```
- (IBAction)storeValueInDictionary:(id)sender;
- (IBAction)retrieveValueFromDictionary:(id)sender;

@end
```

Before doing anything else, switch to the MyDocument.xib file in Interface Builder to link up all these outlets and actions.

The LookItUp application stores information in an NSDictionary object, so we're going to need access to one of those, much like we use the existing shoppingListArray mutable array in the Shopping List application.

Since we're going to need the dictionary object to exist as long as the document exists, we can add an instance variable into the @interface for the MyDocument object. And, since we're going to need to add items into the dictionary object after it's been created, we need to use the changeable variety, an NSMutableDictionary.

Add a mainDictionary instance variable in MyDocument.h:

```
@interface MyDocument : NSDocument
{
    NSMutableDictionary *mainDictionary;

    IBOutlet NSTextField *keyToStoreTextField;
    IBOutlet NSTextField *valueToStoreTextField;
    «interface continues»
```

Remember how we maintain access to the dictionary throughout the life of the MyDocument object? We allocate and initialize the dictionary in the MyDocument's init method, using alloc] init] so the dictionary is retained until we release it in the MyDocument's dealloc method.

Let's implement these two methods next, in MyDocument.m. The template file includes an init method, so we need to modify this to create our dictionary and then add the dealloc method (don't forget to call [super dealloc] at the end):

```
@implementation MyDocument

- (id)init
{
    self = [super init];
    if (self) {
        mainDictionary = [[NSMutableDictionary alloc] init];
    }
    return self;
}

- (void)dealloc
{
    [mainDictionary release];

    [super dealloc];
}
«implementation continues»
```

We'll leave the rest of the methods in the template file for now and instead focus on how we implement the two action methods to store and retrieve information in the dictionary.

Storing Information in a Dictionary

Before we see the code to store values in the dictionary, let's analyze what we need the storeValueInDictionary: method to do:

1. Get the stringValue from the keyToStoreTextfield.

2. Get the stringValue from the valueToStoreTextfield.

3. Store the value in the dictionary using the specified key.

4. Clear the two text fields so they're ready for more information.

Steps 1, 2, and 4 are easy to implement, so let's start by writing a method that implements them:

```
- (IBAction)storeValueInDictionary:(id)sender
{
    NSString *keyToStore = [keyToStoreTextField stringValue];
    NSString *valueToStore = [valueToStoreTextField stringValue];

    // Store the value in the dictionary using the specified key

    [keyToStoreTextField setStringValue:@""];
    [valueToStoreTextField setStringValue:@""];
}
```

Take a look at the documentation for NSMutableDictionary, and you'll find that there are several methods listed under the heading "Adding Entries to a Mutable Dictionary." The one that we'll use is the setValue:forKey: method.

This looks pretty straightforward—as the method name implies, it stores the value in the dictionary using the specified key. Let's use it:

```
- (IBAction)storeValueInDictionary:(id)sender
{
    NSString *keyToStore = [keyToStoreTextField stringValue];
    NSString *valueToStore = [valueToStoreTextField stringValue];

    [mainDictionary setValue:valueToStore forKey:keyToStore];

    [keyToStoreTextField setStringValue:@""];
    [valueToStoreTextField setStringValue:@""];
}
```

If you Build & Run the application, you'll find that you can type a value and a key into the top half of the document window; clicking the Store button will clear the two text fields, and we'll just have to assume that the information is actually being stored in the dictionary.

We obviously can't *retrieve* anything from the dictionary, since we have not written the retrieveValueFromDictionary: method yet.

Retrieving Information from a Dictionary

Before we write the next method, let's consider what it needs to do:

1. Get the stringValue from the keyToRetrieve text field.

2. Get the value from the mainDictionary that was stored using that key.

3. Set the stringValue of the retrieveValueLabel to the retrieved value.

Once again, we'll check the documentation for NSMutableDictionary to see how to retrieve the value. Huh? There seem to be no methods listed relating to value retrieval—only for setting or removing values.

Don't panic: an NSMutableDictionary is just the *mutable* version of a plain NSDictionary. If you look up at the top of the class documentation for the NSMutableDictionary, you'll see its class inheritance—it inherits from NSDictionary, which in turn inherits from NSObject. Click NSDictionary to view its class reference instead.

If you look under the section "Accessing Keys and Values," you'll find the companion method to our earlier setValue:forKey: method, which is called valueForKey:. This method returns the value stored in the dictionary with the specified key, meaning we're ready to implement our retrieval method:

```
- (IBAction)retrieveValueFromDictionary:(id)sender
{
    NSString *keyToRetrieve = [keyToRetrieveTextField stringValue];

    NSString *retrievedValue = [mainDictionary valueForKey:keyToRetrieve];

    [retrievedValueLabel setStringValue:retrievedValue];
}
```

Build & Run the application, and you'll find that you can now retrieve a value stored in the dictionary using a specified key. Note that because we haven't implemented any kind of Save or Open functionality yet, you will have to add values for keys each time you run the application or create new documents.

If you try to access a value for a key that hasn't previously been stored or don't specify a key at all, you'll find that the retrieved value field doesn't get updated. To see why not, take a look at the Console Log window in Xcode (⇧-⌘-R).

You'll see messages along these lines:

```
*** Assertion failure in -[NSTextFieldCell _objectValue:forString:errorDescription:]
          /SourceCache/AppKit/AppKit-1038.11/AppKit.subproj/NSCell.m:1531
Invalid parameter not satisfying: aString != nil
```

These messages indicate that there's a problem trying to pass a nil string pointer to an NSTextFieldCell. This cell is an object used by an NSTextField object to handle the actual text display or editing. We'll look at the relationship between cells and views in the next chapter, in Section 12.6, *Views and Cells*, on page 305.

The only place in our retrieveValueFromDictionary: method where we're passing an object pointer *to* a text field, and therefore to its text field cell, is the following line:

```
[retrievedValueLabel setStringValue:retrievedValue];
```

Since the value we pass, held in retrievedValue, is set when we ask the dictionary for its valueForKey:, we can infer that there are some cases when valueForKey: will return nil.

It just so happens that valueForKey: will return nil if it can't find a value for the specified key. If you check the documentation for valueForKey:, this isn't immediately easy to confirm, so we'll just have to accept it for now.

We can make use of this feature by adding a conditional statement to check the retrievedValue pointer variable before we try to display it. If it's nil, we can instead display an error message. Change the retrieveValue-FromDictionary: method to this:

```
- (IBAction)retrieveValueFromDictionary:(id)sender
{
    NSString *keyToRetrieve = [keyToRetrieveTextField stringValue];

    NSString *retrievedValue = [mainDictionary valueForKey:keyToRetrieve];

    if( retrievedValue )
        [retrievedValueLabel setStringValue:retrievedValue];
    else
        [retrievedValueLabel setStringValue:@"Sorry, key not found"];
}
```

Here we make use of the fact that a *non*-nil variable will evaluate as true in a conditional statement, as described in Section 9.2, *Every Value Is a Winner*, on page 194. If you Build & Run, you'll find that you now see an error message if you enter an undefined key.

Persisting Dictionary Contents to Disk

We haven't written very much code in this section, but the two important points to take away are that you can *store* something in a dictionary, using a specified key in the method setValue:forKey:, and then *fetch* it later, using valueForKey:. As the name implies, an NSDictionary object functions just like a real-world dictionary; it contains information (the values), which it makes available by looking up keywords.

We've implemented as much of the LookItUp application as we need for this illustration, but you might like to test your Cocoa prowess by adding the methods to read and write files on disk.

If you look in the documentation for NSDictionary, you will find that dictionary objects have the same initWithContentsOfURL: and writeToURL: atomically: methods we're using in the Shopping List application. You might want to refer to Section 8.4, *Adding Spice*, on page 171 to remind yourself of the NSDocument methods we implemented.

The sample code for this chapter, available via the book's website, includes example methods to save and open files.

11.3 Reworking the Shopping List Application

Now that you have a good understanding of dictionaries, values, and keys, let's redesign the underlying data structure for our Shopping List application. Instead of the earlier strategy of using an array of *arrays*, we'll use an array of *dictionaries*.

For each row in the table view, we need a dictionary that will hold the item name and the quantity required for that item. We'll start by looking at all the places in our application that need to be changed. Close anything currently open in Xcode, and open the Shopping List project again.

Before we look at code changes, we need to modify the interface to display our new quantity information in the table view and enable the users to specify a quantity when they add an item. Open the MyDocument.xib file in Interface Builder. If the other MyDocument.xib file (from the LookItUp application) is still open, make sure you close it before continuing to avoid any confusion!

We need to add a new column to the shopping list table view. The easiest way to do this is to view the main MyDocument.xib window in list view mode; keep expanding the objects under the main Window object until you see the Table View, which is under the Bordered Scroll View object. Click the Table View object in this list to select it, switch to its Attributes inspector, and increase the number of columns to 2.

You'll find that Interface Builder adds a new column, listed below the existing Shopping List Items column. Click this new column, and use its inspector to change the title to "Quantity." Next, click and drag this new column in the list view *above* the existing column; if you look at the visual representation for the window and table view itself, you'll find your table view looks like Figure 11.3, on the following page.

This figure also shows an extra label and text field to allow the user to specify quantity information when they add a new shopping list item; add these to your interface as well.

Switch to Xcode, and open the MyDocument.h file to see whether we need to change anything.

The existing shoppingListArray instance variable can stay as it is; we still need only one main shopping list array—we'll just be filling it with dictionary objects, rather than strings.

We need to add an IBOutlet for the new quantity text field, and thinking ahead to how we'll provide values to the table view, we're going to need to differentiate between the two table columns. The easiest way to do this is to add IBOutlets to refer to each NSTableColumn:

```
@interface MyDocument : NSDocument
{
    IBOutlet NSTableView *shoppingListTableView;
    IBOutlet NSTextField *newItemNameTextField;
    IBOutlet NSTextField *newItemQuantityTextField;

    IBOutlet NSTableColumn *quantityColumn;
    IBOutlet NSTableColumn *itemNameColumn;

    NSMutableArray *shoppingListArray;
«interface continues»
```

Switch to Interface Builder, and connect these outlets—Figure 11.4, on page 249 shows how to connect the table columns.

That's it for the MyDocument interface. Open the MyDocument.m file in Xcode, and let's see how much of that needs to be changed:

- The numberOfRowsInTableView: method is fine as it is; we still have only one table view, and we still have a single array of shopping list items. The count from the array is still the number of rows.
- The tableView:objectValueForTableColumn:row: is going to need to be changed, as we saw earlier in the chapter, to respond correctly depending on which table column is specified.

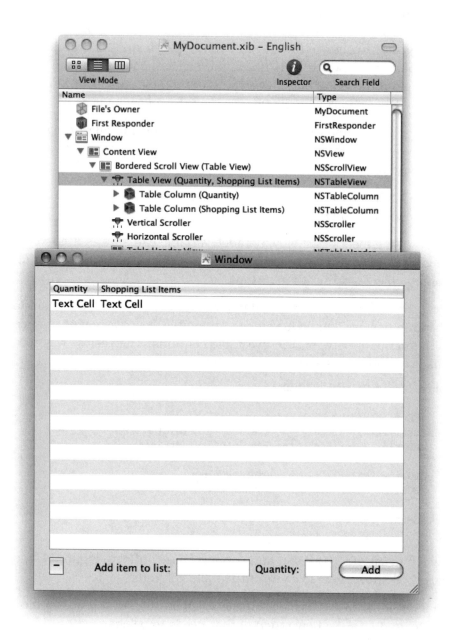

Figure 11.3: THE REVISED SHOPPING LIST INTERFACE IN INTERFACE BUILDER

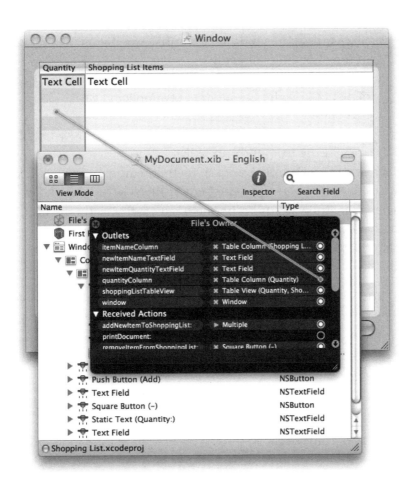

Figure 11.4: CONNECTING THE NSTABLECOLUMN OUTLETS IN INTERFACE BUILDER

- The tableView:setObjectValue:forTableColumn:row: is going to need to be changed in the same way so that the users can edit the value held in either table column.
- The addNewItemToShoppingList: method will need to be changed so that it does the following:
  1. Makes use of the amount specified in the Quantity text field
  2. Stores the name and the quantity correctly using a dictionary in the shopping list array
  3. Checks for duplicates in the values already held in the array of dictionaries (in the interest of simplicity, we're going to skip this step)
  4. Empties the name text field and sets the quantity text field to 1 when the user adds an object
- The removeItemFromShoppingList: method can stay as it is because we still need it to remove the item at the selected row index.
- The init method needs to be modified to create the default items using dictionaries.
- The dealloc method can stay as is, as can the other methods in the file.

Let's start with the init method so we see how to add items into the shopping list.

Adding the Initial Items

We need to decide on two strings to use as the keys for our two values; let's use @"itemNameKey" and @"itemQuantityKey".

The other important decision is how we are going to store the quantity value. We could just store it as another NSString object, which would mean that the user could type "4 pints," rather than just being allowed to type an integer. For the purposes of learning about dictionaries and model objects, however, let's store a *number* in the array.

There's one vital piece of information to be aware of when we work with arrays and dictionaries—both NSArray and NSDictionary are designed to collect pointers to other *objects*. This means that we can't just stick an int value (or even a pointer to an int) in our item dictionary. To store the quantity value, we need to use an object that holds a number.

Back in Section 7.3, *Creating Objects in Code*, on page 118, we wrote just such a class, the WonderfulNumber class, which held a number internally as a float and offered various methods to retrieve that value or output it as a string. It would be perfectly acceptable to use WonderfulNumber objects in the Shopping List application, but there is another class available to us.

The Cocoa framework offers us a great class for working with numbers, with a particularly predictable name of NSNumber. Its behavior is similar to our own WonderfulNumber class, but it offers a lot of extra functionality. You can set the value of an NSNumber object using set...Value:, where the ... is one of the C number types, like int or float.

Let's write the init method for the Shopping List document object and create those initial shopping list item dictionaries using an NSString for the item name and an NSNumber for the quantity. We'll still create the same three items we had before (milk, eggs, and butter), but we'll need to create a mutable dictionary for each item, adding each dictionary into the main shoppingListArray:

```
- (id)init
{
    self = [super init];
    if (self) {
        // Create the main shopping list array
        shoppingListArray = [[NSMutableArray alloc] init];

        // Add the Milk
        NSDictionary *milkItem = [NSMutableDictionary dictionary];
        [milkItem setValue:@"Milk" forKey:@"itemNameKey"];
        [milkItem setValue:[NSNumber numberWithInt:4] forKey:@"itemQuantityKey"];

        [shoppingListArray addObject:milkItem];

        // Add the Eggs
        NSDictionary *eggsItem = [NSMutableDictionary dictionary];
        [eggsItem setValue:@"Eggs" forKey:@"itemNameKey"];
        [eggsItem setValue:[NSNumber numberWithInt:12] forKey:@"itemQuantityKey"];

        [shoppingListArray addObject:eggsItem];

        // Add the Butter
        NSDictionary *butterItem = [NSMutableDictionary dictionary];
        [butterItem setValue:@"Butter" forKey:@"itemNameKey"];
        [butterItem setValue:[NSNumber numberWithInt:1] forKey:@"itemQuantityKey"];

        [shoppingListArray addObject:butterItem];
    }
    return self;
}
```

This method is quite a bit longer than it was before, and the margin for typo errors is high! Xcode's automatic syntax highlighting and suggestion features should help you along the way.

This code obviously populates each item dictionary in the same way: it starts by creating an *autoreleased* mutable dictionary, using the dictionary class factory method provided by NSMutableDictionary.

Why do we create autoreleased dictionaries? Surely we need them to be retained so they last as long as the main shoppingListArray container and indeed the MyDocument object? Actually, both NSArray and NSDictionary (and their subclasses) will retain any objects that they collect. Every time we add one of our item dictionaries into the main shoppingListArray, that dictionary is retained by the array. The same applies to the objects we add into the dictionary: the @"Milk" string is retained by the item dictionary, as is the NSNumber quantity object.

When an array or dictionary is subsequently deallocated, it empties itself of all its items first; when it does, all those items are sent a release message, balancing the retain they were sent when they were added. In our Shopping List application, the only model object that we specifically retain is the main shoppingListArray (created through alloc] init]). When we release the shoppingListArray in the MyDocument object's dealloc method, that release triggers a cascade of array and dictionary emptying and object releasing, with the end result that we don't leak any memory.

Pretty amazing, considering we've only had to take responsibility for the alloc] init] and release of a single Cocoa object!

Displaying the Items

Now that we've set up our initial shopping list contents, it's time to modify the method that displays them in the table view. With our new dictionaries for items, this is now quite easy, so let's implement it:

```
- (id)tableView:(NSTableView *)aTableView
        objectValueForTableColumn:(NSTableColumn *)aTableColumn
                            row:(NSInteger)rowIndex
{
    NSDictionary *itemDictionary = [shoppingListArray objectAtIndex:rowIndex];

    if( aTableColumn == quantityColumn )
        return [itemDictionary valueForKey:@"itemQuantityKey"];
    else if( aTableColumn == itemNameColumn )
        return [itemDictionary valueForKey:@"itemNameKey"];
    else // Unknown Column!
        return nil;
}
```

Build & Run the Shopping List application to make sure that our initial shopping list contents are displayed correctly. You should see the "4 Milk," "12 Eggs," and "1 Butter" items displayed across the two columns of the table view. If you don't, double-check your method that creates the initial dictionaries!

If you try to add any new items or edit existing items, you'll find that you get lots of errors in the debugger console in Xcode. We still have a few methods to change before our application is fully functional again.

Editing the Items

Next, let's change the method that gets called if the user tries to edit values in the table view itself. Again, we need to fetch the dictionary for the row being edited and then set the proposed value for the key relevant to the current column:

```
- (void)tableView:(NSTableView *)aTableView
                        setObjectValue:(id)anObject
                        forTableColumn:(NSTableColumn *)aTableColumn
                                   row:(NSInteger)rowIndex
{
    NSDictionary *itemDictionary = [shoppingListArray objectAtIndex:rowIndex];

    if( aTableColumn == quantityColumn )
        [itemDictionary setValue:anObject forKey:@"itemQuantityKey"];
    else if( aTableColumn == itemNameColumn )
        [itemDictionary setValue:anObject forKey:@"itemNameKey"];
}
```

Build & Run once again to check whether you can edit the values in the main table view: try changing the word "Eggs" to something like "Lamb Chops" and its quantity to "4." This should work just fine, and you'll also find that you can still save and reopen the shopping list files, just like you did before.

Checking the Class of the Proposed Value

There's something worth pointing out here. In the MyDocument object's init method, we store the quantity as an NSNumber object. The code we've just written takes the object value provided when the method is called and stores it directly in the dictionary. Because the user is editing *text* in the table, with the editing behavior provided in the same way as in an NSTextField, this object will be a *string* object.

Let's test that theory:

```
- (void)tableView:(NSTableView *)aTableView
                  setObjectValue:(id)anObject
                  forTableColumn:(NSTableColumn *)aTableColumn
                             row:(NSInteger)rowIndex
{
    NSDictionary *itemDictionary = [shoppingListArray objectAtIndex:rowIndex];

    NSLog(@"Class of anObject is: %@", [anObject class]);

    if( aTableColumn == quantityColumn )
        [itemDictionary setValue:anObject forKey:@"itemQuantityKey"];
    else if( aTableColumn == itemNameColumn )
        [itemDictionary setValue:anObject forKey:@"itemNameKey"];
}
```

Here, we're using a call to NSLog to log a message to the debugger console. We ask anObject for its class, and include the result in the log string using the %@ string substitution.

Build & Run the application, and try changing a quantity; you'll see the following in the debugger console window in Xcode:

```
Class of anObject is: NSCFString
```

The *CF* in this class stands for "Core Foundation" and represents the fundamental object type used to store a CFString, which is itself the Core Foundation type for a string of characters under Mac OS X. You'll often see *CF* in a class name when examining object types, such as NSCFArray or NSCFDictionary, but you don't need to worry about them. In general, treat them as if they were the standard NSString, NSArray, or NSDictionary you were expecting.

If we want to maintain the quantity as an NSNumber in our item dictionary, we need to change the code to this:

```
- (void)tableView:(NSTableView *)aTableView
                  setObjectValue:(id)anObject
                  forTableColumn:(NSTableColumn *)aTableColumn
                             row:(NSInteger)rowIndex
{
    NSDictionary *itemDictionary = [shoppingListArray objectAtIndex:rowIndex];

    if( aTableColumn == quantityColumn ) {
        NSNumber *newQuantity = [NSNumber numberWithInt:[anObject intValue]];
        [itemDictionary setValue:newQuantity forKey:@"itemQuantityKey"];
    } else if( aTableColumn == itemNameColumn )
        [itemDictionary setValue:anObject forKey:@"itemNameKey"];
}
```

Note that we have added braces to the quantityColumn's if statement because there is more than one line of code to be executed for that condition.

Adding New Items

There's one final piece of functionality that we haven't yet implemented: the rather important method that adds new objects into the shopping list. Given the way that we created the dictionaries for the initial three items, this is quite straightforward. Implement it like this:

```
- (IBAction)addNewItemToShoppingList:(id)sender
{
    NSString *newItemName = [newItemNameTextField stringValue];
    int quantityInt = [newItemQuantityTextField intValue];
    NSNumber *newItemQuantity = [NSNumber numberWithInt:quantityInt];

    NSMutableDictionary *newItem = [NSMutableDictionary dictionary];
    [newItem setValue:newItemName forKey:@"itemNameKey"];
    [newItem setValue:newItemQuantity forKey:@"itemQuantityKey"];
    [shoppingListArray addObject:newItem];

    [shoppingListTableView reloadData];
}
```

We've stripped out all the old code from this method to make it simpler. It now adds new items and their quantities immediately, without performing any duplication checks. It also doesn't empty either of the text fields.

You might like to test your knowledge of conditional statements by adding code that checks to see whether the users added the item by pressing ↵ either in the item name text field or in the quantity text field. If they did, empty the item name text field, and set the quantity text field to 1. You'll need to connect the selector for the quantity text field in Interface Builder so that it calls the addNewItemToShoppingList: method, then use the Attributes inspector to set its Action property to "Sent on Enter Only," just like you did for the name text field in Section 9.6, *Additional Conditionals*, on page 210.

The sample code for this chapter shows one possible implementation and also includes a line of code that moves the cursor to the item name text field so that it is ready to receive new text straightaway.

The Problem with Keys

While writing the code for the revised Shopping List application, you may already have encountered a few problems related to the fact that we've been typing the same @"keyName" strings each time we want to get or set a value for a particular key. The word *key* means exactly what it says—if you misspell the string in your code, the value you want to use will effectively be locked away because you're not using the correct key.

Consider a dictionary where an object is stored with the key @"door-Color". If I work on this code from the United Kingdom, I make no guarantees about remembering to spell *color* in the same way as somebody living in the United States. If I add some functionality to the code that stores an object with the key @"doorColour", that object clearly won't be accessible anymore using the old key @"doorColor".

Xcode syntax highlighting and automatic suggestions as you type are great for working with variables, class names, methods, and so on, but there's no help when you're typing a string key name. If you're writing the name of a particularly long key, like @"someRidiculouslyLongName-ForAKeyThatItMakesItEasierToReadTheCodeWeThink", it's extremely likely you will misspell part of the key name at some point in your code, leaving you with a bug that's quite difficult to track down.

There are a couple of solutions to this problem; one of them is to define a *global* variable, marked as a *constant*, with the key name value that you're using. We'll look at the exact syntax for this in Section 13.2, *Declaring Global Variables*, on page 339; for now, it's a variant of something like this:

```
NSString *myKeyName = @"myKeyName";
```

This variable is declared globally and can be made available to any code within your project, which means that you can now use code like this:

```
{
    [someDictionary setValue:someObject forKey:myKeyName];
}
```

It might not look like much of a difference, but because myKeyName is now the name of a variable, Xcode will help autocomplete it when you start typing. The compiler will also complain if you misspell the key name when you try to build your project—it will only allow you to use a variable name that has previously been defined.

11.4 Creating a Shopping List Item Object

You've already covered a lot of ground in this chapter; you took a brief high-level overview of the architecture of models, views, and controllers, before revising the data structure of the Shopping List application using NSDictionary objects.

You might have been wondering, while we were working with dictionaries, whether we couldn't just write a new class description for a ShoppingListItem object. Naturally, we can, and we're going to do this right now.

Object Encapsulation

We've written several of our own custom objects so far; our Wonderful-Number class turns out not to be so wonderful in comparison to Cocoa's NSNumber class, but it was a good example of how a value can be *encapsulated*, along with some useful behavior, inside an object.

Let's start defining a new ShoppingListItem object right now. In your Xcode project for the Shopping List application, right-click (or ^-click) the Classes group, and select Add > New File.... Create a new Cocoa Objective-C class (inheriting from NSObject) called "ShoppingListItem."

Xcode will generate the two files for the class—ShoppingListItem.h and .m.

A ShoppingListItem object needs to store an item name and a quantity—so add two instance variables to the ShoppingListItem.h interface:

```
@interface ShoppingListItem : NSObject {
    NSString *itemName;
    int quantity;
}

@end
```

Note that only one of these instance variables is an object: the itemName string. Since the quantity is a number, and because an object can quite happily have a standard C scalar instance variable, we'll use an int.

There are no interface outlets or actions for this object, because it's a model object—as mentioned earlier in this chapter, model objects should never need to talk directly to any view objects, and vice versa.

Both these instance variables need to exist for the lifetime of the ShoppingListItem object, so the itemName object needs to be retained for the life of the object. We're going to need to allocate it in an init method and release it in dealloc, as usual. The scalar value just needs to be given an initial value to avoid any weird behavior resulting from the use of an uninitialized variable.

When we wrote our original WonderfulNumber class, we wrote two init methods. In Section 7.6, *Initializing with Arguments*, on page 131, you learned how to write one init method to create an object with a specified value for an instance variable, and you learned how you should also implement our superclass's *designated initializer* so that your object is properly initialized, no matter how it is created. You even wrote a class factory method to return a newly created, autoreleased WonderfulNumber object.

We'll do all of these things again, so add these two method signatures to your ShoppingListItem interface:

```
@interface ShoppingListItem : NSObject {
    NSString *itemName;
    int quantity;
}

- (id)initWithName:(NSString *)newName quantity:(int)newQuantity;
+ (id)shoppingListItemWithName:(NSString *)newName quantity:(int)newQuantity;

@end
```

Switch to the ShoppingListItem.m file, and implement these methods first:

```
@implementation ShoppingListItem

- (id)initWithName:(NSString *)newName quantity:(int)newQuantity
{
    if( self = [super init] )
    {
        itemName = [newName retain];
        quantity = newQuantity;
    }

    return self;
}

+ (id)shoppingListItemWithName:(NSString *)newName quantity:(int)newQuantity
{
    return [[[ShoppingListItem alloc]
            initWithName:newName quantity:newQuantity] autorelease];
}

@end
```

We also need to implement a standard init method to call our designated initializer, along with a dealloc method to release the object instance variable:

```
- (id)init
{
    return [self initWithName:@"Bread" quantity:1];
}

- (void)dealloc
{
    [itemName release];

    [super dealloc];
}
```

There are a few other methods we need to implement to allow other objects to set the values of the instance variables.

Protection from the Outside World

Technically speaking, because of the way Objective-C adds object-oriented features to the non-object-oriented C language, it is possible for one object to access the internal variables of another object directly; in practice, this is generally best avoided, as we'll see a little later in the chapter.

To provide access to its internal values, an object should supply *accessor methods* for those values. In Section 7.3, *Adding a New Class*, on page 119, we wrote a setStoredNumber: method to set the value stored by the WonderfulNumber object. We also wrote a sister method, storedNumber, that returned the number stored by the object. We'll need to do the same thing here. Start by adding four method signatures to the ShoppingListItem interface:

```
@interface ShoppingListItem : NSObject {
    NSString *itemName;
    int quantity;
}

- (id)initWithName:(NSString *)newName quantity:(int)newQuantity;
+ (id)shoppingListItemWithName:(NSString *)newName quantity:(int)newQuantity;

- (void)setItemName:(NSString *)newName;
- (NSString *)itemName;
- (void)setQuantity:(int)newQuantity;
- (int)quantity;

@end
```

Notice the naming convention used here. The setter method names are setCapitalizedInstanceVariableName:; the getter method names are the same as the instance variable name. This convention exists for several reasons, some of which will become clear in a moment.

We can implement the accessor methods for the quantity quite easily— they just need to set or return the value held by the variable. Switch to the ShoppingListItem.m file, and implement them like this:

```
- (void)setQuantity:(int)newQuantity
{
    quantity = newQuantity;
}

- (int)quantity
{
    return quantity;
}
```

The methods for the itemName variable need to do a little more than this: the setItemName: method needs to release the existing string object pointed to by the itemName instance variable. It should then point item-Name to the provided newName and call retain on that new object to ensure it stays in memory for use by the ShoppingListItem object until specifically released.

```
- (void)setItemName:(NSString *)newName
{
    [itemName release];

    itemName = [newName retain];
}
```

If you examine lots of sample code, you'll sometimes see setter methods for objects written like this:

```
- (void)setItemName:(NSString *)newName
{
    [itemName release];

    itemName = [newName copy];
}
```

Calling copy on an object does exactly what it sounds like: it creates a completely new object, with all its internal instance variables copied across. It also returns that object to you with a retain count set in the same way as an object you receive by calling alloc] init], so you should treat it in the same way (i.e., it needs to be released somewhere).

When to Use Copy and Retain

Using copy or retain is a frequently debated topic. For an object to be copyable, it needs to implement a copyWithZone: class method that decides how an instance and its internal values are copied. Most of the classes in the Cocoa framework can be copied, including NSString and NSMutableString. In the case of mutable classes, if you are specifically passing around a pointer to an NSMutableString, it's possible for an object to do this:

```
{
    NSMutableString *someString = [someObject mutableStringPlease];
    [someString appendString:@" changed you!!!"];
}
```

If the string object returned by the mutableStringPlease method is the same object held in the instance variable, the receiving object can change that instance variable, which is a bad thing: it breaks the whole encapsulation idea. If mutableString-Please returned a *copy* of someObject's instance variable string object, any changes to that copy won't have any effect on someObject's internal string.

You can't borrow the original Declaration of Independence in Washington, D.C.; you have to borrow (well, buy) a copy. If you were allowed to borrow the original, you might change the text or maybe discover a map on the back. Treat object encapsulation in the same way; if it's possible for a requested object to be damaged, copy it (and autorelease it) before it is returned.

The accessor can again be quite simple; it just returns the value held by the itemName instance variable:

```
- (NSString *)itemName
{
    return itemName;
}
```

To avoid the problem outlined in the sidebar on the current page, you may also see accessor methods written like this:

```
- (NSString *)itemName
{
    return [[itemName copy] autorelease];
}
```

This time, the internal object is first copied and then autoreleased to avoid leaking memory, and the newly copied object is returned.

Why Use Accessor Methods?

You may be wondering why it's such a bad idea for one object to modify another object's instance variables; after all, if we're implementing setter methods that allow a value to be changed, surely that defeats the purpose?

These are good points, and it's definitely worth addressing them now. For a start, there may be instance variables you specifically do not want any other objects to be able to access, such as a secure password cached inside an object that connects to a secure Internet resource. For these variables, you may decide either not to provide access at all or to write a getter method that just returns a bogus value and warns the user.

It's also possible that one value in an object depends on another value. You might decide to write functionality in our ShoppingListItem object that checks to see whether a provided quantity for an item is greater than 1; if so, it could ensure that the name of the object is plural or that it's singular for a quantity of 1. This might help avoid having a list containing "1 eggs" or "2 lettuce."

You might even want an object to perform validation checks before changing its instance variables; you might want to prevent the user from specifying any values less than 1 (that is, 0 or -1, and so on) for the quantity of an item, for example.

In the future, you might decide to change the way an object holds its information. Consider a case where a ContactInformation object has accessor methods for a phone number; as far as other objects are concerned, a ContactInformation object *stores a phone number*. There's nothing to say that you couldn't rewrite the accessor methods to change the way the phone number gets stored. You may decide it makes sense for a ContactInformation object to store a phone number using one instance variable for a country code, one for the exchange, one for the rest of the phone number, and one for any extension.

To the outside world, the object is still storing a phone number—exactly *how* doesn't matter. There is a setPhoneNumber: and a phoneNumber method that work correctly, so everything will be fine. If the outside world had been allowed to access a single phoneNumber instance variable directly, all that outside code would be broken if the phoneNumber variable no longer existed or if it just contained a small portion of the whole phone number.

So, always make sure you recognize the data abstraction and encapsulation offered by object-oriented design; don't try to modify another object's internal values directly, unless you have exceptional, justifiable reasons.

Accessor Methods for Internal Use

Now that we have accessor methods for our ShoppingListItem object, it's worth considering whether we should use them from within the ShoppingListItem class itself, with code like this:

```
- (void)someMethod
{
    [self setItemName:@"Baked Beans"];
}
```

This is absolutely fine and a very good idea. If you have accessor methods that either validate values before setting them or need to make changes to other values when one value is set, it's obviously easiest if an object uses its own accessor method rather than having to duplicate any validation code, and so on, every time it accesses an instance variable directly.

The only places where this doesn't apply is in init and dealloc methods. The init method is meant to set up *initial* values in an object—at the time an init method is called, the rest of the object may not yet be completely set up. If an object's setter methods have any additional functionality beyond setting values (and some objects will, automatically, without you writing any extra code, through a process known as *Key-Value Observing*), using those setter methods from within init could have all sorts of undesirable effects.

The dealloc method is called just before an object is removed from memory; it's designed so an object can do all necessary destructive work in terms of releasing any objects it retains, thereby avoiding memory leaks. As with init, using a setter method in a dealloc method can cause problems.

For our ShoppingListItem class, we need to leave our init and dealloc methods as they are.

11.5 Reworking the Shopping List Application... Again

Now that we have a new class of ShoppingListItem available, let's modify the Shopping List application to make use of it. All the code we need to modify is in the MyDocument.m file, so open it up.

To be able to refer to ShoppingListItem objects from within our MyDocument object, we'll need to start by **#import**ing the header file at the top of MyDocument.m:

```
#import "MyDocument.h"
#import "ShoppingListItem.h"

@implementation MyDocument
«code continues»
```

The methods we need to modify are the same as those back in Section 11.3, *Reworking the Shopping List Application*, on page 246. Let's once again start with the init method:

```
- (id)init
{
    self = [super init];
    if (self) {
        // Create the main shopping list array
        shoppingListArray = [[NSMutableArray alloc] init];

        // Add the Milk
        ShoppingListItem *milkItem =
            [ShoppingListItem shoppingListItemWithName:@"Milk" quantity:4];
        [shoppingListArray addObject:milkItem];

        // Add the Eggs
        ShoppingListItem *eggsItem =
            [ShoppingListItem shoppingListItemWithName:@"Eggs" quantity:12];
        [shoppingListArray addObject:eggsItem];

        // Add the Butter
        ShoppingListItem *butterItem =
            [ShoppingListItem shoppingListItemWithName:@"Butter" quantity:1];
        [shoppingListArray addObject:butterItem];
    }
    return self;
}
```

That's cut down quite a few lines of code! The code is able to make use of our class factory method to create each autoreleased ShoppingListItem before adding it to the array.

Next up is the method to display the items:

```
- (id)tableView:(NSTableView *)aTableView
        objectValueForTableColumn:(NSTableColumn *)aTableColumn
                         row:(NSInteger)rowIndex
{
    ShoppingListItem *currentItem = [shoppingListArray objectAtIndex:rowIndex];

    if( aTableColumn == quantityColumn )
        return [NSNumber numberWithInt:[currentItem quantity]];
    else if( aTableColumn == itemNameColumn )
        return [currentItem itemName];
    else
        return nil;
}
```

This time we get the ShoppingListItem at the relevant rowIndex. We then make use of our accessor methods; for the itemNameColumn, we just pass back the string returned by itemName method on our item.

Notice that the name of the method we're implementing is *object*Value-For...; because we decided to implement our ShoppingListItem using an int for the quantity value, we have to generate an NSNumber object from that int before we can pass it back to the table view.

The method that allows the user to change values in the table view rows now needs to look like this:

```
- (void)tableView:(NSTableView *)aTableView
                    setObjectValue:(id)anObject
                    forTableColumn:(NSTableColumn *)aTableColumn
                               row:(NSInteger)rowIndex
{
    ShoppingListItem *currentItem = [shoppingListArray objectAtIndex:rowIndex];

    if( aTableColumn == quantityColumn )
        [currentItem setQuantity:[anObject intValue]];
    else if( aTableColumn == itemNameColumn )
        [currentItem setItemName:anObject];
}
```

Notice how much more readable this code is? Again, because the method passes us a proposed *object*Value, we ask that proposed object for its intValue to pass on as the new quantity.[1]

---

1. This code makes the assumption that whatever object we might receive will definitely respond to the intValue message. This will certainly be the case for table views using the standard cell objects, like the text cells we are using to display the items in the table view.

Last, but not least, the method that adds in new objects to the list needs to be updated as well:

```
- (IBAction)addNewItemToShoppingList:(id)sender
{
    ShoppingListItem *newItem = [ShoppingListItem
            shoppingListItemWithName:[newItemNameTextField stringValue]
                            quantity:[newItemQuantityTextField intValue]];

    [shoppingListArray addObject:newItem];

    [shoppingListTableView reloadData];
}
```

Again, this method is quite a bit simpler than it was before. We're just passing the results, returned by asking the text fields for their respective string and int values, straight into the class factory method used to create our new shopping list item.

That's it! Build & Run the application to make sure it still behaves as it should.

You'll find that you can add, edit, and remove items in the list as much as you like. If you try to save the list, however, you'll unfortunately end up with an error. Oops. What did we break?

For an NSArray to be able to archive itself using the writeToURL:atomically: method, every object in that array needs either to be another NSArray or NSDictionary or to be an object that can save as an NSString.[2]

Now that we are storing our shopping list items using an NSObject subclass of our own, we'll need to use an *archiver* object to archive the array to disk. For now, you won't be able to save and reopen your shopping lists; don't despair, though, we'll see how to work with archivers and unarchivers in Section 13.5, *Archiving with NSCoding*, on page 362.

11.6 Introducing Objective-C 2.0 Properties

Most objects need accessor methods. If you compare the methods we wrote for the storedNumber variable in Section 7.3, *Adding a New Class*, on page 119 with the quantity accessors we wrote in this chapter, (in Section 11.4, *Protection from the Outside World*, on page 259), you'll notice that the methods follow the same pattern.

---

2. These are all the objects available for use in *p-list* files (property lists), the file format used by the writeToURL:atomically: method

```
// For a scalar variable named: myVariable

// Accessor method:
- («variable type»)myVariable
{
    return myVariable;
}

// Setter method:
- (void)setMyVariable:(«variable type»)newValue
{
    myVariable = newValue;
}
```

If you have an object with a large number of instance variables and need to offer up access to those variables to other objects, you're going to need to write lots of accessor methods. We'll look at objects in a moment, but if each variable is a scalar variable, like an int or a float, you're going to end up with endless methods, all following the same pattern as the methods shown earlier. Surely there must be a "Don't Repeat Yourself" alternative?

In Section 10.1, *Introducing Array Enumeration*, on page 213, you learned about the syntax of fast enumeration, a technique introduced with Objective-C 2.0. There are a number of other important additions in Objective-C 2.0, including *Objective-C properties*.

Declaring Properties

Objective-C properties allow us to declare that an object has a *property*, with a specific *type*. Once we've declared that property, we can use a keyword to specify that the methods relevant to that property be *synthesized* automatically for us.

Let's look at what this means for our existing ShoppingListItem object. Open the ShoppingListItem.h file to check the existing accessor methods for the integer quantity instance variable:

```
@interface ShoppingListItem : NSObject {
    «other instance variables»
    int quantity;
}

«other methods»

- (void)setQuantity:(int)newQuantity;
- (int)quantity;

@end
```

The syntax to *declare a property* looks like this:

```
@property («keyword») «variable type» «variable name»;
```

The keyword portion of the declaration specifies how the proposed values passed in through setter methods should relate to the instance variables. For our scalar int type quantity variable, we just *assign* the newQuantity value directly to the instance variable, like this:

```
- (void)setQuantity:(int)newQuantity
{
    quantity = newQuantity;
}
```

The property syntax keyword for this type of property is **assign**. So, remove the existing setter and getter methods (setQuantity: and quantity), and replace them with a property declaration:

```
@interface ShoppingListItem : NSObject {
    NSString *itemName;
    int quantity;
}

- (id)initWithName:(NSString *)newName quantity:(int)newQuantity;
+ (id)shoppingListItemWithName:(NSString *)newName quantity:(int)newQuantity;

- (void)setItemName:(NSString *)newName;
- (NSString *)itemName;

@property (assign) int quantity;

@end
```

The new line of code indicates that there is a quantity property on a ShoppingListItem object; this means that another object can access or set the value of that property using standard accessor methods, even though those accessor methods aren't specifically listed in the interface of the class description.

Synthesizing Properties

By declaring a property in the *interface*, we can also remove the *implementation* of the accessor methods from ShoppingListItem.m altogether, replacing them with a simple directive requesting that the methods be synthesized automatically for us, using this syntax:

```
@synthesize «property name»;
```

Switch to the ShoppingListItem.m file, and remove the setQuantity: and quantity method implementations. Replace them with this single line of code:

```
@implementation ShoppingListItem

@synthesize quantity;

- (void)setItemName:(NSString *)newName
«implementation continues»
```

Note that the **@synthesize** keyword goes *inside* the **@implementation** for the ShoppingListItem. Most of the sample code you'll see puts any **@synthesize** declarations just under the opening **@implementation** keyword.

By using **@property** and **@synthesize**, we've cut out two methods from our ShoppingListItem class. This might not seem so amazing right now, but when you're working with objects that need to maintain a large number of instance variables, not having to write out all those identical-looking access methods is quite a bonus.

Before we continue, Build & Run the Shopping List application to make sure that it still works and that you can still change the quantities of items in the table view. You'll find that it appears to behave exactly as it did before; we're still using the setQuantity and quantity methods from within the MyDocument.m file, even though we haven't specifically written out those methods.

It's also now becoming apparent why it's so important that accessor method names follow standard conventions; unless you specifically request otherwise, properties will be synthesized using the setVariableName:, variableName naming conventions.

Declaring Properties for Object Types

So far, we've seen how to use properties to work with a scalar int variable using the **assign** keyword. What about objects?

Our setter method for the itemName instance variable currently looks like this:

```
- (void)setItemName:(NSString *)newName
{
    [itemName release];

    itemName = [newName retain];
}
```

That looks pretty formulaic—release the existing object and retain and assign the new value. Surely there must be a keyword for this type of property? Of course! For an object property that should be retained when it is set, specify the **retain** keyword.

Open the ShoppingListItem.h file again, and replace the existing accessor methods for the itemName with a property declaration:

```
@interface ShoppingListItem : NSObject {
    NSString *itemName;
    int quantity;
}

- (id)initWithName:(NSString *)newName quantity:(int)newQuantity;
+ (id)shoppingListItemWithName:(NSString *)newName quantity:(int)newQuantity;

@property (retain) NSString *itemName;
@property (assign) int quantity;

@end
```

Again, this declaration specifies that the itemName property may be accessed or set using standard accessor methods. And, just like the quantity property, we can synthesize the property and remove the setItemName: and itemName methods from ShoppingListItem.m:

```
@implementation ShoppingListItem

@synthesize itemName;
@synthesize quantity;

- (id)initWithName:(NSString *)newName quantity:(int)newQuantity
«implementation continues»
```

Well, that was pretty easy—surely as you progress through a book on learning Mac programming, you should be *adding* code rather than *removing* it? On the other hand, it really is a good thing to be able to delete chunks of code. Those are lines of code that you won't have to worry about maintaining in the future.

Your ShoppingListItem.m file now has only four methods in it, and two of those have only one line of code in them. That's pretty manageable for a simple shopping list item! It's even perfectly acceptable to consolidate multiple **@synthesize** statements onto one line, like this:

```
@implementation ShoppingListItem

@synthesize quantity, itemName;

- (id)initWithName:(NSString *)newName quantity:(int)newQuantity
«implementation continues»
```

That's another line's worth of code gone! Hooray!

Build & Run the application once again to make sure that it still works; just like before, the name of an item can still be set using the setItem-Name: method, even though we haven't specifically written it. From a user's perspective, nothing appears to have changed. Excellent!

Dot Syntax

There's another side effect to using property notation that I need to mention, and it involves something that is still considered slightly controversial amongst the Mac developer community: *dot syntax.*

Dot syntax, or dot notation, enables us to access or set the properties on an object using a very different notation from what we've seen before:

```
// Accessor Method:
id variable = [someObject someValue];

// Dot Syntax:
id variable = someObject.someValue;
```

This might not look particularly controversial, but it does bear a striking resemblance to the way we work with a non-object type that we haven't yet discussed in this book: the *structure,* offered by the C language.

We'll be looking at structures in the next chapter, in Section 12.1, *Keeping Track of Locations on Screen,* on page 275, but for the moment, let's finish our property examination and try to forget they've even been mentioned.

Along with *access*ing a property on an object using dot syntax, we can also *set* a property on an object using dot syntax:

```
// Setter Method:
[someObject setSomeValue:newValue];

// Dot Syntax:
someObject.someValue = newValue;
```

Even though the word *set* doesn't appear anywhere in the dot syntax version, by using the assignment operator (=) with dot notation, the receiving object's property will still be set using a setter method. If the property is declared as a **retain**ed property, the someValue instance variable will still be set correctly and retained when you use this notation.

While you're trying to get your head around instance variables and accessor methods, you might like to stick with using the [someObject setSomeValue:newValue] version for now. If you do plan on writing software for the iPhone, though, you'll find that much of the available sample code and documentation for iPhone development uses dot notation *everywhere*.

If you're not convinced that using dot notation is a good idea, that's fine. Some people love it, and some people hate it. Personally, I quite like being able to do this:

```
[myObject.someProperty doSomething];
```

Rather than this:

```
[[myObject someProperty] doSomething];
```

Either is acceptable, and both work just as well.

11.7 Chapter Summary

We covered an enormous amount of ground in this chapter. We started by looking at the Model-View-Controller design pattern used when writing Mac OS X applications. We then went through several design iterations of our Shopping List application and learned all about dictionaries that hold collections of objects ready to be accessed using keys.

We also looked in some detail at how an object encapsulates information and behavior, hiding its internal instance variables behind public accessor methods. We finished by looking at Objective-C 2.0 property syntax, which makes it possible to specify properties on objects such that accessor methods can be generated for us without having to write them out in full.

In the next chapter, we're going to look in more detail at the *View* part of Model-View-Controller, seeing how to write our own custom objects to display information on screen.

Chapter 12

All About Views

The previous chapter introduced you to the separation between models, views, and controllers. You saw a number of different ways to structure the *model* data for an application, and you reworked the Shopping List application's data structure.

We've been using *controller* objects all the way through the book, from our NotifyingClass object in TextApp through the MyDocument object in the Shopping List application. In this chapter, it's time to learn about the *view* objects in Model-View-Controller. You'll see how Mac OS X software displays information on screen using a view hierarchy, and you'll find out how to do some simple drawing tasks using custom views.

Before we talk about views, though, we need to look at some very basic geometry used to describe position and size on screen.

12.1 Simple Geometry in Two Dimensions

Most of the Mac software you interact with on a daily basis displays its information in at least one window. Apple's iTunes application, for example, uses a single window to display various types of information depending on whether you are searching through your music library, playing an album, or browsing the iTunes Store.

For now, let's ignore all the information displayed *inside* the window, instead focusing on the window itself. In terms of its physical characteristics, a window has a specific **shape**, a **location** on screen, and a **size**.

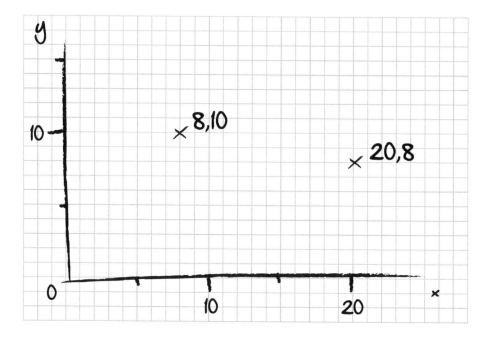

Figure 12.1: LINE DRAWING OF GRAPH

Nearly all the windows you'll come across are rectangular in shape.[1] Some windows have a fixed size; others are resizable. The iTunes window, for example, can be shrunk down to a minimum size or made as large as you like to fill a big screen. If you exit and relaunch iTunes, the window will even reappear with the size and position you last set.

To keep track of the size and position of a window on screen, we make use of some simple geometry.

X and Y Coordinates

Back in school, you probably had to make up lots of graphs like the one in Figure 12.1. *Points* on the graph are defined in terms of coordinates, given relative to the x-axis (running horizontally from left to right) and the y-axis (running vertically, bottom to top).

---

1. And even those that don't appear to be rectangular are still defined by their *enclosing* rectangle.

Think of a computer screen as being like a big piece of graph paper. The *origin* (that's the point where the x- and y-axes intersect at the bottom left) corresponds to the bottom left of your screen.[2]

A window's location on screen is defined by the location of the point at its bottom-left corner, relative to the bottom-left corner of the screen.

It's tempting to think of this coordinate system as being specified in *pixels*, or the tiny dots that make up the image on a computer screen, but coordinates are in fact specified in units called *points*—see the sidebar on the next page to find out why.

Keeping Track of Locations on Screen

To keep track of a location on screen, we obviously need some kind of scalar or object variable type. The type provided by Apple is an NSPoint.

Although it might look like an object, with the NS prefix like NSObject and NSTableView, an NSPoint is *not* an object. It's one example of something we mentioned briefly in Section 11.6, *Dot Syntax*, on page 271: a *structure* offered by the C language.

A structure is a special kind of variable type that stores more than one piece of information. Conceptually, it's just like an object with multiple instance variables (like our ShoppingListItem object in the previous chapter), but without any behavior defined in methods.[3]

A single NSPoint variable is used to hold two pieces of information, a value for an x-coordinate and a value for a y-coordinate. It's used like this:

```
NSPoint myPoint;
myPoint.x = 250;
myPoint.y = 300;
```

Notice that there's no asterisk on the front of the myPoint declaration; NSPoint isn't a type of object, and we're not using a pointer. An NSPoint variable is just like an int or a float, but it has subvariables known as *members*, accessible using the previously shown dot syntax.

---

2. If you have multiple screens, things get a little more complicated. For the most part, though, Mac OS X and Cocoa handle most of the problems for you, and you don't need to worry too much unless you're writing a screen saver or a full-screen application.

3. If you go on to learn more about how Objective-C works behind the scenes, you'll find that this is a somewhat backward way of looking at things; in fact, an object is itself made up of one of these *structures* of information, with some associated behavior.

When Is a Pixel Not a Pixel?

Your Mac screen can display several resolutions. The maximum resolution of a 30-inch Apple Cinema display is 2560x1600, so the screen is 2560 pixels wide by 1600 pixels high. At this maximum resolution, each point corresponds to one pixel, so you could, for example, display a very large window with a maximum size of 2560 by 1600, filling the screen.

You might also choose to use your display at a different resolution, 1280x800. At this resolution, everything appears much larger than it does at 2560x1600. The biggest window you can display is now only 1280x800, but it still fills the screen. Each of the 1280 horizontal *points* across the window now corresponds to two *pixels* rather than one.

If a window has a position of {640,200}, the left side of the window will be 640 *points* away from the left edge of the screen. At a resolution of 1280x800, the bottom-left corner will start exactly halfway across the screen and a quarter of the way up. At a resolution of 2560x1600, the bottom-left corner starts only a quarter of the way across the screen and an eighth of the way up.

By specifying coordinates in points, rather than pixels, we don't have to worry about screen resolutions. The Cocoa framework and operating system handle all of this for us. A dot that's 1 point by 1 point is essentially the smallest thing we can draw on a screen at its current resolution. This might use 1 physical pixel; it might use 4.

From a memory management point of view, treat an NSPoint just like you would an int or a float. You can't retain or release it, so it's valid only in the code block in which it is defined. As with all other variables, it's also a good idea to set the initial values at declaration time.

A location on screen is, as the name NSPoint implies, just a point; it has no physical size. You can't draw a point, but you can use it together with a second type of variable that defines a *size* to define a rectangular area on screen.

The variable type used to hold a size is another C structure, with the predictable name of NSSize. Again, it has two members, allowing you to specify both a width and a height, and is used like this:

```
NSSize mySize;
mySize.width = 500;
mySize.height = 350;
```

With this information in mind, we can define the outer *frame* of the window in terms of a location and size. Its origin is {250, 300}, and its size is {500,350}.

Given that it's so common to need to combine a location and size to define a rectangular area on screen, Apple also provides us with a structure to define a rectangle. It's called an NSRect and is used like this:

```
NSPoint myPoint;
myPoint.x = 5;
myPoint.y = 5;

NSSize mySize;
mySize.width = 17;
mySize.height = 9;

NSRect myRect;
myRect.origin = myPoint;
myRect.size = mySize;
```

This code ends up with an NSRect variable called myRect defining the rectangle shown in Figure 12.2, on the next page.

12.2 Working with Windows and Views

Now that you've seen how to work with locations, sizes, and rectangles in code, we're going to write a very simple application to put it all into practice.

Open Xcode, and create another new project. Use the Mac OS X Cocoa Application template (if you're using Xcode 3.2, make sure the "Create document-based application" checkbox isn't selected), and call the application "Windows and Views."

When running, the application looks like Figure 12.3, on page 279; it displays the location and the size of the window on screen when the button is clicked. It may not look like the most exciting application you've ever seen, but you will be adding extra functionality to it as

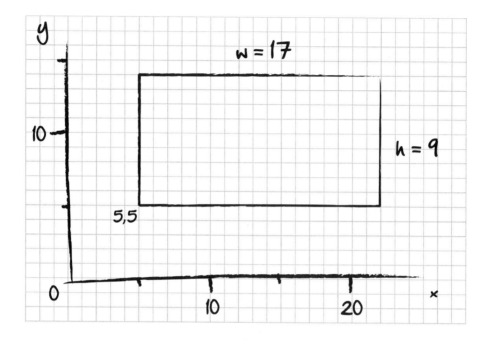

Figure 12.2: A RECTANGLE DEFINED BY AN NSRECT

you learn more about the relationships between windows, views, and coordinate systems.

We'll start with the interface first. Open the new project's MainMenu.xib in Interface Builder. Drag out an NSBox instance onto the window interface, and use the Attributes inspector to set its title to "Main Window."

Add the rest of the controls (an NSButton, two editable text fields, and two labels) so that the interface resembles the application in Figure 12.3, on the next page.

Next, we'll write the code that makes this work, so we're going to need some kind of controller object. If you're using Xcode 3.2 under Snow Leopard, the template projects automatically include what's known as an *application delegate*[4] class description, together with an instance of that class already included inside the MainMenu.xib file. This object would be perfect to handle our measuring requirements, but since some

---

4. So-called for reasons that will become clear in Chapter 13, *Mac OS X and Cocoa Mechanisms*, on page 315

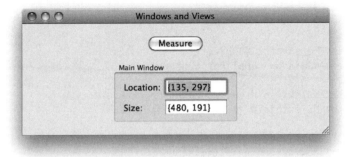

Figure 12.3: THE WINDOWS AND VIEWS APPLICATION

readers might still be running Leopard or only have access to Xcode 3.1, we'll create our own dedicated measuring object.

Switch to Xcode, and right-click (or ^-click) the Classes group in the Groups & Files list. Select Add > New File..., and choose the Mac OS X Cocoa Objective-C class in the New File template picker. If you're running Xcode 3.2 under Snow Leopard, make sure that the "Subclass of" drop-down menu shows NSObject.

We need to decide on a suitable name for this class; since it will be measuring various things, we could call it "Measurer." The problem is that's a pretty common word. Somebody else might write a class with the same name that we want to use in the future. We wouldn't be able to use it because of the name clash.

Way back near the beginning of the book, in Section 3.4, *Objective-C File Types for a Class*, on page 35, I mentioned that it's common to prefix the names of classes with letters (like *NS*) to avoid clashes. Let's start adopting this practice now and give our new class a prefixed name. If this was a class that might be reusable in other applications, we could choose a prefix related either to our own name or to a company name, like *PP* for Pragmatic Programmers. This measuring class probably won't get used outside of the current application, so instead we'll use the prefix *WV*, standing for Windows and Views. Name the new class WVMeasurer.

Once Xcode has created the files, open the WVMeasurer.h file to add the necessary interface outlets and actions, as usual. To measure the application's main window, you'll need an outlet for that too. Add all of these into the @interface, like this:

```
@interface WVMeasurer : NSObject {
    IBOutlet NSWindow *applicationWindow;

    IBOutlet NSTextField *windowLocationTextField;
    IBOutlet NSTextField *windowSizeTextField;
}

- (IBAction)showMeasurements:(id)sender;

@end
```

Open the WVMeasurer.m file next, ready to write the showMeasurements: method.

This method needs to ask the window for its frame (which will be an NSRect containing the window's location on screen along with its size). It then needs to extract the origin and size from the NSRect and display these in the two text fields.

Extracting the values is relatively straightforward, so let's deal with these first:

```
@implementation WVMeasurer

- (IBAction)showMeasurements:(id)sender
{
    NSRect windowFrame = [applicationWindow frame];

    NSPoint windowLocation = windowFrame.origin;
    NSSize windowSize = windowFrame.size;
}

@end
```

But how can we display an NSPoint or an NSSize in a string of characters? It seems likely that we could build up an NSString using the stringWithFormat: method, but unfortunately there isn't a format specifier we can use to display a structure. Instead, we have to output each member value within the structure separately.

Both NSPoint and NSSize use the same variable type for their member subvariables: an Apple-defined CGFloat. The CG here stands for "Core Graphics." As the rest of the word suggests, you can think of these as being just like basic float variables,[5] meaning that we could use the following to generate a string from an NSPoint:

```
NSString *valueString =
    [NSString stringWithFormat:@"{%f,%f}", myPoint.x, myPoint.y];
```

There's a slightly simpler way to do this, however, using an Apple-defined *function* called NSStringFromPoint():

```
NSString *valueString = NSStringFromPoint(myPoint);
```

This function accomplishes the same thing as the format string version. Helpfully, there's also a corresponding function, NSStringFromSize(), that generates an NSString from an NSSize, so let's use both of these functions to output the relevant information:

```
- (IBAction)showMeasurements:(id)sender
{
    NSRect windowFrame = [applicationWindow frame];

    NSPoint windowLocation = windowFrame.origin;
    NSSize windowSize = windowFrame.size;

    [windowLocationTextField setStringValue:NSStringFromPoint(windowLocation)];
    [windowSizeTextField setStringValue:NSStringFromSize(windowSize)];
}
```

That's as much code as we need right now; all that's left is to create an instance of our new WVMeasurer class and connect everything up in Interface Builder.

Switch to Interface Builder, and drag out one of the generic blue cube NSObjects; use the Identity inspector to change its class to WVMeasurer, and then link up all the outlets and the action.

Save the MainMenu.xib file, return to Xcode, and Build & Run the application.

Move the main application window near the bottom left of your screen, and click the button; then move the window to the bottom right of the screen, and click the button to see how the Location information changes. The first value of the two location numbers increases as you move the window to the right.

Try moving the window up the screen, and click the button; the second location value increases as you move the window higher on your screen.

---

5. This isn't strictly true in a 64-bit world, but don't worry about it now!

Note that the Size information hasn't changed yet because we've just been changing the position of the window on screen. Try making the window bigger by dragging down its bottom-right resize handle. Click the button, and the new size will be displayed.

Note that the location has also changed following the resize. The bottom of the window (which is the origin for the window) is now lower than it was before, even though to the user it seems as if the window hasn't *moved* on screen.

This is a common source of confusion and is one of the side effects of working in a bottom-to-top, x- and y-axes coordinate system when we're so used to thinking in terms of starting at the top and working downward. If you ever need to adjust the height of a window using code, you'll probably want to adjust the origin too so that it appears as if the top of the window doesn't move.

View Relationships

We're about to add a few more interface items to the Windows and Views application, but before we do, let's tidy up some annoying problems that occur when the window is resized.

If you resize the window, it would be nice if the size and location information moved to stay in the middle of the window. Right now, it's also possible to make the window too small to see any information at all; it would be nice if we could specify a minimum size for the window.

If you wanted to accomplish all of this using your own code, you'd need to do quite a bit of work. You'd need to watch out for the window resizing, find out the window's height and width, then work out where each item needs to be moved to, and so on. Thankfully, Interface Builder offers us an incredibly easy way to do all this, and we don't need to write any code at all.

Let's start by setting the minimum size for the window. Switch to Interface Builder, and use the list view mode of the MainMenu.xib file to select the Window object; open the Size inspector for the Window object (that's the yellow ruler icon), and you'll see the palette shown in Figure 12.4, on the facing page.[6]

---

6. Your inspector might look slightly different if you are running Xcode 3.1.

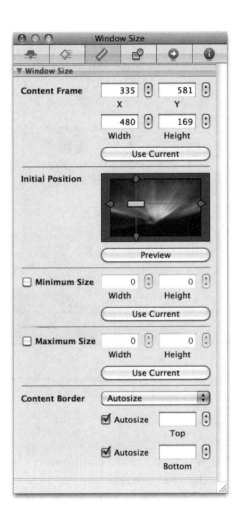

Figure 12.4: The Size inspector for a Window object

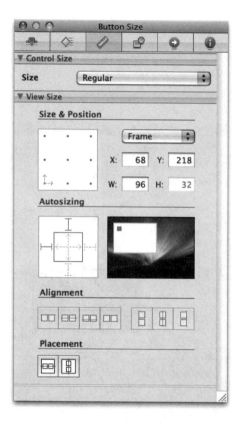

Figure 12.5: THE SIZE INSPECTOR FOR A CONTROL

This inspector allows you to set both a minimum and a maximum size for the window; click the Use Current button to set the minimum size to be the size of the window as it is designed in the xib file.

Save the file, and switch to Xcode to Build & Run the application again. You'll find that you can't make the window any smaller than the size specified in the Size inspector.

The other problem to sort out is how the controls in the window move around when the window is resized. Quit the Windows and Views application, and return to Interface Builder. Click the Measure button in the interface to select it, and open its Size inspector. The Size inspector for a control is shown in Figure 12.5.

Under the Autosizing heading in this inspector, you'll see what looks like a mini Mac OS X desktop, with an animating rectangle,[7] showing how the selected item will move or resize relative to its enclosure. The default settings for controls are that they are tied to the top left: in the animating view, the white enclosure is increasing in size, but the red item stays stuck in its top-left corner.

Next to the animating view is a strange-looking square control, used to change how the control resizes or moves. By default, the top and left anchors are set. Click the left anchor to turn it off, and you'll find that the red box in the animating view now stays in the top middle of the white box as it changes size.

Feel free to experiment with the other resizing features to see how they affect the animation. The inner arrows are used to define how an object will resize; the outer options anchor the object to an edge.

Turn off all the red arrows and anchors, except for the top anchor, before you proceed.

Click the NSBox instance once in the interface to select it, and use the Size inspector to set its autoresizing information to the same as the button (i.e., leaving just the top anchor). Don't make any changes to the other controls yet.

Switch to Xcode, and Build & Run the application to see how we're getting on. You should now find that when you resize the window, the button and the box stay in the middle of the window.

What's also worth noting is that the controls *inside* the NSBox object move with their box container. We didn't change the autosizing settings on those controls, yet they are moving as we require.

Let's find out why!

12.3 The View Hierarchy

When displaying information on screen, we use what's known as the *view hierarchy.*

At the top of the hierarchy, from our Cocoa perspective, is the NSWindow object. As we've already seen, this window object keeps track of its location and size on screen. As well as a huge amount of functionality

---

7. It may animate only when you move the mouse pointer over it.

Figure 12.6: THE HIERARCHY OF VIEWS IN OUR WINDOWS AND VIEWS APPLICATION

relating to how it draws itself, an NSWindow object also keeps track of its *content view*, which is an NSView object that marks the next step down the view hierarchy.

Switch to Interface Builder, and view the MainMenu.xib file in list view mode. Click the triangle next to the Window object to expand it, and you'll find it contains a Content View item. Expand this as well, and you'll find the NSBox and NSButton instances. If you expand the Box item, you'll see the labels and text fields, as shown in Figure 12.6.

Notice that each of the NSTextField instances and the NSButton instance also have triangles next to them; we will see why a little later in this chapter.

Views and Subviews

The list of views shown in Figure 12.6, on the preceding page, represents the view hierarchy for our simple application. The basic view class, NSView, provides all sorts of functionality related both to displaying information on screen and to keeping track of subviews in the view hierarchy. In our application, the NSBox is a *subview* of the window's *content view*. The NSTextFields are in turn subviews of the NSBox.

When you created the interface earlier in this chapter, you might have noticed that Interface Builder provided some visual feedback on adding the text fields into the box. If you click and drag one view over another, the receiving view will be highlighted to show that you are making the inserted view a subview of the receiving view.

This may all sound overly complicated, but it offers some huge benefits. For a start, if you move the NSBox instance in Interface Builder, you'll find that the NSTextField objects inside move with it. If you were to move the NSBox instance programmatically, using code, the same thing would happen.

This explains why we didn't need to make any modifications to the autosizing properties for the text field controls. When the box moves, its subviews move too. Since the default autoresizing properties are anchored to the top left of the enclosing view, the text fields stay anchored to the top left of the box.

There's another important benefit of having this view hierarchy system, relating to view coordinates. To investigate, let's change our Windows and Views application so that it also displays the size and location of the main window's content view.

Switch to Xcode, and open the WVMeasurer.h file. Add an outlet for the content view, along with outlets for a couple extra text fields:

```
@interface WVMeasurer : NSObject {
  IBOutlet NSWindow *applicationWindow;
  IBOutlet NSView *mainView;

  IBOutlet NSTextField *windowLocationTextField;
  IBOutlet NSTextField *windowSizeTextField;
  IBOutlet NSTextField *viewLocationTextField;
  IBOutlet NSTextField *viewSizeTextField;
}

- (IBAction)showMeasurements:(id)sender;

@end
```

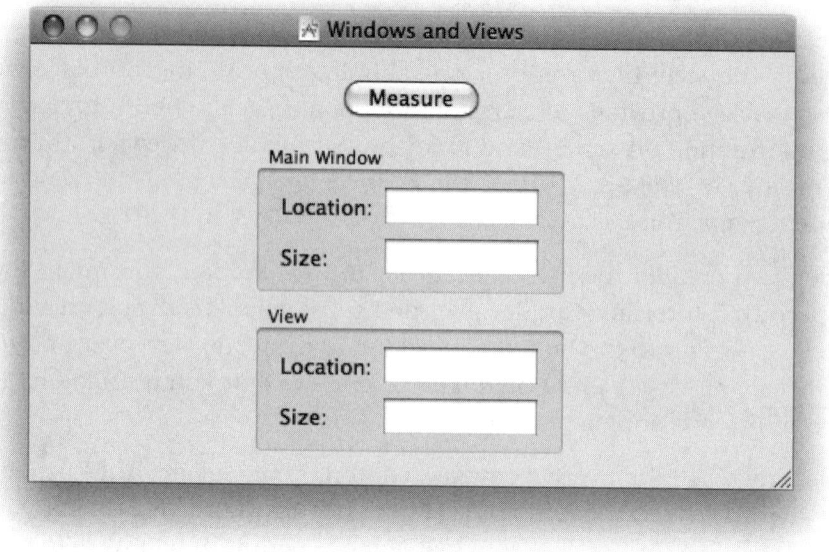

Figure 12.7: ADDING EXTRA CONTROLS TO THE WINDOWS AND VIEWS APPLICATION

Switch to Interface Builder, and add another NSBox object (with its title set to "View"), along with labels and text fields, so that your interface matches Figure 12.7. Set the autosizing for the box so that it's also anchored at the top.

Connect up the text field outlets from the existing WVMeasurer object to the new controls. Connect the mainView outlet to the window's content view by dragging from the connection HUD down to an empty portion of the main Window interface (the whole window content area needs to be highlighted before you release the mouse).

Switch to Xcode, open the WVMeasurer.m, and change the showMeasurements: method to display the information about the content view:

```
- (IBAction)showMeasurements:(id)sender
{
    «beginning of method»

    [windowLocationTextField setStringValue:NSStringFromPoint(windowLocation)];
    [windowSizeTextField setStringValue:NSStringFromSize(windowSize)];
```

```
    NSRect viewFrame = [mainView frame];

    NSPoint viewLocation = viewFrame.origin;
    NSSize viewSize = viewFrame.size;

    [viewLocationTextField setStringValue:NSStringFromPoint(viewLocation)];
    [viewSizeTextField setStringValue:NSStringFromSize(viewSize)];
}
```

Build & Run the application, and click the button. As before, the size and location for the window change as the window is resized and moved; the size of the content view also changes, but the location of the content view remains set at {0,0}.

This is one of the greatest benefits of the view-subview hierarchy system. Each view in the hierarchy has its own coordinate space, with its origin at the bottom left.

A subview is positioned *relative to its superview's origin*. In the case of the content view, its origin is the bottom left of the window, that is, {0,0}. Notice that its width is the same as that of the window, because the content view is scaled to fill the entire window, but the height is less than the height of the window. Why? Because the window also has to display its title bar. The height of the content view is equal to the height of the window less the height of the title bar.

To test a different example, use Interface Builder to set the autosizing properties of the "View" NSBox so that it is anchored to the bottom left of its enclosing view. You'll need to turn off the top anchor, leaving just the left and bottom anchors enabled.

Then change the mainView outlet of the WVMeasurer object to point to that box rather than the window's content view, and Build & Run the application again. This time when you resize the window and click the button, you'll end up with something looking like Figure 12.8, on the next page.

In this particular case, the location of the box stays fixed at 141 points away from the left edge of the content view (i.e., the window's left edge) and 16 points away from the bottom edge. These coordinates are the coordinates of the box relative to the content view's origin, which is the bottom left of the window.

If you try changing the mainView outlet to point to one of the text fields, you'll find that the text field location is given relative to the NSBox item's origin.

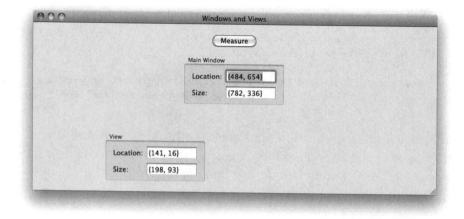

Figure 12.8: LOCATION OF THE BOX OBJECT

12.4 Custom Views

To get a better understanding of working with coordinate systems, we're going to write our own very simple custom view. We'll be subclassing NSView and seeing how to write code to draw various shapes in the interface for the Windows and Views application.

Let's start by adding a new class for our view, in Xcode. As before, right-click (or ^-click) the Classes group, and choose Add > New File...; if you are running Xcode 3.2, choose the Mac OS X Cocoa Objective-C class, and use the "Subclass of" drop-down menu to select NSView. If you are running Xcode 3.1, you'll need to look through the available project file templates to find the NSView Subclass.

Call the new class WVShapesView. We won't need any instance variables for this simple class, so ignore the WVShapesView.h file when Xcode has created it, and open the WVShapesView.m file. The template file includes two methods in the implementation:

```
@implementation WVShapesView

- (id)initWithFrame:(NSRect)frame {
    self = [super initWithFrame:frame];
    if (self) {
        // Initialization code here.
    }
    return self;
}
```

```
- (void)drawRect:(NSRect)dirtyRect {
    // Drawing code here.
}
```

@end

The first method, initWithFrame:, is the *designated initializer* for an NS-View object. If you were creating a view in code, you'd use this method to initialize an instance with a specific frame, before you added it into the view hierarchy. We'll be creating our instance using Interface Builder, so we won't get to call this method directly. And, since we haven't got any instance variables in our WVShapesView, we don't need to do any of our own initialization in this method, so leave it as it is in the template file.

The second method, drawRect:, is the method that will be called to tell our view that it needs to draw its contents. This is the method where we'll be doing all our work in this example.

The dirtyRect parameter[8] passed to drawRect: is used to specify which rectangular portion of the view needs to be redrawn. If we were writing a complicated 3D-drawing package, where it was expensive in terms of processor cycles and memory to recalculate and redraw the entire view all the time, we could use this parameter to decide which 3D objects needed to be redrawn and just recalculate and redraw those.

Our view will be using extremely simple drawing code, so we will just ignore the dirtyRect parameter and redraw the entire view whenever the method is called.

The first step to draw our view is to fill it with white and give it a thin black frame so that it feels like we have a blank canvas.

Remember how I said that each view maintains its own coordinate system? Well, this applies to our custom view as well. The coordinates of the bottom left of our blank canvas are {0, 0}. But how do we know how big the canvas is?

Frames and Bounds

Earlier in this chapter, we asked various objects for their frame; this returned us an NSRect structure with the relevant information. The difficulty here is that the frame method returns the NSRect values in the

---

8. Depending on the version of Xcode you're running, this parameter may be called rect rather than dirtyRect.

> ### When Does a View Need Only a Partial Redraw?
>
> You might be wondering why we might only need to redraw a small portion of a view, and there are several reasons:
>
> - The view might be resized. If it grows, the part that was already visible doesn't necessarily need to be redrawn, just the new view area.
>
> - You might specifically request a small portion of a view be redrawn. If you were writing a simple game application using a custom view, you might have a complicated fixed background with just a few moving objects. Rather than redrawing the entire view every time an object moves, you could instead choose just to redraw the area affected by the moving object by calling the method set-NeedsDisplayInRect:.

superview's coordinates. The window's frame was provided in coordinates relative to the bottom left of the screen, the window's content view frame was provided in coordinates relative to the bottom left of the window, the NSBox frame was provided relative to the content view, and so on.

Luckily for us, an NSView object also has a bounds property, which will again return an NSRect describing the frame of the view, but this time it will be relative to the view's own coordinate system.

That sorts out how we can get an NSRect describing the area to be filled, but how do we do the actual filling? Well, we use what's known as *Quartz* drawing code.

Quartz and C Functions

Quartz is a collection of code that's relatively old. Much of it is non-object-oriented and uses standard C rather than Objective-C. We've already seen some of its NSRect, NSPoint, and NSSize structures. We've also used some of its C functions, like NSStringFromPoint().

Up until this point in the book, we've glossed over what a *function* actually is, so it's worth taking a moment to explain. From our perspective, a function behaves just like an object's *method*, but it is called by itself, without using an object. A function doesn't share the nicety of Objective-C's method names to indicate what each argument does;

instead, the arguments are supplied, separated only by commas, inside parentheses tagged on the end of the function name.

In code terms, Objective-C methods and functions are related like this:

```
// Objective C method
[someObject doSomething:something withAnObject:anObject];
```

```
// C function
getSomeObjectToDoSomethingWithAnObject(someObject, something, anObject);
```

We've previously made use of the NSLog() function to output information to the Xcode console. The NSStringFromPoint() and NSStringFromSize() functions are used to return strings describing the contents of the provided point or size structure. When we're drawing with Quartz, we need to make use of a variety of other functions, which we'll cover as we use them.

Working with Colors

We know that we have to use bounds to get the view's rectangle, and we know that we have to deal with a few C functions to do our drawing; can we write our code now? We're nearly ready, but there's just one more thing we need to know. To do any drawing in a specific color, we need to *set* that color before we draw anything.

Drawing with Quartz is a bit like working with an eager and very obedient group of kindergarten children. You tell Quartz to use a color and then say what to draw, and it will carry on drawing everything you tell it in the same color until you give it another one.

Cocoa provides us with color *objects*, using the NSColor class. If you want to be able to pick any color, you can do so either by specifying a color using RGB values or by specifying a color using hues and saturations, and so on. If you take a look at the documentation for NSColor, however, you'll find it has some useful utility class methods that return certain named colors, like redColor or blueColor.

So, replace the // drawing code here comment in our view's drawRect: method with the following:

```
- (void)drawRect:(NSRect)dirtyRect {
    NSLog(@"drawRect: was called!");

    NSRect viewBounds = [self bounds];
    NSColor *currentColor = [NSColor whiteColor];
    [currentColor set];
    NSRectFill(viewBounds);
}
```

How Objective-C Translates into C

As with C structures and Objective-C objects, the way we've been looking at methods and functions is a little backward. If you ever decide to investigate how Objective-C adds its object-oriented additions to the C language, you'll find that the methods on an object end up being translated into plain C functions.

Whenever you use an Objective-C method, like this:

```
[someObject doSomething:something];
```

the code is translated into a call to a C function called objc_msgSend(). This function takes at least two arguments; the first argument refers to the "object" that will receive the message (which is really just a pointer to a plain *C* structure). The second argument is a *selector*, used to keep track of the name of the method called. The remaining arguments are the arguments that were originally provided to the method.

So the Objective-C method call shown earlier is equivalent to this:

```
objc_msgSend(someObject, @selector(doSomething:), something);
```

You can even rewrite method calls to use this syntax, if you feel so inclined, and everything will still work.

Don't worry if you can't follow all this now. You don't *need* to understand it unless you really want to delve into the inner workings of Objective-C.

We start with a call to NSLog() to let us know that the drawRect: method has been called. We then create an NSRect containing the bounds of the view. Next, we get hold of a color object, using the whiteColor class method provided by NSColor, and we use the set method on that color to specify that any drawing from now on should be done in white. Finally, we use a Quartz C method, NSRectFill(), to fill the rectangle.

Instantiating the View

To see whether this works, we need to add an instance of the view into MainMenu.xib, so open this file now in Interface Builder.

Rearrange the interface so that the existing NSBox objects and the Measure button are moved to the left of the existing window. Use the Size

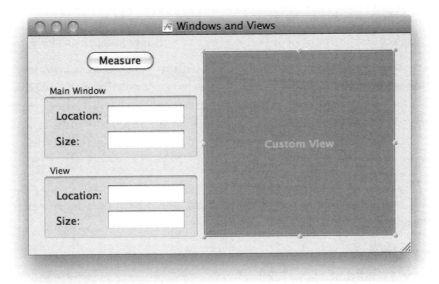

Figure 12.9: ADDING A CUSTOM VIEW TO THE WINDOWS AND VIEWS APPLICATION

inspector for the two boxes and the button to anchor them all to the top left of the containing view.

Next, drag out a Custom View from the Interface Builder Library palette, drop it into the space in the right of the window, and resize it to look like Figure 12.9.

Use the Identity inspector for this custom view object to change its class from NSView to WVShapesView. Then use the Size inspector to turn on every single anchor and resizing arrow in the Autosizing section. In the animating view, the red box should expand with its white container.

Save the file, and switch back to Xcode to Build & Run. You'll find that the custom view appears and is filled with white. If you resize the window, you'll find that the view expands. As you drag the resizing handle on the window, the view will keep receiving drawRect: calls until you release the mouse; this means that as you resize the window, the view will be continually redrawn.

Check the contents of Xcode's debugger console to see when the draw-Rect: method is triggered; this will be when the view is first displayed (at application launch) or if you resize the window (and thus the view).

Notice how drawRect: gets called continuously while the window is changing size. This is known as *live resizing*. If you have a view that's particularly expensive to redraw, you can check to see whether you are currently inLiveResize and perhaps just draw a simple box outline, waiting to do the complete redraw until the mouse is released and the view has finished changing size.

That's quite a lot of theory we have gone through just to display a blank white canvas; we're going to move forward much more quickly from now on.

Framing the View

Earlier, I said that we wanted to frame the view with a thin black line; let's do this next. We already have a suitable NSRect that we can use for the frame; we'll need to set the current color to blackColor and use another Quartz function NSFrameRect() to draw the line. Remove the NSLog() call, and add the following code to the drawRect: method:

```
- (void)drawRect:(NSRect)dirtyRect {
    NSRect viewBounds = [self bounds];
    NSColor *currentColor = [NSColor whiteColor];
    [currentColor set];
    NSRectFill(viewBounds);

    currentColor = [NSColor blackColor];
    [currentColor set];
    NSFrameRect(viewBounds);
}
```

Build & Run the application, and you'll see that our blank canvas now has a definite frame, as shown in Figure 12.10, on the next page.

Drawing a Square

Let's add a square to our custom view next. Since we are drawing using the local coordinates of our view, the bottom-left corner is the origin, {0,0}. We'll draw a square with bottom-left coordinates of {15,15} and give it a fixed height and width:

```
- (void)drawRect:(NSRect)dirtyRect {
    «beginning of method»
    [currentColor set];
    NSFrameRect(viewBounds);
```

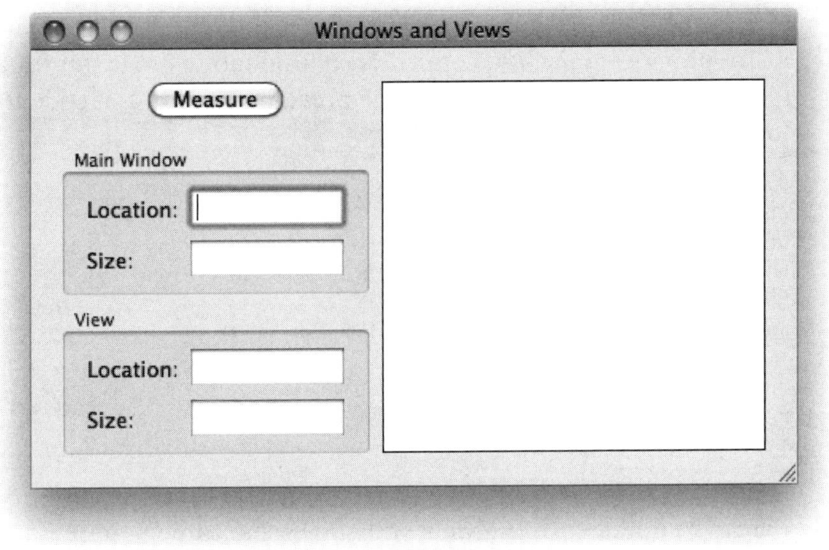

Figure 12.10: THE NEWLY FRAMED CUSTOM VIEW

```
    NSRect squareRect;
    squareRect.origin.x = 15;
    squareRect.origin.y = 15;
    squareRect.size.width = 150;
    squareRect.size.height = 150;

    currentColor = [NSColor lightGrayColor];
    [currentColor set];
    NSRectFill(squareRect);
}
```

Notice how we're using multiple dots to traverse the members of each structure; the x is a member of an NSPoint structure called origin, which is a member of the NSRect structure called squareRect.

Build & Run the application again, and you'll see that the new, gray square is drawn a little way up from the bottom left of the view and has a fixed height and width. If you resize the window, and therefore the view, the square stays fixed in size and remains in the same place relative to the bottom of the view as it's redrawn.

The code we're currently using to set up the NSRect for the square seems to have a lot of lines of code for something that's so straightforward. Quartz also provides us with a convenience function to create an NSRect given four CGFloat values, so replace the previous five lines of code that create and set the squareRect with this:

```
- (void)drawRect:(NSRect)dirtyRect {
    «beginning of method»
    [currentColor set];
    NSFrameRect(viewBounds);

    NSRect squareRect = NSMakeRect(15, 15, 150, 150);

    currentColor = [NSColor lightGrayColor];
    [currentColor set];
    NSRectFill(squareRect);
}
```

Build & Run to make sure the view still shows the same square.

What about changing the square into a rectangle with its size set relative to the bounds of the view? In other words, the rectangle should grow or shrink as the view grows or shrinks.

For this, we need to set the squareRect values to be the values of the viewBounds rect, with some adjustments.

We could use this code:

```
NSRect squareRect;
squareRect.origin.x = viewBounds.origin.x + 15.0;
squareRect.origin.y = viewBounds.origin.y + 15.0;
squareRect.size.width = viewBounds.size.width - 30.0;
squareRect.size.height = viewBounds.size.height - 30.0;
```

which would set the squareRect to be exactly 15 points less on each side than the viewBounds rectangle.

Again, though, there is a handy convenience Quartz function to *inset* one rectangle based on another, called NSInsetRect(). It returns an NSRect made from the provided rectangle but shrunk by a specified amount horizontally and vertically. Change the code to this:

```
- (void)drawRect:(NSRect)dirtyRect {
    «beginning of method»

    NSRect squareRect = NSInsetRect(viewBounds, 15, 15);

    «end of method»
}
```

Build & Run again to test. The gray rectangle is now exactly 15 points from each edge of the view; as you resize the window, and therefore the view, the rectangle appears to resize with it.

Drawing an Oval

It's about time we added a bit of color to our custom view, so let's draw an oval, filled with purple. There aren't any Quartz functions with names like NSOvalFill(), so we need to take a different approach. We still start off with a rectangle to contain the oval, which we'll generate using the same NSInsetRect() method as before, but we'll need to use a drawing *object*, called an NSBezierPath.

An NSBezierPath instance keeps track of one or more path components, ready for drawing on screen. If you've ever used a vector drawing application like Adobe Illustrator, you'll have worked with straight and curved lines that behave in a similar way to an NSBezierPath. We'll see how to work with the components of a path a little later in the chapter; for now, we'll use a class factory method provided by NSBezierPath that works out all the necessary path information for an oval contained within a specified rectangle.

Add the following code to the drawRect: method:

```
(void)drawRect:(NSRect)dirtyRect {
    «beginning of method»

    currentColor = [NSColor lightGrayColor];
    [currentColor set];
    NSRectFill(squareRect);

    NSRect ovalRect = NSInsetRect(squareRect, 40.0, 40.0);
    NSBezierPath *ovalPath = [NSBezierPath bezierPathWithOvalInRect:ovalRect];

    currentColor = [NSColor purpleColor];
    [currentColor set];
    [ovalPath fill];
}
```

First, we generate a rectangle by insetting the squareRect. We then request a Bezier path instance made by making an oval inside that rectangle. Finally, we set a stunning purple color and then *tell the path to fill itself*. The Bezier path object figures out what it has to do to draw itself on screen, so we don't have to worry about changing the color of individual pixels, or anything like that.

Build & Run the application to make sure it works.

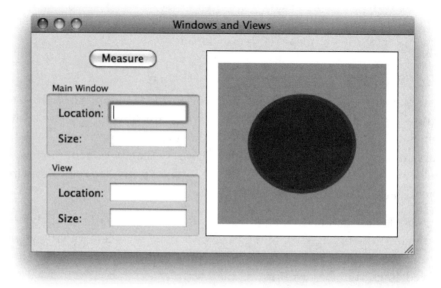

Figure 12.11: THE CUSTOM VIEW WITH A SQUARE AND OVAL

It might be nice to draw an outline around the oval rather than just having a solid fill, so we'll add what's called a *stroke*. We'll need to set a color, as usual, but we'll also need to set a line width for the stroke:

```
- (void)drawRect:(NSRect)dirtyRect {
    «beginning of method»

    [currentColor set];
    [ovalPath fill];

    currentColor = [NSColor darkGrayColor];
    [currentColor set];
    [ovalPath setLineWidth:5.0];
    [ovalPath stroke];
}
```

When you Build & Run, you'll find that the oval now has a dark gray line around it, 5 pixels in width, as shown in Figure 12.11.

Feel free to experiment with other shapes and colors by looking up the documentation for NSBezierPath and NSColor.

Figure 12.12: THE REVISED SHOPPING LIST APPLICATION

12.5 Back to the Shopping List Application

Now that we've seen how to work with simple drawing code, let's add a new feature to the Shopping List application. We're going to make it possible to mark an item in a shopping list as *purchased*; for any item that has been purchased, we'll display the name of the item as if it's been crossed off, as shown in Figure 12.12.

We need to take several steps here. First, we need to add a new property to the ShoppingListItem model object to indicate whether an item has been purchased. Next, we need to add another column to the interface, containing a checkbox to indicate the purchase. Finally, and most importantly for this chapter, we need to figure out how to draw the item name with a line through it.

Let's deal with the easy parts first.

Changing the Model

Close any windows currently open in Xcode and Interface Builder, and then open the Shopping List application project.

Find the ShoppingListItem.h file, and add a new property to indicate whether an item has been purchased. We'll need a BOOL instance variable, together with a property declaration for that variable.

Since a BOOL variable is a scalar, not an object, the property declaration should use the keyword assign:

```
@interface ShoppingListItem : NSObject {
    NSString *itemName;
    int quantity;
    BOOL purchased;
}

- (id)initWithName:(NSString *)newName quantity:(int)newQuantity;
+ (id)shoppingListItemWithName:(NSString *)newName quantity:(int)newQuantity;

@property (retain) NSString *itemName;
@property (assign) int quantity;
@property (assign) BOOL purchased;

@end
```

Switch to the ShoppingListItem.m implementation, and add a declaration to @synthesize the new property. Also use the init method to set the initial state of the purchased instance variable to NO:

```
@implementation ShoppingListItem

@synthesize quantity, itemName, purchased;

- (id)initWithName:(NSString *)newName quantity:(int)newQuantity
{
    if( self = [super init] )
    {
        itemName = [newName retain];
        quantity = newQuantity;
        purchased = NO;
    }

    return self;
}
«code continues»
```

Changing the Interface

Next, let's add the extra column into the shopping list table view.

Open MyDocument.xib in Interface Builder, and follow the instructions given earlier in Section 11.3, *Reworking the Shopping List Application*, on page 246 to add an extra column. Use the Attributes inspector to set the title of the column to "Purchased."

Unless you specify otherwise, the table column will use an NSTextFieldCell to display its content. We want to use a checkbox rather than a text field, so use the Library palette to find a Check Box Cell, which is an instance of NSButtonCell. Drag one of these out of the library and onto the new Purchased column; you'll find that the "Text Cell" is replaced by a box and the word "Check."

While the check box cell is still selected, use its Attributes inspector to set the Position value for the checkbox to the second option; that's the one with just a square but no line. You'll find that the cell in the column now shows only the checkbox without the word "Check."

To supply the table view with the relevant information for the new column, we need to add some extra code to the MyDocument object. We'll need an outlet for the new column, so switch back to Xcode and add one into MyDocument.h:

```
@interface MyDocument : NSDocument
{
    «other outlets»

    IBOutlet NSTableColumn *quantityColumn;
    IBOutlet NSTableColumn *itemNameColumn;
    IBOutlet NSTableColumn *purchasedColumn;

    NSMutableArray *shoppingListArray;
}

«methods»

@end
```

Switch straight back to Interface Builder, and connect this outlet to the new column.

We need to change the method that supplies the table view with values and the one that lets us know if the user changes a value in a column. Switch to Xcode, open the MyDocument.m file, and make the following changes:

```
- (id)tableView:(NSTableView *)aTableView
          objectValueForTableColumn:(NSTableColumn *)aTableColumn
                              row:(NSInteger)rowIndex
{
    ShoppingListItem *currentItem = [shoppingListArray objectAtIndex:rowIndex];

    if( aTableColumn == quantityColumn )
        return [NSNumber numberWithInt:[currentItem quantity]];
    else if( aTableColumn == itemNameColumn )
        return [currentItem itemName];
    else if( aTableColumn == purchasedColumn )
        return [NSNumber numberWithBool:[currentItem purchased]];
    else
        return nil;
}

- (void)tableView:(NSTableView *)aTableView
                    setObjectValue:(id)anObject
                    forTableColumn:(NSTableColumn *)aTableColumn
                              row:(NSInteger)rowIndex
{
    ShoppingListItem *currentItem = [shoppingListArray objectAtIndex:rowIndex];

    if( aTableColumn == quantityColumn ) {
        [currentItem setQuantity:[anObject intValue]];
    } else if( aTableColumn == itemNameColumn )
        [currentItem setItemName:anObject];
    else if( aTableColumn == purchasedColumn )
        [currentItem setPurchased:[anObject boolValue]];
}
```

As before, the methods need to work with an *object* value, so we have to use an NSNumber object to represent the BOOL, just like we used one to represent the integer quantity.

Build & Run the application to check that you can mark an item as purchased; you still won't be able to save shopping lists, though, so don't spend too long adding any items.

That's it for the simple modifications. Now all we need to do is figure out how to change the way we display the item name.

12.6 Views and Cells

In Section 11.2, *Retrieving Information from a Dictionary*, on page 243, we saw a brief indication that there was something other than an NSText-Field being used to display the text inside the field.

For various reasons, including the way the view hierarchy works and the fact that there are lots of coordinate transformations happening, views are reasonably expensive in terms of memory and processor cycles. This doesn't matter for an interface containing 20 or so views, but there are cases when it could be extremely problematic.

As you may have realized from our earlier modification of the Purchased table view column, table views use *cells* to display their contents. If every cell of every row in a table view was instead drawn using a *view*, it could very quickly become a problem if your table view had thousands of rows and several columns. Table views avoid this by keeping track of a *prototype cell* for each *column*; each column's contents are then drawn using the column's prototype cell.

Because there is so much shared functionality related to text display and editing between an NSTextField and a text cell in a table view, an NSTextField also uses a text field cell to handle all the text-related details rather than duplicating all the functionality itself. Most controls work in similar ways, keeping track of one or more cell objects.

In Section 12.3, *The View Hierarchy*, on page 285, we clicked the triangles next to various views to see their subviews, as shown in Figure 12.6, on page 286. The text fields and labels also had triangles, but if you happened to click to expand these controls, you'd find that you'd be shown their internal cell objects.

Given that we want to be able to show purchased items in our table view with a line through their name, we need to decide how best to proceed.

We could take several different paths:

- We could write a complete custom NSView subclass to display all the shopping list items; this would replace the existing NSTableView altogether, instead using custom code to draw the list, and each item in the list.

- We could leave the table view as is but write a completely custom NSCell subclass to draw just the shopping list item name, using code to handle drawing the string of text and drawing the crossed-out line if required. We'd also need to write code that handled editing the name of the item in the table view.

- We could leave the table view as is and still write a custom cell for our item name, but this time subclass NSTextFieldCell. We would inherit all the existing textual display abilities, as well as editing. The only thing we'd need to change would be some additional drawing of a line across the text, if it was required.

As you might be able to guess, the best option is to subclass NSTextField-Cell. When you're writing your own custom user interface items, it's always best to find the *most specific* object, with as much built-in functionality as possible so you don't have to reinvent the wheel.

Subclassing NSTableViewCell

As before, we need to decide on a suitable name for our new cell object. Since this is functionality that might be useful to a future application, let's use a more generic prefix for the class name, PP (for Pragmatic Programmers), and call it PPStrikeThroughCell.

Follow the usual class creation procedure to add a new class to the Shopping List project, for now using the NSObject template (which means that if you're using Xcode 3.2, you'll need to change the "Subclass of" drop-down menu back to NSObject) called PPStrikeThroughCell.

Change the PPStrikeThroughCell.h file so that the object inherits from NSTextFieldCell:

```
@interface PPStrikeThroughCell : NSTextFieldCell {

}

@end
```

Next we need to work out which method to override to do our custom drawing. Open the Xcode documentation for NSTextFieldCell to see what's available. The only methods that have anything to do with drawing seem to involve backgrounds, which isn't what we want. Scroll to the top of the documentation, and click the next item in the inheritance chain, NSActionCell.

An NSActionCell is a type of cell that can handle targets and actions, just like we've been using with buttons and text fields throughout our code in this book. It's actually the *cells* internal to these controls that have offered us that ability, rather than the controls themselves.

Again, there doesn't really appear to be anything useful to us in terms of drawing, so move on to the next class in the hierarchy, NSCell. There's quite a lot of functionality in an NSCell object, so scroll down until you find the heading "Drawing and Highlighting." There are two methods here that look hopeful, drawWithFrame:inView: and drawInteriorWith-Frame:inView:.

The drawWithFrame:inView: method is similar to the drawRect: method[9] that we used for our custom NSView. It draws the outside of the cell, that is, its "frame," and then calls the drawInteriorWithFrame:inView: method to draw the contents of the cell. Ah-ha! This drawInterior... method looks like the one we want.

We need to implement this method in our custom subclass. We will want to call the super implementation as well to draw the text; all we are worried about is drawing a line through the cell.

Open PPStrikeThroughCell.m, and start by writing the method just to call the overridden implementation:

```
@implementation PPStrikeThroughCell

- (void)drawInteriorWithFrame:(NSRect)cellFrame inView:(NSView *)controlView
{
    [super drawInteriorWithFrame:cellFrame inView:controlView];

    NSLog(@"Cell Frame is %@", NSStringFromRect(cellFrame));
}

@end
```

We've also put in a call to NSLog() to output a string from the cellFrame using another utility function, NSStringFromRect(). We'll see why this is useful in a minute.

To make sure the Item Name column in the Shopping List application interface uses our new cell, we need to make a simple change to MyDoc-ument.xib. Switch to Interface Builder, and use the list view mode to find the "Shopping List Items" table column. Click the triangle next to the column in the list view, and you'll see its internal Text Cell object. Click

---

9. Except that the drawRect: method provided by NSView takes a parameter indicating the rectangle to be displayed; these NSCell methods take a parameter indicating the entire rectangle for the cell.

this cell, and use the Identity inspector to change the class to our new PPStrikeThroughCell.

Save the file, switch back to Xcode, and open the Xcode debugger console (⇧-⌘-R). Build & Run the application. The shopping list should appear as normal, and you'll see something like this in the console:

```
Shopping List[3922:a0f] Cell Frame is {{129, 1}, {334, 17}}
Shopping List[3922:a0f] Cell Frame is {{129, 20}, {334, 17}}
Shopping List[3922:a0f] Cell Frame is {{129, 39}, {334, 17}}
```

The call to NSLog() shows us the cell frame for each of the three cells in the table view. If you click any of the rows, you'll find that more information appears in the console. We're only interested in the first three lines at the moment—the lines that relate to the initial drawing of our standard milk, eggs, and butter items.

The first pair of numbers from the cell frame represent its location; the second pair represents its size. The cell frame is just that, a *frame*, so the coordinates are relative to its enclosing view. A cell doesn't maintain its own local coordinate system, so any drawing that we do has to be given in coordinates relative to the frame of the cell.

Since we know the coordinates of the cell's frame, all we have to do is work out a midpoint in its height and draw a horizontal line from its left edge to its right edge.

Replace the NSLog() call with the following code:

```
- (void)drawInteriorWithFrame:(NSRect)cellFrame inView:(NSView *)controlView
{
    [super drawInteriorWithFrame:cellFrame inView:controlView];

    CGFloat middleY = cellFrame.origin.y + (cellFrame.size.height / 2);

    NSPoint leftPoint = NSMakePoint(cellFrame.origin.x, middleY);
    NSPoint rightPoint =
            NSMakePoint(cellFrame.origin.x + cellFrame.size.width, middleY);

    // draw the line here...
}
```

There's some reasonably simple math involved here. First, we work out the vertical middle of the cell by adding half the cell's height to its origin, storing the result in a CGFloat variable.

Next, we make two NSPoint objects to keep track of the start and end of the line; the start of the line is on the left edge of the cell frame, at the height held in our middleY variable. The end of the line is at the same height but on the *right* edge of the cell frame, calculated by adding the cell's width to its horizontal origin.

How do we draw a line? Well, we can use the NSBezierPath class we used earlier. Drawing lines with this class is a bit like working with those same, super-obedient kindergarten children as before, but this time they each have an Etch A Sketch set to a specific color.

You start by creating an empty Bezier path object, move to a point, then draw a line from that point to another point, and so on. Implement the rest of the method like this:

```
- (void)drawInteriorWithFrame:(NSRect)cellFrame inView:(NSView *)controlView
{
    [super drawInteriorWithFrame:cellFrame inView:controlView];

    CGFloat middleY = cellFrame.origin.y + (cellFrame.size.height / 2);

    NSPoint leftPoint = NSMakePoint(cellFrame.origin.x, middleY);
    NSPoint rightPoint =
            NSMakePoint(cellFrame.origin.x + cellFrame.size.width, middleY);

    NSBezierPath *straightLine = [NSBezierPath bezierPath];
    [straightLine moveToPoint:leftPoint];
    [straightLine lineToPoint:rightPoint];
    [[NSColor redColor] set];
    [straightLine stroke];
}
```

Build & Run the application, and you'll find that each cell is drawn with a red line from one side to the other, as shown in Figure 12.13, on the following page.

We're getting closer to what we need, but it would be nice if the crossing-out line only went across the word rather than across the whole cell.

There are several ways to accomplish this; the one we will use is to measure the size of the text being displayed and set the line length accordingly.

Measuring the Text

There are some useful additions available to the NSString class on the desktop, including a method called sizeWithAttributes:. This method takes a dictionary argument, describing information like the font and size of the text, and returns an NSSize structure indicating how big the string would be if it were drawn with those attributes.

Figure 12.13: The PPStrikeThroughCell with strikethrough lines

Since we are working with the cell used to display the item name, we can access the string for that item name by asking ourselves (well, the inherited NSCell) for our objectValue, which is the value that gets passed to the table view for this particular cell, i.e., an NSString containing the item name.

We can also find out the font used to display the text using NSCell's font method and put this in a dictionary using the key NSFontAttributeName, ready to pass to the sizeWithAttributes: method.

Change the method to this:

```
- (void)drawInteriorWithFrame:(NSRect)cellFrame inView:(NSView *)controlView
{
    [super drawInteriorWithFrame:cellFrame inView:controlView];

    CGFloat middleY = cellFrame.origin.y + (cellFrame.size.height / 2);

    NSString *displayedText = [self objectValue];
    NSDictionary *attributes = [NSDictionary
                                dictionaryWithObject:[self font]
                                forKey:NSFontAttributeName];
```

```
NSSize textSize = [displayedText sizeWithAttributes:attributes];
CGFloat lineLength = textSize.width;

NSPoint leftPoint = NSMakePoint(cellFrame.origin.x, middleY);
NSPoint rightPoint = NSMakePoint(cellFrame.origin.x + lineLength, middleY);

NSBezierPath *straightLine = [NSBezierPath bezierPath];
[straightLine moveToPoint:leftPoint];
[straightLine lineToPoint:rightPoint];
[[NSColor redColor] set];
[straightLine stroke];
}
```

Make sure you change the code that determines the position of the
rightPoint so that it uses this new lineLength variable.

Build & Run the application to see what happens. The line is now drawn
only across the displayed item name.

There are a couple of issues, though. First, the line doesn't quite extend
all the way across an item name, because it doesn't allow for the fact
that NSCell draws the string with a slight offset from the immediate left
edge of the cell. We can correct this easily enough by adding an extra 4
points to the length.

The second issue, which isn't immediately apparent, is that if you have
more text than will fit inside the cell, the line will be too long, extending
into the area used by other cells, which is a Very Bad Thing. To test this,
try changing one of the item names into a really long string, and then
drag the column header for the item name column so that it becomes
the first column in the table view. Make the column smaller by dragging
the resize line in the header between it and the next column.

You'll see something like Figure 12.14, on the next page.

We need to make sure that the line is either as long as the width of the
text, or the width of the cell, whichever is shorter.

Change the method to this:

```
- (void)drawInteriorWithFrame:(NSRect)cellFrame inView:(NSView *)controlView
{
    «beginning of method»
    NSDictionary *attributes = [NSDictionary
                                    dictionaryWithObject:[self font]
                                    forKey:NSFontAttributeName];
    NSSize textSize = [displayedText sizeWithAttributes:attributes];
    CGFloat lineLength = textSize.width + 4.0;
```

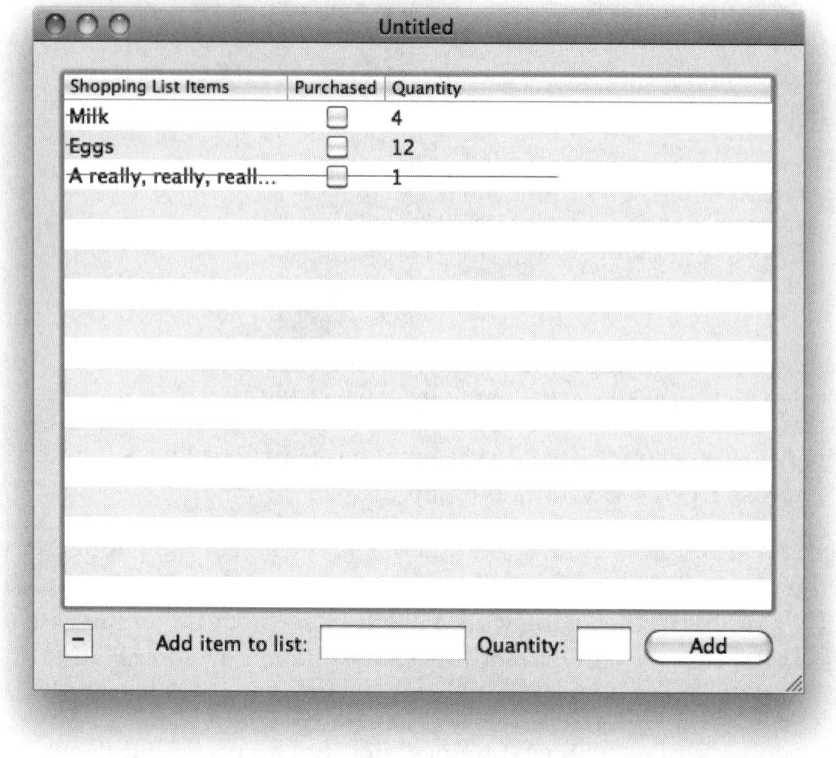

Figure 12.14: DRAWING OUTSIDE THE PROPER CELL AREA

```
if( lineLength > cellFrame.size.width )
    lineLength = cellFrame.size.width;

NSPoint leftPoint = NSMakePoint(cellFrame.origin.x, middleY);
NSPoint rightPoint = NSMakePoint(cellFrame.origin.x + lineLength, middleY);

«end of method»
}
```

Here we've added an extra 4 points to the end of the line so that it extends as much over the end of the text as it does at the beginning. We then check to see whether the line length is greater than the width of the cell and change the length if it is.

Build & Run again, and you'll find that we've solved the two earlier problems. Our cell is displaying perfectly.

Just One Small Problem

Yes, the cell is displaying perfectly, but there's one ever-so-slightly-important problem remaining. Every cell has a line through it, regardless of whether the item has been purchased.

That's a bit of a pain—all this work, and it's still not right? We need to figure out how to set the line on the cell to be shown *only* if an item is purchased. Should we in some way be trying to get two values out to this cell rather than just the string value for display? Perhaps we could package up an NSDictionary containing the item name string and a number object to say whether the item is purchased.

That would certainly work, but it takes us back to having a cell that's useful in only one situation. It would be better if we continue passing just a single string for display and instead find a way to set a flag on the cell each time it's displayed to say whether the line should be drawn.

This is actually pretty easy, but you need to learn about another Mac OS X and Cocoa concept called *delegation* before we can proceed. You'll be glad to hear that this is the first topic covered by the next chapter.

12.7 Chapter Summary

You now know all about how views fit into Cocoa and Mac OS X software. We've covered coordinate systems for displaying information on screen, in windows, and in views and we even created our own custom shape-drawing view to try some simple Quartz drawing.

You've seen how Interface Builder lets you set the autosizing properties on views and controls, defining how they resize or move when their containing view resizes or moves. You might like to test your understanding of these features by setting the autosizing properties on the Shopping List application interface items. The main table view needs every single anchor and sizing flag turned on; the controls along the bottom of the window need to be anchored to the bottom of the window. You might like to anchor the -- button so that it stays at the bottom left of the window and anchor all the other controls to the bottom right of the window.

We've also looked at the relationship between views and cells and seen how a view often uses at least one cell to handle common functionality. We added an extra feature to the Shopping List application, creating

our own custom cell and overriding the Cocoa class with the most functionality common to what we needed, the NSTextFieldCell.

As promised, the next chapter looks at delegation, which, as the name
implies, allows one object to delegate decisions to another object. We'll
also be looking at the Responder chain, seeing how Cocoa objects can
respond to user interaction, and covering various other important
mechanisms offered by Mac OS X and the Cocoa framework.

Chapter 13

Mac OS X and Cocoa Mechanisms

The Cocoa framework makes heavy use of common object-oriented design patterns. Over the previous two chapters, you learned about Model-View-Controller (MVC), describing the separation between model objects and the views that display information on screen. In this chapter, we'll look at some of the other patterns and mechanisms available to us, as well as the underlying Objective-C techniques used to implement these patterns.

It's impossible for an introductory book to cover every single design pattern used on the Mac platform—we simply don't have enough space. Instead, the main focus of this chapter is on some of the most important patterns used in Objective-C, Cocoa, and Mac OS X, including topics such as delegation, notifications, and responders, which allow objects to communicate with each other. We'll also be looking at events, seeing how applications respond to user input.

Although Objective-C objects can only *inherit* behavior from one super-object, Cocoa objects can declare that they will implement established methods, defined in *protocols*, ready to be used by other objects to carry out different tasks, such as filling out a table view, as we saw in Section 8.4, *Working with Table Views*, on page 167. Objective-C protocols form the basis for many of the patterns we'll be looking at, and we'll finish the chapter seeing how they are used to enable us to archive objects to disk and how to restore our Shopping List application's ability to save and open shopping list files.

We'll start this chapter by looking at simple *delegation*, where one object can ask another object to help make a decision or do something to change the default behavior.

13.1 Delegation

By the end of the previous chapter, we'd made a great table view cell that displayed its text contents with a line through the middle. The only problem was that this cell was used for every row in the table view, and the strikethrough line appeared whether we wanted it to or not.

In the Shopping List application, the strikethrough cell should display a line only if the item in the table view has been marked as purchased. In Section 12.6, *Just One Small Problem*, on page 313, I mentioned that we might be able to change the object that was passed to this table view column, instead passing a dictionary containing the item name together with a flag to indicate whether the line should be displayed.

Unfortunately, that solution makes the strikethrough cell less useful in the future. Anybody who wants to use the cell needs to know exactly which string *keys* to use for the objects in the dictionary before they can get the cell to display the information. It makes the cell more difficult to reuse.

It would be better to find a way to intercept the table view's behavior, jumping in when it's about to display a particular cell in a row and setting a flag *on the cell itself* to indicate whether the line should be drawn. This way, the cell continues to behave just like a standard NSTextFieldCell but can be told to draw the strikethrough line when required. Wouldn't it be nice if there was some way to do that without having to write a custom table view?

It just so happens that we can provide an NSTableView with a *delegate* object. This object will be sent various messages whenever the table view thinks it might need a second opinion. One of these messages will be sent just before the table view uses a cell to display the value for a particular column and row, which is exactly what we need.

To find out what method to implement, you need to learn how Objective-C uses *protocols* to define a list of messages that such a delegate object might implement.

Introducing Objective-C Protocols

When we wrote the table view data source methods, back in Section 8.4, *Implementing the Required Methods*, on page 167, we looked in the documentation for NSTableViewDataSource. This showed a list of messages used to provide information to a table view.

Let's see how these are defined in Objective-C terms. Open Xcode, and select File > Open Quickly… (⇧-⌘-D). Type in "NSTableView," and click the Open button to open NSTableView.h, the interface file for a Cocoa NSTableView. There's a lot of information in this file. If you scroll down about 70 lines, you'll find a standard @interface declaration for the NSTableView class itself, which looks like this:

```
@interface NSTableView : NSControl <NSUserInterfaceValidations, NSTextViewDelegate>
```

This is just like our normal @interface declarations but with some additional information between angle brackets. We'll see what this information means in a moment.

Keep scrolling through the list of methods for NSTableView,[1] until you find the lines of code that look like this:

```
@protocol NSTableViewDataSource <NSObject>
@optional

/* Required Methods
*/
- (NSInteger)numberOfRowsInTableView:(NSTableView *)tableView;
- (id)tableView:(NSTableView *)tableView
        objectValueForTableColumn:(NSTableColumn *)tableColumn row:(NSInteger)row;
«code continues»
```

This is the definition for a *protocol* called NSTableViewDataSource. A protocol is used to list the methods that can be overridden by an object wishing to *conform* to that protocol. The first two methods listed inside this protocol are the methods we use to provide information to the table view in the Shopping List application.

The general syntax to declare a protocol looks like this:

```
@protocol «protocol name»

«list of required methods»

@optional

«list of optional methods»

@end
```

---

1. Note that the method signatures have comments around them, between /* and */ tags. The interface files for Cocoa classes are often a useful place to look for further documentation.

Any methods listed *before* the @optional keyword are *required* methods. If a particular object states that it is going to conform to the protocol, it *must* implement these methods. Methods listed after the @optional keyword are, as you might have guessed, optional.

All the methods listed for the NSTableViewDataSource are listed after the @optional keyword, so, technically, you don't need to implement any of them. The comment in this file that indicates the first two methods are "Required Methods" is there just to say that for *most* data sources, you will need to include these two methods.[2] Try to ignore this comment, though, while we're learning about protocol syntax!

Conforming to a Protocol

If an object says it's going to *conform to a protocol*, it must implement any required methods and can implement as many optional methods as it likes. These methods can then be called, if they exist. How do we say that the object will conform to the protocol? That's where those angle brackets come in.

To say that an object conforms to a specific protocol, you put the name of the protocol inside angle brackets and tag it on the end of the @interface declaration, like this:

```
@interface MyObject : NSObject <MyProtocol>
```

This code defines a class, MyObject, which inherits from NSObject and conforms to the MyProtocol protocol.

Now we see why the @class declaration for NSTableView has those extra bits of information:

```
@interface NSTableView : NSControl <NSUserInterfaceValidations, NSTextViewDelegate>
```

NSTableView conforms to two protocols (separated by commas): NSUserInterfaceValidations and NSTextViewDelegate.

As you might already have realized, the NSTextViewDelegate protocol defines the methods for any object that wants to be the delegate to an NSTextView. Take a guess at what the protocol name is for an NSTableView delegate.... Yes, it's NSTableViewDelegate.

---

2. There are cases where a table view can be provided with information without using the basic data source methods, such as with *bindings*. You might still need to use the data source to work with drag and drop, though, so the data-providing methods can't be marked as required by the protocol syntax, or the compiler will complain if you don't implement them.

Scroll back up the NSTableView.h file, and you'll see the definition for this protocol. The first few lines look like this:

```
@protocol NSTableViewDelegate <NSControlTextEditingDelegate>
@optional

/* Allows the delegate to provide further setup for 'cell' in ... */

- (void)tableView:(NSTableView *)tableView willDisplayCell:(id)cell
        forTableColumn:(NSTableColumn *)tableColumn row:(NSInteger)row;
- (BOOL)tableView:(NSTableView *)tableView
        shouldEditTableColumn:(NSTableColumn *)tableColumn row:(NSInteger)row;
- (BOOL)selectionShouldChangeInTableView:(NSTableView *)tableView;
```

Notice that the NSTableViewDelegate protocol looks like it's set to conform to an NSControlTextEditingDelegate protocol. This just means that any object conforming to NSTableViewDelegate may also provide methods from the NSControlTextEditingDelegate protocol; it's the protocol equivalent of class inheritance.

All the methods in the NSTableViewDelegate protocol appear after the @optional keyword, so it's fine just to implement the ones we need.

Take a look at the first method listed:

```
- (void)tableView:(NSTableView *)tableView willDisplayCell:(id)cell
    forTableColumn:(NSTableColumn *)tableColumn row:(NSInteger)row;
```

That looks just like the method we need for our Shopping List table view. Open the Xcode Documentation window, and search for "NSTableViewDelegate" to make sure; as the name implies, the method will be called just before the table view displays each cell visible in the table view.

Conforming to the NSTableViewDelegate Protocol

Now that you know all about protocols, let's implement the table view delegate protocol in our Shopping List application's MyDocument object.

Open the Shopping List project in Xcode, and find the MyDocument.h file. We need to use the angle bracket syntax to indicate that we are conforming to the NSTableViewDelegate protocol. We are *already* implementing methods from the NSTableViewDataSource protocol, so let's do the right thing and indicate this as well.

Change the MyDocument.h interface declaration to this:

```
@interface MyDocument : NSDocument <NSTableViewDelegate, NSTableViewDataSource>
{
    «outlets and instance variables»
}

«action methods»

@end
```

Because we set our MyDocument object as the data source for the table view by linking the two objects together in Interface Builder, Xcode didn't know to issue a warning about not conforming to the proper protocol. If, instead, we'd set the data source programmatically, using the NSTableView method setDataSource:, Xcode would have issued this warning: class 'MyDocument' does not implement the 'NSTableViewDataSource' protocol.[3]

We'll use Interface Builder again to set the delegate, so open the MyDocument.xib file, and set the delegate for the table view to be File's Owner (i.e. the MyDocument object), just like you did the data source.

Switch back to Xcode, and let's implement the delegate method that we need. We'll just log a message to the Xcode console for now to let us know whenever it gets called. Open the MyDocument.m file, and add the method:

```
- (void)tableView:(NSTableView *)tableView willDisplayCell:(id)cell
            forTableColumn:(NSTableColumn *)tableColumn row:(NSInteger)row
{
    NSLog(@"willDisplayCell just got called!");
}
```

Make sure the Xcode console is visible (⇧-⌘-[R]), and Build & Run the project. You'll find that the message gets logged quite a few times. This delegate method will be called every time the table view is about to use a cell to display some information. Since an initial shopping list document contains three items over three rows, you'll see nine messages each time the entire table view is displayed. When I first run the application, I see eighteen messages in the console.

One of the arguments provided to this method is the cell that's about to be displayed. We can send a message to this cell object to change its

---

3. You may not see these sorts of warnings under Xcode 3.1.

appearance, but before we can do this for our custom cell, we need to add some functionality to the PPStrikeThroughCell object.

Setting Up the Custom Cell Object

Let's add a *property* to the cell that allows us to specify whether a line should be drawn. We need a simple BOOL instance variable, along with an assign property declaration. We can then check the value of this flag when drawing the cell's contents and skip the line drawing if necessary.

Change the PPStrikeThroughCell.h interface to the following:

```
@interface PPStrikeThroughCell : NSTextFieldCell {
    BOOL shouldDrawLine;
}

@property (assign) BOOL shouldDrawLine;

@end
```

You'll need to synthesize the new property at the top of the implementation and then check the value of this property inside the drawInterior-WithFrame: method. Make the following changes in PPStrikeThroughCell.m:

```
@implementation PPStrikeThroughCell
@synthesize shouldDrawLine;

- (void)drawInteriorWithFrame:(NSRect)cellFrame inView:(NSView *)controlView
{
    [super drawInteriorWithFrame:cellFrame inView:controlView];

    if( !self.shouldDrawLine ) return;

    CGFloat middleY = cellFrame.origin.y + (cellFrame.size.height / 2);

    NSString *displayedText = [self objectValue];
    «code continues»
```

Once we've called the inherited NSTextFieldCell behavior to draw the cell's string contents, we check to see whether we need to draw the line. If not, we **return** immediately, avoiding any of the work involved in calculating the coordinates, etc.

Using the Table View Delegate to Change the Cell

Now that we have behavior in the cell to specify whether the line gets drawn, we can reimplement the table view delegate method to take advantage of it.

- Since the delegate method will be called for every cell visible in the table view, we start by checking to see whether the table column argument matches the column containing the custom cell. If not, we can return immediately.

- Next, we use the provided row argument to fetch the relevant shopping list item from the main array. We can then set the flag on the cell to specify whether the line should be drawn.

Open the MyDocument.m file, and change the delegate method to this:

```
- (void)tableView:(NSTableView *)tableView willDisplayCell:(id)cell
            forTableColumn:(NSTableColumn *)tableColumn row:(NSInteger)row
{
    if( tableColumn != itemNameColumn ) return;

    ShoppingListItem *currentItem = [shoppingListArray objectAtIndex:row];
    if( [currentItem purchased] )
        [cell setShouldDrawLine:YES];
    else
        [cell setShouldDrawLine:NO];
}
```

You'll also need to #import the PPStrikeThroughCell.h file at the top of My-Document.m to avoid a warning about the setShouldDrawLine: method being "unknown."

Build & Run the application, and you'll find that at first launch, none of the items has red lines through them. So far, so good! Click a checkbox on an item to mark it as purchased; the line doesn't appear. Huh?

Before panicking, let's try marking another item as purchased. The second item doesn't get a line, but the first one does. Try deselecting any objects by clicking an empty row. Ah! The line now appears for the second item.

What's happening is that our custom cell isn't being used to *redraw* the item name with or without its line when the purchased checkbox is selected. It's only when you force the cell to redraw, either by clicking another cell to remove the highlight from the first cell or by deselecting all the cells, that the line appears. What we need to do is to get the table view to reload the item name cell when a purchased checkbox is turned on or off.

Reloading the Table View

We can accomplish this task in several ways. The easiest way is just to reload the entire table view when a value in the purchased checkbox column is changed.

The method that gets called whenever the purchased checkbox is selected is the tableView:setObjectValue:forTableColumn:row: data source method. Change this method to the following:

```
- (void)tableView:(NSTableView *)aTableView setObjectValue:(id)anObject
        forTableColumn:(NSTableColumn *)aTableColumn row:(NSInteger)rowIndex
{
    ShoppingListItem *currentItem = [shoppingListArray objectAtIndex:rowIndex];

    if( aTableColumn == quantityColumn )
        [currentItem setQuantity:[anObject intValue]];
    else if( aTableColumn == itemNameColumn )
        [currentItem setItemName:anObject];
    else if( aTableColumn == purchasedColumn ) {
        [currentItem setPurchased:[anObject boolValue]];
        [shoppingListTableView reloadData];
    }
}
```

Build & Run the application to see whether this has solved the problem. You'll find that it has, and the line is drawn at the right time.

However, it's pretty expensive to redraw the entire table view just to redisplay a single cell. For a small shopping list of items, it won't matter much, but if users have particularly long shopping lists, they might start to see some sluggish performance.

The solution is to figure out the row and column for the cell that needs to be redrawn and tell the table view just to reload that cell. This isn't quite as easy as it sounds, but it's still a good idea from a performance perspective, so let's persevere.

Take a look at the documentation for NSTableView. Under the "Loading Data" heading, you will find both the reloadData method that we've been using up until now and another method, reloadDataForRowIndexes: columnIndexes:.

This second method takes two arguments, both of which are NSIndexSet objects. As the name implies, an NSIndexSet object collects a set of indices. To use this method to reload a specific cell, we need to create an index set for the row index and another index set for the column index.

The data source method from which we'll be creating these index sets provides us with the index of the current row, but it just passes in a pointer to a table column object, rather than the index of that column. The column being passed will also be the Purchased column; we need the index of the Item Name column.

The index of a column indicates which column it is in a table view from left to right. If you've followed the interface screenshots in the book up to this point, you may remember that the Item Name column is the third column from the left, meaning it has a zero-based index of 2. Can we just use this as the index?

Sadly, no. Unless we specify otherwise, the columns in a table view can be reordered by the user, as we saw at the end of Section 12.6, *Subclassing NSTableViewCell*, on page 306. Nifty behavior, but it complicates matters a bit!

We could disable the column-moving behavior by setting the table view's Reordering flag for its columns, but it seems a shame. There must be another way.

Look back at the documentation for NSTableView; it provides access to an array of its columns via the tableColumns method. The order in the array will match the order of the columns in the table view at run-time; we can ask this array for the index of the relevant table column object (the item name column), and . . . hooray! We now have everything we need.

Reimplement the data source method like this:

```
- (void)tableView:(NSTableView *)aTableView setObjectValue:(id)anObject
        forTableColumn:(NSTableColumn *)aTableColumn row:(NSInteger)rowIndex
{
    ShoppingListItem *currentItem = [shoppingListArray objectAtIndex:rowIndex];

    if( aTableColumn == quantityColumn )
        [currentItem setQuantity:[anObject intValue]];
    else if( aTableColumn == itemNameColumn )
        [currentItem setItemName:anObject];
    else if( aTableColumn == purchasedColumn ) {
        [currentItem setPurchased:[anObject boolValue]];

        NSIndexSet *rowIndexSet = [NSIndexSet indexSetWithIndex:rowIndex];

        NSArray *columnsArray = [shoppingListTableView tableColumns];
        NSInteger columnIndex = [columnsArray indexOfObject:itemNameColumn];
```

```
    NSIndexSet *columnIndexSet = [NSIndexSet indexSetWithIndex:columnIndex];

    [shoppingListTableView reloadDataForRowIndexes:rowIndexSet
                                    columnIndexes:columnIndexSet];
    }
}
```

Note that we use an NSInteger to hold the columnIndex in order to match the NSInteger argument type for the rowIndex. An NSInteger is another Apple-defined scalar variable type, like the CGFloat we saw in the previous chapter. You can think of it as being a bit like a basic int variable, but as with a CGFloat, the C variable type used to hold its value is something else.[4]

Build & Run the application to check that the purchased lines still appear correctly, but only when an item is marked as purchased.

Other Important Types of Delegate

So far, we've only looked at NSTableViewDelegate. Lots of objects in the Cocoa framework make use of delegates, and it's worth taking a moment to point out some of the most important ones.

The Application Delegate

Back in Section 12.2, *Working with Windows and Views*, on page 277, I mentioned that Xcode 3.2 automatically includes what's called an *application delegate* object in non-document-based applications. If you're running Snow Leopard and Xcode 3.2, open the Windows and Views project from the previous chapter, and take a look at the autogenerated Windows_and_ViewsAppDelegate.h and .m files.

The interface for the object looks like this:

```
@interface Windows_and_ViewsAppDelegate : NSObject <NSApplicationDelegate> {
    NSWindow *window;
}

@property (assign) IBOutlet NSWindow *window;

@end
```

---

4. And, again, it varies depending on whether you are running under 32-bit or 64-bit.

Properties for IBOutlets _____

Notice how the code for the Windows_and_ViewsAppDelegate also defines an **IBOutlet** for the application's main window and declares this as a _property_.

If you declare properties for your own outlets, you should put the **IBOutlet** keyword in the _property_ declaration, rather than the _instance variable_ declaration, because it's technically possible to specify a different property name from the instance variable name.

Using a different name for instance variables is a great way to avoid confusion when you have code featuring instance variables, locally declared variables, and property declarations. Keeping track of which variable is an instance variable and which is locally declared is easier if you choose to name your instance variables with an underscore (_) at the front, such as _window. This means you then have a window property and a _window instance variable.

The main reason for using properties for **IBOutlet**s is that the properties are the public connections from the object to the outside world, i.e., the interface items in the nib. Connecting interface items _directly_ to instance variables, rather than through properties, breaks the whole encapsulation of the object.

It specifies that this object conforms to the NSApplicationDelegate protocol. The implementation for the application delegate looks like this:

```
@implementation Windows_and_ViewsAppDelegate

@synthesize window;

- (void)applicationDidFinishLaunching:(NSNotification *)aNotification {
    // Insert code here to initialize your application
}

@end
```

As the name implies, the applicationDidFinishLaunching: method will be called once the application has launched successfully. Other useful application delegate methods include applicationShouldTerminateAfterLast-WindowClosed: (if you return YES for this, the application will automatically quit once the user closes the last open window) and applica-

Initializing Objects

It's important to mention that an object's init method should be used only for very basic initialization of an object's instance variables.

If you need to do additional setup work when an object is created, there are a number of options.

An application delegate can use methods like applicationWillFinishLaunching: if it needs to perform any initial setup at application launch, such as opening reference files, establishing network connections, or displaying multiple application windows.

If you're working with interface items that are loaded from a nib file, you won't be able to do any interface modifications in init because the rest of the objects in the nib may not have loaded completely at the time init is called. Instead, you should do setup work either in a suitable delegate method or in an awakeFromNib method. The awakeFromNib method is called on every object once it has been instantiated from a nib file.

tionWillFinishLaunching:. This method is similar to the applicationDidFinishLaunching: method but gets called just before the launch finishes. You can use this to do any initial interface setup.

Window Delegates

NSWindow has a number of useful delegate methods, like windowShouldClose:, which asks whether a particular window should be closed if the user tries to close it.

Let's make some modifications to the Windows and Views application from the previous chapter to test some of these window delegate methods.

Open the Windows and Views project in Xcode, and find the WVMeasurer.h file. We'll be setting our existing measurer instance to be the delegate of the application's main window, so let's indicate that the WVMeasurer class will adopt the NSWindowDelegate protocol.

Figure 13.1: SETTING THE WINDOW DELEGATE

```
@interface WVMeasurer : NSObject <NSWindowDelegate> {
    «instance variables»
}

- (IBAction)showMeasurements:(id)sender;

@end
```

Next, open the MainMenu.xib file in Interface Builder, and right-click (or ^-click) the Window object in the xib file. Drag to set the delegate of the window to be the Measurer object, as shown in Figure 13.1.

In the previous chapter, you saw how Interface Builder makes it easy to set minimum and maximum size constraints on a window. Sometimes, though, you might need a little more control.

If you were writing a video-display application, for example, like Apple's DVD Player, you might want to be able to constrain the proportions of the window to a specific aspect ratio, such as 4:3 or 16:9. Interface Builder doesn't offer a "width:height ratio" box, so you'd have to find another way.

Save the MainMenu.xib file, and return to Xcode. Search the Developer Documentation for "NSWindowDelegate" to see if there are any delegate methods that might help in this situation. There are six methods under the "Sizing Windows" heading:

```
- windowWillUseStandardFrame:defaultFrame:
- windowShouldZoom:toFrame:
- windowWillResize:toSize:
- windowDidResize:
- windowWillStartLiveResize:
- windowDidEndLiveResize:
```

Notice how there are naming conventions both in these six methods and throughout the other methods in the documentation? A method called just before something will happen takes the form windowWill..., and a method called just after something has happened uses windowDid.... If a decision is to be made about whether something should be allowed to happen, the method will be called windowShould.... These conventions exist throughout Apple's delegate protocols; when you're writing your own, it's a good idea to follow them.

Click the windowWillResize:toSize: method in the "Sizing Windows" section to jump down to its documentation.

This method is called just before a window is resized to a new size and includes a frameSize argument specifying that new size. What's particularly helpful about this method is that it also needs an NSSize return value, meaning that you can either return the proposed frameSize or specify your own.

Let's use this method to constrain the window's size such that its width must be twice its height, a simple ratio of 1:2.

Copy the method signature to the clipboard, and implement it in WV-Measurer.m, like this:

```
- (NSSize)windowWillResize:(NSWindow *)sender toSize:(NSSize)frameSize
{
    frameSize.width = (frameSize.height * 2);

    return frameSize;
}
```

Build & Run to test the application, and you'll find that when you try to resize the window, it is constrained with the 1:2 ratio.

Note that there is still a minimum size for the window, but because of the simple calculation used, this size is smaller than the minimum size specified in Interface Builder. Any constraints that we set for minimum or maximum size will be applied to a proposed size *before* the windowWill-Resize:toSize: method is called, so if we change the proposed frameSize, it's easy to end up with a window smaller than the specified minimum size. For our simple Windows and Views application, this doesn't matter.

At the moment, the user has to click the Measure button in the interface in order to display the calculated information. It would be nice if this information was automatically updated when the window was resized.

We could add a line to the windowWillResize:toSize: method that calls the showMeasurements: action method, but this isn't the correct place to do it. As we've already said, this method is called just *before* the window is resized; we want to display the measurements *after* the resize has happened.

Looking back at the list of window delegate methods, there's a window-DidResize: method that looks like it might be helpful. Checking the documentation for this method, it's exactly what we need. Copy the method signature to the clipboard, paste it into WVMeasurer.m, and implement it to call the showMeasurements: method. Since the showMeasurements: method is an **IBAction** method, it expects an argument to indicate which object triggered the action. Specify nil for now:

```
- (void)windowDidResize:(NSNotification *)notification
{
    [self showMeasurements:nil];
}
```

Build & Run the application; whenever you resize the window, the location and size information is automatically updated.

It seems like we've accomplished what we wanted; the only downside is that we specified nil when calling the showMeasurements: method. As you've seen earlier in the book, it's often helpful to know exactly which object triggered an **IBAction**, so let's see whether we can find out the relevant window object to specify as the sender of the action.

Often, delegate method signatures include an argument to specify the relevant object. The first argument provided in windowWillResize:toSize:, for example, is a pointer to the window object in question.

In the documentation for NSWindowDelegate, we can see two main types of delegate method. The first type includes a specific argument for the window, like this:

```
- (NSSize)windowWillResize:(NSWindow *)sender toSize:(NSSize)frameSize;
- (id)windowWillReturnFieldEditor:(NSWindow *)sender toObject:(id)client;
- (NSUndoManager *)windowWillReturnUndoManager:(NSWindow *)window;
```

The other type of method includes only one argument, an NSNotification, like this:

```
- (void)windowDidResize:(NSNotification *)notification;
- (void)windowWillMove:(NSNotification *)notification;
- (void)windowDidEndLiveResize:(NSNotification *)notification;
```

In the documentation for any of the methods with an NSNotification argument, we'll find that it states, "you can retrieve the window object in question by sending object to *notification*."

That solves the immediate problem of specifying the object that triggered the action when calling the showMeasurements: method. Change the windowDidResize: method to this:

```
- (void)windowDidResize:(NSNotification *)notification
{
    [self showMeasurements:[notification object]];
}
```

Before we test the application, let's add a line of code to the showMeasurements: method to inspect the sender:

```
- (IBAction)showMeasurements:(id)sender
{
    NSLog(@"Sender was: %@", sender);

    NSRect windowFrame = [applicationWindow frame];

    «method continues»
}
```

Build & Run the application, click the Measure button, and then resize the window. Looking in the console log, you can see a series of messages like this:

```
Windows and Views[2102:a0f] Sender was: <NSButton: 0x10012e600>
Windows and Views[2102:a0f] Sender was: <NSWindow: 0x100413090>
Windows and Views[2102:a0f] Sender was: <NSWindow: 0x100413090>
```

We now know how to extract the relevant object from an NSNotification, but this raises the question as to what these notifications are all about.

13.2 Notifications

Over the course of this book, we've seen a number of different ways to pass messages between objects. In straightforward code, one object can send a message to itself, or another object, like this:

```
[self doSomething];
[someObject doSomethingElse];
```

We've also seen how the target-action mechanism enables one object to be set as the target of another, with a specific action to be triggered. In the Windows and Views application, the Measure button is set to target a WVMeasurer instance, sending it the showMeasurements: message when the button is pressed.

It's fairly obvious that in order for one object to communicate with another object, the first object needs to keep hold of a pointer to the second object. You might have an **IBOutlet** in an interface in order to communicate with a text view, as in our TextApp application, or set one object as the delegate of another.

This is all very well for closely connected objects, but sometimes an object might want to send a message that could be received by multiple objects and not be concerned about who receives that message.

Consider an application in which multiple objects need to react when something happens, such as a window resizing on screen. A window has only a single delegate, so to send one message to multiple recipients, it might seem like we'd have to do something terribly complicated in the delegate method we implemented earlier, perhaps keeping hold of an array of interested objects and passing on the message to each one.

In fact, we have access to a great mechanism for exactly this type of situation under Mac OS X using a system of *notifications*.

Distributing Information

Working with notifications is a bit like working with a mailing list. A list administrator keeps track of the addresses of people who have expressed interest in receiving certain information; whenever new information is produced, it's sent out to all the interested parties.

On Mac OS X, the list administrator is an instance of NSNotificationCenter, an object that keeps track of other objects who have specifically registered to receive certain types of information. These receiving objects are known as *observers* and, when they register, can specify exactly what they want to know about.

If we were signing up to a charity's mailing list in the real world, we might be given the option to specify whether we wanted to receive information about fundraising events, merchandise, financial statements, or all of the above. In the world of NSNotificationCenter, an object can choose not only to register for specific *types* of information but also specify that it only wants to receive information originating from a specific sender *object*.

The NSNotification Object

Before we delve any further into notification centers and observers, let's examine an actual NSNotification object to see what it contains.

Start by removing the NSLog() call from the showMeasurements: method, and then add a new log statement to the windowDidResize: method:

```
- (void)windowDidResize:(NSNotification *)notification
{
    NSLog(@"Notification: %@", notification);
    [self showMeasurements:[notification object]];
}
```

Build & Run the application, and resize the window. You get a series of statements in the Xcode console that looks like this:

```
Windows and Views[2430:a0f] Notification: NSConcreteNotification 0x10014cb80
    {name = NSWindowDidResizeNotification; object = <NSWindow: 0x10021e4a0>}
Windows and Views[2430:a0f] Notification: NSConcreteNotification 0x100131630
    {name = NSWindowDidResizeNotification; object = <NSWindow: 0x10021e4a0>}
```

Each notification object you're sent appears to be an instance of NSConcreteNotification,[5] with two important pieces of information:

- A **name**, used as a unique identifier for this particular type of notification.

- An **object**, used to refer to the object that sent the notification. As we've already seen, in this case, it's the window itself.

---

5. Ignore the Concrete part of the classname; this is just the internal object type used when a notification is sent out. Treat it as if it were an NSNotification.

If you open the documentation for NSWindow and scroll right to the bottom, you find a list of notifications sent out by NSWindow. Among these is the NSWindowDidResizeNotification that you've just seen, along with a number of others, all following the same naming convention:

«*ClassName*»«*Will/Did*»«*Action*»Notification

Notice that each of these notifications has a corresponding method in the NSWindowDelegate protocol. These methods will be called automatically on the delegate when notifications are sent out, but it's also possible for an object *other than the delegate* to register to receive them.

To see what this means, start by opening MainMenu.xib in Interface Builder and then disconnecting the window's delegate outlet by right-clicking (or ^-clicking) the Window object and pressing the little x button next to the delegate outlet.

Save the file, and return to Xcode. Build & Run the application to check that the windowDidResize: method is no longer being called: the interface won't update to show the new measurements when the window is resized.

Registering to Receive a Notification

To register for a notification, we need to talk to the relevant notification center. Although it's possible to create our own notification center when we start posting our own notifications, we'll normally be dealing with just one center, already in existence, that's used by most Cocoa classes to post their notifications. We access this system center using a handy class method, defaultCenter, provided by NSNotificationCenter.

Once we've got hold of a notification center, we can register to receive notifications in various ways. The most common is to use a method with the following signature:

```
- (void)addObserver:(id)notificationObserver selector:(SEL)notificationSelector
              name:(NSString *)notificationName object:(id)notificationSender
```

Although it looks a bit scary, this method isn't all that complicated. Let's look at each of the method arguments in order:

- The first argument, notificationObserver, is used to specify the object that needs to receive notifications.

- The second argument, notificationSelector, is used to refer to a method that should be called on the receiving object in response to the notification.

- The third argument, notificationName, specifies which type of notification we want to receive.

  If we specify nil, we'll receive all notifications sent out by the specified sender.

- The final argument, notificationSender, specifies the object that we want to observe for notifications.

  If we specify nil, we'll receive all notifications with the specified name.

We want to register our WVMeasurer object to receive any NSWindowDidResize notifications sent out by the application's main window, and we'll need to specify the name of a method to be called.

This method must have a very specific signature:

```
- (void)«methodName»:(NSNotification *)notification;
```

Look familiar? We already have a method matching exactly this signature, which we wrote as our NSWindowDelegate method:

```
- (void)windowDidResize:(NSNotification *)notification;
```

We could call our method anything that we wanted, but this name seems pretty suitable, so let's keep it.

Now that we have everything we need to register for the notification, we need to decide *when* to register. As described by the sidebar on page 327, the best time to do this for our WVMeasurer instance is when it is instantiated from the MainMenu.xib file. So, let's write an awakeFromNib method, like this:

```
- (void)awakeFromNib
{
    NSNotificationCenter *center = [NSNotificationCenter defaultCenter];

    [center addObserver:self
               selector:@selector(windowDidResize:)
                   name:NSWindowDidResizeNotification
                 object:applicationWindow];
}
```

We start by getting a reference to the system notification center, and then we add ourselves as an observer for an NSWindowDidResize notification sent out by the applicationWindow (an outlet we set in the previous chapter) and use an **@selector()** call to refer to the method that should be called. Note that the method name is very important—as the method has a single argument, its name has a trailing colon. If we don't include this colon, we're effectively referring to a different method altogether, and our application will crash because the method doesn't exist.

Build & Run the application, and then try resizing the window. As before, we find that the interface is updated with the relevant sizing information whenever the window resizes.

This might seem like a lot of work just to accomplish the same thing as we had back when we were the window's delegate, but bear in mind that we could register as many objects as we like to respond to the resize notification. We're not limited by needing to be the window's delegate, and the window itself doesn't need to have any knowledge whatsoever about which objects will receive its notifications. All the message distribution is handled by the notification center.

Just as a quick demonstration, let's register our WVMeasurer object to receive *any* notification sent out by *any* object in our application; let's add a new method (following the correct signature) just to log the notification to the console:

```
- (void)awakeFromNib
{
    NSNotificationCenter *center = [NSNotificationCenter defaultCenter];

    [center addObserver:self
            selector:@selector(windowDidResize:)
                name:NSWindowDidResizeNotification
              object:applicationWindow];

    [center addObserver:self
            selector:@selector(receivedNotification:)
                name:nil
              object:nil];
}

- (void)receivedNotification:(NSNotification *)notification
{
    NSLog(@"Notification: %@", notification);
}
```

As described earlier, if we specify nil for the name of the notification but provide an object to observe, we'll be sent all notifications sent out by that object. Similarly, if we specify nil for the object but provide a notification name, we'll be sent notifications with that name sent out by *any* object.

If we don't specify a name *or* an object, we receive *everything*. Typically, you won't want to do this very often, but it's useful just to take a quick peek into what's happening behind the scenes.

Build & Run the application, and take a look at the console log in Xcode; there are an enormous number of messages flying around, which give a sense of what's possible as far as system notifications are concerned.

Remove this extra code (shown in bold in the earlier code) before continuing.

Sending Notifications

Now that we've seen how to receive notifications, let's look at how to send them. We'll change the target-action link between the button in the Windows and Views application so that it posts a notification whenever the Measure button is clicked.

We will then write a method to receive the notification and do the measurement-showing functionality.

Start by moving the lines of code from the showMeasurements: method into a new notification method, handleShowMeasurements::

```
- (void)handleShowMeasurements:(NSNotification *)notification
{
    NSRect windowFrame = [applicationWindow frame];

    NSPoint windowLocation = windowFrame.origin;
    NSSize windowSize = windowFrame.size;

    [windowLocationTextField setStringValue:NSStringFromPoint(windowLocation)];
    [windowSizeTextField setStringValue:NSStringFromSize(windowSize)];

    NSRect viewFrame = [mainView frame];

    NSPoint viewLocation = viewFrame.origin;
    NSSize viewSize = viewFrame.size;

    [viewLocationTextField setStringValue:NSStringFromPoint(viewLocation)];
    [viewSizeTextField setStringValue:NSStringFromSize(viewSize)];
}

- (IBAction)showMeasurements:(id)sender
{

}
```

We'll use the showMeasurements: method (that's the method specified as the action to be called when the button is clicked) to post a notification.

In the documentation for NSNotificationCenter, three methods are listed that relate to posting notifications:

```
- postNotification:
- postNotificationName:object:
- postNotificationName:object:userInfo:
```

The second method is the simplest for our purposes; it requires that we provide a notification name and an object to specify as the sender.

We need to define a name for our new notification, so let's use "WVMeasurerShowMeasurementsNotification."

Add the following code to the showMeasurements: method:

```
- (IBAction)showMeasurements:(id)sender
{
    NSNotificationCenter *center = [NSNotificationCenter defaultCenter];

    [center postNotificationName:@"WVMeasurerShowMeasurementsNotification"
                          object:self];
}
```

If you test the application at this point, nothing seems to happen when you click the Measure button. We haven't yet registered the WVMeasurer to receive our new notification.

Before we add the necessary registration code, it's worth pointing out that when we registered for the NSWindowDidResizeNotification earlier, we were able to type this notification name directly, rather than specifying the name as a string, like @"NSWindowDidResizeNotification".

As I mentioned in Section 11.3, *The Problem with Keys*, on page 256, it's very easy to mistype a string such as @"NSWindowDidResizeNotification", causing an error that won't be picked up by the compiler. One way to avoid this is to declare a *global* string *variable*; you can then use this variable in place of the @"string" notation, and the compiler will complain if it comes across a variable name it doesn't recognize.

This is exactly what Apple provides us for the NSWindowDidResizeNotification; they've defined a global variable to save us the possible problems of mistyping @"NSWindowDidResizeNotification".

Let's create our own global string variable for the new notification name.

Declaring Global Variables

As the name implies, a *global* variable is a variable accessible throughout the code in a project. It isn't held within an object instance; it exists in its own right from launch until termination.

To declare a global variable, we need to write the declaration outside any @implementation blocks in Objective-C class files. Typically, global variables are declared at the top of a file, just under any #import statements.

Scroll up to the top of the WVMeasurer.m file, and add the following:

```
#import "WVMeasurer.h"

NSString *WVMeasurerShowMeasurementsNotification =
                    @"WVMeasurerShowMeasurementsNotification";


@implementation WVMeasurer
«implementation continues»
```

This code declares the variable globally, but there's still one slight problem: because it's a global *vari*able, its value could change in the future, which could cause even more problems than just mistyping @"string".

Luckily, the C language provides us with a keyword to make sure that the value of a variable can never be changed, **const**.

Change the global variable declaration to this:

```
NSString * const WVMeasurerShowMeasurementsNotification =
                    @"WVMeasurerShowMeasurementsNotification";
```

It's essential we put the const keyword in the right place; it needs to specify that the WVMeasurerShowMeasurementsNotification pointer cannot be changed to point to any other string. Since the @"string" notation indicates an immutable (unchangeable) string, this guarantees that WVMeasurerShowMeasurementsNotification will always have the correct string value. If we were to try to change the value of this variable, the compiler would complain and refuse to build the project.

Change the showMeasurements: method so that it uses this new variable name:

```
- (IBAction)showMeasurements:(id)sender
{
    NSNotificationCenter *center = [NSNotificationCenter defaultCenter];

    [center postNotificationName:WVMeasurerShowMeasurementsNotification
                    object:self];
}
```

> ### Working with Global Variables Across Files
>
> We've declared the global variable at the top of WVMeasurer.m and can access it in any of the methods in that file.
>
> If you need access to this global variable from another file, you'll need to add a line to that other file using the keyword **extern** and exclude any variable assignment, like this:
>
> extern NSString * const WVMeasurerShowMeasurementsNotification;
>
> Typically, you'd include this line in a header file **#import**ed by any files needing to work with the global variable—in this case, either the WVMeasurer.h file or a separate WVNotifications.h file just containing possible notifications for use in the Windows and Views project.

Finally, we're ready to register to receive our own notifications. Add the following code to awakeFromNib:

```
- (void)awakeFromNib
{
    NSNotificationCenter *center = [NSNotificationCenter defaultCenter];

    [center addObserver:self
            selector:@selector(windowDidResize:)
                name:NSWindowDidResizeNotification
              object:applicationWindow];

    [center addObserver:self
            selector:@selector(handleShowMeasurements:)
                name:WVMeasurerShowMeasurementsNotification
              object:nil];
}
```

Build & Run the application, and click the Measure button; the measurements appear just like they did before.

Again, this may seem like we've done more work to use notifications than we did to use standard target-action, particularly since our WV-Measurer object is sending a notification to be received by itself! But it would technically be possible for any object in our application to trigger the measuring code, such as an object instance from another nib file, with absolutely no way of referring directly to our existing WVMeasurer instance.

Notification Considerations

In practice, notifications shouldn't really be used for triggering actions in this way; they are designed to be used, as the name implies, to *notify* other objects either that something is about to happen or that it already has happened, such as a window being minimized.

Apart from anything else, there's no easy way for an object posting a notification to know whether any other object has reacted to the notification. As far as interface buttons go, you usually want to use Target-Action.

A related downside to notifications is that they can't be used to change behavior. There's no easy way to use a notification to change the way a window resizes; if you need to modify behavior like this, you typically need to use a delegate, as we did earlier in the chapter.

It's also worth knowing that most system notifications are sent *synchronously*. This means that when one object posts a notification, the notification center passes the notification on to all the observers, individually, before returning control to the originating object. So, if we have 500 objects looking out for a particular notification, we would end up with the following code order:

```
1. Object A posts a notification
2.      Notification Center distributes the notification to:
3.              Observer 1 receives the notification and does something
                Observer 2 receives the notification and does something
                ...
                Observer 500 receives the notification and does something
4.      Once all observers have been notified,
5. Control returns to Object A
```

Generally, this isn't a problem, but it's important to keep in mind that the following, fairly innocuous-looking code:

```
- (void)doSomethingQuickly
{
    [[NSNotificationCenter defaultCenter] postNotificationName:DoingSomething
                                                        object:self];

    NSLog(@"I did it really quickly!");
}
```

might trigger lots of other objects to do various things, making a two-line method take more time to execute than you expect.

It is possible to avoid this problem by sending notifications using other methods, *asynchronously*. Sadly, that's outside the scope of this book.

Apple's *Notification Programming Topics for Cocoa* documentation is a good place to start to learn more. In general, though, synchronous notifications will work just fine.

We've now covered a number of different ways for objects to communicate directly, but there's one topic we haven't really touched on yet: *events.*

13.3 Working with Events

An event is simply something that happens—usually triggered by the user, such as a keypress or mouse-click—that requires action in the application code.

So far, we haven't looked in much detail at how Cocoa applications respond to external input. We've obviously been working with standard Cocoa controls (like NSButton and NSTextField) that cope well enough if we click them or type characters, but these don't give us much of an idea about what's happening behind the scenes.

In this section, we'll start by rewriting our WVShapesView class from the Windows and Views application so that it responds to the user clicking the mouse. We'll see how the system decides which of our application's classes should receive an event and learn how to retrieve information from an NSEvent object to enable our view to respond appropriately.

Before we add the event-handling code, let's simplify the view.

Simplifying the Interface

Open the Windows and Views application project in Xcode, and find the WVShapesView.m file. We'll rewrite the view's drawRect: method to display two rectangles, one red (on the left) and one blue (on the right), as shown in Figure 13.2, on the facing page.

First, we need to remove all the existing shape drawing code, leaving only the initial lines that fill and frame the canvas:

```
- (void)drawRect:(NSRect)dirtyRect {
    NSRect viewBounds = [self bounds];
    NSColor *currentColor = [NSColor whiteColor];
    [currentColor set];
    NSRectFill(viewBounds);

    currentColor = [NSColor blackColor];
    [currentColor set];
    NSFrameRect(viewBounds);
}
```

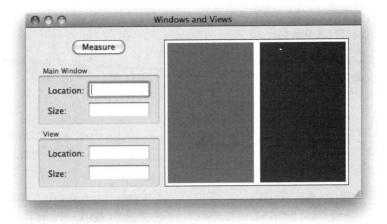

Figure 13.2: THE REVISED WVSHAPESVIEW, DRAWING RED AND BLUE
RECTANGLES

To write the code to display the two rectangles, we could do all the
calculations ourselves, working out how to create two new rectangles
based on the view's bounds, but Quartz provides us with a function
that will do most of the work for us. It looks like this:

```
NSDivideRect(NSRect inRect, NSRect *slice, NSRect *rem, CGFloat amount,
                                                  NSRectEdge edge)
```

The inRect parameter is the rectangle we want to divide. The slice and
rem parameters are pointers to NSRect variables, ready to receive the
coordinates of the divided rectangles, split by the specified amount relative to an edge.

Don't worry if this isn't immediately clear; it's easier to understand in
action. Add the following code to the drawRect: method:

```
- (void)drawRect:(NSRect)dirtyRect {
    «canvas framing code»

    NSRect redRect = NSZeroRect;
    NSRect blueRect = NSZeroRect;
    CGFloat halfWidth = (viewBounds.size.width / 2);
    NSDivideRect(viewBounds, &redRect, &blueRect, halfWidth, NSMinXEdge);

    redRect = NSInsetRect(redRect, 5, 5);
    blueRect = NSInsetRect(blueRect, 5, 5);
```

```
    currentColor = [NSColor redColor];
    [currentColor set];
    NSRectFill(redRect);

    currentColor = [NSColor blueColor];
    [currentColor set];
    NSRectFill(blueRect);
}
```

We start by defining two rectangles, redRect and blueRect, and assign them both the initial value of NSZeroRect,[6] just in case the subsequent NSDivideRect function fails.

We then figure out half the width of the view's bounds and use this width to divide the bounding rectangle exactly in half—we use NSMinX-Edge to refer to the left edge of the view. We could also use NSMaxXEdge to refer to the right edge, and even NSMinYEdge or NSMaxYEdge if we wanted to split the rectangle horizontally. Note that the NSDivideRect() function takes *references* to our redRect and blueRect variables, so it can change their values.

Once we have the two rectangles, we inset them both by 5 points so that there is a white border around and between them, before filling one with red and one with blue.

Build & Run the application to make sure that the view is drawn correctly, as shown in Figure 13.2, on the previous page.

Now all we need to do is figure out how to handle mouse clicks.

Working with Mouse Events

When the user clicks the mouse button in a Cocoa application, various mechanisms jump into action at the system level. If the user clicks in a window that isn't part of the frontmost application, for example, that application will be brought forward by Mac OS X; if that application has multiple windows and the user clicks in a window other than the frontmost window, the clicked window will be brought forward.

Once these mechanisms have completed, it's up to the application to determine what to do with the mouse click. Assuming the user clicks in a window, Cocoa will figure out which view was clicked.

Working out which view was clicked is a fairly nontrivial task, so it's great that we don't have to do this ourselves. In general, Cocoa finds

---

6. NSZeroRect is a rectangle with coordinates of {0,0} and size of {0,0},

the *deepest* view in the view hierarchy that contains the click location. In the Windows and Views application, if the user clicks over one of the measurement text fields, that text field will be the view that receives the click because it is the deepest view in the hierarchy, since it is inside an NSBox, inside the window's content view, inside the window itself.

There are a number of messages associated with mouse events, including the following:

```
- mouseDown:
- mouseDragged:
- mouseUp:
```

These methods relate to the *main* mouse button; on a multibutton mouse, this will be the *left* button. There are also related rightMouse-Down: and otherMouseDown: (and so on) methods to deal with other buttons.

When the user presses the mouse button, the mouseDown: message is sent; if the mouse is moved while the button is held down, the mouse-Dragged message will be sent; when the user finally releases the mouse button, the mouseUp: message is sent.

Each of these methods provides a single argument, an NSEvent object, which contains all the information necessary relative to the current event. This information includes the mouse location and time at which the event occurred, the window associated with the event, if applicable, and whether any *modifier* keys were held down (such as ⌘, ^, or ⌥).

Let's implement a few mouse-handling methods in our WVShapesView class and log a message to the console showing the location of the event.

In the documentation for NSEvent, we can see that it has a locationInWindow method that returns the location of the mouse pointer at the time a mouse-related event occurred. With this in mind, add the following three methods to WVShapesView.m:

```
- (void)mouseDown:(NSEvent *)theEvent {
    NSPoint mouseLocation = [theEvent locationInWindow];
    NSLog(@"Mouse down at %@", NSStringFromPoint(mouseLocation));
}

- (void)mouseUp:(NSEvent *)theEvent {
    NSPoint mouseLocation = [theEvent locationInWindow];
    NSLog(@"Mouse up at %@", NSStringFromPoint(mouseLocation));
}
```

```
- (void)mouseDragged:(NSEvent *)theEvent {
    NSPoint mouseLocation = [theEvent locationInWindow];
    NSLog(@"Mouse dragged to %@", NSStringFromPoint(mouseLocation));
}
```

Make sure the Xcode console is visible (⇧-⌘-R), and then Build & Run the application. Click once near the bottom-left corner of the shapes view, releasing the mouse button immediately. The following messages appear in the console:

```
Windows and Views[2328:a0f] Mouse down at {223, 24}
Windows and Views[2328:a0f] Mouse up at {223, 24}
```

Now click-hold near the top left corner, drag down to the bottom-right corner, and release the mouse button:

```
Windows and Views[2328:a0f] Mouse down at {224, 244}
Windows and Views[2328:a0f] Mouse dragged to {225, 243}
Windows and Views[2328:a0f] Mouse dragged to {233, 237}
...
Windows and Views[2328:a0f] Mouse dragged to {504, 26}
Windows and Views[2328:a0f] Mouse dragged to {508, 23}
Windows and Views[2328:a0f] Mouse up at {508, 23}
```

This shows us that a standard mouse *click-release* consists of two *separate* events, a mouseDown: and a mouseUp:. If the mouse moves while the button is pressed, we also receive one or more mouseDragged: events.

The other thing to notice is that the coordinates of the event are given in the coordinate system of the *containing window*, as the method name locationInWindow implies. To work out which part of the view is hit, we're going to need the click locations to be given in the view's coordinate system, i.e., relative to its bottom-left corner at {0,0}.

Luckily for us, NSView provides a great helper method, convertPoint:fromView:. If we know a point is in some *other* view's coordinate system, we can use this method to convert to the *current* view's coordinates. If we pass nil for fromView:, the point will be converted from the enclosing *window*'s coordinate system.

Insert the following line of code in each of the previously shown three methods:

```
- (void)mouse«Down, Up, Dragged»:(NSEvent *)theEvent {
    NSPoint mouseLocation = [theEvent locationInWindow];
    mouseLocation = [self convertPoint:mouseLocation fromView:nil];
    NSLog(«log statement»);
}
```

When you Build & Run the application, you find that a mouse click near the bottom left of the view is now shown in the view's coordinates:

```
Windows and Views[2541:a0f] Mouse down at {3, 4}
Windows and Views[2541:a0f] Mouse up at {3, 4}
```

You've seen how to determine the location of a click, so you're ready to modify WVShapesView to react when the user clicks in one of the colored rectangles.

Refactoring the Drawing Code

To determine which rectangle is clicked, we'll need to have access to an NSRect for each of the rectangles to test. We could repeat the code we used in the drawRect: method, but as I've said throughout the book, repeated code is bad. It would be better to *refactor* the code that calculates the rectangles, placing it inside a separate method that we can reuse.

Start by writing the implementation for a new method, calculateRedRect:blueRect:, and place this *before* the drawRect: method:

```
- (void)calculateRedRect:(NSRect *)redRect blueRect:(NSRect *)blueRect {

}

- (void)drawRect:(NSRect)dirtyRect {
    «code continues»
```

By placing this method before the drawRect: method in WVShapesView.m, we don't need to add a method signature to WVShapesView.h, provided we only call the method from within methods that are written *after* it. This method won't be recognized by the compiler outside WVShapes-View.m, but that's OK, because it's only for *internal* use.[7]

---

7. If you try to call this method from another method written *before* its implementation, or from a method in a different file, it will still work, but you'll receive an Xcode warning when you try to compile the application. This method is not designed to be called on the object *publicly*, so it's good that it doesn't appear in the interface, but there's the side effect that any *private* code that uses it must be written after it (this side effect can be avoided with the use of Objective-C *categories*). The compiler warning is designed to show you that you were trying to access either a method that doesn't exist or a method that you're not supposed to use outside the object itself. Always aim to compile a project *clean*, i.e., without any warnings—warnings generally indicate that you are doing something that may cause a crash in the future or at the very least cause confusion when you come back to the code in a month's time!

Write the method like this:

```
- (void)calculateRedRect:(NSRect *)redRect blueRect:(NSRect *)blueRect {
    NSRect viewBounds = [self bounds];
    CGFloat halfWidth = (viewBounds.size.width / 2);
    NSDivideRect(viewBounds, redRect, blueRect, halfWidth, NSMinXEdge);
    *redRect = NSInsetRect(*redRect, 5, 5);
    *blueRect = NSInsetRect(*blueRect, 5, 5);
}
```

This code is very similar to the code we used earlier, but notice that because the method accepts two NSRect *pointers*, we need to dereference those pointers when we use NSInsetRect().

Change the drawRect: method to use this new method:

```
- (void)drawRect:(NSRect)dirtyRect {
    «canvas framing code»

    NSRect redRect = NSZeroRect;
    NSRect blueRect = NSZeroRect;
    [self calculateRedRect:&redRect blueRect:&blueRect];

    currentColor = [NSColor redColor];
    [currentColor set];
    NSRectFill(redRect);

    currentColor = [NSColor blueColor];
    [currentColor set];
    NSRectFill(blueRect);
}
```

Build & Run the application to make sure the view is still displayed correctly.

Checking Which Rectangle Was Hit

Now that we have easy access to the relevant rectangles in our view, let's log a message to the console when the user clicks in either the red area or the blue area.

The expected Mac behavior is to trigger an action when the user *releases* the mouse button over a control; this allows users to click-hold a button, for example, and then change their minds and drag the mouse outside the button before releasing so that the click is effectively ignored.

Start by removing the existing calls to NSLog() from the mouseDown:, mouseUp:, and mouseDragged: methods so that for now, nothing happens if the user clicks the view.

To check whether the click occurred within one of the rectangles, we can use another helpful function, NSPointInRect(), which returns a Boolean value to indicate whether a point is contained within a rectangle.[8]

Implement the mouseUp: method like this:

```
- (void)mouseUp:(NSEvent *)theEvent {
    NSPoint mouseLocation = [theEvent locationInWindow];
    mouseLocation = [self convertPoint:mouseLocation fromView:nil];

    NSRect redRect = NSZeroRect;
    NSRect blueRect = NSZeroRect;
    [self calculateRedRect:&redRect blueRect:&blueRect];

    if( NSPointInRect(mouseLocation, redRect) )
        NSLog(@"User clicked red rect");
    else if( NSPointInRect(mouseLocation, blueRect) )
        NSLog(@"User clicked blue rect");
}
```

Note that our mouseUp: method implementation needs to be written *after* the calculateRedRect:blueRect: method to avoid any compiler warnings. This method creates NSRect variables for the red and blue rectangles, as before, and then uses NSPointInRect() to determine whether the mouse location is within either of the rectangles.

Build & Run the application, and check what happens when the mouse is clicked.

If you click in one of the white portions of the view, i.e., outside the two rectangles, nothing appears in the Xcode console log. You'll see the relevant message if you do click a rectangle, but if you click-hold a rectangle and then decide to drag outside the view before releasing the button, you won't see anything in the log window.

That's the basic functionality for our view, but we have a couple of issues. The first is that there is no visual feedback to the user in response to clicks. Most Cocoa controls highlight when they are clicked, indicating that the user has hit a clickable object; if the mouse moves outside the clickable area, the highlight disappears.

The second issue is more serious: if you click-hold the red rectangle and then drag to the blue rectangle and release the button, you see a message in the console to indicate that we clicked the blue rectangle,

---

8. If we were working with path objects, rather than rectangles, we could use NSBezier-Path's containsPoint: method to accomplish the same thing.

which is incorrect. We shouldn't see anything in the console, because we effectively clicked the red rectangle and then changed our minds, such that the click should be ignored.

Let's fix this problem first.

Handling Clicks When the Mouse Is Dragged

To determine whether the mouseUp: should be ignored, we need a way to check whether the original mouseDown: event occurred within the same rectangle.

An NSEvent object doesn't provide us with any kind of originalMouseDown-LocationInWindow, so we need to cache this value from within our mouse-Down: method.

Open WVShapesView.h, and add an NSPoint instance variable to hold this initial mouse point:

```
@interface WVShapesView : NSView {
    NSPoint mouseDownPoint;
}

@end
```

Switch to WVShapesView.m, and set the value of the variable from within mouseDown::

```
- (void)mouseDown:(NSEvent *)theEvent {
    mouseDownPoint = [theEvent locationInWindow];
    mouseDownPoint = [self convertPoint:mouseDownPoint fromView:nil];
}
```

All we need to do now is modify the mouseUp: method to check *both* this location *and* the location when the button is released:

```
- (void)mouseUp:(NSEvent *)theEvent {
    NSPoint mouseLocation = [theEvent locationInWindow];
    mouseLocation = [self convertPoint:mouseLocation fromView:nil];

    NSRect redRect = NSZeroRect;
    NSRect blueRect = NSZeroRect;
    [self calculateRedRect:&redRect blueRect:&blueRect];

    if( NSPointInRect(mouseDownPoint, redRect) &&
                       NSPointInRect(mouseLocation, redRect) )
        NSLog(@"User clicked red rect");
    else if( NSPointInRect(mouseDownPoint, blueRect) &&
                       NSPointInRect(mouseLocation, blueRect) )
        NSLog(@"User clicked blue rect");
}
```

Build & Run to test that the correct message appears in the console *only* if you click and release the mouse within the same rectangle.

Now let's tackle the problem of highlighting a rectangle when the user clicks it.

Providing Visual Feedback

Determining whether a highlight should be displayed is fairly straightforward:

- The highlight should be displayed when mouseDown: occurs.
- The highlight should disappear when mouseUp: occurs.
- If the user drags outside the clicked rectangle, the highlight should disappear.
- If the user drags back into the rectangle they originally clicked, the highlight should reappear.

Let's handle the easy cases first and display a highlight on mouseDown:, removing it on mouseUp:.

The only time a view should draw itself is in response to the drawRect: message—we can't just draw something to the screen in mouseDown: and clear it in mouseUp:. We need a way for drawRect: to determine whether it should draw the highlight.

To keep things simple, let's use two Boolean instance variables to indicate whether the red or blue rectangles should be highlighted. Open WVShapesView.h, and add the following:

```
@interface WVShapesView : NSView {
    NSPoint mouseDownPoint;

    BOOL shouldHighlightRedRect;
    BOOL shouldHighlightBlueRect;
}

@end
```

Switch to WVShapesView.m, and set the relevant flag in mouseDown:, setting both flags to NO in mouseUp::

```
- (void)mouseDown:(NSEvent *)theEvent {
    mouseDownPoint = [theEvent locationInWindow];
    mouseDownPoint = [self convertPoint:mouseDownPoint fromView:nil];

    NSRect redRect = NSZeroRect;
    NSRect blueRect = NSZeroRect;
    [self calculateRedRect:&redRect blueRect:&blueRect];
```

```
        if( NSPointInRect(mouseDownPoint, redRect) )
            shouldHighlightRedRect = YES;
        else if( NSPointInRect(mouseDownPoint, blueRect) )
            shouldHighlightBlueRect = YES;
}

- (void)mouseUp:(NSEvent *)theEvent {
    «beginning of method»

    if( NSPointInRect(mouseDownPoint, redRect) &&
                        NSPointInRect(mouseLocation, redRect) )
        NSLog(@"User clicked red rect");
    else if( NSPointInRect(mouseDownPoint, blueRect) &&
                        NSPointInRect(mouseLocation, blueRect) )
        NSLog(@"User clicked blue rect");

    shouldHighlightRedRect = NO;
    shouldHighlightBlueRect = NO;
}
```

Next, modify the drawing code to draw a rectangle in dark gray if it should be highlighted:

```
- (void)drawRect:(NSRect)dirtyRect {
    «canvas framing code»

    NSRect redRect = NSZeroRect;
    NSRect blueRect = NSZeroRect;
    [self calculateRedRect:&redRect blueRect:&blueRect];

    if( shouldHighlightRedRect )
        currentColor = [NSColor darkGrayColor];
    else
        currentColor = [NSColor redColor];
    [currentColor set];
    NSRectFill(redRect);

    if( shouldHighlightBlueRect )
        currentColor = [NSColor darkGrayColor];
    else
        currentColor = [NSColor blueColor];
    [currentColor set];
    NSRectFill(blueRect);
}
```

If you Build & Run at this point, you find that despite all our best efforts, the highlights aren't drawn. The problem here is that drawRect: isn't being called.

One suggestion might be to call drawRect: directly, but this is something you should *never* do.

Back in the sidebar on page 292, I mentioned briefly that it's possible to trigger a partial redraw of a view using the setNeedsDisplayInRect: method. Since our view is extremely simple, it's fine just to request that the entire view is redrawn by using the setNeedsDisplay: method, passing in YES.

Add a call to this method at the end of both the mouseDown: and mouseUp: methods:

```
- (void)mouseDown:(NSEvent *)theEvent {
    «beginning of method»

    if( NSPointInRect(mouseDownPoint, redRect) )
        shouldHighlightRedRect = YES;
    else if( NSPointInRect(mouseDownPoint, blueRect) )
        shouldHighlightBlueRect = YES;

    [self setNeedsDisplay:YES];
}

- (void)mouseUp:(NSEvent *)theEvent {
    «beginning of method»

    shouldHighlightRedRect = NO;
    shouldHighlightBlueRect = NO;

    [self setNeedsDisplay:YES];
}
```

This line of code indicates that the view needs to be redrawn but delays the actual redraw until the current event loop has finished (that is, all the code relating to the current event has been executed). This happens so quickly that it appears to the users as if the rectangle highlights immediately when they click it.

Build & Run to check this; the highlight displays when a rectangle is clicked and disappears when the mouse button is released.

All that remains is to remove the highlight if the user drags outside the rectangle and redisplay it if they reenter. Add the following code to the mouseDragged: method:

```
- (void)mouseDragged:(NSEvent *)theEvent {
    NSPoint mouseLocation = [theEvent locationInWindow];
    mouseLocation = [self convertPoint:mouseLocation fromView:nil];

    NSRect redRect = NSZeroRect;
    NSRect blueRect = NSZeroRect;
    [self calculateRedRect:&redRect blueRect:&blueRect];
```

```
        shouldHighlightRedRect = NO;
        shouldHighlightBlueRect = NO;

        if( NSPointInRect(mouseDownPoint, redRect) &&
                            NSPointInRect(mouseLocation, redRect) )
            shouldHighlightRedRect = YES;
        else if( NSPointInRect(mouseDownPoint, blueRect) &&
                            NSPointInRect(mouseLocation, blueRect) )
            shouldHighlightBlueRect = YES;

        [self setNeedsDisplay:YES];
}
```

This method is pretty simple, considering what it achieves. We start by getting our usual red and blue rectangles and then set *both* the should-Highlight... flags to NO. We check whether the original mouse-down point *and* the current location are within either of the rectangles, setting the relevant flag if so, before making a final call to redisplay the view.

Build & Run to make sure that it works. You can click-drag in and out of a rectangle as much as you like, and the highlight provides the correct visual feedback.

One thing that's worth noticing about our Windows and Views application is what happens when you click and type something into one of the text fields in the window and then click the view.

With the application still running, click in one of the Location text fields. The usual text cursor appears and flashes to indicate that the text field is ready to accept keyboard entry. If you click the custom view, the cursor continues to flash, and the text field continues to accept keystrokes.

If you click in a different text field, the flashing cursor now appears for that field, and it will accept keystrokes, even if you click the custom view.

Have we neglected to do something to our view in order to make it "selectable?" Or is there something more important happening?

13.4 Responders and the Responder Chain

When the user clicks a view, that view receives the relevant mouse event messages, as we've seen earlier. However, mouse clicks are obviously not the only kind of event that might occur. A keystroke event, for example, might occur if the user types a keyboard shortcut, or it might just be a character that the user expects to appear on screen in a text field or text view. Where should this typed character appear?

From a user's point of view, it should be wherever the text cursor (or *caret*) is flashing. From a programming point of view, however, life is more complicated. How do we determine which view object is currently ready to accept such keyboard entry?

The Cocoa framework helps us with what's known as the *first responder*.

Introducing First Responder

When an event occurs, the internal Mac OS X and Cocoa mechanisms mentioned in Section 13.3, *Working with Mouse Events*, on page 344 deal with the event if it's some kind of system event, such as the user pressing the Eject button on a Mac keyboard. Otherwise, the event is processed and then passed to an application's first responder.

There can be only one first responder object at a time, and only a few objects can accept first responder status. NSTextField is one such example of an object that can become first responder.

When a text field is the current first responder, it will display the usual flashing caret and receive any keystroke events that occur, along with most other nonsystem events.

The text field will also be sent *all* other events, regardless of whether they seem relevant. What happens to events that the text field can't handle?

The answer to this problem is provided by the *responder chain*.

The Responder Chain

Any object that responds to events must inherit from NSResponder. If an event is sent to a responder such as a text field and that responder doesn't handle the event, the event will be passed to the *next responder*.

Each responder in an application fits into a responder chain, and conceptually, this chain is just an *inverse* view hierarchy. It starts with the first responder, such as a text field. The text field's next responder would be its enclosing view (NSView is a subclass of NSResponder), and that view's next responder would be *its* enclosing view, and so on, until you reach the enclosing window.

This responder chain is maintained automatically, so you don't have to worry about it.

Becoming the First Responder

Given that NSView inherits from NSResponder and we're already receiving mouse events in our custom WVShapesView, why doesn't first responder status pass to the view when it is clicked?

When the user tries to make an object the first responder—for instance, by clicking it—the object will be asked whether it acceptsFirstResponder. The default implementation of this method returns NO, which is why our view never becomes the first responder.

Let's implement the acceptsFirstResponder method to see what happens if we return YES. Open WVShapesView.m, and add the following method:

```
- (BOOL)acceptsFirstResponder {
    return YES;
}
```

Build & Run the application, click one of the Location fields to make it the first responder, and then click the custom view.

The text view loses its first responder status, and the caret stops flashing. The shapes view is now the first responder, and any events from now on will be sent to the view, until some other object becomes first responder.

When you press any keys on the keyboard, the keystroke events are passed up the chain, since WVShapesView doesn't implement any of the NSResponder methods relating to keys, such as keyDown: and keyUp:. In this case, a simple keystroke doesn't have any meaning to any other responders in the chain, so there's an alert sound to let you know the key press is an invalid input.

Working with Actions

Responders can also be used for action messages. So far, we've seen how to send action messages directly using the target-action mechanism. Let's look at a case where target-action can't be used.

Close the Windows and Views project, and open the Shopping List application project instead. We'll add a menu item to the Edit menu to allow the users to remove a selected shopping list item, one that behaves as if they had clicked the - button in the interface.

The menu bar for the application is located in MainMenu.xib, rather than the MyDocument.xib file, so we can't just use Interface Builder to link the menu bar directly to a MyDocument object.

This obviously makes sense because there may be multiple shopping list windows open on screen, and the menu item needs to remove the selected item in the frontmost document window. This window will be the shopping list the user is currently editing, meaning that this window will *contain the first responder.*

You might be wondering whether we could make use of notifications, since I mentioned earlier that notifications can be used for communication between objects in different nib files. Unfortunately, there are a number of problems with this solution. First, *every* shopping list document would be listening for the notification, so each shopping list would need to check whether it was currently the *main window*—in other words, contained the first responder—before reacting. Second, as I've already discussed, notifications aren't really designed for this kind of communication. In the case of our menu item, we really need to have some way to connect that menu item *directly* to the shopping list related to the current first responder.

If we can set a menu item to target the first responder itself, the action will be sent to whichever object is first responder at the time the menu item is chosen and then passed up the responder chain, if necessary, until an object can deal with it.[9] This solution sounds promising; let's see whether it's possible.

We'll start by creating the new menu item. Open MainMenu.xib in Interface Builder, and double-click the Main Menu object to open the menu editor.

Click the Edit menu header in this editor to display the menu items, and then drag a Separator Menu Item from the Library palette and drop it under the Select All menu item. Drag out a standard Menu Item from the library, and drop it below the new separator.

---

9. The responder chain for action messages is just like the one for events but slightly extended. If none of the responders up to the enclosing window can deal with the action, the window's *delegate* is given the opportunity to respond. If the window delegate can't respond, the action is passed up to the *application* object; if the application can't respond, the action passes to the application's delegate. These delegate objects are the only responder objects that don't need to inherit from NSResponder.

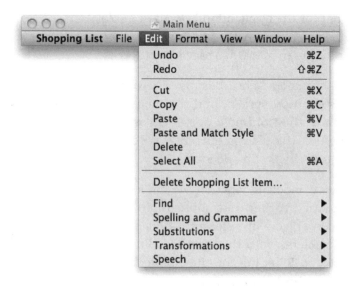

Figure 13.3: Adding a new menu item

Later in this section, we'll be setting this menu item to call the removeItemFromShoppingList: method, which displays an NSAlert to check that the users are absolutely sure they want to remove the item. We need to follow the Mac OS X naming convention of using an ellipsis (...) to indicate that a menu item will require further input.

Set the title of the new menu item to "Delete Shopping List Item..." (those aren't three separate dot characters; they are one ellipsis character, typed by pressing ⌥-;). The finished menu looks like Figure 13.3.

Targeting the First Responder

You may already have noticed that interface files contain an icon called First Responder. This object is used as a *placeholder* to represent any possible first responder object at runtime.

If you click this First Responder object to select it and then look in its Attributes inspector, you get a list of system-defined actions supported as standard by an object inheriting from NSResponder.

Since we need to target the removeItemFromShoppingList: action, which obviously isn't a system-defined action, we'll need to add this manually to the list of possible first responder actions.

Figure 13.4: ADDING AN ACTION TO FIRST RESPONDER

Click the + button in the First Responder's Attributes inspector, and change the name of the new action to "removeItemFromShoppingList:" (don't forget the trailing colon), as shown in Figure 13.4.

All that remains is to link the menu item to the new action. Make sure both the menu editor and the MainMenu.xib document window are visible, and then right-click (or ^-click) the menu item. Drag from its Sent Actions selector over to the First Responder object, and choose the removeItemFromShoppingList: from the pop-up list, as shown in Figure 13.5, on the following page.

Save the file, and switch over to Xcode. Build & Run the application, then select a shopping list item in the Untitled shopping list. Choose our new menu item from the Edit menu, and you'll see the NSAlert asking if you're sure you want to remove the item.

Wow, that was pretty easy. What happens if no shopping lists are visible? Close the Untitled shopping list document so that no shopping lists are left open, and then open the Edit menu. Now our menu item is disabled. Huh? How did that happen?

Figure 13.5: ADDING AN ACTION TO FIRST RESPONDER

User Interface Validation

What appears to be absolute magic is actually the result of a complex target/first-responder/validation interaction, happening behind the scenes.

When you click to display the Edit menu, the application *validates* each item in that menu. You can customize this validation if you need to, but the default behavior will go through each menu item in turn to see whether the first responder, or any other items in the responder chain, can respond to that menu's action. If so, the menu will be enabled; otherwise, it will be disabled.

If we were to add another action to the First Responder object in Main-Menu.xib but give it a name that isn't used by any method in the project, we'd find that any linked menu item would always be disabled, since no responder will ever be able to respond to a method with that name.

The only downside to this automatic validation for our Delete Shopping List Item... menu item is that it has the same problem as the - button in the interface; if there's a shopping list on screen, the item is always enabled, even if no item is selected in the list.

You might like to look at the documentation for User Interface Validation to see how to perform validation to enable or disable the menu item. The sample code for this chapter includes a validation method that will enable the menu item only if the user has selected a row in the shopping list table view.

Setting Keyboard Shortcuts for Menu Items

We still have one major feature left to implement in our Shopping List application, the all-important ability to save. Before we do this, let's make one simple change to the menu item we just created and add a keyboard shortcut.

Open the MainMenu.xib file in Interface Builder, and select the Delete Shopping List Item... menu item. Open its Attributes inspector, and click in the box next to Key Equiv.; the box will show a *focus ring*, indicating that it is Interface Builder's current first responder, awaiting keyboard entry.

Hold down the ⌘ key, press the ⌫ key, and then release the ⌘ key. When you release the keys, the focus ring disappears, indicating that the box has resigned first responder status, and the keyboard shortcut is set as ⌘-⌫, as shown in Figure 13.6, on the next page.

Save the file, return to Xcode, and Build & Run the application. Now you can delete selected rows from the shopping list by typing the keyboard shortcut ⌘-⌫.

Keyboard shortcuts are handled slightly differently than standard keystrokes. When a keyboard shortcut is received, the window containing the first responder is given a chance to respond (you might have a keyboard shortcut that doesn't have a corresponding menu item, such as using ⌥ with the arrow keys to move the text cursor in big jumps). If no object in the responder chain can deal with the shortcut, it is passed to the menus.

With the Shopping List application almost complete, it's time to add the code we need to allow the shopping lists to save. To do this, we're going to need to know about NSCoding.

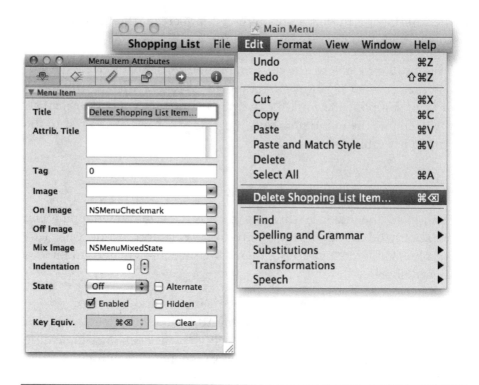

Figure 13.6: SETTING A KEYBOARD SHORTCUT

13.5 Archiving with NSCoding

When we started using a shopping list item *object* to hold an item's information, back in Section 11.5, *Reworking the Shopping List Application... Again*, on page 264, we lost the ability to save the array of shopping list items to a file using NSArray's writeToURL:atomically: method. This method requires that every object held within the array is either another array, a dictionary, or an object that can be saved as a string. Our ShoppingListItem obviously doesn't fall under any of these types, so the writeToURL:atomically: method no longer works.

To save the shopping list items, we need to use one of several mechanisms offered under Mac OS X and Cocoa to archive or serialize an object to disk.

The easiest way for us to archive our shopping lists is through the use of an object called *NSKeyedArchiver*.

Working with Keyed Archivers

As the name suggests, NSKeyedArchiver offers us the ability to archive objects to disk using string keys.

There are various ways to work with keyed archivers, but the simplest is through a convenience class method:

```
+ archiveRootObject:toFile:
```

This method accepts an object that forms the top of a hierarchy of objects to be saved, which is why it's called the *Root* object, and saves that object to a file. In the case of our Shopping List application, this root object will be the main shoppingListArray of items.

The code we will be using to start the archival process looks like this (but don't implement anything in the shopping list application yet):

```
[NSKeyedArchiver archiveRootObject:shoppingListArray toFile:«path to save»];
```

When this code executes, the keyed archiver starts by telling the root object to *encode* itself. This object must conform to a protocol called NSCoding; in the case of our Shopping List application, the root is an NSArray, which does conform to that protocol. When it's told to encode, the shopping list array will then cycle through its subitems, telling each one to encode in turn.

If the root object were an array of arrays of arrays, this iterative process would walk through each item of each array, archiving it to disk. Alternatively, if we ended up in a situation where we have multiple root objects rather than one object containing them all (such as an invoicing application keeping track of separate arrays of customers, invoices, receipts, bank accounts, and so on), we'd need to create a root *dictionary* holding each of these arrays under a different key, ready to be restored later.

Once we've created an archive using archiveRootObject:toFile:, the whole object hierarchy can be restored by using the *un*archiving relative of NSKeyedArchiver, called NSKeyedUnarchiver, using code like this:

```
NSArray *restoredArray = [NSKeyedUnarchiver unarchiveObjectWithFile:«path to read»];
```

As far as our Shopping List application is concerned, it's fine to archive our single shopping list items array as the root, but every subitem in that array (each one being an instance of the ShoppingListItem class) will need to conform to the NSCoding protocol.

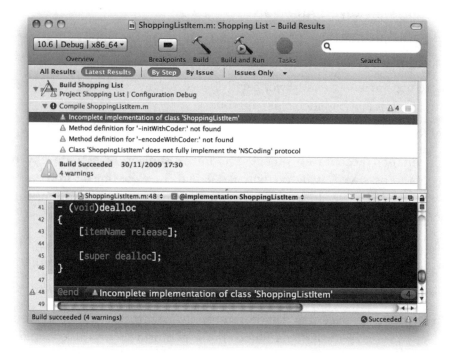

Figure 13.7: WARNINGS ABOUT NOT FULLY IMPLEMENTING A PROTOCOL

Adopting NSCoding

Open the ShoppingListItem.h file inside the Shopping List project. As we've just learned, any object we want to be able to archive using NSKeyed-Archiver must adopt the NSCoding protocol, so let's indicate this in the interface file:

```
@interface ShoppingListItem : NSObject <NSCoding> {
    «instance variables»
}

«method signatures and properties»

@end
```

If you're running Xcode 3.2 under Snow Leopard, try building the project (⌘-B) before you do anything else. You'll find that the compiler will complain with four warnings, which are shown in Figure 13.7.

These warnings show what happens if you state that a class will adopt a protocol, but fail to implement one or more of its required methods.

Select File > Open Quickly... (⇧-⌘-D); then type in "NSCoding" and press ↵. Xcode will locate the protocol definition inside NSObject.h, so click the Open button to jump to the declaration.

We see that the protocol defines two methods, neither of which is listed as **@optional**:

```
@protocol NSCoding

- (void)encodeWithCoder:(NSCoder *)aCoder;
- (id)initWithCoder:(NSCoder *)aDecoder;

@end
```

These correspond with the warnings shown in Figure 13.7, on the facing page, and we'll need to implement both these methods in our ShoppingListItem class.

Encoding Information with NSCoder

Let's start by implementing the method to *en*code our shopping list item. The method passes us a pointer to an instance of the NSCoder class.

NSCoder is what's known as an *abstract* class, which means that we never work directly with an instance of NSCoder; we always work with a *concrete* subclass. Because we'll be using NSKeyedArchiver's class method to encode the root object and start the cascade of subitem encoding, the NSCoder we'll be passed will itself be an instance of NSKeyedArchiver (which is a subclass of NSCoder).

This coder is what we'll use to save enough information from a Shopping List item object so that it can be resurrected at a later date. Working with a keyed archive NSCoder is a bit like working with an NSDictionary; it stores values for keys, but it stores them in a way that can be saved straight to disk.

Since we'll be working with keys once again and will need to make sure we encode the information with the same keys we use to decode it, let's declare some global variables to hold the string keys. There are three pieces of information relevant to each shopping list item: its name, the quantity, and whether it has already been purchased; i.e., the information that's *encapsulated* by each object.

Add the following global variable declarations at the top of ShoppingListItem.m, just like we did for our WVMeasurerShowMeasurementsNotification, earlier in the chapter:

```
#import "ShoppingListItem.h"

NSString * const kShoppingListItemName = @"kShoppingListItemName";
NSString * const kShoppingListQuantity = @"kShoppingListQuantity";
NSString * const kShoppingListPurchased = @"kShoppingListPurchased";


@implementation ShoppingListItem
«implementation continues»
```

We could call these global variables anything we wanted; the previous names follow a common convention of starting the variable name with a "k" to indicate a key.

Now that we've defined the keys, let's see how to implement the encodeWithCoder: method. Looking at the documentation for NSCoder, we find that it has a number of methods listed under the "Encoding Data" heading that follow the convention:

```
encode«dataType»:forKey:
```

For example:

```
- encodeBool:forKey:
- encodeInt:forKey:
- encodeObject:forKey:
```

Also notice that there are corresponding decodeTypeForKey: methods for each data type, listed under the "Decoding Data" heading.

The quantity for our shopping list item can be encoded using the encodeInt:forKey: method, and we can use encodeBool:forKey: to encode the purchased property. But notice that there is no encodeString:forKey: method. Instead, we have to use the encodeObject:forKey: method, which requires that the specified object supports NSCoding. Luckily for us, NSString is one of many Cocoa classes that do.

Implement the encodeWithCoder: method for the shopping list item like this:

```
- (void)encodeWithCoder:(NSCoder *)aCoder
{
    [aCoder encodeObject:itemName forKey:kShoppingListItemName];
    [aCoder encodeInt:quantity forKey:kShoppingListQuantity];
    [aCoder encodeBool:purchased forKey:kShoppingListPurchased];
}
```

These lines of code are all that's required to make our object encodable. We just need to set the relevant values for our keys in the coder, and Cocoa handles the rest for us.

What about decoding?

Decoding Information with NSCoder

We've already seen from the documentation that NSCoder has corresponding decoding methods for each of the variable types, and these are available to us when we use NSKeyedUnarchiver. The method we need to implement in our ShoppingListItem class to handle the decoding is an init method, with the signature:

```
- (id)initWithCoder:(NSCoder *)aCoder;
```

This method needs to work in the same way as our designated initializer, initWithName:quantity:, which looks like this:

```
- (id)initWithName:(NSString *)newName quantity:(int)newQuantity
{
    if( self = [super init] )
    {
        itemName = [newName retain];
        quantity = newQuantity;
        purchased = NO;
    }

    return self;
}
```

but set the values of the instance variables to the values extracted from the coder for the relevant keys.

Implement it like this (the differences from the designated initializer are highlighted in bold):

```
- (id)initWithCoder:(NSCoder *)aDecoder
{
    if( self = [super init] )
    {
        itemName = [[aDecoder decodeObjectForKey:kShoppingListItemName] retain];
        quantity = [aDecoder decodeIntForKey:kShoppingListQuantity];
        purchased = [aDecoder decodeBoolForKey:kShoppingListPurchased];
    }

    return self;
}
```

That's all there is to it! Our ShoppingListItem class is now fully archivable and restorable, using NSKeyedArchiver, NSKeyedUnarchiver, and the NSCoding protocol.

There's just one last thing we need to add to the Shopping List application before we can save our shopping lists. We still need to write the code that triggers the archive process when the user saves to a file and that unarchives the data when they open an existing shopping list.

Saving and Reopening Shopping List Files

As I mentioned earlier in this chapter, NSKeyedArchiver has a handy class method to archive data to disc, archiveRootObject:toFile:. This method returns a Boolean value to indicate success, just like NSArray's write-ToURL:atomically: method.

The only issue is that we need to specify a string for the path to the file rather than an NSURL. Luckily, NSURL has a method called path, which returns an NSString representing the URL's path.

Open MyDocument.m, find the writeToURL:ofType:error: method, and rewrite it like this:

```
- (BOOL)writeToURL:(NSURL *)absoluteURL ofType:(NSString *)typeName
                                    error:(NSError **)outError
{
    return [NSKeyedArchiver archiveRootObject:shoppingListArray
                             toFile:[absoluteURL path]];
}
```

That's all we need to do to save a shopping list. Let's see whether opening existing files is as straightforward.

The existing method (which no longer works) looks like this:

```
- (BOOL)readFromURL:(NSURL *)absoluteURL ofType:(NSString *)typeName
                                    error:(NSError **)outError
{
    [shoppingListArray release];
    shoppingListArray = [[NSMutableArray alloc] initWithContentsOfURL:absoluteURL];
    [shoppingListTableView reloadData];

    return YES;
}
```

We still need to release the existing array and reload the table view, but we'll need to revise the line of code that resurrects the array from the archive so that it uses NSKeyedUnarchiver's unarchiveObjectWithFile: method.

As before, this method expects a string path to the file to open, so we'll need to use NSURL's path method again.

Because this method doesn't have the word alloc or copy in it, it will return us an autoreleased array. We'll need to retain this array, or the shopping list will be deallocated from memory just when we need it!

If the unarchiving process fails, this method returns nil; we can check for this and return NO to indicate that there was a problem opening the file.

Implement the method like this:

```
- (BOOL)readFromURL:(NSURL *)absoluteURL ofType:(NSString *)typeName
                                     error:(NSError **)outError
{
    [shoppingListArray release];

    NSArray *restoredList = [NSKeyedUnarchiver
                         unarchiveObjectWithFile:[absoluteURL path]];
    if( !restoredList ) return NO; // couldn't open the file

    shoppingListArray = [restoredList retain];
    [shoppingListTableView reloadData];

    return YES;
}
```

We start by releasing the existing shopping list array and then try unarchiving an array from disc. If this fails, we return NO so the user will be informed that the file couldn't be opened. Otherwise, we set the shoppingListArray variable, retaining the array, before reloading the table view as before.

Build & Run the application to check that this all works. You'll find that you can now save a shopping list to disk and then reopen it. The items reappear exactly as they were when they were saved, with the names, quantities, and purchased information all set correctly.

13.6 Chapter Summary

That brings us to the end of this chapter, and to the end of the main learning chapters in this book.

We've covered an enormous amount of ground, looking at a number of mechanisms offered by Mac OS X and Cocoa, with a particular focus on messaging and event handling. You've also learned about Objective-C protocols and seen how to work with Cocoa protocols relating both to delegation, and to archiving.

The Shopping List application is pretty functional at this point and even includes a menu item (complete with shortcut) to allow the users to remove an item from their shopping list. We've put back the ability to archive shopping lists to files, along with the equally important ability to reopen them, so the application is ready for use and initial testing.

The pace of this chapter was fast, designed to give you an idea of what's available to you in the future. Although the Shopping List application is functional at a basic level, it's really still the beginning of its journey into what can be achieved through the Cocoa framework.

The next chapter gives you some ideas of where to go next to learn more and what to look out for, and it highlights some key features in the future of Mac development offered by Snow Leopard and subsequent Mac OS X releases.

Chapter 14

Where to Go from Here

One of the inherent problems with programming books for beginners is that the example applications they build don't really have anything like the amount of functionality expected in a shipping Mac application. Although it feels great to get these basic applications working, the moment you finish the book and want to start on your own projects, you're quickly overwhelmed by how much you *haven't* learned.

The aim of this chapter is to introduce some of the major topics we haven't been able to cover, partly so you'll know the terms to search for when you want to take your code to the next level. We'll look at some of the technologies that are shaping the future of Mac applications, as well as several important mechanisms available in Cocoa that there wasn't room to talk about in the previous chapter.

Once you have an overview of these topics, we'll look at where to go to find more information. As the Mac and iPhone gain exponentially in popularity, the number of Mac-related books, websites, and forums increases to match demand. It's frequently the case that if you know the right terms to Google, you'll find lots of sources explaining exactly what you're trying to achieve. If you prefer a more structured approach to learning, we'll mention some books along the way that are available to help you.

Let's start by looking at some of the other important mechanisms offered by Cocoa and Mac OS X.

14.1 Important Technologies

We've only scratched the surface of what's available under Cocoa on the desktop. As we'll see in Section A, *Introducing Cocoa Touch and UIKit*, on page 388, *Cocoa* is really an umbrella term for a large collection of frameworks available to us when we write Mac OS X software.

Mac OS X versions 10.4 Tiger and 10.5 Leopard saw Apple introduce a number of *Core* technologies to Cocoa, making key areas of an application's functionality much easier to implement. These technologies are mostly *higher-level* technologies, meaning they add an extra level of abstraction on top of the underlying frameworks, mechanisms, and terrifying-looking low-level C functions.

Let's start with the prettiest Core technology, Core Animation.

Core Animation

The award for the greatest wow factor in a Cocoa framework would probably have to go to Core Animation, which makes it easy to add animated effects to your application's user interface.

Although you might be tempted to think that animating your application is the desktop equivalent of flashing text and autoplaying sound files on websites, animation can actually be an essential part of making the *user experience* as great as possible. The user experience in software relates to how the users perceive the application, including how well it helps them achieve their goals, how easy it is to use, and how fast it is to learn.

Consider what happens when you minimize a window on Mac OS X; the window shrinks itself down to the Dock, using what's known as the *genie effect*. Yes, it looks pretty impressive, but its *primary* function is to show how the window can be redisplayed.

Imagine if there was no animation—the window would seem to disappear into thin air. To a first-time user, the Dock is probably the last place they'd look to find out where the window had gone. By animating the window and shrinking it down to its Dock representation, the users are able to see exactly what's happened. They already know that clicking something on the Dock causes it to open, so they know that clicking the window will restore it. The learning experience is enhanced by the fact that their *expectation is confirmed* when the window animates back up on screen when clicked.

Core Animation works on a keyframe principle, where you define the start and end *frames* for an animation, and the underlying framework figures out how to display the rest of the animation on screen, making it relatively simple to accomplish extremely impressive effects.

To find out more, you might like to start by looking at Apple's *Core Animation Programming Guide*.[1] There are currently two books on the subject, Bill Dudney's *Core Animation for Mac OS X and the iPhone: Creating Compelling Dynamic User Interfaces* [Dud08] and Marcus Zarra and Matt Long's *Core Animation: Simplified Animation Techniques for Mac and iPhone Development* [ZL09]. As the titles imply, Core Animation is also available on the iPhone, where animation is used for almost everything!

Core Data

Over the course of the book, we've looked at a number of ways to persist information to disk. Each of these involved keeping track of a network of objects in memory, collected in dictionaries or arrays, and saving those collections to disk when required.

The Core Data framework takes data storage to a whole new level. Instead of worrying about how to handle the object persistence ourselves, it allows us to work with *managed* objects tied, through an intermediary *context* that keeps track of changes, to the underlying data stored on disk.

Working with Core Data involves modeling an application's data into *entities*, which are rather like class descriptions. These entities contain properties that may be either *attributes*, like the properties on our shopping list object, or *relationships* to other objects.

It would be very straightforward to use Core Data to store a lot more information in our Shopping List application, keeping track of items on a list, relating them to the shops that sell those items, and recording the times (and prices) at which the items had previously been purchased. From a data point of view, Core Data would manage this network of related objects automatically, making it incredibly easy to find out which shop sells an item or to see how many items can be purchased from one shop, leaving us "just" to worry about how to design the interface and controllers to make everything work!

---

1. http://developer.apple.com/mac/library/documentation/cocoa/Conceptual/CoreAnimation_guide

Core Data is one of the more advanced Cocoa frameworks, and it can take a while to get your head around the basic features. It's also a good idea to have a reasonable understanding of some of the mechanisms we'll talk about in Section 14.1, *Other Cocoa Mechanisms*, on the facing page before starting out.

To get an immediate idea of the power of the Core Data framework, several tutorials are available that allow you to build relatively impressive data-saving applications using absolutely no code at all. Start by looking at Apple's Core Data tutorials and guides. Alternatively, see Marcus Zarra's *Core Data: Apple's API for Persisting Data on Mac OS X* [Zar09] or one of my own books, such as *Building Data-Driven Desktop Applications for Mac OS X* [Ist10a] or *Core Data for iPhone: Building Data-Driven Applications for the iPhone and iPod Touch* [Ist10b].

Garbage Collection

In Chapter 7, *Objects and Memory Management*, on page 113, you spent some time learning all about manual memory management, including seeing how to use retain, release, and autorelease to make sure objects stay in memory only as long as they are needed to avoid memory leaks.

When Apple released Objective-C 2.0, which added support for properties and fast enumeration (as you saw earlier in the book), it also added support for *garbage collection*. Garbage collection simplifies and automates memory management, so you no longer need to use the retain and release mechanism.

It's very simple to enable garbage collection; it requires only a single change to be made in a project's build settings. Once enabled, calling retain or release on an object has no effect, because the Objective-C 2.0 runtime handles the memory management automatically. When the garbage collector collects, it searches through the network of objects in memory, looking for orphaned objects that are no longer in use by any other object (i.e., there are no references to them), and frees up the memory that they occupy.

If you're wondering why you've had to endure the torture of learning about manual memory management in this book, when it seems unnecessary given you can use garbage collection, there are a number of reasons.

First, garbage collection doesn't completely remove the need to worry about how much memory your application is using. If you work with an enormous collection of objects in memory, each keeping references to objects that they no longer need, the garbage collector won't free up the memory. Given that you understand manual memory management, you also understand the need to worry about whether you really need to keep track of some enormous array object (with all its contents), for example, or whether you can safely "release" that array by setting any pointers to it to nil.

You'll also find that a large amount of sample code and tutorials still use manual memory management, so even if you adopt garbage collection in your own desktop projects, you won't be able to forget about retain and release altogether.

Furthermore, if you like what you see in Appendix A, on page 383 and decide to write software for iPhone, you'll *have* to use manual memory management because at the time of writing, there's no garbage collector on the iPhone. Given that an iPhone has such a tiny memory allowance compared to a desktop machine, it's absolutely imperative to minimize the amount of memory you use, or the iPhone OS will terminate your application.

To find out more about garbage collection, start by looking at Apple's *Garbage Collector Programming Guide*.[2]

Other Cocoa Mechanisms

Cocoa has a number of "nuts-and-bolts" mechanisms that are either needed in order to make use of the higher-level frameworks or that simplify common tasks in an application's code.

One such mechanism is *Key-Value Coding* (KVC). KVC makes it possible to refer to the properties (*values*) of an object using string *keys*, rather like the way you work with an NSDictionary.

If an object has a property backgroundColor, that object is said to be *KVC-compliant* for the property if the accessor methods follow the conventions mentioned in Section 11.4, *Protection from the Outside World*, on page 259. For a backgroundColor property, the getter method should be called backgroundColor, and the setter method should be called set-BackgroundColor:.

---

2. http://developer.apple.com/mac/library/documentation/cocoa/conceptual/
GarbageCollection/

If these conventions are followed, the backgroundColor property can also be accessed using code like this:

```
NSColor *someColor = [someObject valueForKey:@"backgroundColor"];

[someObject setValue:someColor forKey:@"backgroundColor"];
```

There are various reasons why this is useful, not least because it enables us to use *Key-Value Observing* (KVO), where one object can register to observe the value held at a specific key in another object. When the value at the observed key is changed, the observing object is notified.

You'll remember that we had to write code in our Shopping List application to reload the relevant row in the table whenever a shopping list item was modified. There's another Cocoa technology, Bindings, that makes it possible to link a user interface item with a value on a model object such that we could bind a specific cell in the table view to the shopping list object's purchased value and have that cell update automatically whenever the purchased value changed. In reverse, if the user changed the state of the checkbox representing the purchased value, the related shopping list item's purchased attribute would be updated automatically.

Bindings, alongside KVC and KVO, make it possible to build simple Core Data–backed applications without writing any additional code beyond what is already in the Xcode template project. You model the data visually using the Xcode data modeler and then design the interface, binding interface items to special controller objects that access the underlying model, all using Interface Builder.

For more information, check out Apple's *Key-Value Coding Programming Guide*, *Key-Value Observing Programming Guide*, and *Cocoa Bindings Programming Topics*.

Concurrency

At the time of writing, the cheapest current-model Mac is the Mac Mini, which has an Intel Core 2 Duo processor. As the name implies, it has two *cores*. The top-of-the-line Mac Pros currently have two Quad Core processors, meaning they have a total of eight cores. It's not hard to imagine that future Mac lines will feature sixteen, thirty-two, or more cores.

In the past, technological advances in the computer world were shown by increasing processor speeds, amounts of RAM, and storage capacity. Recently, however, increases in standard RAM and hard drive sizes have slowed down, and processor speeds are reaching the upper limit of what's physically possible with today's technology.

Rather than increasing the *speed* of a processor to run more quickly, the new trend is to increase the number of *cores*. For your software to take advantage of this, you need to change the way you write code, splitting any long operation into multiple short operations that can be run across multiple CPU cores simultaneously.[3]

Cocoa and Objective-C 2.0 offer us a number of different ways to make use of concurrency; the highest-level of these require us to divide up our code into *tasks* or *operations*, which are passed to a queue, ready to be executed as soon as processor time becomes available. Under Mac OS X 10.6 Snow Leopard, we have access to Grand Central Dispatch (GCD), which simplifies the process of working with *asynchronous* tasks and offers great efficiency.

When you are writing your own software and deciding which framework or technique to use, it's always best to start at the top and find the highest-level option that hides away as much of the low-level drudgery as possible. Concurrency is no exception. If you can make use of operations and queues, then you should; otherwise, consider working directly with GCD. In an ideal world, you really want to avoid having to work with the more traditional and lower-level approach of using *threads*.

Check out Apple's *Concurrency Programming Guide* to learn more. Writing code that takes maximum advantage of multiprocessor environments is a complex topic, so don't put off if you struggle with some of the terminology, mechanisms, and syntax.

14.2 Finding Information

Now that you've got a brief overview of some of the topics you might want to investigate next, let's look at some of the best sources of information.

---

3. It's even possible to make use of something known as OpenCL to write code that can be run on the *GPU* cores available in graphics cards.

Books

We've already mentioned a few topic-specific books that cover some of the Core technologies in Cocoa. If you're looking for a more general Cocoa book, take a look at Daniel Steinberg's *Cocoa Programming: A Quick-Start Guide for Developers* [Ste09] or Aaron Hillegass's *Cocoa Programming for Mac OS X* [Hil08], currently in its third edition.

If you would like to learn more about the Objective-C language, check out Stephen Kochan's *Programming in Objective-C 2.0, Second Edition* [Koc09], or Mark Dalrymple and Scott Knaster's *Learn Objective-C on the Mac* [DK09].

Developer Documentation

As we've seen throughout this book, Xcode provides a built-in set of documentation that's a great place to find out which method does what or to look up the exact signature for any particular delegate method you might want to implement.

A number of guides and tutorials give an overview, rather than a reference, of certain key technologies and frameworks, some of which I mentioned earlier in the chapter.

One of the most important documents (though it's frequently overlooked) is the *Human Interface Guidelines* (HIG), which describe the way a Mac application is expected to look and behave. If you want a user to be able to sit down and immediately be comfortable working with your application, make sure it works in the same way as all their other software. Certain menu commands should always be found under certain menus, for example, and if you design your own custom user interface items, they should follow certain guidelines.

There's also a separate HIG document for the iPhone. Designing a user interface for the iPhone is very different from designing for the Mac desktop—you can't just shrink the contents of a 17-inch desktop display so that they fit on a 3.5-inch iPhone screen!

The header files for Cocoa classes (accessed most easily using Xcode's File > Open Quickly... command) can be another useful source of information, in the form of code comments. If you're not sure why a method isn't being called or a value isn't set correctly, you might find a note in the header file explaining why something doesn't behave quite as expected.

The Internet

When it comes to finding information on specific tools and techniques, or to solve a particular problem, Internet search engines are definitely the first place to start, but the success of this strategy depends on knowing the exact terms used to describe what it is you want to do.

If you didn't know that a dialog box that drops down from the top of a window (like the standard Mac OS X Print dialog box) was actually called a *sheet*, rather than a *dialog box*, for example, you might have some difficulty locating the relevant information. If you're not sure about the correct terminology for something, try looking in Apple's overview guides for the general topic or the Human Interface Guidelines if you're not sure what to call a particular interface element. Sheets, for example, are introduced under the "Dialogs" section in the *Windows* chapter of the HIG.

There are many Mac developer blogs out there that are a great source for undocumented tips and tricks, warnings about common misunderstandings, through to tutorials that walk you through very specific tasks.

Asking Questions

If you've exhausted the documentation options and can't find a relevant blog post, there are several ways to ask other people for help:

- StackOverflow.com is a website for developers from all platforms and languages, and it allows anybody to ask (or answer) questions on any programming topic.

- There are several Apple-run email lists for Mac developers. The most common of these is cocoa-dev,[4] for asking questions about anything to do with Cocoa. There's also an Xcode-specific list, and some of the more advanced frameworks have their own separate lists.

  Try subscribing to cocoa-dev for a while, even if you don't post anything. You'll see a huge amount of information pass through the list, some of which you'll want to ignore, but you'll often catch nuggets of information directly useful to something you are working on.

---

4. http://lists.apple.com/mailman/listinfo/cocoa-dev

- Apple also has its own developer forums; at the time of writing, these are in beta and available only to paid members of the Apple developer programs (the cheapest of which is currently $499 per year). The iPhone forum is accessible to paid members of the iPhone developer program (currently $99 per year).

Before you ask for help, there are some important points to bear in mind. First, don't ask other people to do your work for you. Don't post a message that simply asks "How do I write a program to download web pages?" You will either be ignored or greeted with a barrage of abusive replies.

Start by searching the archives for the mailing list (or previous forum entries) to make sure your question hasn't already been asked and answered. Assuming it hasn't, start by explaining the problem clearly, describe exactly what you've tried so far, and state clearly what hasn't worked.

You can take a look at Matt Gemmell's blog post on this topic, available at http://www.whathaveyoutried.com, for a more detailed explanation of how to ask questions. The fact that the blog post has a dedicated domain name should give you some idea how important it is to follow the correct etiquette.

Making Contacts

Twitter is an excellent way to get connected with other Mac developers. You can follow conversations about interesting problems or see the latest and greatest tools and techniques get summed up in less than 140 characters.

The best networking (the social kind) is done in person at Mac developer events. Check http://www.cocoaheads.org/ and http://nscodernight.com to see whether there's a local developer group near you. These events are great for getting together, usually with drinks, and sharing coding problems with like-minded people.

The major Mac developer conference is WWDC (http://developer.apple.com/wwdc/), run by Apple each year in San Francisco. This is a mammoth event with several thousand attendees, so it can be a bit daunting for first-timers, but there are also lots of independent conferences run throughout the year on a smaller scale, such as C4 (http://c4.rentzsch.com/) in Chicago, and NSConference (http://www.nsconference.com/), which I coorganize, in the United States and Europe. These conferences are often as much about networking as they are about technical content, and they have only a few hundred attendees, so it's easy for everybody to get to talk to everybody else.

14.3 Book Summary

That's it! (Well, almost...)

Congratulations on making it through the early stages of becoming a software developer. I hope you feel confident enough to venture out on your own, start designing your own applications from scratch, and figure out where to go when you need help.

It's an overwhelming feeling when you start your first Xcode project for your first application. You'll probably very quickly discover that you don't yet know enough to do exactly what you want, but don't panic. Work out the general topic that you need to learn, Google a few search terms, look at some overview guides, read a few blog posts, and everything really will be OK.

As you become more accomplished, keep in mind that you should never have any code in your project that you don't fully understand or know exactly why it's there and what it does. In the beginning, this is obviously going to be difficult, and it's tempting to copy and paste code from any source that looks like it might work. Try to examine why each line of code that you use is necessary, and experiment a little to see whether you can't make it work better.

Unless you're writing a virus,[5] working with very low-level code, or trying to write information to protected directories, it's hard to do any permanent damage to your system, so experiment to see what works and what doesn't. If you find something that does work, however, make sure you understand *why* it works. Don't just assume that because you've fiddled a method to work in the way you want this time, it will *always* work in the right way!

This isn't quite the end of the book. Now that you've learned about Mac desktop programming, you might like to try your hand at writing software for the iPhone; if so, Appendix A, on page 383 might be just what you're looking for.

---

5. Please don't.

Appendix A

Developing for the iPhone OS

Even though this book is titled *Beginning **Mac** Programming*, there's so much overlap between what we've already learned and what's needed to write software for the iPhone OS, that it's worth taking a quick peek at what's possible on the "other Apple platform."

The iPhone OS is the operating system running on iPhones, iPod touches, and also on Apple's new iPad device. At the time of writing, the tools and techniques used to build iPad applications are under Non-Disclosure Agreement, so I can't discuss them here. Rest assured, however, that a standard iPhone OS application will run just fine on the iPad. From now on, when I talk about the "iPhone," take it to mean any device that runs the iPhone OS.

In this chapter, we're going to build a fairly simple iPhone application that displays a message to the user when a button is pushed on screen. To make it a little more interesting, we'll allow the user to specify the message to be shown, storing this preference in what's known as *user defaults*. This will be restored any time the application is run in the future.

We'll be learning about how the iPhone works with views and view controllers and seeing how to tap into the view cycle to change interface elements just before they appear on screen. Along the way, we'll learn about some of the differences between Mac and iPhone development and look at how to work with Cocoa Touch on iPhone OS devices, rather than the Cocoa classes we've been using on the desktop.

Everything that we'll learn about user defaults also applies on the desktop, so even if you never plan on writing your own iPhone software, the information will still be useful.

Figure A.1: THE NEW PROJECT WINDOW FOR IPHONE APPLICATIONS

Before we can get started, make sure that you have followed the instructions in Section B, *Installing the iPhone SDK*, on page 403. You don't need to have an iPhone developer account (or even an iPhone) to follow this chapter, because we'll be working entirely in the iPhone Simulator.

Once the iPhone SDK is installed, we're ready to make our first iPhone application!

Creating an iPhone Project

Launch Xcode, and choose File > New Project... (⇧-⌘-N). Then click Application, under the iPhone OS heading, as shown in Figure A.1.

Xcode offers a number of different templates for iPhone applications:[1]

- An app based on the Navigation-Based Application template allows the user to navigate back and forth through screens of information, like Apple's own Mail application on the iPhone, which navigates into and out of mail inboxes and subfolders.
- An app based on the OpenGL ES Application template uses 3D rendering with OpenGL to display its interface; this template is often used for developing games.
- An app based on the Tab Bar Application template uses tabs along the bottom of the interface so that the user can tap to switch between different screens of information, like the iPhone's all-important Phone application, with its tabs for Favorites, Recents, Contacts, Keypad, and Voicemail.
- The View-based and Window-based Application templates are simple starting templates, leaving you to decide how you want to structure the application.

We'll be using the Utility Application template for our application, so select it in the New Project window, and click Choose.... Call the application "MessageTapper," and click Save.

Before we examine any of the files in the project, click Build & Run to compile the project and launch it in the iPhone Simulator.

Once the simulator has appeared on your screen, the new application will be installed and run, so we can see what we get bundled up for free with the Utility Application template.

The simulator screen will fill with gray, along with a single i button. Tap (click) this button, and you'll be treated to a veritable masterpiece of Core Animation technology, flipping the screen around to display what appears on the reverse side, as shown in Figure A.2, on the next page.

Tap the Done button, and the screen will flip back again. Press the simulator's Home button to exit the application, and then switch back to Xcode to see how much code it takes to make all this work.

---

1. Bear in mind that just because you choose one type of application template when you create your project, it doesn't mean you can't incorporate features from the other types later—many iPhone applications exhibit characteristics from each of the Xcode template projects. The templates are just there to give you a head start.

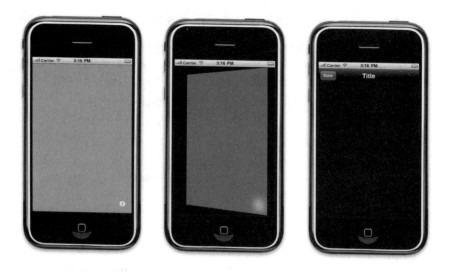

Figure A.2: A UTILITY APPLICATION IN THE SIMULATOR

Examining the Files

The important code and interface files from this template are organized into groups—expand the Main View, Flipside View, Application Delegate, and Resources groups to see their contents.

You'll find that the Resources group contains a MainWindow.xib file, which is similar to the standard MainMenu.xib file found in desktop apps—it sets up a "window" (which you can think of as a portal through which information is displayed on the iPhone screen) and the application delegate. If you open MessageTapperAppDelegate.m, you'll see that the template class includes two methods, applicationDidFinishLaunching: and dealloc, just like you might find in any desktop app delegate object.

The applicationDidFinishLaunching: method creates a new *view controller*, an instance of MainViewController, using the contents of the MainView.xib interface file.

We've talked quite a bit about *controller* objects on the desktop. On the iPhone, if you have a view that fills the screen (like a list of email messages), that view will usually have an accompanying *view controller*. We'll look at iPhone view controllers in a minute; for now, open Main-View.xib in Interface Builder to see how the view is set up.

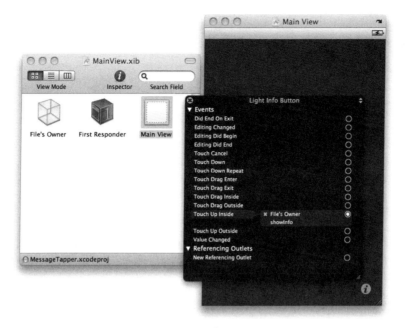

Figure A.3: THE INTERFACE BUILDER FILE FOR AN IPHONE VIEW

When the file opens, double-click the Main View object to open the view, and then right-click (or ^-click) the little i button at the bottom right of the view editor, as shown in Figure A.3.

You'll find that a button object on the iPhone has a number of different *events* available to connect to different *actions*. The Touch Up Inside outlet of the button is connected to the showInfo method on File's Owner, which means that if a user taps the button and then releases their finger still over the button, this method will be called. This is usual button behavior, allowing a user to change their mind and drag out of the button before releasing their finger, and it mimics the behavior we wrote into our WVShapesView in Section 13.3, *Providing Visual Feedback*, on page 351.

The File's Owner object in MainView.xib will be a MainViewController object, so switch back to Xcode, and open MainViewController.h to see how the class is defined.

The interface for the MainViewController class looks like this:

```
@interface MainViewController : UIViewController <FlipsideViewControllerDelegate> {
}

- (IBAction)showInfo:(id)sender;

@end
```

You'll notice that this class adopts a *delegate* protocol, FlipsideViewControllerDelegate, which we'll look at later. The most important thing, however, is that it inherits from UIViewController.

Although we haven't covered them in this book, view controller objects are also available on the Mac desktop,[2] with a classname of **NS**ViewController. On the iPhone, the classname is **UI**ViewController, which is the first class we've seen belonging to UIKit.

Introducing Cocoa Touch and UIKit

Every single chapter of this book has referred to objects from the Cocoa framework—so far, always bearing the initials **NS**. What I haven't yet mentioned is that "the Cocoa framework" is actually made up of multiple frameworks, including *Foundation* and *Application Kit*.

The Foundation framework includes objects sch as NSObject, NSArray, and NSDictionary—the basic building blocks for our code. The Application Kit (or *AppKit*) framework includes objects such as NSWindow, NSTextView, and NSMenuItem—the visual elements that define Mac OS X desktop applications.

Since a window on the desktop is a very different concept from a window on an iPhone, and the iPhone doesn't run Mac OS X, we don't have access to any of the AppKit classes when we develop software for the iPhone. Instead, we have access to *UIKit*, containing objects like UIWindow and UITextView. As you might already have realized, these classes generally have names beginning with *UI*.

Although we don't have AppKit on the iPhone, the fundamental objects provided by the Foundation framework *are* available. Together with UIKit (and lots more besides), they're referred to as *Cocoa Touch*, the iPhone-equivalent of Cocoa on the desktop.

---

2. They're normally used to split a complex window interface into more manageable components.

Now that you know about UIKit, let's get back to looking at how our iPhone application works.

Flipping the View

Open MainViewController.m, and find the implementation for the showInfo: method (the method called when the user taps the i button). It looks like this:

```
- (IBAction)showInfo:(id)sender {
    FlipsideViewController *controller = [[FlipsideViewController alloc]
                                initWithNibName:@"FlipsideView" bundle:nil];
    controller.delegate = self;

    controller.modalTransitionStyle = UIModalTransitionStyleFlipHorizontal;
    [self presentModalViewController:controller animated:YES];

    [controller release];
}
```

This method creates the new view controller, using an alloc] init...] call, sets itself as the delegate, sets a *transition style*, and then calls present-ModalViewController:animated: to display the view controller *modally*. A modal view controller is like a modal dialog box on the desktop—it prevents the user from doing anything else in the application until it's dismissed. Finally, the controller is released (it will be retained elsewhere while it's on screen) to match the initial alloc.

Next, open FlipsideViewController.m to see what's happening inside this file. There's another **IBAction**, done:,[3] which is connected (in Flipside-View.xib) to the Done button. This method looks like this:

```
- (IBAction)done:(id)sender {
    [self.delegate flipsideViewControllerDidFinish:self];
}
```

A modal UIViewController has to be dismissed from the screen by the same view controller that originally called presentModalViewController:animated: to display it, which, in this case, is the MainViewController.

For the two view controllers to communicate, the MainViewController sets itself as the *delegate* of the FlipsideViewController object, as we've already seen, and conforms to a protocol defined in FlipsideViewController.h.

---

3. You may find that some of the IBAction methods in Xcode template files are missing the :(id)sender. It won't make any difference; you just won't be able to find out which object sent the message in the first place.

MainViewController implements the delegate message flipsideViewControllerDidFinish: to dismiss the modal view controller, like this:

```
- (void)flipsideViewControllerDidFinish:(FlipsideViewController *)controller {
    [self dismissModalViewControllerAnimated:YES];
}
```

This has the effect of reversing the animation effect used to display the flip-side view.

Note that the *views* displayed by the view controllers are each a subclass of UIView, allowing us to customize their appearance; if you look in the code files for these views, however, you'll find that, as in MainView.m, the method implementations inside don't actually do anything, so they are effectively standard UIView instances.

Adding Our Messaging Behavior

Now that we've been introduced to the underlying structure of our application, let's add some simple messaging functionality. We'll start by adding a button to the main view, so open MainView.xib.

Drag a UIButton from the Library palette, drop it in the middle of the view, and change its title to "Tap Me!"

Next, drag out a UILabel object to display the message.[4] Resize it to stretch across the view, and then use the Attributes inspector to change the text Layout to centered and the Color to white so that your view looks like Figure A.4, on the facing page.

Switch to Xcode, and open MainViewController.h; add an outlet for the label and an action method to display the message, like this:

```
@interface MainViewController : UIViewController <FlipsideViewControllerDelegate> {
    IBOutlet UILabel *messageLabel;
}

- (IBAction)showInfo:(id)sender;
- (IBAction)displayMessage:(id)sender;

@end
```

---

4. Note that a label in UIKit is its own object, a UILabel, rather than just an uneditable variety of an NSTextField under AppKit on the desktop.

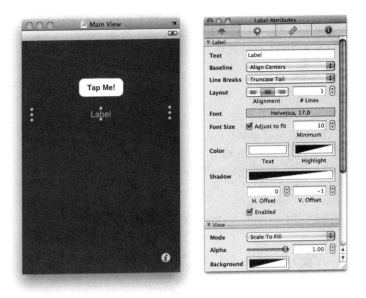

Figure A.4: THE BUTTON AND LABEL IN INTERFACE BUILDER

Return to the MainView.xib file in Interface Builder, link up the message-Label outlet, and then connect the displayMessage action to the button's Touch Up Inside event. Save the file, and return to Xcode.

Open MainViewController.m, and implement the displayMessage: method, like this:

```
- (IBAction)displayMessage:(id)sender
{
    [messageLabel setText:@"Hello World!"];
}
```

Before we test the application, there's one very important point to notice: **IBOutlet**s in iPhone applications need to be specifically released from memory, unlike their desktop counterparts.

So, find the MainViewController's dealloc method and release the outlet:

```
- (void)dealloc {
    [messageLabel release];
    [super dealloc];
}
```

Build & Run the application to test this in the simulator. When you press the button, you'll see the message displayed by the label; the only problem is that the label shows the text "Label" when you first start the application.

We could fix this just by removing the label's initial title in the xib file, but it would be even better if the label was hidden whenever the view appeared. This would have the added benefit that if the user presses the i button to flip the view and then presses Done, the label will be hidden, ready to be redisplayed when the Tap Me! button is pressed.

Making Use of Inherited View Controller Functionality

There are a number of useful UIViewController methods that are called when a controller is loaded into memory or its view displayed:

```
- viewDidLoad        // called when a view controller is loaded into memory
- viewWillAppear:    // called just before a view appears on screen
- viewDidAppear:     // called just after a view has appeared on screen
- viewWillDisappear: // called just before a view disappears from screen
- viewDidDisappear:  // called just after a view disappears from screen
- viewDidUnload      // called when a view controller is unloaded from memory
```

We can use the viewWillAppear: method to hide the label just before the view is displayed on screen; we'll also have to show the label again after we've set its text in displayMessage:. So, add the following into MainView-Controller.m:

```
- (void)viewWillAppear:(BOOL)animated {
    [super viewWillAppear:animated];

    [messageLabel setHidden:YES];
}

- (IBAction)displayMessage:(id)sender
{
    [messageLabel setText:@"Hello World!"];
    [messageLabel setHidden:NO];
}
```

Note that we need to call the inherited viewWillAppear: method before we do anything ourselves.[5]

---

5. The animated argument specifies whether the view appeared on screen with animation or whether it was displayed with a call like [self presentModalViewController:controller animated:NO], which would cause the view to appear immediately.

Build & Run the application again; this time the label will be hidden at launch, reappear when the button is pressed, and then disappear once more if you flip in and out of the other view. That was pretty easy!

Next, let's make use of the flip-side view to allow users to set their own message texts.

Allowing the User to Change the Text

We're going to be working with a text field, an instance of the UIKit class UITextField, so let's add an outlet for this into FlipsideViewController.h before setting up the interface.

The messageLabel outlet we created earlier in the chapter was declared in the same way as every other outlet in this book, using the **IBOutlet** keyword on the front of the instance variable declaration. If you look at a lot of iPhone sample code, however, you'll find that outlets in iPhone code are normally specified using properties. As mentioned in the side-bar on page 326, if you declare a @property for the outlet, the **IBOutlet** should go in the *property* declaration, rather than the *instance variable* declaration.

Let's declare the outlet for the text field using a property, in FlipsideView-Controller.h:

```
@interface FlipsideViewController : UIViewController {
    id <FlipsideViewControllerDelegate> delegate;

    UITextField *messageTextField;
}

@property (nonatomic, assign) id <FlipsideViewControllerDelegate> delegate;
@property (retain) IBOutlet UITextField *messageTextField;
- (IBAction)done:(id)sender;

@end
```

You will need to @synthesize the property in FlipsideViewController.m and release it in the dealloc method:

```
@implementation FlipsideViewController

@synthesize delegate;
@synthesize messageTextField;

- (void)dealloc {
    [messageTextField release];
    [super dealloc];
}
```

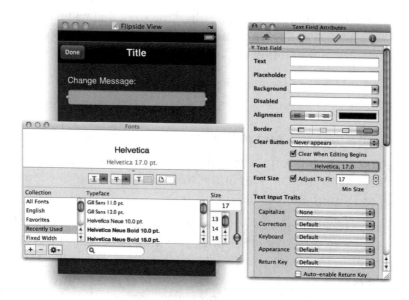

Figure A.5: CONFIGURING THE UITEXTFIELD IN INTERFACE BUILDER

We're now ready to add this text field to the interface, so open Flipside-View.xib in Interface Builder.

Start by adding a UILabel object near the top of the view, with its title set to "Change Message:" and the Text Color set to white.

Next, drag a UITextField from the Library palette, and drop it under the label. Resize it to fill the view horizontally, and use the Attributes inspector to change the font to Helvetica, 17pt, as shown in Figure A.5.

Connect the messageTextField outlet from File's Owner to the text field, save the file, and then return to Xcode.

Build & Run the project to see what you have so far. Once the application has launched in the simulator, tap the i button to display the flip-side view; tap the text field to make it *first responder*, and the standard iPhone keyboard will appear, ready for you to type a message.

If you click the Done button, the modal dialog box will disappear, along with the keyboard. The only thing we haven't yet implemented is a means to pass the typed message over to the main view controller, ready for display in the label.

We might implement this behavior in several ways. One example would be to add a method to the FlipsideViewControllerDelegate protocol to allow us to send a message back to the main view controller.

Since we also need to be able to keep track of the message for later retrieval, let's see how to store the value in *user defaults*, giving us the added benefit that the stored value can be accessed by the other view controller without us having to pass it directly.

Working with User Defaults

It's extremely common for applications, both on the desktop and on the iPhone, to allow the user to specify *preferences*. An email application might allow the user to change the font used to display the text of a message, for example, or change the signature used at the bottom of outgoing messages.

Both Cocoa and Cocoa Touch make it extremely easy to save this kind of information, through the use of a class called *NSUserDefaults*.

Working with NSUserDefaults is just like working with a dictionary object; you set values for specified keys, and those values are saved into a suitable preferences file, ready to be accessed at a later stage.

Let's see how to modify our MessageTapper application to save any user-defined message into the user defaults; we'll do this when the user presses the Done button on the flip-side view.

We will need to have access to an NSUserDefaults instance—luckily, NSUserDefaults offers a class method, standardUserDefaults, which returns just what we need.

So, open FlipsideViewController.m, and change the done: action to the following:

```
- (IBAction)done:(id)sender {
    NSString *messageString = [self.messageTextField text];
    NSUserDefaults *userDefaults = [NSUserDefaults standardUserDefaults];
    [userDefaults setObject:messageString forKey:@"kMessageString"];

    [self.delegate flipsideViewControllerDidFinish:self];
}
```

We start by asking the messageTextField for its text; then, we get hold of the standardUserDefaults object and use it to set the message string under the key @"kMessageString".[6]

Add a viewWillAppear: method to display the current message string in the text field when this flip-side view appears:

```
- (void)viewWillAppear:(BOOL)animated {
    NSString *messageString = [[NSUserDefaults standardUserDefaults]
                                      stringForKey:@"kMessageString"];
    [self.messageTextField setText:messageString];
}
```

Next, we need to change the code that displays the message on the main view so that the string is taken from the user defaults.

Open MainViewController.m, and change the displayMessage: method to this:

```
- (IBAction)displayMessage:(id)sender
{
    NSString *messageString = [[NSUserDefaults standardUserDefaults]
                                      stringForKey:@"kMessageString"];
    [messageLabel setText:messageString];
    [messageLabel setHidden:NO];
}
```

Don't test the application yet—there's a problem with this solution: the first time a user runs the application, there won't be a string stored in user defaults, so there won't be any message to display when the button is tapped.

We could run a test to check whether a string exists and generate one if not, but there's a better way. NSUserDefaults allows us to register *default values* for specific keys; these values will be used until the user overrides them.[7]

---

6. You might prefer to consolidate these three lines of code into one: [[NSUserDefaults standardUserDefaults] setObject:[self.messageTextField text] forKey:@"kMessageString"]; and/or use a global string variable to keep track of the key, as described in Section 13.2, *Declaring Global Variables*, on page 339 (you'll need to refer to the sidebar on page 340 to find out how to make that global variable accessible from other files that want to use it).

7. There's also the added benefit that we can *reset* the user defaults to their original values at any time, allowing a user to get rid of non-default preferences and return the application to its "factory" state.

Setting Default Values

The method we need to use to set these initial values is registerDefaults:, which takes a dictionary containing the values we want set for each key. This seems easy enough; the only question is *when* should we do this?

To set the initial defaults to be ready the first time they are requested, we need to register them as early as possible after the application is launched. Any ideas when this might be?

I hope you remembered that the application delegate object has an applicationDidFinishLaunching: method, which will be called just after the application launches. This is the perfect place, so open MessageTapper-AppDelegate.m, and add the following:

```
- (void)applicationDidFinishLaunching:(UIApplication *)application {
    NSDictionary *initialDefaults =
                    [NSDictionary dictionaryWithObject:@"Hello World!"
                                               forKey:@"kMessageString"];
    [[NSUserDefaults standardUserDefaults] registerDefaults:initialDefaults];

    MainViewController *aController = [[MainViewController alloc]
                                        initWithNibName:@"MainView" bundle:nil];
    self.mainViewController = aController;
    [aController release];

    mainViewController.view.frame = [UIScreen mainScreen].applicationFrame;
    [window addSubview:[mainViewController view]];
    [window makeKeyAndVisible];
}
```

Build & Run the application, and you'll find that the *Hello World!* message is still displayed when you tap the button. You can change the message if you want, and this message will be saved; if you exit the application and relaunch, the message will still be there. Hooray!

Summary

This appendix has taken us on a whistle-stop tour of a simple iPhone application. We've covered a lot of technical concepts—some specific to the iPhone and some that also apply to the desktop.

Developing for the iPhone involves working with Cocoa Touch, which includes some of the functionality from Cocoa on the desktop, but the AppKit classes (like NSWindow) are replaced by UIKit classes (like UIWindow).

We've seen how to work with user defaults (which work in the same way on the desktop) to store user *preferences* for an application—you don't want to use them to store any data that users might want to locate on disk, though, not least because most users aren't too comfortable trawling through Library directories, looking for unusually named files where the values are stored.

If you are now hooked on iPhone development, you might want to consider signing up as a registered iPhone developer through http:// developer.apple.com/iphone. This will enable you to *provision* an iPhone (or iPod touch) for use as a development machine so that you can test your applications on a real device. Once you've developed the killer application you've got in mind, you'll be able to submit it for sale on the App Store and then sit back and watch the money roll in!

Installing Xcode

One of the great things about Apple's developer tools is that they are available free of charge to anybody who wants them.

There are two options for getting hold of the software, either from Apple's Developer Connection website or from a Mac OS X install disc. This could be either the system disc that came with your Mac or a Snow Leopard installation disc if you bought the upgrade later.

If you have a previous version of Xcode on your machine and want to upgrade to the latest version, then continue reading—the process is similar. You may find that you have some remnants of the older version even after running the installation scripts, and we'll look at a few ways to clear these out.

Developer Tools Installation

The best option is to download the Developer Tools from the Web to ensure you have the most recent version—it's a sizeable download, though (a gigabyte or more).

If you don't have a fast Internet connection or don't want to have to register for any developer accounts, skip to Section B, *Using System Discs*, on the next page, to locate the tools on your Mac OS X system install discs.

Downloading the Tools

If you want to be able to take advantage of the iPhone information in Appendix A, on page 383, it's worth downloading the iPhone SDK package now, because it includes *both* Mac and iPhone support. You'll need to register for a free iPhone developer account before you can download anything, though, and you'll also need an Intel-based Mac. Here are the steps:

1. Go to http://developer.apple.com/iphone/.

2. Click the Register link (at the time of writing, this can be accessed directly via http://developer.apple.com/iphone/sdk1/), and follow the instructions.

3. Once you've registered your account and logged in, find the Downloads section. There may be two different download headings, depending on whether you're running Mac OS X 10.5 Leopard or Mac OS X 10.6 Snow Leopard, so make sure you pick the right file under the correct heading.

4. There should be two files listed, one with a title like iPhone SDK 3.1.2 with Xcode 3.2.1 (the version numbers may be higher) and the other with a title like iPhone SDK 3.1.2 with Xcode 3.2.1 Readme. You want the first of these files—don't worry about the Readme, because it's included inside the SDK package anyway.

If you don't have an Intel-based Mac or don't want to install the whole iPhone SDK as well as the Mac, you can download an Xcode package without the iPhone SDK. You'll need to register for a free Mac Developer Program account:

1. Go to http://developer.apple.com/products/membership.html, and follow the instructions to register for a free ADC online membership.

2. Once you've registered and logged in, find the link to download Xcode; the name should be something like Xcode 3.2.1 under Snow Leopard or Xcode 3.1.4 for Leopard (the version numbers may be higher).

When the download completes, you'll end up with a .dmg disk image; double-click this in the Finder to mount it, and then skip to Section B, *The Installation Process*, on the next page.

Using System Discs

The Mac-only Developer Tools are included on the system discs that originally came with your Mac; they're also on any OS Installation discs if you purchased an OS upgrade at a later date.

You'll find Xcode inside the Optional Installs directory, as an installer package with a name like Xcode.mpkg.

The Installation Process

Once you've located the installer, double-click it to launch it. You'll need to agree to a license agreement (two if you're installing from the iPhone SDK package) before continuing.

You'll be asked to customize the installation, selecting various options in the list—it's usually fine just to accept the default options. If you're given the option of installing Mac OS X 10.4 Support, you might want to leave this unchecked; if you specifically need to write software that will run under earlier versions of Mac OS X, you can always install this later.

Follow the rest of the instructions on screen to install the Developer Tools package on your system.

What's Been Installed?

When the installation finishes, it might not be immediately obvious what's been installed, or where.

The Developer Tools package is a collection of applications, software development kits (SDKs), and documentation, most of which is installed inside the Developer directory at the root level of your main hard disk. Rather confusingly, the term *Xcode* can be used to refer either to the entire Developer Tools collection or just to the specific Xcode application. When you see Xcode mentioned in the main body of this book, it's generally referring to the application.

You can find Xcode in the *Developer* directory's Applications directory. You might want to add Xcode to your Dock to save having to locate it every time you want to use it. You don't necessarily need to add Interface Builder to the Dock because you can launch it when you need it by double-clicking an interface file from within an Xcode project.

This should be everything you need to work through the book!

Upgrade Problems

If you already have an older version of Xcode on your system before you run through the installation process, you may run into some issues where the older templates continue to show up for new projects. This seems to happen occasionally when upgrading from Xcode 3.1 to Xcode 3.2 on Snow Leopard.

If you run into this problem, there are various things you can do to try to fix it—some of these fixes involve working in the command line, some with removing files by hand from library directories, so exercise caution!

The first thing to do is to try uninstalling the Developer Tools completely and then starting the whole installation process from scratch. The Release Notes or Readme included with the latest version that you have will include a section titled "Uninstalling Xcode Developer Tools"; at the time of this writing, this involves using a Terminal window and typing commands.

To find the Terminal application, open your *main* Applications directory (as in, the one with Mail, Safari, and so on), and find the Utilities directory inside. The terminal app allows you to interact with your Mac in a more traditional, command-line way.

The removal instructions in the Xcode Readme involve the use of a command preceded by the word sudo, looking something like this:

```
sudo <Xcode>/Library/uninstall-devtools --mode=all
```

You'll need to replace the <Xcode> part with the location of the developer tools. Assuming you haven't specified a different location, this will be /Developer:

```
sudo /Developer/Library/uninstall-devtools --mode=all
```

The sudo term is used to indicate that the following command should be executed with root privileges, so you'll be asked for your password; type this into the terminal (the password characters won't appear), and press the ↵ key to continue.

Note that it's possible to do various nasty things to your system by typing the wrong command into the Terminal; make sure you have a good backup in place if you don't feel confident with the command line.

Once this uninstall script has completed, start the whole Developer Tools installation process again.

If you find you still have problems, you might want to try removing the necessary files manually. This means removing the entire /Developer directory itself first and then any additional supporting files.

Check in the Library directory, inside your home directory, and open the Application Support directory. A quick Finder shortcut to get to this directory is to select Go > Go to Folder... (⇧-⌘-G) and type the following:

```
~/Library/Application Support
```

The first character is a *tilde* and will be translated into "the user directory for the current user."

Click OK, and you will see the contents of this directory. Look for any directories relating to Xcode or the Developer Tools and remove them; this might include Apple Developer Tools, Xcode, and Developer directories.

The Application Support directory is used to hold user preference and configuration files relating to the current user. Removing these files shouldn't break anything, but again it's a good idea to have a backup of your system before proceeding.[1]

Installing the iPhone SDK

If you previously downloaded only the Mac tools or installed Xcode from a system disk, the only way to get hold of the iPhone SDK is to download it and install it on top.

You'll need to register for an iPhone developer account (there's a free option) and follow the instructions from Section B, *Downloading the Tools*, on page 399 onward. When you run the installer package, you'll find that it now indicates that some files will be installed, but some will either just be upgraded or ignored altogether.

You'll be able to test your iPhone applications in the iPhone simulator, running on your Mac. If you own an iPhone or iPod Touch, you won't be able to test your applications on that device unless you sign up for one of Apple's paid iPhone developer programs (from $99 per year).

---

1. It's always a good idea to have regular backups of your important files! Apple's Time Machine software, built into Mac OS X since 10.5 Leopard, makes it very easy to keep regular backups. Given that large hard disks are now so inexpensive, it's getting more and more difficult to come up with excuses not to have a backup system in place.

Appendix C

Bibliography

[DK09]   Mark Dalrymple and Scott Knaster. *Learn Objective-C on the Mac.* Apress, New York, NY, 2009.

[Dud08]   Bill Dudney. *Core Animation for OS X: Creating Dynamic Compelling User Interfaces.* The Pragmatic Programmers, LLC, Raleigh, NC, and Dallas, TX, 2008.

[Hil08]   Aaron Hillegass. *Cocoa Programming for Mac OS X.* Addison-Wesley, Reading, MA, third edition, 2008.

[Ist10a] Tim Isted. *Building Data-Driven Desktop Applications for Mac OS X.* Addison-Wesley, Boston, MA, 2010.

[Ist10b] Tim Isted. *Core Data for iPhone: Building Data-Driven Applications for the iPhone and iPod Touch.* Addison-Wesley, Boston, MA, 2010.

[Koc09]   Stephen G. Kochan. *Programming in Objective-C 2.0.* Addison-Wesley, Boston, MA, second edition, 2009.

[Ste09]   Daniel H Steinberg. *Cocoa Programming: A Quick-Start Guide for Developers.* The Pragmatic Programmers, LLC, Raleigh, NC, and Dallas, TX, 2009.

[Zar09]   Marcus Zarra. *Core Data: Apple's API for Persisting Data under Mac OS X.* The Pragmatic Programmers, LLC, Raleigh, NC, and Dallas, TX, 2009.

[ZL09]   Marcus Zarra and Matt Long. *Core Animation: Simplified Animation Techniques for Mac and iPhone Development.* Addison-Wesley, Boston, MA, 2009.

Index

Symbols

%p, 85, 87
+ sign, 106, 135
- sign, 106
= sign, 181
@"\n" newline character, 138
@ notation, 151
@%f string, 128
[super dealloc] method, 166
!, 193
++ operator, 218, 219
-- operator, 218, 219
== operator, 195
= operator, 271
@"string", 215
&& operator, 190
|| operator, 189, 198
>= operator, 222
> operator, 220, 222
<= operator, 222
< operator, 220–222

A

Abstract class, 365
acceptsFirstResponder method, 356
Accessor methods, 194, 262, 263
    Objective-C 2.0 properties, 266–272
Action signature, 55
Actions
    connecting button to, 58f
    connecting to, 55
    sent by push button, 59f
addNewItemToShoppingList: method, 250
Address Book application, 177
Address checking, 85
Alert display, 206, 207f
alloc method, 115, 134, 137
Ampersands, 85
AND operator, 190, 191

Angle brackets, 318
Animation frames, 373
Apple developer forums, 380
Apple-run email lists, 379
Application delegate, 279, 325
Application Kit, 388
Application object, 38
applicationDidFinishLaunching: method,
    327, 397
applicationWillFinishLaunching: method,
    327
Archiving, 362–369
Arguments, 53
    initializing with, 131–134
    methods and, 99–104
    rowIndex, 169
Array of arrays, 237
Arrays
    adding items to, 152, 153f
    collecting, 142
    count message, rows, 168
    counting items in, 147
    creating, 166
    defined, 139
    editing items, 170
    efficiency of, 149
    index of items, 145
    indices for, 223
    introduced, 139–142
    list view, in IB, 161f
    memory and, 150
    multiple, 237
    naming conventions, 140
    opening a saved list, 173
    pointers and, 150
    releasing, 166
    saving, 172
    setting up, 164

in shopping list application, 154f,
    154–175
shopping list application,
    dictionaries, 246–256
static, 147
strong object reference, 150
table view, 159f
table views and, 167
using, 142–147
    see also Looping, see also Objects
arrayWithCapacity:, 149
arrayWithObjects: method, 140
ASCII, 79
Ash, Mike, 203
assign keyword, 268
Assignable values, 27
Assignment operator, 74–76, 179, 180,
    203, 209, 271
Asterisks, 53, 60, 87, 111
Asynchronous tasks, 377
aTableColumn, 236
Attribute inspector, 303
Attributes, 28, 172
    Core Data, 373
    inheritance and, 32
Attributes palette, 99
autorelease, 129, 130
Autoreleasing, 134
Autosizing, 285
awakeFromNib method, 327

B

Base object class, 37
Bezier path object, 299
Binary notation, 69
Bindings, 318, 376
Bits, 68, 69, 76
Blocks of code, 40
BOOL keyword, 65
BOOL variable, 193, 195
Boolean values, 65, 193
bounds property, 292
break keyword, 225, 230, 231
break statement, 201
Bugs, 187, 201
Build & Run command, 13, 17, 20, 47,
    52, 64, 65
Buttons
    adding, 99
    changing text on, 121
    distinguishing between, 208

writing code for delete, 209
Byte size, 86
Bytes, 68, 71, 84, 84f, 85, 123

C

C4 conference, 381
Calendar application, 216, 217f
    see also Looping
Camel case, 100
Caret, 355
case keyword, 225
Cells, 235, 245, 310f, 312f, 305–313,
    316
    custom object, 321
    delegate method, 321
    table view of, 159
char keyword, 79
Checkbox, 241
Choose... button, 10
Circle example, 94–107, 121
circumferenceFromRadius: method, 102,
    103
@class declaration, 318
Class description, 28, 30, 36
Class methods, 105–109
class of an object, checking, 254
Classes
    adding new, 119
    controller, 158, 162
    descriptions for, writing, 34
    file types for, 35
    inheritance, 32, 38, 118
    mutable, 149
    naming, 37
    pointers, declaring, 61
    protocols, 167
    public interface, 39
    subclassing, 37
    types of, 234
    writing new, 105–109
    see also specific class names
Click-release, 346
Cocoa application, 8, 10
Cocoa Bindings Programming Topics
    (Apple), 376
Cocoa document-based application, 8
Cocoa framework, 14–15
    base object class and, 37
    concurrency, 377
    control types in, 241
    Core Animation, 372–373

Core Data, 373
defined, 14
Foundation and Application Kit, 388
multiple frameworks of, 388
reference counting technique, 125
see also Target-action mechanism
Cocoa Programming for Mac OS X, 3rd
    Ed (Hillegass), 378
*Cocoa Programming: A Quick-Start
    Guide for Developers* (Steinberg),
    378
Cocoa Touch, 388
cocoa-dev, 379
Code blocks, 45
Code compiler, 55
Code consolidation, 103–104
Code readability, 80, 104, 238
Code, downloading, 21
Collecting an array, 142
Colons, 53, 100–102
Color coding, 12, 39
Colors, 293
Columns, 324
Comma separated list, 141
Comment out code, 12
Comments
    about, 12
    color coding in, 12
    method signatures, 317
    uses for, 12
Comparative operators, 220
Comparing objects, 195
Compile-time, 67
componentsJoinedByString: method, 214
Concrete subclass, 365
Concurrency, 376
Concurrency Programming Guide
    (Apple), 377
condition, 220
Conditional blocks, 197
Conditional statements, 157, 193
    adding to shopping list application,
        204–211
    init methods, 202–204
    multiple checks for, 199
Conferences, 381
Conforming, to protocol, 317, 318
Connections palette, 99
Consolidation, of code, 103–104
Constant variable, 256
Constants, 208

Content view, 286
continue keyword, 225, 230, 231
Control types, 241
controller objects, 234
Controller class, 158, 162
Controller objects, 273
Controller, linking interface to, 161
Conventions, 34, 38
    accessor method names, 269
    argument syntax, 53
    blocks of code, 40
    class descriptions, 40
    class method form, 134
    class method syntax, 106
    class names, 37
    file extensions, 158
    instance method syntax, 106
    logical expression syntax, 179
    method syntax, 101
    naming, 100
    naming arrays, 140
    operator syntax, 180
    pointer syntax, 60
    semicolons, 44
    sending messages to text view, 63
    strings, 151
    stylistic, 196
    variable syntax, 72
Coordinates, 274
copy, 261
Core Animation, 372–373
*Core Animation for Mac OS X and the
    iPhone: Creating Compelling
    Dynamic User Interfaces* (Dudney),
    373
Core Animation Programming Guide
    (Apple), 373
*Core Animation: Simplified Animation
    Techniques for Mac and iPhone
    Development* (Zarra & Long), 373
Core Data, 373
*Core Data: Apple's API for Persisting
    Data on Mac OS X* (Zarra), 374
*Core Data for iPhone: Building
    Data-Driven Applications for the
    iPhone and iPod Touch* (Isted), 374
*Building Data-Driven Desktop
    Applications for Mac OS X* (Isted),
    374
Core Foundation, 254
Core Graphics, 281

Cores, 376
count message, 168
Counters, 223
Counting, 147, 216–219
Create document-based application,
    155
Curly braces, 40, 45, 51, 60, 119, 166,
    178, 196, 206
currentIndex variable, 224–226
Cursor, 355
Custom views, 290–300
    adding, 295f
    frame for, 297f
    square and oval in, 300f

D

Data source, 167
dealloc method, 121, 123, 165, 242
Debugger console, 46, 52, 122, 296
Decimal notation, 68
Decimal points, 78
Declaration and assignment, 80
Declaration of Independence, 261
Declaring properties, 267–268
Decrementing values, 219
Delegation, 316–332
    application, 325
    conforming to protocols, 319
    initializing objects, 327
    Objective-C protocols, 316–318
    types of, 325
    window, 327, 328f
Delete button, 209
Deleting information, fail-safe, 177
Deleting items alert, shopping list, 207f
Dereference, pointers, 111
Design patterns, 328f, 315–370
    archiving, 362–369
    delegation, 316–332
    events, 342–354
    notification, 332–342
    responders, 358f, 359f, 360f,
        355–361, 362f
Designated initializer, 133
Designing model objects, 236–246
Developer account, 400
Developer documentation, 378
Developer forums, 380
Developer Tools, 399
Dictionaries, 239f, 240f, 238–246
    persisting contents to disk, 246

retrieving information from, 243–245
shopping list application redesign,
    246–256
storing information from, 242–243
Dirty document, 175
Displaying an alert, 206, 207f
displaySomeText: method, 49, 52, 86, 87
    returning values, 91
    variable values, 93
do...while keyword, 227
Document object, 156
Documentation, 39
    code consolidation, 103–104
    code readability and, 80
    comments and, 12
    developer, 378
    NSArray class, 140
    NSObject, 121
    NSString, 134
    NSWindowDelegate, 331
    User interface validation, 361
    Xcode window for, 63f
doSomethingElse:, 86
Dot notation, 272
Dot syntax, 271
Downloads, for this book, 21
drawInteriorWithFrame: method, 321
drawInteriorWithFrame:inView: method, 307
drawWithFrame:inView: method, 307
Dudney, Bill, 373

E

Elevators, in UK vs. US, 146
else statement, 177–192
Encapsulation, 257–263
encodeWithCoder: method, 366
@end keyword, 39, 40, 44, 50, 102
Enter key, 99
Entities, 373
Enumerating and looping, 213–232
    array enumeration, 213–216
    counting, 216–219
    for loops, 219–226
    overview, 231
    shopping list application, duplicate
        items, 229–231
    while loops, 226–228
Equality operator, 179, 180, 182, 209
Equals sign, 74, 181
error: 'MathUtilities' undeclared, 107, 108f
Error attribute, 172

Errors, Xcode, 93
Etiquette, 380
Events, 342–354
    checking which rectangle was hit,
        348–350
    handling clicks when the mouse is
        dragged, 350–351
    mouse events, 344–347
    refactoring the drawing code,
        347–348
    simplifying the interface, 343f,
        342–344
    visual feedback, 351–354
EXC_BAD_ACCESS error, 187
Expressions, *see* Logical expressions

F

Factory methods, 134, 140
false, 228
False expressions, 179
Fast enumeration, 214, 215, 219, 228,
    229
File's Owner object, 162, 163
File extensions, 158
File types, for classes, 35
Files, *see specific names of files*
Finish, 34
First Responder object, 355, 356, 358
float keyword, 78, 79, 85, 91–93, 95,
    98, 101, 109, 118, 127
Floating-point numbers, 78, 92
for loops, 219–226
Forums, Apple developers, 380
Foundation, 388
Frame, 277
frame method, 292
Frames, animation, 373
Framework
    base object class, 37
    defined, 14
Framing the view, 296, 297f
Functions, 46

G

Garbage collection, 131, 374, 375
Garbage Collector Programming Guide
    (Apple), 375
Gemmell, Matt, 380
generateValue method, 92, 103
genie effect, 372

Geometry overview, 274f, 273–277,
    278f
Global variable, 256
Graph, 274, 274f
Grayed-out commands, 13
Greater than comparison operator,
    220, 222
Greater than or equal to comparison
    operator, 222
Groups of bits, 69
Guidelines, application, 14

H

Header bars, 159
Heads-up display (HUD), 57, 57f
Hexadecimal, 84
Highlights, displaying, 351
Hillegass, Aaron, 378
House developer example, 27–30
"The How and Why of Cocoa
    Initializers" (Ash), 203
Human Interface Guidelines (HIG), 378

I

IBAction keyword, 54, 163
IBOutlet keyword, 60, 97, 114, 161, 163,
    247, 326, 393
id keyword, 54, 136
Identity inspector, 42
Identity inspector, 43f
if statement, 178f, 177–192
    combining logical operators, 189
    evaluating to false, 181
    magic number message, 182f
    multiple expressions, 188
    operators for, 180
    syntax, 196
if keyword, 157, 166
Illegal access message, 184
Implementation, 44, 51
@implementation keyword, 44, 269
#import keyword, 12, 39, 108, 120, 264
Incrementing values, 218
Index, 145, 324
Indices, array, 223
Inheritance, 31–33, 38, 315, 319
    initializing with, 117
    overriding, 32
init method, 118, 157, 165, 166, 242,
    250, 327
    arguments for, 132

calling, 116
as designated initializer, 133
problems with, 133
writing, 202–204
init keyword, 76
Initial assignment, looping, 226
initWithCapacity:, 149
initWithContentsOfURL: method, 237
initWithFormat: method, 131
initWithFrame: method, 291
insertText method, 63
Instance methods, 106
Instance variables, initializing, 117
Instances, 28, 41, 140
int keyword, 76, 85, 111, 183
Interest, in objects, 124, 125
@interface keyword, 39, 40, 49, 60, 114,
    127, 183
Interface Builder, 16, 41
    action, connecting to, 55
    control types, 241
    file extensions, 158
    file for iPhone, 387f
    IBAction keyword, 55
    iPhone, 391f
    iPhone and, 394f
    Library palette, 19f
    list view, 161f
    LookItUp interface, 240f
    MainMenu.xib file, 17f
    NSTableColumn outlets, 249f
    outlets in, 61, 62f, 72
    Xcode communication, 54–55
Interface guidelines, 14
Interface, linking, 97, 98f
Internet, as information tool, 379
iPhone, 383–398
    adding messaging behavior, 390–395
    allowing user to change text, 393
    button and label in IB, 391f
    configuring the UITextField, 394f
    creating a project, 384–390
    default values for keys, 396
    developer account (free), 400
    examining files, 386
    flipping the view, 389
    Garbage collection, 131
    human interface guidelines, 378
    IB file for, 387f
    installing SDK, 403
    memory leaks, 123

new project window, 384f
NSUserDefaults class, 395
registering as developer, 398
simulator, 384, 386f
templates, 385
UIViewController methods, 392
user defaults, 395–397
view controller objects, 388
Xcode and, 8
iPod touch, 398
isa variable, 114, 118
isEqualTo...:, 195
Isted, Tim, 374
Iteration, 139, 142

K

Key-value coding (KVC), 375, 376
Key-Value Coding Programming Guide
    (Apple), 376
*Key-Value Observing Programming
    Guide* (Apple), 376
Key-value observing (KVO), 263
Keyboard shortcuts, 361
Keys, 238, 250, 256
Keystrokes, adding, 99
keyToRetrieve, 243
keyToStoreTextfield, 242
Kill application, 187
Knaster, Scott, 378
Kochan, Stephen, 378

L

Learn Objective-C on the Mac
    (Dalrymple & Knaster), 378
Less than comparison operator,
    220–222
Less than or equal to comparison
    operator, 222
Library palette, 18, 19f, 41, 42f, 56, 96,
    204, 295
Life cycle, of objects, 124–126
List view, 161f
Listservs, 379
Live resizing, 296
location keyword, 273
Location, on screen, 275
Logical expressions
    comparing objects in, 181
    defined, 179
    pointers and, 182
    variables and, 186

see also Conditional statements
Logical operator, 179, 180, 189
Long, Matt, 373
LookItUp interface, 239, 240f, 246
Looping, 213–232
  array enumeration, 213–216
  counting, 216–219
  for loops, 219–226
  initial assignment, 226
  overview, 231
  shopping list application, duplicate
    items, 229–231
  single-line, 226
  while loops, 226–228
Lorum Ipsum text, 61

M

Mac developer events, 380
Mac OS X application
  Cocoa framework and, 14–15
  construction process, 23
  downloads for, 21
  guidelines for, 14
  introduction to, 7–21
    Xcode, 7–10
  quitting, 14
  resources, 16f, 17f, 15–20
  summary, 21
  technologies and, 372
Mac-only Developer Tools, 400
Magic number message, 182f
main.m file, 10
mainDictionary, 242, 244
MainMenu.xib file, 16, 17f, 18, 95
  Generate Text button, 142
Mark, Darlrymple, 378
Measuring text, 309
Memory
  address checking, 85
  allocating for objects, 115–118
  arrays objects and, 150
  byte size, 86
  garbage collection, 131, 374, 375
  for holding variables, 115
  how it works, 67–72
  numbers stored as bytes, 84f
  numbers stored in, 70f
  object structure and, 114
  pointers and, 87–89
  reclaiming, 124
  storing numbers in, 76

  variables and, 72–81
  variables in, 83–87
Memory address, access and, 86
Memory leak, 123, 125
Memory management
  retained counts, 125
  subclassing, 37
Messages
  receiving, 53–57
  sending, 59–66
  sending to objects, 61, 64f
Messaging functionality, 32
Method signatures, 317
Methods
  adding new, 102
  arguments and, 53, 99–104
  calling with arguments, 102
  class methods, 105–109
  combining calls to, 196
  defined, 44
  defining new, 49–52
  implementing, 51
  init methods, writing, 202–204
  Objective-C 2.0 properties, 266–272
  passing multiple values to, 141
  protocols and, 317
  syntax for, 101
  utility class methods, 134–138
  void and, 51
  with a return type, 92
  see also Returning values
Model, 302
model objects, 234, 236–246
Modifier keys, 345
Months application, 216, 217f
  see also Looping
Mouse click-release, 346
Mouse events, 344–347
mouseDown: method, 346, 348, 350,
  351, 353
mouseDragged: method, 353
mouseUp: method, 346, 349–351, 353
Multiple operators, 189
Multiple variables, 141
Mutability, 148–153, 244
MVC, shopping list application, 234,
  235
MyDocument class, 155
MyDocument.m file, 236, 264–266

N

Naming conventions, 100, 140, 269, 329
   see also Conventions; Syntax
Navigation-Based Application template, 385
Negative numbers, 76, 77
Nesting, 104, 116, 196
new line keyword, 64
Next button, 34
Next responder, 355
nib vs. xib file extensions, 158
NO keyword, 66
Non-object-oriented programming, 24–26
NOT operator, 192
Notation, *see* Conventions; Syntax
Notification, 332–342
   distributing information, 332–333
   NSNotification object, 333–334
   registering to receive, 334–337
   sending, 337–342
Notification Programming Topics for Cocoa (Apple), 341
NotifyingClass class, 114
NotifyingClass.h file, 37f, 39, 40, 49, 55, 57f
NSActionCell, 307
NSArray, 139, 144, 147
NSBox object, 239, 285, 288
NSButton class, 53, 54, 183, 241
NSCoder class
   decoding information with, 367, 368
   encoding information with, 365
NSCoding protocol, 364, 364f
NSConference, 381
NSDocument class, 158
NSEnumerator class, 227
NSInsetRect method, 348
NSKeyedArchiver object, 362, 363
NSKeyedUnarchiver object, 363
NSLog, 46, 122, 307
NSMutableArray(), 149
NSMutableDictionary class, 243
NSNotification object, 333–334
NSNotificationCenter object, 334–337
NSObject class, 37
NSObject.h, 41f
NSPoint variable, 275, 276, 281
NSPointInRect() method, 349
NSRect variable, 277, 278f

NSSize, 281
NSString class, 137
NSString object, 234
NSStringFromRect(), 307
NSTableColumn, 249f
NSTableView class, 234
NSTableViewDataSource protocol, 319
NSTextField outlets, 241
NSTextFieldCell, 321
NSUserDefaults class, 395
NSWindow delegate methods, 327, 328f
NSWindowDelegate protocol, 327
numberOfRowsInTableView: method, 247

O

Objective-C class template, 34
objc_msgSend function, 294
Object initialization, 116
Object messaging, 49–66
   defining new methods, 49–52
   overview, 49, 66
   sending messages, 59–66
   target-action mechanism, 53–57
Object pointers, 88
Object-oriented programming (OOP), 24, 26–31
Objective-C 2.0 properties, 266–272
Objective-C protocols, 316–318
Objective-C, translating into C, 294
Objects, 23–48
   allocating an instance of, 120
   allocating memory for, 115–118
   application construction process, 23
   application object, 38
   autoreleasing, 129, 130
   checking class of, 254
   comparing, 195
   conforming to protocols, 319
   creating, 114
   creating in code, 118–124
   as data source, 167
   defined, 114
   defining, 26
   delegation and, 328f, 316–332
   designing model objects, 236–246
   document, 156
   encapsulation and, 257–263
   equality operator and, 182
   in expressions, 181
   implementation, 44
   index of items and, 145

inheritance, 31–33, 315

initializing, 202, 327

initializing with arguments, 131–134

instance variables, initializing, 117

instances of, 41

interest in, 124, 125

leaving in memory, 137

life cycle of, 124–126

message logging, 46

mutability in, 148–153

mutability of, 148

MyDocument.m file, reworking,
    264–266

non-object-oriented programming,
    24–26

notification and, 332–342

object-oriented programming, 26–31

Objective-C 2.0 properties, 266–272

relationships, 373

releasing, 126

responsibility for, 127

retain count of, 126

retaining count on, 125

sending message to self, 94

sending messages to, 61

ShoppingListItem object, 257–263

strings, 63, 74

structure of, 114

table views, 159, 159f

types of, 233–235

writing code for, 33–48

see also Arrays; Object messaging

Observers, 333

One-based index, 146

Open Quickly..., 40

OpenGL ES Application template, 385

Operators, *see* AND operator;
    Assignment operator; Equality
    operator; Logical operator; OR
    operator

@optional keyword, 318, 365

OR operator, 189, 191

Origin, 275, 277

Outlets, 61, 62f, 72, 240

    adding, 163, 183, 184f

    buttons, 183

    IBOutlet, 326

    linking up, 241

Oval, drawing, 299

Overriding inherited behavior, 32

Parents and children application, 198

Parking lot metaphor, 83

Partial redraws, 292

Patterns, *see* Design patterns

Persistent storage, 67

Pixels, 275, 276

Pointers

    arrays and, 139, 150

    declaring, 61

    defined, 59, 182

    dereferencing, 111

    evaluating, 194

    example of, 59

    logical expressions and, 182

    memory and, 67, 87–89, 150

    memory leak and, 123

    method signature and, 109

    objects as, 114

    as outlets, 60

    syntax, 60

    as variables, 72

Points, 274, 276

Power of ten, 68

PPStrikeThroughCell object, 321

pre-loop statement, 220

Programming in Objective-C 2.0, 2nd Ed
    (Kochan), 378

Programming syntax, 34, 38

    arguments, 53

    class descriptions, 40

    class methods, 106

    class names, 37

    code blocks, 40

    file extensions, 158

    instance methods, 106

    logical expressions, 179

    methods, 101

    naming arrays, 140

    naming conventions, 100

    operators, 180

    OR operator, 189

    pointers, 60

    protocols, 317

    semicolons, 44

    sending messages to text view, 63

    strings, 151

    variables, 72

Project window, 10, 11f

Properties, 266–272

    declaring, 267–268

declaring for object types, 269–271
dot syntax, 271
IBOutlet, 326
synthesizing, 268–269
@property keyword, 269
Property declaration, 321
Protocols, 167, 315, 316
Prototype cell, 160
Public interface, 39
Push button, 56f, 59f

Q

Quartz, 292
Questions, where to ask, 379
Quit TextApp command, 14, 17

R

Radius calculation code, *see* Circle
    example
RAM, 67, 68, 123
Readability of code, 80, 104, 238
readFromURL:ofType:error: method, 174
Reclaiming memory, 124
Rectangles, 278f, 344
redefinition of 'anInt' error, 83
Reference counting, 125
registerDefaults: method, 397
Registration, 400
release, 126
Remove button, for shopping list
    application, 204, 205f
removeItemFromShoppingList: method,
    205, 206, 250
Reopening files, 368
Resolution, 276
Resources, application, 16f, 17f, 15–20
Responder chain, 355
Responders, 355–361, 362f
    actions and, 356
    adding a new menu item, 358f
    becoming the First Responder, 356
    chain of, 355
    First Responder, introduced, 355
    keyboard shortcuts, 361
    targeting the First Responder, 358, 359,
        360f
    user interface validation, 360
retain keyword, 261, 270, 271
Retaining count, 125
retrieveInformationFromDictionary: method,
    243

retrieveValueFromDictionary: method, 245
retrieveValueLabel, 244
Return key, 99
return keyword, 93, 104, 117, 173, 197,
    230
Returning values, 91–99
Returning variables, 94
reverseObjectEnumerator class, 228
rowIndex, 169
Runtime, 67

S

Save All..., 55
Saving a shopping list, 172
Saving files, 368
Scalar types, 67, 72, 89, 113, 116
School children application, 198
Scope, 82f, 81–83
    parentheses and, 191
    variables and, 185, 216
Screen locations, 275
Screen resolution, 276
Selector, 294
Selector connection, 99
self keyword, 94, 102, 117, 136
Semicolons, 44–46, 51, 224
Senders, other than expected, 187
setNeedsDisplay: method, 353
setShouldDrawLine: method, 322
setStoredNumber: method, 119
setTitle: method, 65
shape keyword, 273
Shopping list application, 154f,
    154–175
    adding conditional statements to,
        204–211
    adding items, 153f
    adding new items to, 170
    adding outlets and action, 163
    alert display, 206
    buttons, distinguishing between, 208
    caveats with, 174
    connecting table view to data source,
        168f
    connecting to interface, 164f
    creating, 155
    delegation, 316
    deleting items, 207f
    dictionaries and, 246–256
    displaying items, 252
    duplicate items check, 229–231

editing items, 170, 253

interface, 162f

interface button, 161

interface for, 158

keyboard shortcuts, 361

linking to controller, 161

MVC, 234, 235

MyDocument class, 155

MyDocument.m file, reworking,
    264–266

opening a saved list, 173

purchased item feature, 301f,
    301–304

remove button, 204, 205f

revised interface, 248f

saving a list, 172

saving and reopening files, 368

setting up the array, 164

ShoppingListItem object, 257–263

table views, 158

working with table views, 167

ShoppingListItem object, 257–263

Shortcuts

    copying signature from header file,
        51, 52f

    decrementing values, 219

    Developer Documentation, 61

    incrementing values, 218

    save all, 55

    setting, for keyboard, 361

    string object shorthand, 215

showMeasurements: method, 280, 288

Signature, 50, 51, 53, 54, 317, 331

    action, 55

    adding to interface, 102

    implementation method, 55

Signed numbers, 76

Single-line loops, 226

size keyword, 273

Size inspector, 283, 284f

sizeof() method, 86

sizeWithAttributes: method, 309

Sizing Windows methods, 329

Spaces, 74

Square brackets, 63, 64, 88, 93, 104,
    116, 196

Square, drawing, 296

Square Button, 204

StackOverflow developer website, 379

statement for after each loop pass, 220

Static arrays, 147

Steinberg, Daniel, 378

Strikethrough cells, 316

String Format Specifiers link, 128

Strings, 63, 74, 127

    allocating and initializing, 128

    array setup and, 166

    blank, 170

    defined in C, 151

    format, 128

    functionality, 137

    initializing, 127

    keys for, 238, 250

    mutable objects, 151

    newline characters, 138

    object shorthand for, 215

    shorthand creation of, 138

    variables and scope, 185

stringWithFormat: method, 144

Stroke, 300

Strong object reference, 150

Subclassing, 37, 306

Subview, 287, 289

Superclass, 32

switch-case construction, 200, 202, 209

switch keyword, 225

Switch statement, 199

Syntax, 34, 38

    arguments, 53

    class descriptions, 40

    class methods, 106

    class names, 37

    code blocks, 40

    conforming to protocol, 318

    declaring a property, 268

    dot notation, 272

    dot syntax, 271

    fast enumeration, 215, 219, 228

    file extensions, 158

    global variables, 256

    if statements, 196

    increment/decrement values, 218,
        219

    instance methods, 106

    keys, 256

    logical expressions, 179

    message signature, 50

    methods, 101

    naming arrays, 140

    naming conventions, 100

    negating variables, 193

    NOT operator, 192

operators, 180
OR operator, 189
pointers, 60
protocols, 317
semicolons, 44
sending messages to text view, 63
string object shorthand, 215
strings, 151
switch-case construction, 200
synthesizing properties, 268
variables, 72
@synthesize keyword, 269
Synthesizing properties, 268–269
System discs, 400

T

Tab Bar Application template, 385
Table view delegate method, 321
Table views, 158, 159f, 160, 163, 167,
      168, 168f, 323
Tables, 235
tableView:objectValueForTableColumn:row:
      method, 247
tableView:setObjectValue:forTableColumn:row:
      method, 250
Target-action mechanism, 53–57, 100,
      101, 356
Template window, 9f
Testing
   conditional statements, 198
   objects, creating instance of, 41
Text cells, 159
Text field
   adding, 95, 96, 97f
   linking to textField variable, 98f
Text, measuring, 309
TextApp, 10
   adding array items, 152
   application construction process, 23
   arrays in, 142
   conditional branches, 179
   interface, making generic, 143f
   project window for, 11f
   Push button for, 56f
   stopping from Xcode, 187f
   variables, declaring, 72
   window, adding, 19, 20f
TextApp-Info.plist file, 15, 16f
Threads, 377
true, 228
True expressions, 179

Twitter, 380
Type attribute, 172

U

UIKit, 389
UITextField class, 394, 394f
UIViewController methods, 392
unsigned keyword, 77
Unsigned numbers, 76
Upgrades, Xcode and, 402–403
User defaults, 383
User Interface Validation, 360
UTF-8, 79
Utility class methods, 134–138, 140

V

Validation, 360
Value column, 15
valueForKey:, 245
Values
   assignable, 27
   assigning to variables, 73
   Boolean, 65
   passing by reference, 109–111
   passing to a method, 141
   returning, 91–99
valueToStoreTextfield, 242
Variables
   addresses in memory, 85
   addresses of, 86
   changing value of, 74
   declaring, 72, 74, 80
   declaring for single character, 79
   global, 256
   initial value of, 186
   introduced, 72–81
   logical expressions and, 186
   memory and, 83–87, 115
   negating, 193
   passing values by reference, 109
   pointers and, 72, 87–89
   returning, 94
   scope of, 82f, 81–83, 185, 216
   signed and unsigned numbers, 76
   size of, 86
   storing non-number information, 79
   syntax, 72
   unused variable warning, 73f
   validity of, 185
   values assigned to, 73
Versions, of Xcode, 399

Vertical bars, 189

view objects, 234

View-based Application template, 385

Views

    cells and, 310f, 312f, 305–313

    colors and, 293

    custom views, 295f, 297f, 300f, 290–300

    geometry for, 274f, 273–277, 278f

    instantiating, 294

    partial redraws, 292

    shopping list application, purchased item feature, 301f, 301–304

    subviews, 287

    view hierarchy, 286f, 288f, 285–289, 290f

    view relationships, 282

    working with windows, 279f, 283f, 284f, 277–285

viewWillAppear: method, 396

void keyword, 50, 54

W

Warnings, Xcode, 93

while loops, 226–228

Whitespace, 45, 74

Window object, defining, 26

Window delegates, 327, 328f

Window, frame of, 277

Window-based Application template, 385

Windows, sizing methods, 329

WonderfulNumber class factory method, 136

writeToURL: method, 237

WVMeasurer class, 281, 288

WWDC developer conference, 381

X

X and Y coordinates, 274

Xcode

    application resources and, 16f, 17f, 15–20

    Cocoa framework, 14–15

    color coding in, 12

    Debugger Console, 122, 296

    directory location of, 401

    documentation window, 63f

    email list, 379

    environment, 8–10

    errors, 108f

    installation, 399–403

    Interface Builder communication and, 54–55

    introduction to, 7–8

    New File pane, 36f

    New File window, 35f

    NotifiyingClass.h, 37f

    project downloads, 21

    project window, 10, 11f

    protocol definition, 365

    protocol reference, 167

    registering, 400

    stopping TextApp from, 187f

    Template window, 9f

    templates, 156f

    upgrades, 402–403

    uses for, 8

    variable scope error, 82f

    versions of, 399

    warning, unused variable, 73f

    warnings and errors, 93

xib vs. nib file extensions, 158

Z

Zarra, Marcus, 373, 374

Zero-based index, 145, 223

The Pragmatic Bookshelf

Available in paperback and DRM-free eBooks, our titles are here to help you stay on top of your game. The following are in print as of August 2010; be sure to check our website at pragprog.com for newer titles.

Title	Year	ISBN	Pages
Advanced Rails Recipes: 84 New Ways to Build Stunning Rails Apps	2008	9780978739225	464
Agile Coaching	2009	9781934356432	248
Agile Retrospectives: Making Good Teams Great	2006	9780977616640	200
Agile Web Development with Rails, Third Edition	2009	9781934356166	784
Beginning Mac Programming: Develop with Objective-C and Cocoa	2010	9781934356517	300
Behind Closed Doors: Secrets of Great Management	2005	9780976694021	192
Best of Ruby Quiz	2006	9780976694076	304
Cocoa Programming: A Quick-Start Guide for Developers	2010	9781934356302	450
Core Animation for Mac OS X and the iPhone: Creating Compelling Dynamic User Interfaces	2008	9781934356104	200
Core Data: Apple's API for Persisting Data on Mac OS X	2009	9781934356326	256
Data Crunching: Solve Everyday Problems using Java, Python, and More	2005	9780974514079	208
Debug It! Find, Repair, and Prevent Bugs in Your Code	2009	9781934356289	232
Deploying Rails Applications: A Step-by-Step Guide	2008	9780978739201	280
Design Accessible Web Sites: 36 Keys to Creating Content for All Audiences and Platforms	2007	9781934356029	336
Desktop GIS: Mapping the Planet with Open Source Tools	2008	9781934356067	368
Developing Facebook Platform Applications with Rails	2008	9781934356128	200
Domain-Driven Design Using Naked Objects	2009	9781934356449	375
Enterprise Integration with Ruby	2006	9780976694069	360
Enterprise Recipes with Ruby and Rails	2008	9781934356234	416
Everyday Scripting with Ruby: for Teams, Testers, and You	2007	9780977616619	320
ExpressionEngine 2: A Quick-Start Guide	2010	9781934356524	250
FXRuby: Create Lean and Mean GUIs with Ruby	2008	9781934356074	240
From Java To Ruby: Things Every Manager Should Know	2006	9780976694090	160

Continued on next page

Title	Year	ISBN	Pages
GIS for Web Developers: Adding Where to Your Web Applications	2007	9780974514093	275
Google Maps API, V2: Adding Where to Your Applications	2006	PDF-Only	83
Grails: A Quick-Start Guide	2009	9781934356463	200
Groovy Recipes: Greasing the Wheels of Java	2008	9780978739294	264
Hello, Android: Introducing Google's Mobile Development Platform	2010	9781934356562	320
Interface Oriented Design	2006	9780976694052	240
Land the Tech Job You Love	2009	9781934356265	280
Language Implementation Patterns: Create Your Own Domain-Specific and General Programming Languages	2009	9781934356456	350
Learn to Program, 2nd Edition	2009	9781934356364	240
Manage It! Your Guide to Modern Pragmatic Project Management	2007	9780978739249	360
Manage Your Project Portfolio: Increase Your Capacity and Finish More Projects	2009	9781934356296	200
Mastering Dojo: JavaScript and Ajax Tools for Great Web Experiences	2008	9781934356111	568
Metaprogramming Ruby: Program Like the Ruby Pros	2010	9781934356470	240
Modular Java: Creating Flexible Applications with OSGi and Spring	2009	9781934356401	260
No Fluff Just Stuff 2006 Anthology	2006	9780977616664	240
No Fluff Just Stuff 2007 Anthology	2007	9780978739287	320
Pomodoro Technique Illustrated: The Easy Way to Do More in Less Time	2009	9781934356500	144
Practical Programming: An Introduction to Computer Science Using Python	2009	9781934356272	350
Practices of an Agile Developer	2006	9780974514086	208
Pragmatic Project Automation: How to Build, Deploy, and Monitor Java Applications	2004	9780974514031	176
Pragmatic Thinking and Learning: Refactor Your Wetware	2008	9781934356050	288
Pragmatic Unit Testing in C# with NUnit	2007	9780977616671	176
Pragmatic Unit Testing in Java with JUnit	2003	9780974514017	160
Pragmatic Version Control Using Git	2008	9781934356159	200
Pragmatic Version Control using CVS	2003	9780974514000	176
Pragmatic Version Control using Subversion	2006	9780977616657	248
Programming Clojure	2009	9781934356333	304
Programming Cocoa with Ruby: Create Compelling Mac Apps Using RubyCocoa	2009	9781934356197	300

Continued on next page

Title	Year	ISBN	Pages
Programming Erlang: Software for a Concurrent World	2007	9781934356005	536
Programming Groovy: Dynamic Productivity for the Java Developer	2008	9781934356098	320
Programming Ruby: The Pragmatic Programmers' Guide, Second Edition	2004	9780974514055	864
Programming Ruby 1.9: The Pragmatic Programmers' Guide	2009	9781934356081	960
Programming Scala: Tackle Multi-Core Complexity on the Java Virtual Machine	2009	9781934356319	250
Prototype and script.aculo.us: You Never Knew JavaScript Could Do This!	2007	9781934356012	448
Rails Recipes	2006	9780977616602	350
Rails for .NET Developers	2008	9781934356203	300
Rails for Java Developers	2007	9780977616695	336
Rails for PHP Developers	2008	9781934356043	432
Rapid GUI Development with QtRuby	2005	PDF-Only	83
Release It! Design and Deploy Production-Ready Software	2007	9780978739218	368
SQL Antipatterns: Avoiding the Pitfalls of Database Programming	2010	9781934356555	352
Scripted GUI Testing with Ruby	2008	9781934356180	192
Ship It! A Practical Guide to Successful Software Projects	2005	9780974514048	224
Stripes ...and Java Web Development Is Fun Again	2008	9781934356210	375
Test-Drive ASP.NET MVC	2010	9781934356531	296
TextMate: Power Editing for the Mac	2007	9780978739232	208
The Definitive ANTLR Reference: Building Domain-Specific Languages	2007	9780978739256	384
The Passionate Programmer: Creating a Remarkable Career in Software Development	2009	9781934356340	200
ThoughtWorks Anthology	2008	9781934356142	240
Ubuntu Kung Fu: Tips, Tricks, Hints, and Hacks	2008	9781934356227	400
Web Design for Developers: A Programmer's Guide to Design Tools and Techniques	2009	9781934356135	300
iPhone SDK Development	2009	9781934356258	576

More on Cocoa and iPhone

Cocoa Programming

Cocoa Programming shows you how to get productive with Cocoa–fast! You'll learn to use the Apple developer tools to design your user interface, write the code, and create the data model. We'll show you Objective-C concepts when you are ready to apply them throughout the book. By the end of the book, you'll be a Cocoa programmer.

Cocoa Programming: A Quick-Start Guide for Developers
Daniel H Steinberg
(450 pages) ISBN: 978-19343563-0-2. $32.95
http://pragprog.com/titles/dscpq

iPhone SDK Development

Jump into application development for today's most remarkable mobile communications platform, the Pragmatic way. This Pragmatic guide takes you through the tools and APIs, the same ones Apple uses for its applications, that you can use to create your own software for the iPhone and iPod touch. Packed with useful examples, this book will give you both the big-picture concepts and the everyday "gotcha" details that developers need to make the most of the beauty and power of the iPhone OS platform.

iPhone SDK Development
Bill Dudney, Chris Adamson, Marcel Molina
(545 pages) ISBN: 978-1-9343562-5-8. $38.95
http://pragprog.com/titles/amiphd

More Mac Frameworks

Core Animation for OS X/iPhone

Have you seen Apple's Front Row application and Cover Flow effects? Then you've seen Core Animation at work. It's about making applications that give strong visual feedback through movement and morphing, rather than repainting panels. This comprehensive guide will get you up to speed quickly and take you into the depths of this new technology.

Core Animation for Mac OS X and the iPhone: Creating Compelling Dynamic User Interfaces
Bill Dudney
(220 pages) ISBN: 978-1-9343561-0-4. $34.95
http://pragprog.com/titles/bdcora

Core Data

Learn the Apple Core Data APIs from the ground up. You can concentrate on designing the model for your application, and use the power of Core Data to do the rest. This book will take you from beginning with Core Data through to expert level configurations that you will not find anywhere else. Learn why you should be using Core Data for your next Cocoa project, and how to use it most effectively.

Core Data: Apple's API for Persisting Data under Mac OS X
Marcus S. Zarra
(256 pages) ISBN: 978-1-93435-632-6. $32.95
http://pragprog.com/titles/mzcd

Tools and Tips

TextMate

If you're coding Ruby or Rails on a Mac, then you owe it to yourself to get the TextMate editor. And, once you're using TextMate, you owe it to yourself to pick up this book. It's packed with information that will help you automate all your editing tasks, saving you time to concentrate on the important stuff. Use snippets to insert boilerplate code and refactorings to move stuff around. Learn how to write your own extensions to customize it to the way you work.

TextMate: Power Editing for the Mac
James Edward Gray II
(200 pages) ISBN: 0-9787392-3-X. $29.95
http://pragprog.com/titles/textmate

Debug It!

Debug It! will equip you with the tools, techniques, and approaches to help you tackle any bug with confidence. These secrets of professional debugging illuminate every stage of the bug life cycle, from constructing software that makes debugging easy; through bug detection, reproduction, and diagnosis; to rolling out your eventual fix. Learn better debugging whether you're writing Java or assembly language, targeting servers or embedded micro-controllers, or using agile or traditional approaches.

Debug It! Find, Repair, and Prevent Bugs in Your Code
Paul Butcher
(232 pages) ISBN: 978-1-9343562-8-9. $34.95
http://pragprog.com/titles/pbdp

For Your Career

Land the Tech Job You Love

You've got the technical chops—the skills to get a great job doing what you love. Now it's time to get down to the business of planning your job search, focusing your time and attention on the job leads that matter, and interviewing to wow your boss-to-be.

You'll learn how to find the job you want that fits you and your employer. You'll uncover the hidden jobs that never make it into the classifieds or Monster. You'll start making and maintaining the connections that will drive your future career moves.

You'll land the tech job you love.

Land the Tech Job You Love
Andy Lester
(280 pages) ISBN: 978-1934356-26-5. $23.95
http://pragprog.com/titles/algh

The Passionate Programmer

This book is about creating a remarkable career in software development. Remarkable careers don't come by chance. They require thought, intention, action, and a willingness to change course when you've made mistakes. Most of us have been stumbling around letting our careers take us where they may. It's time to take control.

This revised and updated second edition lays out a strategy for planning and creating a radically successful life in software development *(the first edition was released as My Job Went to India: 52 Ways To Save Your Job)*.

The Passionate Programmer: Creating a Remarkable Career in Software Development
Chad Fowler
(232 pages) ISBN: 978-1934356-34-0. $23.95
http://pragprog.com/titles/cfcar2

For Your Head

Pragmatic Thinking and Learning

Software development happens in your head. Not in an editor, IDE, or design tool. In this book by Pragmatic Programmer Andy Hunt, you'll learn how our brains are wired, and how to take advantage of your brain's architecture. You'll master new tricks and tips to learn more, faster, and retain more of what you learn.

• Use the Dreyfus Model of Skill Acquisition to become more expert • Leverage the architecture of the brain to strengthen different thinking modes
• Avoid common "known bugs" in your mind
• Learn more deliberately and more effectively
• Manage knowledge more efficiently

Pragmatic Thinking and Learning:
Refactor your Wetware
Andy Hunt
(288 pages) ISBN: 978-1-9343560-5-0. $34.95
http://pragprog.com/titles/ahptl

Pomodoro Technique Illustrated

Do you ever look at the clock and wonder where the day went? You spent all this time at work and didn't come close to getting everything done. Tomorrow, try something new. In *Pomodoro Technique Illustrated*, Staffan Nöteberg shows you how to organize your work to accomplish more in less time. There's no need for expensive software or fancy planners. You can get started with nothing more than a piece of paper, a pencil, and a kitchen timer.

Pomodoro Technique Illustrated: The Easy Way to Do More in Less Time
Staffan Nöteberg
(144 pages) ISBN: 9781934356500. $24.95
http://pragprog.com/titles/snfocus

The Pragmatic Bookshelf

The Pragmatic Bookshelf features books written by developers for developers. The titles continue the well-known Pragmatic Programmer style and continue to garner awards and rave reviews. As development gets more and more difficult, the Pragmatic Programmers will be there with more titles and products to help you stay on top of your game.

Visit Us Online

Beginning Mac Programming's Home Page
http://pragprog.com/titles/tibmac
Source code from this book, errata, and other resources. Come give us feedback, too!

Register for Updates
http://pragprog.com/updates
Be notified when updates and new books become available.

Join the Community
http://pragprog.com/community
Read our weblogs, join our online discussions, participate in our mailing list, interact with our wiki, and benefit from the experience of other Pragmatic Programmers.

New and Noteworthy
http://pragprog.com/news
Check out the latest pragmatic developments, new titles and other offerings.

Save on the eBook

Save on the eBook versions of this title. Owning the paper version of this book entitles you to purchase the electronic versions at a terrific discount.

PDFs are great for carrying around on your laptop—they are hyperlinked, have color, and are fully searchable. Most titles are also available for the iPhone and iPod touch, Amazon Kindle, and other popular e-book readers.

Buy now at pragprog.com/coupon.

Contact Us

Online Orders:	www.pragprog.com/catalog
Customer Service:	support@pragprog.com
Non-English Versions:	translations@pragprog.com
Pragmatic Teaching:	academic@pragprog.com
Author Proposals:	proposals@pragprog.com
Contact us:	1-800-699-PROG (+1 919 847 3884)